ANALYTICAL STUDIES

ANALYTICAL STUDIES

HONORE DE BALZAC,
J. WALKER MCSPADDEN,
PAUL BOURGET

ISBN: 978-93-89821-77-2

Published: -

LECTOR HOUSE LLP
E-MAIL: lectorpublishing@gmail.com

THE CLANDESTINE VISIT

Photogravure From Drawing bv J. Allen St. John

ANALYTICAL STUDIES:

THE PHYSIOLOGY OF MARRIAGE
AND
PETTY TROUBLES OF MARRIED LIFE

BY

HONORE DE BALZAC

WITH INTRODUCTIONS BY
J. WALKER MCSPADDEN
AND
PAUL BOURGET

DEDICATION

Notice the words: *The man of distinction to whom this book is dedicated.* Need I say: "You are that man." — THE AUTHOR.

The woman who may be induced by the title of this book to open it, can save herself the trouble; she has already read the work without knowing it. A man, however malicious he may possibly be, can never say about a woman as much good or as much evil as they themselves think. If, in spite of this notice, a woman will persist in reading the volume, she ought to be prevented by delicacy from despising the author, from the very moment that he, forfeiting the praise which most artists welcome, has in a certain way engraved on the title page of his book the prudent inscription written on the portal of certain establishments: Ladies must not enter.

CONTENTS

THIRD PART
RELATING TO CIVIL WAR.

PETTY TROUBLES OF MARRIED LIFE

PART FIRST

PART SECOND

INTRODUCTION

The two Analytical Studies, *Physiology of Marriage* and *Petty Troubles of Married Life*, belong quite apart from the action of the *Comedie Humaine*, and can only be included therein by virtue of a special dispensation on the part of their author, who made for them an eighth division therein, thus giving them a local habitation and a name. Although they come far down in the list of titles, their creation belongs almost to the formative era. Balzac had just shaken his skirts clear of the immature dust of the *Oeuvres de Jeunesse*, and by the publication, in 1829, of *The Chouans*, had made his first real bow to his larger public. In December of that same year appeared the *Physiology of Marriage*, followed eleven months later by a few papers belonging to *Petty Troubles of Married Life*. Meanwhile, between these two Analytical Studies, came a remarkable novelette, *At the Sign of the Cat and Racket*, followed soon after by one of the most famous stories of the entire *Comedie, The Magic Skin*.

We are thus particular to place the two Analytical Studies in time and in environment, that the wonderful versatility of the author may become apparent—and more: that Balzac may be vindicated from the charge of dullness and inaccuracy at this period. Such traits might have been charged against him had he left only the Analytical Studies. But when they are preceded by the faithful though heavy scene of military life, and succeeded by the searching and vivid philosophical study, their faults and failures may be considered for the sake of their company.

It is hard to determine Balzac's full purpose in including the Analytical Studies in the *Comedie*. They are not novels. The few, lightly-sketched characters are not connected with those of the *Comedie*, save in one or two remote instances. They must have been included in order to make one more room in the gigantic mansion which the author had planned. His seventh sense of subdivision saw here fresh material to classify. And so these grim, almost sardonic essays were placed where they now appear.

In all kindness, the Balzac novitiate is warned against beginning an acquaintance with the author through the medium of the Analytical Studies. He would be almost certain to misjudge Balzac's attitude, and might even be tempted to forsake his further cultivation. The mistake would be serious for the reader and unjust to the author. These studies are chiefly valuable as outlining a peculiar—and, shall we say, forced?—mood that sought expression in an isolated channel. All his life long, Balzac found time for miscellaneous writings —critiques, letters, reviews, essays, political diatribes and sketches. In early life they were his "pot-boilers," and he never ceased writing them, probably urged partly by continued need of money, partly through fondness for this sort of thing. His *Physiology* is fairly representative of the material, being analysis in satirical vein of sundry foibles of society. This class of composition was very popular in the time of Louis Philippe.

The *Physiology of Marriage* is couched in a spirit of pseudo-seriousness that leaves one in doubt as to Balzac's faith with the reader. At times he seems honestly to be trying to analyze a particular phase of his subject; at other times he appears to be ridiculing the whole institution of marriage. If this be not the case, then he would seem unfitted for his task—through the ignorance of a bachelor—and adds to error the element of slander. He is at fault through lack of intimate experience. And yet the flashes of keen penetration preclude such a charge as this. A few bold touches of his pen, and a picture is drawn which glows with convincing reality. While here and there occur paragraphs of powerful description or searching philosophy which proclaim Balzac the mature, Balzac the observant.

On the publication of *Petty Troubles of Married Life* in *La Presse*, the publishers of that periodical had this to say: "M. de Balzac has already produced, as you know, the *Physiology of Marriage*, a book full of diabolical ingenuity and an analysis of society that would drive to despair Leuwenhoech and Swammerdam, who beheld the entire universe in a drop of water. This inexhaustible subject has again inspired an entertaining book full of Gallic malice and English humor, where Rabelais and Sterne meet and greet him at the same moment."

In *Petty Troubles* we have the sardonic vein fully developed. The whole edifice of romance seems but a card house, and all virtue merely a question of utility. We must not err, however, in taking sentiments at their apparent value, for the real Balzac lies deeper; and here and there a glimpse of his true spirit and greater power becomes apparent. The bitter satire yields place to a vein of feeling true and fine, and gleaming like rich gold amid baser metal. Note "Another Glimpse of Adolphus" with its splendid vein of reverie and quiet inspiration to higher living. It is touches like this which save the book and reveal the author.

Petty Troubles of Married Life is a pendant or sequel to *Physiology of Marriage*. It is, as Balzac says, to the *Physiology* "what Fact is to Theory, or History to Philosophy, and has its logic, as life, viewed as a whole, has its logic also." We must then say with the author, that "if literature is the reflection of manners, we must admit that our manners recognize the defects pointed out by the *Physiology of Marriage* in this fundamental institution;" and we must concede for *Petty Troubles* one of those "terrible blows dealt this social basis."

The *Physiologie du Mariage, ou Meditations de philosophie eclectique sur le bonheur et le malheur conjugal* is dated at Paris, 1824-29. It first appeared anonymously, December, 1829, dated 1830, from the press of Charles Gosselin and Urbain Canel, in two octavo volumes with its present introduction and a note of correction now omitted. Its next appearance was signed, in 1834, in a two-volume edition of Ollivier. In 1846 it was entered, with its dedication to the reader, in the first edition of *Etudes Analytiques*—the first edition also of the *Comedie Humaine*—as Volume XVI. All the subsequent editions have retained the original small division heads, called Meditations.

Petites Miseres de la Vie Conjugale is not dated. Its composition was achieved piecemeal, beginning shortly after its predecessor appeared. But it was not till long after—in 1845-46—that its present two-part form was published in a single octavo volume by Chlendowski. A break had ensued between the first and second parts, the latter having appeared practically in full in *La Presse* of December, 1845. The sub-headings have remained unchanged since the original printing.

J. WALKER MCSPADDEN.

THE PHYSIOLOGY OF MARRIAGE;

OR,
THE MUSINGS OF AN ECLECTIC PHILOSOPHER ON THE HAPPINESS AND UNHAPPINESS OF MARRIED LIFE

INTRODUCTION

"Marriage is not an institution of nature. The family in the east is entirely different from the family in the west. Man is the servant of nature, and the institutions of society are grafts, not spontaneous growths of nature. Laws are made to suit manners, and manners vary.

"Marriage must therefore undergo the gradual development towards perfection to which all human affairs submit."

These words, pronounced in the presence of the Conseil d'Etat by Napoleon during the discussion of the civil code, produced a profound impression upon the author of this book; and perhaps unconsciously he received the suggestion of this work, which he now presents to the public. And indeed at the period during which, while still in his youth, he studied French law, the word ADULTERY made a singular impression upon him. Taking, as it did, a prominent place in the code, this word never occurred to his mind without conjuring up its mournful train of consequences. Tears, shame, hatred, terror, secret crime, bloody wars, families without a head, and social misery rose like a sudden line of phantoms before him when he read the solemn word ADULTERY! Later on, when he became acquainted with the most cultivated circles of society, the author perceived that the rigor of marriage laws was very generally modified by adultery. He found that the number of unhappy homes was larger than that of happy marriages. In fact, he was the first to notice that of all human sciences that which relates to marriage was the least progressive. But this was the observation of a young man; and with him, as with so many others, this thought, like a pebble flung into the bosom of a lake, was lost in the abyss of his tumultuous thoughts. Nevertheless, in spite of himself the author was compelled to investigate, and eventually there was gathered within his mind, little by little, a swarm of conclusions, more or less just, on the subject of married life. Works like the present one are formed in the mind of the author with as much mystery as that with which truffles grow on the scented plains of Perigord. Out of the primitive and holy horror which adultery caused him and the investigation which he had thoughtlessly made, there was born one morning a trifling thought in which his ideas were formulated. This thought was really a satire upon marriage. It was as follows: A husband and wife found themselves in love with each other for the first time after twenty-seven years of marriage.

He amused himself with this little axiom and passed a whole week in delight, grouping around this harmless epigram the crowd of ideas which came to him unconsciously and which he was astonished to find that he possessed. His humorous mood yielded at last to the claims of serious investigation. Willing as he was to take a hint, the author returned to his habitual idleness. Nevertheless, this slight germ of science and of joke grew to perfection, unfostered, in the fields of thought. Each phase of the work which had been condemned by others took root and gathered strength, surviving like the slight branch of a tree which, flung upon the sand by a winter's storm, finds itself covered at morning with white and fantastic icicles, produced by the caprices of nightly frosts. So the sketch lived on and became the starting point of myriad branching moralizations. It was like a polypus which multiplies itself by generation. The feelings of youth, the observations which a favorable opportunity led him to make, were verified in the most trifling events of his after life. Soon this mass of ideas became harmonized, took life, seemed, as it were, to become a living individual and moved in the midst of those domains of fancy, where the soul loves to give full rein to its wild creations. Amid all the distractions of the world and of life, the author always heard a voice ringing in his ears and mockingly revealing the secrets of things at the very moment he was watching a woman as she danced, smiled, or talked. Just as Mephistopheles pointed out to Faust in that terrific assemblage at the Brocken, faces full of frightful augury, so the author was conscious in the midst of the ball of a demon who would strike him on the shoulder with a familiar air and say to him: "Do you notice that enchanting smile? It is a grin of hatred." And then the demon would strut about like one of the captains in the old comedies of Hardy. He would twitch the folds of a lace mantle and endeavor to make new the fretted tinsel and spangles of its former glory. And then like Rabelais he would burst into loud and unrestrainable laughter, and would trace on the street-wall a word which might serve as a pendant to the "Drink!" which was the only oracle obtainable from the heavenly bottle. This literary Trilby would often appear seated on piles of books, and with hooked fingers would point out with a grin of malice two yellow volumes whose title dazzled the eyes. Then when he saw he had attracted the author's attention he spelt out, in a voice alluring as the tones of an harmonica, *Physiology of Marriage*! But, almost always he appeared at night during my dreams, gentle as some fairy guardian; he tried by words of sweetness to subdue the soul which he would appropriate to himself. While he attracted, he also scoffed at me; supple as a woman's mind, cruel as a tiger, his friendliness was more formidable than his hatred, for he never yielded a caress without also inflicting a wound. One night in particular he exhausted the resources of his sorceries, and crowned all by a last effort. He came, he sat on the edge of the bed like a young maiden full of love, who at first keeps silence but whose eyes sparkle, until at last her secret escapes her.

"This," said he, "is a prospectus of a new life-buoy, by means of which one can pass over the Seine dry-footed. This other pamphlet is the report of the Institute on a garment by wearing which we can pass through flames without being burnt. Have you no scheme which can preserve marriage from the miseries of excessive cold and excessive heat? Listen to me! Here we have a book on the *Art* of preserving foods; on the *Art* of curing smoky chimneys; on the *Art* of making good mortar; on the *Art* of tying a cravat; on the *Art* of carving meat."

In a moment he had named such a prodigious number of books that the author felt his head go round.

"These myriads of books," says he, "have been devoured by readers; and while everybody does not build a house, and some grow hungry, and others have no cravat, or no fire to warm themselves at, yet everybody to some degree is married. But come look yonder."

He waved his hand, and appeared to bring before me a distant ocean where all the books of the world were tossing up and down like agitated waves. The octodecimos bounded over the surface of the water. The octavos as they were flung on their way uttered a solemn sound, sank to the bottom, and only rose up again with great difficulty, hindered as they were by duodecimos and works of smaller bulk which floated on the top and melted into light foam. The furious billows were crowded with journalists, proof-readers, paper-makers, apprentices, printers' agents, whose hands alone were seen mingled in the confusion among the books. Millions of voices rang in the air, like those of schoolboys bathing. Certain men were seen moving hither and thither in canoes, engaged in fishing out the books, and landing them on the shore in the presence of a tall man, of a disdainful air, dressed in black, and of a cold, unsympathetic expression. The whole scene represented the libraries and the public. The demon pointed out with his finger a skiff freshly decked out with all sails set and instead of a flag bearing a placard. Then with a peal of sardonic laughter, he read with a thundering voice: *Physiology of Marriage*.

The author fell in love, the devil left him in peace, for he would have undertaken more than he could handle if he had entered an apartment occupied by a woman. Several years passed without bringing other torments than those of love, and the author was inclined to believe that he had been healed of one infirmity by means of another which took its place. But one evening he found himself in a Parisian drawing-room where one of the men among the circle who stood round the fireplace began the conversation by relating in a sepulchral voice the following anecdote:

A peculiar thing took place at Ghent while I was staying there. A lady ten years a widow lay on her bed attacked by mortal sickness. The three heirs of collateral lineage were waiting for her last sigh. They did not leave her side for fear that she would make a will in favor of the convent of Beguins belonging to the town. The sick woman kept silent, she seemed dozing and death appeared to overspread very gradually her mute and livid face. Can't you imagine those three relations seated in silence through that winter midnight beside her bed? An old nurse is with them and she shakes her head, and the doctor sees with anxiety that the sickness has reached its last stage, and holds his hat in one hand and with the other makes a sign to the relations, as if to say to them: "I have no more visits to make here." Amid the solemn silence of the room is heard the dull rustling of a snowstorm which beats upon the shutters. For fear that the eyes of the dying woman might be dazzled by the light, the youngest of the heirs had fitted a shade to the candle which stood near that bed so that the circle of light scarcely reached the pillow of the deathbed, from which the sallow countenance of the sick woman stood out like a figure of Christ imperfectly gilded and fixed upon a cross of tarnished silver. The flickering rays shed by the blue flames of a crackling fire were therefore the sole light of this sombre chamber, where the denouement of a drama was just ending. A log suddenly rolled from the fire onto the floor, as if presaging some catastrophe. At the sound of it the sick woman quickly rose to a sitting posture. She opened two eyes, clear as those of a cat, and all present eyed her in astonishment. She saw the log advance, and before any one could check an unexpected movement which seemed prompted by a kind of delirium, she bounded from her bed, seized the tongs and threw the coal back into the fireplace. The nurse, the doctor, the relations rushed to her assistance; they took the dying woman in their arms. They put her back in bed; she laid her head upon her pillow and after a few minutes died, keeping her eyes fixed even after her death upon that plank in the floor which the burning brand had touched. Scarcely had the Countess Van Ostroem expired when the three co-heirs exchanged looks of suspicion, and thinking no more about their aunt, began to examine the mysterious floor. As they were Belgians their calculations were as rapid as their glances. An agreement was made by three words uttered in a low voice that none of them should leave the chamber. A servant was sent to fetch a carpenter. Their collateral hearts beat excitedly as they gathered round the treasured flooring, and watched their young apprentice giving the first blow with his chisel. The plank was cut through.

"My aunt made a sign," said the youngest of the heirs.

"No; it was merely the quivering light that made it appear so," replied the eldest, who kept one eye on the treasure and the other on the corpse.

The afflicted relations discovered exactly on the spot where the brand had fallen a certain object artistically enveloped in a mass of plaster.

"Proceed," said the eldest of the heirs.

The chisel of the apprentice then brought to light a human head and some odds and ends of clothing, from which they recognized the count whom all the town believed to have died at Java, and whose loss had been bitterly deplored by his wife.

The narrator of this old story was a tall spare man, with light eyes and brown hair, and the author thought he saw in him a vague resemblance to the demon who had before this tormented him; but the stranger did not show the cloven foot. Suddenly the word ADULTERY sounded in the ears of the author; and this word woke up in his imagination the most mournful countenances of that procession which before this had streamed by on the utterance of the magic syllables. From that evening he was haunted and persecuted by dreams of a work which did not yet exist; and at no period of his life was the author assailed with such delusive notions about the fatal subject of this book. But he bravely resisted the fiend, although the latter referred the most unimportant incidents of life to this unknown work, and like a customhouse officer set his stamp of mockery upon every occurrence.

Some days afterwards the author found himself in the company of two ladies. The first of them had been one of the most refined and the most intellectual women of Napoleon's court. In his day she occupied a lofty position, but the sudden appearance of the Restoration caused her downfall; she became a recluse. The second, who was young and beautiful, was at that time living at Paris the life of a fashionable woman. They were friends, because, the one being forty and the other twenty-two years old, they were seldom rivals on the same field. The author was considered quite insignificant by the first of the two ladies, and since the other soon discovered this, they carried on in his presence the conversation which they had begun in a frank discussion of a woman's lot.

"Have you noticed, dear, that women in general bestow their love only upon a fool?"

"What do you mean by that, duchess? And how can you make your remark fit in with the fact that they have an aversion for their husbands?"

"These women are absolute tyrants!" said the author to himself. "Has the devil again turned up in a mob cap?"

"No, dear, I am not joking," replied the duchess, "and I shudder with fear for myself when I coolly consider people whom I have known in other times. Wit always has a sparkle which wounds us, and the man who has much of it makes us fear him perhaps, and if he is a proud man he will be capable of jealousy, and is not therefore to our taste. In fact, we prefer to raise a man to our own height rather than to have to climb up to his. Talent has great successes for us to share in, but the fool affords enjoyment to us; and we would sooner hear said 'that is a very handsome man' than to see our lover elected to the Institute."

"That's enough, duchess! You have absolutely startled me."

And the young coquette began to describe the lovers about whom all the women of her acquaintance raved; there was not a single man of intellect among them.

"But I swear by my virtue," she said, "their husbands are worth more."

"But these are the sort of people they choose for husbands," the duchess answered gravely.

"Tell me," asked the author, "is the disaster which threatens the husband in France quite inevitable?"

"It is," replied the duchess, with a smile; "and the rage which certain women breathe out against those of their sex, whose unfortunate happiness it is to entertain a passion, proves what a burden to them is their chastity. If it were not for fear of the devil, one would be Lais; another owes her virtue to the dryness of her selfish heart; a third to the silly behaviour of her first lover; another still—"

The author checked this outpour of revelation by confiding to the two ladies his design for the work with which he had been haunted; they smiled and promised him their assistance. The youngest, with an air of gaiety suggested one of the first chapters of the undertaking, by saying that she would take upon herself to prove mathematically that women who are entirely virtuous were creatures of reason.

When the author got home he said at once to his demon:

"Come! I am ready; let us sign the compact."

But the demon never returned.

If the author has written here the biography of his book he has not acted on the prompting of fatuity. He relates facts which may furnish material for the history of human thought, and will without doubt explain the work itself. It may perhaps be important to certain anatomists of thought to be told that the soul is feminine. Thus although the author made a resolution not to think about the book which he was forced to write, the book, nevertheless, was completed. One page of it was found on the bed of a sick man, another on the sofa of a boudoir. The glances of women when they turned in the mazes of a waltz flung to him some thoughts; a gesture or a word filled his disdainful brain with others. On the day when he said to himself, "This work, which haunts me, shall be achieved," everything vanished; and like the three Belgians, he drew forth a skeleton from the place over which he had bent to seize a treasure.

A mild, pale countenance took the place of the demon who had tempted me; it wore an engaging expression of kindliness; there were no sharp pointed arrows of criticism in its lineaments. It seemed to deal more with words than with ideas, and shrank from noise and clamor. It was perhaps the household genius of the honorable deputies who sit in the centre of the Chamber.

"Wouldn't it be better," it said, "to let things be as they are? Are things so bad? We ought to believe in marriage as we believe in the immortality of the soul; and you are certainly not making a book to advertise the happiness of marriage. You will surely conclude that among a million of Parisian homes happiness is the exception. You will find perhaps that there are many husbands disposed to abandon their wives to you; but there is not a single son who will abandon his mother. Certain people who are hit by the views which you put forth will suspect your morals and will misrepresent your intentions. In a word, in order to handle social sores, one ought to be a king, or a first consul at least."

Reason, although it appeared under a form most pleasing to the author, was not listened to; for in the distance Folly tossed the coxcomb of Panurge, and the author wished to seize it; but, when he tried to catch it, he found that it was as heavy as the club of Hercules. Moreover, the cure of Meudon adorned it in such fashion that a young man who was less pleased with producing a good work than with wearing fine gloves could not even touch it.

"Is our work completed?" asked the younger of the two feminine assistants of the author.

"Alas! madame," I said, "will you ever requite me for all the hatreds which that work will array against me?"

She waved her hand, and then the author replied to her doubt by a look of indifference.

"What do you mean? Would you hesitate? You must publish it without fear. In the present day we accept a book more because it is in fashion than because it has anything in it."

Although the author does not here represent himself as anything more than the secretary of two ladies, he has in compiling their observations accomplished a double task. With regard to marriage he has here arranged matters which represent what everybody thinks but no one dares to say; but has he not also exposed himself to public displeasure by expressing the mind of the public? Perhaps, however, the eclecticism of the present essay will save it from condemnation. All the while that he indulges in banter the author has attempted to popularize certain ideas which are particularly consoling. He has almost always endeavored to lay bare the hidden springs which move the human soul. While undertaking to defend the most material interests of man, judging them or condemning them, he will perhaps bring to light many sources of intellectual delight. But the author does not foolishly claim always to put forth his pleasantries in the best of taste; he has merely counted upon the diversity of intellectual pursuits in expectation of receiving as much blame as approbation. The subject of his work was so serious that he is constantly launched into anecdote; because at the present day anecdotes are the vehicle of all moral teaching, and the anti-narcotic of every work of literature. In literature, analysis and investigation prevail, and the wearying of the reader increases in proportion with the egotism of the writer. This is one of the greatest misfortunes that can befall a book, and the present author has been quite aware of it. He has therefore so arranged the topics of this long essay as to afford resting places for the reader. This method has been successfully adopted by a writer, who produced on the subject of Taste a work somewhat parallel to that which is here put forth on the subject of Marriage. From the former the present writer may be permitted to borrow a few words in order to express a thought which he shares with the author of them. This quotation will serve as an expression of homage to his predecessor, whose success has been so swiftly followed by his death:

"When I write and speak of myself in the singular, this implies a confidential talk with the reader; he can examine the statement, discuss it, doubt and even ridicule it; but when I arm myself with the formidable WE, I become the professor and demand submission." — Brillat-Savarin, Preface to the *Physiology of Taste*.

DECEMBER 5, 1829.

FIRST PART.
A GENERAL CONSIDERATION.

We will declaim against stupid laws until they are changed, and in the meantime blindly submit to them. —Diderot, *Supplement to the Voyage of Bougainville.*

MEDITATION I.

THE SUBJECT.

Physiology, what must I consider your meaning?

Is not your object to prove that marriage unites for life two beings who do not know each other?

That life consists in passion, and that no passion survives marriage?

That marriage is an institution necessary for the preservation of society, but that it is contrary to the laws of nature?

That divorce, this admirable release from the misfortunes of marriage, should with one voice be reinstated?

That, in spite of all its inconveniences, marriage is the foundation on which property is based?

That it furnishes invaluable pledges for the security of government?

That there is something touching in the association of two human beings for the purpose of supporting the pains of life?

That there is something ridiculous in the wish that one and the same thoughts should control two wills?

That the wife is treated as a slave?

That there has never been a marriage entirely happy?

That marriage is filled with crimes and that the known murders are not the worst?

That fidelity is impossible, at least to the man?

That an investigation if it could be undertaken would prove that in the transmission of patrimonial property there was more risk than security?

That adultery does more harm than marriage does good?

That infidelity in a woman may be traced back to the earliest ages of society, and that marriage still survives this perpetuation of treachery?

That the laws of love so strongly link together two human beings that no human law can put them asunder?

That while there are marriages recorded on the public registers, there are others over which nature herself has presided, and they have been dictated either by the mutual memory of thought, or by an utter difference of mental disposition, or by corporeal affinity in the parties named; that it is thus that heaven and earth are constantly at variance?

That there are many husbands fine in figure and of superior intellect whose wives have lovers exceedingly ugly, insignificant in appearance or stupid in mind?

All these questions furnish material for books; but the books have been written and the questions are constantly reappearing.

Physiology, what must I take you to mean?

Do you reveal new principles? Would you pretend that it is the right thing that woman should be made common? Lycurgus and certain Greek peoples as well as Tartars and savages have tried this.

Can it possibly be right to confine women? The Ottomans once did so, and nowadays they give them their liberty.

Would it be right to marry young women without providing a dowry and yet exclude them from the right of succeeding to property? Some English authors and some moralists have proved that this with the admission of divorce is the surest method of rendering marriage happy.

Should there be a little Hagar in each marriage establishment? There is no need to pass a law for that. The provision of the code which makes an unfaithful wife liable to a penalty in whatever place the crime be committed, and that other article which does not punish the erring husband unless his concubine dwells beneath the conjugal roof, implicitly admits the existence of mistresses in the city.

Sanchez has written a dissertation on the penal cases incident to marriage; he has even argued on the illegitimacy and the opportuneness of each form of indulgence; he has outlined all the duties, moral, religious and corporeal, of the married couple; in short his work would form twelve volumes in octavo if the huge folio entitled *De Matrimonio* were thus represented.

Clouds of lawyers have flung clouds of treatises over the legal difficulties which are born of marriage. There exist several works on the judicial investigation of impotency.

Legions of doctors have marshaled their legions of books on the subject of marriage in its relation to medicine and surgery.

In the nineteenth century the *Physiology of Marriage* is either an insignificant compilation or the work of a fool written for other fools; old priests have taken their balances of gold and have weighed the most trifling scruples of the marriage consciences; old lawyers have put on their spectacles and have distinguished between every kind of married transgression; old doctors have seized the scalpel and drawn it over all the wounds of the subject; old judges have mounted to the bench and have decided all the cases of marriage dissolution; whole generations have passed unuttered cries of joy or of grief on the subject, each age has cast its vote into the urn; the Holy Spirit, poets and writers have recounted everything from the days of Eve to the Trojan war, from Helen to Madame de Maintenon, from the mistress of Louis XIV to the woman of their own day.

Physiology, what must I consider your meaning?

Shall I say that you intend to publish pictures more or less skillfully drawn, for the purpose of convincing us that a man marries:

From ambition—that is well known;

From kindness, in order to deliver a girl from the tyranny of her mother;

From rage, in order to disinherit his relations;

From scorn of a faithless mistress;

From weariness of a pleasant bachelor life;

From folly, for each man always commits one;

In consequence of a wager, which was the case with Lord Byron;

From interest, which is almost always the case;

From youthfulness on leaving college, like a blockhead;

From ugliness,—fear of some day failing to secure a wife;

Through Machiavelism, in order to be the heir of some old woman at an early date;

From necessity, in order to secure the standing to *our* son;

From obligation, the damsel having shown herself weak;

From passion, in order to become more surely cured of it;

On account of a quarrel, in order to put an end to a lawsuit;

From gratitude, by which he gives more than he has received;

From goodness, which is the fate of doctrinaires;

From the condition of a will when a dead uncle attaches his legacy to some girl, marriage with whom is the condition of succession;

From custom, in imitation of his ancestors;

From old age, in order to make an end of life;

From *yatidi*, that is the hour of going to bed and signifies amongst the Turks all bodily needs;

From religious zeal, like the Duke of Saint-Aignan, who did not wish to commit sin?[1]

But these incidents of marriage have furnished matter for thirty thousand comedies and a hundred thousand romances.

Physiology, for the third and last time I ask you—What is your meaning?

So far everything is commonplace as the pavement of the street, familiar as a crossway. Marriage is better known than the Barabbas of the Passion. All the an-

[1] The foregoing queries came in (untranslatable) alphabetic order in the original.— Editor

In spite of this, here is my first proposition: marriage is a fight to the death, before which the wedded couple ask a blessing from heaven, because it is the rashest of all undertakings to swear eternal love; the fight at once commences and victory, that is to say liberty, remains in the hands of the cleverer of the two.

Undoubtedly. But do you see in this a fresh idea?

Well, I address myself to the married men of yesterday and of to-day; to those who on leaving the Church or the registration office indulge the hope of keeping their wives for themselves alone; to those whom some form or other of egotism or some indefinable sentiment induces to say when they see the marital troubles of another, "This will never happen to me."

I address myself to those sailors who after witnessing the foundering of other ships still put to sea; to those bachelors who after witnessing the shipwreck of virtue in a marriage of another venture upon wedlock. And this is my subject, eternally now, yet eternally old!

A young man, or it may be an old one, in love or not in love, has obtained possession by a contract duly recorded at the registration office in heaven and on the rolls of the nation, of a young girl with long hair, with black liquid eyes, with small feet, with dainty tapering fingers, with red lips, with teeth of ivory, finely formed, trembling with life, tempting and plump, white as a lily, loaded with the most charming wealth of beauty. Her drooping eyelashes seem like the points of the iron crown; her skin, which is as fresh as the calyx of a white camelia, is streaked with the purple of the red camelia; over her virginal complexion one seems to see the bloom of young fruit and the delicate down of a young peach; the azure veins spread a kindling warmth over this transparent surface; she asks for life and she gives it; she is all joy and love, all tenderness and candor; she loves her husband, or at least believes she loves him.

The husband who is in love says in the bottom of his heart: "Those eyes will see no one but me, that mouth will tremble with love for me alone, that gentle hand will lavish the caressing treasures of delight on me alone, that bosom will heave at no voice but mine, that slumbering soul will awake at my will alone; I only will entangle my fingers in those shining tresses; I alone will indulge myself in dreamily caressing that sensitive head. I will make death the guardian of my pillow if only I may ward off from the nuptial couch the stranger who would violate it; that throne of love shall swim in the blood of the rash or of my own. Tranquillity, honor, happiness, the ties of home, the fortune of my children, all are at stake there; I would defend them as a lioness defends her cubs. Woe unto him who shall set foot in my lair!"

Well now, courageous athlete, we applaud your intention. Up to the present moment no geographer has ventured to trace the lines of longitude and latitude in the ocean of marriage. Old husbands have been ashamed to point out the sand banks, the reefs, the shallows, the breakers, the monsoons, the coasts and currents which have wrecked their ships, for their shipwrecks brought them shame. There was no pilot, no compass for those pilgrims of marriage. This work is intended to supply the desideratum.

Without mentioning grocers and drapers, there are so many people occupied in discovering the secret motives of women, that it is really a work of charity to classify for them, by chapter and verse, all the secret situations of marriage; a good table of contents will enable them to put their finger on each movement of their wives' heart, as a table of logarithms tells them the product of a given multiplication.

And now what do you think about that? Is not this a novel undertaking, and one which no philosopher has as yet approached, I mean this attempt to show how a woman may be prevented from deceiving her husband? Is not this the comedy of comedies? Is it not a second *speculum vitae humanae.* We are not now dealing with the abstract questions which we have done justice to already in this Meditation. At the present day in ethics as in exact science, the world asks for facts for the results of observation. These we shall furnish.

Let us begin then by examining the true condition of things, by analyzing the forces which exist on either side. Before arming our imaginary champion let us reckon up the number of his enemies. Let us count the Cossacks who intend to invade his little domain.

All who wish may embark with us on this voyage, all who can may laugh. Weigh anchor; hoist sail! You know exactly the point from which you start. You have this advantage over a great many books that are written.

As for our fancy of laughing while we weep, and of weeping while we laugh, as the divine Rabelais drank while he ate and ate while he drank; as for our humor, to put Heraclitus and Democritus on the same page and to discard style or premeditated phrase—if any of the crew mutiny, overboard with the doting cranks, the infamous classicists, the dead and buried romanticists, and steer for the blue water!

Everybody perhaps will jeeringly remark that we are like those who say with smiling faces, "I am going to tell you a story that will make you laugh!" But it is the proper thing to joke when speaking of marriage! In short, can you not understand that we consider marriage as a trifling ailment to which all of us are subject and upon which this volume is a monograph?

"But you, your bark or your work starts off like those postilions who crack their whips because their passengers are English. You will not have galloped at full speed for half a league before you dismount to mend a trace or to breathe your horses. What is the good of blowing the trumpet before victory?"

Ah! my dear pantagruellists, nowadays to claim success is to obtain it, and since, after all, great works are only due to the expansion of little ideas, I do not see why I should not pluck the laurels, if only for the purpose of crowning those dirty bacon faces who join us in swallowing a dram. One moment, pilot, let us not start without making one little definition.

Reader, if from time to time you meet in this work the terms virtue or virtuous, let us understand that virtue means a certain labored facility by which a wife keeps her heart for her husband; at any rate, that the word is not used in a general sense, and I leave this distinction to the natural sagacity of all.

MEDITATION II.
MARRIAGE STATISTICS.

The administration has been occupied for nearly twenty years in reckoning how many acres of woodland, meadow, vineyard and fallow are comprised in the area of France. It has not stopped there, but has also tried to learn the number and species of the animals to be found there. Scientific men have gone still further; they have reckoned up the cords of wood, the pounds of beef, the apples and eggs consumed in Paris. But no one has yet undertaken either in the name of marital honor or in the interest of marriageable people, or for the advantage of morality and the progress of human institutions, to investigate the number of honest wives. What! the French government, if inquiry is made of it, is able to say how many men it has under arms, how many spies, how many employees, how many scholars; but, when it is asked how many virtuous women, it can answer nothing! If the King of France took into his head to choose his august partner from among his subjects, the administration could not even tell him the number of white lambs from whom he could make his choice. It would be obliged to resort to some competition which awards the rose of good conduct, and that would be a laughable event.

Were the ancients then our masters in political institutions as in morality? History teaches us that Ahasuerus, when he wished to take a wife from among the damsels of Persia, chose Esther, the most virtuous and the most beautiful. His ministers therefore must necessarily have discovered some method of obtaining the cream of the population. Unfortunately the Bible, which is so clear on all matrimonial questions, has omitted to give us a rule for matrimonial choice.

Let us try to supply this gap in the work of the administration by calculating the sum of the female sex in France. Here we call the attention of all friends to public morality, and we appoint them judges of our method of procedure. We shall attempt to be particularly liberal in our estimations, particularly exact in our reasoning, in order that every one may accept the result of this analysis.

The inhabitants of France are generally reckoned at thirty millions.

Certain naturalists think that the number of women exceeds that of men; but as many statisticians are of the opposite opinion, we will make the most probable calculation by allowing fifteen millions for the women.

We will begin by cutting down this sum by nine millions, which stands for those who seem to have some resemblance to women, but whom we are compelled to reject upon serious considerations.

Let us explain:

Naturalists consider man to be no more than a unique species of the order bimana, established by Dumeril in his *Analytic Zoology*, page 16; and Bory de Saint Vincent thinks that the ourang-outang ought to be included in the same order if we would make the species complete.

If these zoologists see in us nothing more than a mammal with thirty-two vertebrae possessing the hyoid bone and more folds in the hemispheres of the brain than any other animal; if in their opinion no other differences exist in this order than those produced by the influence of climate, on which are founded the nomenclature of fifteen species whose scientific names it is needless to cite, the physiologists ought also to have the right of making species and sub-species in accordance with definite degrees of intelligence and definite conditions of existence, oral and pecuniary.

Now the nine millions of human creatures which we here refer to present at first sight all the attributes of the human race; they have the hyoid bone, the coracoid process, the acromion, the zygomatic arch. It is therefore permitted for the gentlemen of the Jardin des Plantes to classify them with the bimana; but our Physiology will never admit that women are to be found among them. In our view, and in the view of those for whom this book is intended, a woman is a rare variety of the human race, and her principal characteristics are due to the special care men have bestowed upon its cultivation, — thanks to the power of money and the moral fervor of civilization! She is generally recognized by the whiteness, the fineness and softness of her skin. Her taste inclines to the most spotless cleanliness. Her fingers shrink from encountering anything but objects which are soft, yielding and scented. Like the ermine she sometimes dies for grief on seeing her white tunic soiled. She loves to twine her tresses and to make them exhale the most attractive scents; to brush her rosy nails, to trim them to an almond shape, and frequently to bathe her delicate limbs. She is not satisfied to spend the night excepting on the softest down, and excepting on hair-cushioned lounges, she loves best to take a horizontal position. Her voice is of penetrating sweetness; her movements are full of grace. She speaks with marvelous fluency. She does not apply herself to any hard work; and, nevertheless, in spite of her apparent weakness, there are burdens which she can bear and move with miraculous ease. She avoids the open sunlight and wards it off by ingenious appliances. For her to walk is exhausting. Does she eat? This is a mystery. Has she the needs of other species? It is a problem. Although she is curious to excess she allows herself easily to be caught by any one who can conceal from her the slightest thing, and her intellect leads her to seek incessantly after the unknown. Love is her religion; she thinks how to please the one she loves. To be beloved is the end of all her actions; to excite desire is the motive of every gesture. She dreams of nothing excepting how she may shine, and moves only in a circle filled with grace and elegance. It is for her the Indian girl has spun the soft fleece of Thibet goats, Tarare weaves its airy veils, Brussels sets in motion those shuttles which speed the flaxen thread that is purest and most fine, Bidjapour wrenches from the bowels of the earth its sparkling pebbles, and the Sevres gilds its snow-white clay. Night and day she reflects upon new costumes and spends her life in considering dress and in plaiting her apparel. She moves about exhibiting her brightness and freshness to people she does not know, but whose homage flatters her, while the desire she excites charms her, though she is indifferent to those who feel it. During the hours which she spends in private, in pleasure, and in the care of her person, she amuses herself by caroling the sweetest strains. For her France and Italy ordain delightful concerts and Naples imparts to the strings of the violin an harmonious soul. This species is in fine at once the queen of the world and the slave of passion. She dreads marriage because it ends by spoiling her figure, but she surrenders herself to it because it promises happiness. If she bears children it is by pure chance, and when they are grown up she tries to conceal them.

These characteristics taken at random from among a thousand others are not found amongst those beings whose hands are as black as those of apes and their skin tanned like the ancient parchments of an *olim*; whose complexion is burnt brown by the sun and whose neck is wrinkled like that of a turkey; who are covered with rags; whose voice is hoarse; whose intelligence is nil; who think of nothing but the bread box, and who are incessantly bowed in toil towards the ground; who dig; who harrow; who make hay, glean, gather in the harvest, knead the bread and strip hemp; who, huddled among domestic beasts, infants and men, dwell in holes and dens scarcely covered with thatch; to whom it is of little importance from what source children rain down into their homes. Their work it is to produce many and to deliver them to misery and toil, and if their love is not like their labor in the fields it is at least as much a work of chance.

Alas! if there are throughout the world multitudes of trades-women who sit all day long between the cradle and the sugar-cask, farmers' wives and daughters who milk the cows, unfortunate women who are employed like beasts of burden in the manufactories, who all day long carry the loaded basket, the hoe and the fish-crate, if unfortunately there exist these common human beings to whom the life of the soul, the benefits of education, the delicious tempests of the heart are an unattainable heaven; and if Nature has decreed that they should have coracoid processes and hyoid bones and thirty-two vertebrae, let them remain for the physiologist classed with the ourang-outang. And here we make no stipulations for the leisure class; for those who have the time and the sense to fall in love; for the rich who have purchased the right of indulging their passions; for the intellectual who have conquered a monopoly of fads. Anathema on all those who do not live by thought. We say Raca and fool to all those who are not ardent, young, beautiful and passionate. This is the public expression of that secret sentiment entertained by philanthropists who have learned to read and can keep their own carriage. Among the nine millions of the proscribed, the tax-gatherer, the magistrate, the law-maker and the priest doubtless see living souls who are to be ruled and made subject to the administration of justice. But the man of sentiment, the philosopher of the boudoir, while he eats his fine bread, made of corn, sown and harvested by these creatures, will reject them and relegate them, as we do, to a place outside the genus Woman. For them, there are no women excepting those who can inspire love; and there is no living being but the creature invested with the priesthood of thought by means of a privileged education, and with whom leisure has developed the power of imagination; in other words that only is a human being whose soul dreams, in love, either of intellectual enjoyments or of physical delights.

We would, however, make the remark that these nine million female pariahs produce here and there a thousand peasant girls who from peculiar circumstances are as fair as Cupids; they come to Paris or to the great cities and end up by attaining the rank of *femmes comme il faut*; but to set off against these two or three thousand favored creatures, there are one hundred thousand others who remain servants or abandon themselves to frightful irregularities. Nevertheless, we are obliged to count these Pompadours of the village among the feminine population.

Our first calculation is based upon the statistical discovery that in France there are eighteen millions of the poor, ten millions of people in easy circumstances and two millions of the rich.

There exist, therefore, in France only six millions of women in whom men of sentiment are now interested, have been interested, or will be interested.

Let us subject this social elite to a philosophic examination.

We think, without fear of being deceived, that married people who have lived twenty years together may sleep in peace without fear of having their love trespassed upon or of incurring the scandal of a lawsuit for criminal conversation.

From these six millions of individuals we must subtract about two millions of women who are extremely attractive, because for the last forty years they have seen the world; but since they have not the power to make any one fall in love with them, they are on the outside of the discussion now before us. If they are unhappy enough to receive no attention for the sake of amiability, they are soon seized with ennui; they fall back upon religion, upon the cultivation of pets, cats, lap-dogs, and other fancies which are no more offensive than their devoutness.

The calculations made at the Bureau of Longitudes concerning population authorize us again to subtract from the total mentioned two millions of young girls, pretty enough to kill; they are at present in the A B C of life and innocently play with other children, without dreading that these little hobbledehoys, who now make them laugh, will one day make them weep.

Again, of the two millions of the remaining women, what reasonable man would not throw out a hundred thousand poor girls, humpbacked, plain, crossgrained, rickety, sickly, blind, crippled in some way, well educated but penniless, all bound to be spinsters, and by no means tempted to violate the sacred laws of marriage?

Nor must we retain the one hundred thousand other girls who become sisters of St. Camille, Sisters of Charity, monastics, teachers, ladies' companions, etc. And we must put into this blessed company a number of young people difficult to estimate, who are too grown up to play with little boys and yet too young to sport their wreath of orange blossoms.

Finally, of the fifteen million subjects which remain at the bottom of our crucible we must eliminate five hundred thousand other individuals, to be reckoned as daughters of Baal, who subserve the appetites of the base. We must even comprise among those, without fear that they will be corrupted by their company, the kept women, the milliners, the shop girls, saleswomen, actresses, singers, the girls of the opera, the ballet-dancers, upper servants, chambermaids, etc. Most of these creatures excite the passions of many people, but they would consider it immodest to inform a lawyer, a mayor, an ecclesiastic or a laughing world of the day and hour when they surrendered to a lover. Their system, justly blamed by an inquisitive world, has the advantage of laying upon them no obligations towards men in general, towards the mayor or the magistracy. As these women do not violate any oath made in public, they have no connection whatever with a work which treats exclusively of lawful marriage.

Some one will say that the claims made by this essay are very slight, but its limitations make just compensation for those which amateurs consider excessively padded. If any one, through love for a wealthy dowager, wishes to obtain admittance for her into the remaining million, he must classify her under the head of Sisters of Charity, ballet-dancers, or hunchbacks; in fact we have not taken more than five hundred thousand individuals in forming this last class, because it often happens, as we have seen above, that the nine millions of peasant girls make a large accession to it. We have for the same reason omitted the working-girl class and the hucksters; the women of these two sections are the product of efforts made by nine millions of female bimana to rise to the higher civilization. But for its scrupulous exactitude many persons might regard this statistical meditation as a mere joke.

We have felt very much inclined to form a small class of a hundred thousand individuals as a crowning cabinet of the species, to serve as a place of shelter for women who have fallen into a middle estate, like widows, for instance; but we have preferred to estimate in round figures.

It would be easy to prove the fairness of our analysis: let one reflection be sufficient.

The life of a woman is divided into three periods, very distinct from each other: the first begins in the cradle and ends on the attainment of a marriageable age; the second embraces the time during which a woman belongs to marriage; the third opens with the critical period, the ending with which nature closes the passions of life. These three spheres of existence, being almost equal in duration, might be employed for the classification into equal groups of a given number of women. Thus in a mass of six millions, omitting fractions, there are about two million girls between one and eighteen, two millions women between eighteen and forty and two millions of old women. The caprices of society have divided the two millions of marriageable women into three main classes, namely: those who remain spinsters for reasons which we have defined; those whose virtue does not reckon in the obtaining of husbands, and the million of women lawfully married, with whom we have to deal.

You see then, by the exact sifting out of the feminine population, that there exists in France a little flock of barely a million white lambs, a privileged fold into which every wolf is anxious to enter.

Let us put this million of women, already winnowed by our fan, through another examination.

To arrive at the true idea of the degree of confidence which a man ought to have in his wife, let us suppose for a moment that all wives will deceive their husbands.

On this hypothesis, it will be proper to cut out about one-twentieth, viz., young people who are newly married and who will be faithful to their vows for a certain time.

Another twentieth will be in ill-health. This will be to make a very modest allowance for human infirmities.

Certain passions, which we are told destroy the dominion of the man over the heart of his wife, namely, aversion, grief, the bearing of children, will account for another twentieth.

Adultery does not establish itself in the heart of a married woman with the promptness of a pistol-shot. Even when sympathy with another rouses feelings on first sight, a struggle always takes place, whose duration discounts the total sum of conjugal infidelities. It would be an insult to French modesty not to admit the duration of this struggle in a country so naturally combative, without referring to at least a twentieth in the total of married women; but then we will suppose that there are certain sickly women who preserve their lovers while they are using soothing draughts, and that there are certain wives whose confinement makes sarcastic celibates smile. In this way we shall vindicate the modesty of those who enter upon the struggle from motives of virtue. For the same reason we should not venture to believe that a woman forsaken by her lover will find a new one on the spot; but this discount being much more uncertain than the preceding one, we will estimate it at one-fortieth.

These several rebates will reduce our sum total to eight hundred thousand women, when we come to calculate the number of those who are likely to violate married faith. Who would not at the present moment wish to retain the persuasion that wives are virtuous? Are they not the supreme flower of the country? Are they not all blooming creatures, fascinating the world by their beauty, their youth, their life and their love? To believe in their virtue is a sort of social religion, for they are the ornament of the world, and form the chief glory of France.

It is in the midst of this million we are bound to investigate:

The number of honest women;

The number of virtuous women.

The work of investigating this and of arranging the results under two categories requires whole meditations, which may serve as an appendix to the present one.

cient ideas which it calls to light permeate literature since the world is the world, and there is not a single opinion which might serve to the advantage of the world, nor a ridiculous project which could not find an author to write it up, a printer to print it, a bookseller to sell it and a reader to read it.

Allow me to say to you like Rabelais, who is in every sense our master:

"Gentlemen, God save and guard you! Where are you? I cannot see you; wait until I put on my spectacles. Ah! I see you now; you, your wives, your children. Are you in good health? I am glad to hear it."

But it is not for you that I am writing. Since you have grown-up children that ends the matter.

Ah! it is you, illustrious tipplers, pampered and gouty, and you, tireless pie-cutters, favorites who come dear; day-long pantagruellists who keep your private birds, gay and gallant, and who go to tierce, to sexts, to nones, and also to vespers and compline and never tire of going.

It is not for you that the *Physiology of Marriage* is addressed, for you are not married and may you never be married. You herd of bigots, snails, hypocrites, dotards, lechers, booted for pilgrimage to Rome, disguised and marked, as it were, to deceive the world. Go back, you scoundrels, out of my sight! Gallows birds are ye all—now in the devil's name will you not begone? There are none left now but the good souls who love to laugh; not the snivelers who burst into tears in prose or verse, whatever their subject be, who make people sick with their odes, their sonnets, their meditation; none of these dreamers, but certain old-fashioned pantagruellists who don't think twice about it when they are invited to join a banquet or provoked to make a repartee, who can take pleasure in a book like *Pease and the Lard* with commentary of Rabelais, or in the one entitled *The Dignity of Breeches*, and who esteem highly the fair books of high degree, a quarry hard to run down and redoubtable to wrestle with.

It no longer does to laugh at a government, my friend, since it has invented means to raise fifteen hundred millions by taxation. High ecclesiastics, monks and nuns are no longer so rich that we can drink with them; but let St. Michael come, he who chased the devil from heaven, and we shall perhaps see the good time come back again! There is only one thing in France at the present moment which remains a laughing matter, and that is marriage. Disciples of Panurge, ye are the only readers I desire. You know how seasonably to take up and lay down a book, how to get the most pleasure out of it, to understand the hint in a half word—how to suck nourishment from a marrow-bone.

The men of the microscope who see nothing but a speck, the census-mongers—have they reviewed the whole matter? Have they pronounced without appeal that it is as impossible to write a book on marriage as to make new again a broken pot?

Yes, master fool. If you begin to squeeze the marriage question you squirt out nothing but fun for the bachelors and weariness for the married men. It is everlasting morality. A million printed pages would have no other matter in them.

MEDITATION III.

OF THE HONEST WOMAN.

The preceding meditation has proved that we possess in France a floating population of one million women reveling in the privilege of inspiring those passions which a gallant man avows without shame, or dissembles with delight. It is then among this million of women that we must carry our lantern of Diogenes in order to discover the honest women of the land.

This inquiry suggests certain digressions.

Two young people, well dressed, whose slender figures and rounded arms suggest a paver's tool, and whose boots are elegantly made, meet one morning on the boulevard, at the end of the Passage des Panoramas.

"What, is this you?"

"Yes, dear boy; it looks like me, doesn't it?"

Then they laugh, with more or less intelligence, according to the nature of the joke which opens the conversation.

When they have examined each other with the sly curiosity of a police officer on the lookout for a clew, when they are quite convinced of the newness of each other's gloves, of each other's waistcoat and of the taste with which their cravats are tied; when they are pretty certain that neither of them is down in the world, they link arms and if they start from the Theater des Varietes, they have not reached Frascati's before they have asked each other a roundabout question whose free translation may be this:

"Whom are you living with now?"

As a general rule she is a charming woman.

Who is the infantryman of Paris into whose ear there have not dropped, like bullets in the day of battle, thousands of words uttered by the passer-by, and who has not caught one of those numberless sayings which, according to Rabelais, hang frozen in the air? But the majority of men take their way through Paris in the same manner as they live and eat, that is, without thinking about it. There are very few skillful musicians, very few practiced physiognomists who can recognize the key in which these vagrant notes are set, the passion that prompts these floating words. Ah! to wander over Paris! What an adorable and delightful existence is that! To saunter is a science; it is the gastronomy of the eye. To take a walk is to vegetate; to saunter is to live. The young and pretty women, long contemplated with ardent eyes, would be much more admissible in claiming a salary than the cook who asks for twenty sous from the Limousin whose nose with inflated nostrils took in the perfumes of beauty. To saunter is to enjoy life; it is to indulge the flight of fancy; it is to enjoy the sublime pictures of misery, of love, of joy, of gracious or grotesque physiognomies; it is to pierce with a glance the abysses of a thousand existences; for the young it is to desire all, and to possess all; for the old it is to live the life of the youthful, and to share their passions. Now how many answers have not the sauntering artists heard to the categorical question which is always with us?

"She is thirty-five years old, but you would not think she was more than twenty!" said an enthusiastic youth with sparkling eyes, who, freshly liberated from college, would, like Cherubin, embrace all.

"Zounds! Mine has dressing-gowns of batiste and diamond rings for the evening!" said a lawyer's clerk.

"But she has a box at the Francais!" said an army officer.

"At any rate," cried another one, an elderly man who spoke as if he were standing on the defence, "she does not cost me a sou! In our case — wouldn't you like to have the same chance, my respected friend?"

And he patted his companion lightly on the shoulder.

"Oh! she loves me!" said another. "It seems too good to be true; but she has the most stupid of husbands! Ah!—Buffon has admirably described the animals, but the biped called husband—"

What a pleasant thing for a married man to hear!

"Oh! what an angel you are, my dear!" is the answer to a request discreetly whispered into the ear.

"Can you tell me her name or point her out to me?"

"Oh! no; she is an honest woman."

When a student is loved by a waitress, he mentions her name with pride and takes his friends to lunch at her house. If a young man loves a woman whose husband is engaged in some trade dealing with articles of necessity, he will answer, blushingly, "She is the wife of a haberdasher, of a stationer, of a hatter, of a linen-draper, of a clerk, etc."

But this confession of love for an inferior which buds and blows in the midst of packages, loaves of sugar, or flannel waistcoats is always accompanied with an exaggerated praise of the lady's fortune. The husband alone is engaged in the business; he is rich; he has fine furniture. The loved one comes to her lover's house; she wears a cashmere shawl; she owns a country house, etc.

In short, a young man is never wanting in excellent arguments to prove that his mistress is very nearly, if not quite, an honest woman. This distinction originates in the refinement of our manners and has become as indefinite as the line which separates *bon ton* from vulgarity. What then is meant by an honest woman?

On this point the vanity of women, of their lovers, and even that of their husbands, is so sensitive that we had better here settle upon some general rules, which are the result of long observation.

Our one million of privileged women represent a multitude who are eligible for the glorious title of honest women, but by no means all are elected to it. The principles on which these elections are based may be found in the following axioms:

APHORISMS.

I.

An honest woman is necessarily a married woman.

II.

An honest woman is under forty years old.

III.

A married woman whose favors are to be paid for is not an honest woman.

IV.

A married woman who keeps a private carriage is an honest woman.

V.

A woman who does her own cooking is not an honest woman.

VI.

When a man has made enough to yield an income of twenty thousand francs, his wife is an honest woman, whatever the business in which his fortune was made.

VII.

A woman who says "letter of change" for letter of exchange, who says of a man, "He is an elegant gentleman," can never be an honest woman, whatever fortune she possesses.

VIII.

An honest woman ought to be in a financial condition such as forbids her lover to think she will ever cost him anything.

IX.

A woman who lives on the third story of any street excepting the Rue de Rivoli and the Rue de Castiglione is not an honest woman.

X.

The wife of a banker is always an honest woman, but the woman who sits at the cashier's desk cannot be one, unless her husband has a very large business and she does not live over his shop.

XI.

The unmarried niece of a bishop when she lives with him can pass for an honest woman, because if she has an intrigue she has to deceive her uncle.

XII.

An honest woman is one whom her lover fears to compromise.

XIII.

The wife of an artist is always an honest woman.

By the application of these principles even a man from Ardeche can resolve all the difficulties which our subject presents.

In order that a woman may be able to keep a cook, may be finely educated, may possess the sentiment of coquetry, may have the right to pass whole hours in her boudoir lying on a sofa, and may live a life of soul, she must have at least six thousand francs a year if she lives in the country, and twenty thousand if she lives at Paris. These two financial limits will suggest to you how many honest women are to be reckoned on in the million, for they are really a mere product of our statistical calculations.

Now three hundred thousand independent people, with an income of fifteen thousand francs, represent the sum total of those who live on pensions, on annuities and the interest of treasury bonds and mortgages.

Three hundred thousand landed proprietors enjoy an income of three thousand five hundred francs and represent all territorial wealth.

Two hundred thousand payees, at the rate of fifteen hundred francs each, represent the distribution of public funds by the state budget, by the budgets of the cities and departments, less the national debt, church funds and soldier's pay, (i.e. five sous a day with allowances for washing, weapons, victuals, clothes, etc.).

Two hundred thousand fortunes amassed in commerce, reckoning the capital at twenty thousand francs in each case, represent all the commercial establishments possible in France.

Here we have a million husbands represented.

But at what figure shall we count those who have an income of fifty, of a hundred, of two, three, four, five, and six hundred francs only, from consols or some other investment?

How many landed proprietors are there who pay taxes amounting to no more than a hundred sous, twenty francs, one hundred francs, two hundred, or two hundred and eighty?

At what number shall we reckon those of the governmental leeches, who are merely quill-drivers with a salary of six hundred francs a year?

How many merchants who have nothing but a fictitious capital shall we admit? These men are rich in credit and have not a single actual sou, and resemble the sieves through which Pactolus flows. And how many brokers whose real capital does not amount to more than a thousand, two thousand, four thousand, five thousand francs? Business!—my respects to you!

Let us suppose more people to be fortunate than actually are so. Let us divide this million into parts; five hundred thousand domestic establishments will have an income ranging from a hundred to three thousand francs, and five thousand women will fulfill the conditions which entitle them to be called honest women.

After these observations, which close our meditation on statistics, we are entitled to cut out of this number one hundred thousand individuals; consequently we can consider it to be proven mathematically that there exist in France no more than four hundred thousand women who can furnish to men of refinement the exquisite and exalted enjoyments which they look for in love.

And here it is fitting to make a remark to the adepts for whom we write, that love does not consist in a series of eager conversations, of nights of pleasure, of an occasional caress more or less well-timed and a spark of *amour-propre* baptized by the name of jealousy. Our four hundred thousand women are not of those concerning whom it may be said, "The most beautiful girl in the world can give only what she has." No, they are richly endowed with treasures which appeal to our ardent imaginations, they know how to sell dear that which they do not possess, in order to compensate for the vulgarity of that which they give.

Do we feel more pleasure in kissing the glove of a grisette than in draining the five minutes of pleasure which all women offer to us?

Is it the conversation of a shop-girl which makes you expect boundless delights?

In your intercourse with a woman who is beneath you, the delight of flattered *amour-propre* is on her side. You are not in the secret of the happiness which you give.

In a case of a woman above you, either in fortune or social position, the ticklings of vanity are not only intense, but are equally shared. A man can never raise his mistress to his own level; but a woman always puts her lover in the position that she herself occupies. "I can make princes and you can make nothing but bastards," is an answer sparkling with truth.

If love is the first of passions, it is because it flatters all the rest of them at the same time. We love with more or less intensity in proportion to the number of chords which are touched by the fingers of a beautiful mistress.

Biren, the jeweler's son, climbing into the bed of the Duchesse de Courlande and helping her to sign an agreement that he should be proclaimed sovereign of the country, as he was already of the young and beautiful queen, is an example of the happiness which ought to be given to their lovers by our four hundred thousand women.

If a man would have the right to make stepping-stones of all the heads which crowd a drawing-room, he must be the lover of some artistic woman of fashion. Now we all love more or less to be at the top.

It is on this brilliant section of the nation that the attack is made by men whose education, talent or wit gives them the right to be considered persons of importance with regard to that success of which people of every country are so proud; and only among this class of women is the wife to be found whose heart has to be defended at all hazard by our husband.

What does it matter whether the considerations which arise from the existence of a feminine aristocracy are or are not equally applicable to other social classes? That which is true of all women exquisite in manners, language and thought, in whom exceptional educational facilities have developed a taste for art and a capacity for feeling, comparing and thinking, who have a high sense of propriety and politeness and who actually set the fashion in French manners, ought to be true also in the case of women whatever their nation and whatever their condition. The man of distinction to whom this book is dedicated must of necessity possess a certain mental vision, which makes him perceive the various degrees of light that fill each class and comprehend the exact point in the scale of civilization to which each of our remarks is severally applicable.

Would it not be then in the highest interests of morality, that we should in the meantime try to find out the number of virtuous women who are to be found among these adorable creatures? Is not this a question of marito-national importance?

MEDITATION IV.

OF THE VIRTUOUS WOMAN.

The question, perhaps, is not so much how many virtuous women there are, as what possibility there is of an honest woman remaining virtuous.

In order to throw light upon a point so important, let us cast a rapid glance over the male population.

From among our fifteen millions of men we must cut off, in the first place, the nine millions of bimana of thirty-two vertebrae and exclude from our physiological analysis all but six millions of people. The Marceaus, the Massenas, the Rousseaus, the Diderots and the Rollins often sprout forth suddenly from the social swamp, when it is in a condition of fermentation; but, here we plead guilty of deliberate inaccuracy. These errors in calculation are likely, however, to give all their weight to our conclusion and to corroborate what we are forced to deduce in unveiling the mechanism of passion.

From the six millions of privileged men, we must exclude three millions of old men and children.

It will be affirmed by some one that this subtraction leaves a remainder of four millions in the case of women.

This difference at first sight seems singular, but is easily accounted for.

The average age at which women are married is twenty years and at forty they cease to belong to the world of love.

Now a young bachelor of seventeen is apt to make deep cuts with his penknife in the parchment of contracts, as the chronicles of scandal will tell you.

On the other hand, a man at fifty-two is more formidable than at any other age. It is at this fair epoch of life that he enjoys an experience dearly bought, and probably all the fortune that he will ever require. The passions by which his course is directed being the last under whose scourge he will move, he is unpitying and determined, like the man carried away by a current who snatches at a green and pliant branch of willow, the young nursling of the year.

XIV.

Physically a man is a man much longer than a woman is a woman.

With regard to marriage, the difference in duration of the life of love with a man and with a woman is fifteen years. This period is equal to three-fourths of the time during which the infidelities of the woman can bring unhappiness to her husband. Nevertheless, the remainder in our subtraction from the sum of men only differs by a sixth or so from that which results in our subtraction from the sum of women.

Great is the modest caution of our estimates. As to our arguments, they are founded on evidence so widely known, that we have only expounded them for the sake of being exact and in order to anticipate all criticism.

It has, therefore, been proved to the mind of every philosopher, however little disposed he may be to forming numerical estimates, that there exists in France a floating mass of three million men between seventeen and fifty-two, all perfectly alive, well provided with teeth, quite resolved on biting, in fact, biting and asking nothing better than the opportunity of walking strong and upright along the way to Paradise.

The above observations entitle us to separate from this mass of men a million husbands. Suppose for an instant that these, being satisfied and always happy, like our model husband, confine themselves to conjugal love.

Our remainder of two millions do not require five sous to make love.

It is quite sufficient for a man to have a fine foot and a clear eye in order to dismantle the portrait of a husband.

It is not necessary that he should have a handsome face nor even a good figure;

Provided that a man appears to be intellectual and has a distinguished expression of face, women never look where he comes from but where he is going to;

The charms of youth are the unique equipage of love;

A coat made by Brisson, a pair of gloves bought from Boivin, elegant shoes, for whose payment the dealer trembles, a well-tied cravat are sufficient to make a man king of the drawing-room;

And soldiers—although the passion for gold lace and aiguillettes has died away—do not soldiers form of themselves a redoubtable legion of celibates? Not to mention Eginhard—for he was a private secretary —has not a newspaper recently recorded how a German princess bequeathed her fortune to a simple lieutenant of cuirassiers in the imperial guard?

But the notary of the village, who in the wilds of Gascony does not draw more than thirty-six deeds a year, sends his son to study law at Paris; the hatter wishes his son to be a notary, the lawyer destines his to be a judge, the judge wishes to become a minister in order that his sons may be peers. At no epoch in the world's history has there been so eager a thirst for education. To-day it is not intellect but cleverness that promenades the streets. From every crevice in the rocky surface of society brilliant flowers burst forth as the spring brings them on the walls of a ruin; even in the caverns there droop from the vaulted roof faintly colored tufts of green vegetation. The sun of education permeates all. Since this vast development of thought, this even and fruitful diffusion of light, we have scarcely any men of superiority, because every single man represents the whole education of his age.

We are surrounded by living encyclopaedias who walk about, think, act and wish to be immortalized. Hence the frightful catastrophes of climbing ambitions and insensate passions. We feel the want of other worlds; there are more hives needed to receive the swarms, and especially are we in need of more pretty women.

But the maladies by which a man is afflicted do not nullify the sum total of human passion. To our shame be it spoken, a woman is never so much attached to us as when we are sick.

With this thought, all the epigrams written against the little sex —for it is antiquated nowadays to say the fair sex—ought to be disarmed of their point and changed into madrigals of eulogy! All men ought to consider that the sole virtue of a woman is to love and that all women are prodigiously virtuous, and at that point to close the book and end their meditation.

Ah! do you not remember that black and gloomy hour when lonely and suffering, making accusations against men and especially against your friends, weak, discouraged, and filled with thoughts of death, your head supported by a fevered pillow and stretched upon a sheet whose white trellis-work of linen was stamped upon your skin, you traced with your eyes the green paper which covered the walls of your silent chamber? Do you recollect, I say, seeing some one noiselessly open your door, exhibiting her fair young face, framed with rolls of gold, and a bonnet which you had never seen before? She seemed like a star in a stormy night, smiling and stealing towards you with an expression in which distress and happiness were blended, and flinging herself into your arms!

"How did you manage it? What did you tell your husband?" you ask.

"Your husband!"—Ah! this brings us back again into the depths of our subject.

XV.

Morally the man is more often and longer a man than the woman is a women.

On the other hand we ought to consider that among these two millions of celibates there are many unhappy men, in whom a profound sense of their misery and persistent toil have quenched the instinct of love;

That they have not all passed through college, that there are many artisans among them, many footmen—the Duke of Gevres, an extremely plain and short man, as he walked through the park of Versailles saw several lackeys of fine appearance and said to his friends, "Look how these fellows are made by us, and how they imitate us"—that there are many contractors, many trades people who think of nothing but money; many drudges of the shop;

That there are men more stupid and actually more ugly than God would have made them;

That there are those whose character is like a chestnut without a kernel;

That the clergy are generally chaste;

That there are men so situated in life that they can never enter the brilliant sphere in which honest women move, whether for want of a coat, or from their bashfulness, or from the failure of a mahout to introduce them.

But let us leave to each one the task of adding to the number of these exceptions in accordance with his personal experience—for the object of a book is above all things to make people think—and let us instantly suppress one-half of the sum total and admit only that there are one million of hearts worthy of paying homage to honest women. This number approximately includes those who are superior in all departments. Women love only the intellectual, but justice must be done to virtue.

As for these amiable celibates, each of them relates a string of adventures, all of which seriously compromise honest women. It would be a very moderate and reserved computation to attribute no more than three adventures to each celibate; but if some of them count their adventures by the dozen, there are many more who confine themselves to two or three incidents of passion and some to a single one in their whole life, so that we have in accordance with the statistical method taken the average. Now if the number of celibates be multiplied by the number of their excesses in love the result will be three millions of adventures; to set against this we have only four hundred thousand honest women!

If the God of goodness and indulgence who hovers over the worlds does not make a second washing of the human race, it is doubtless because so little success attended the first.

Here then we have a people, a society which has been sifted, and you see the result!

XVI.

Manners are the hypocrisy of nations, and hypocrisy is more or less perfect.

XVII.

Virtue, perhaps, is nothing more than politeness of soul.

Physical love is a craving like hunger, excepting that man eats all the time, and in love his appetite is neither so persistent nor so regular as at the table.

A piece of bread and a carafe of water will satisfy the hunger of any man; but our civilization has brought to light the science of gastronomy.

Love has its piece of bread, but it has also its science of loving, that science which we call coquetry, a delightful word which the French alone possess, for that science originated in this country.

Well, after all, isn't it enough to enrage all husbands when they think that man is so endowed with an innate desire to change from one food to another, that in some savage countries, where travelers have landed, they have found alcoholic drinks and ragouts?

Hunger is not so violent as love; but the caprices of the soul are more numerous, more bewitching, more exquisite in their intensity than the caprices of gastronomy; but all that the poets and the experiences of our own life have revealed to us on the subject of love, arms us celibates with a terrible power: we are the lion of the Gospel seeking whom we may devour.

Then, let every one question his conscience on this point, and search his memory if he has ever met a man who confined himself to the love of one woman only!

How, alas! are we to explain, while respecting the honor of all the peoples, the problem which results from the fact that three millions of burning hearts can find no more than four hundred thousand women on which they can feed? Should we apportion four celibates for each woman and remember that the honest women would have already established, instinctively and unconsciously, a sort of understanding between themselves and the celibates, like that which the presidents of royal courts have initiated, in order to make their partisans in each chamber enter successively after a certain number of years?

That would be a mournful way of solving the difficulty!

Should we make the conjecture that certain honest women act in dividing up the celibates, as the lion in the fable did? What! Surely, in that case, half at least of our altars would become whited sepulchres!

Ought one to suggest for the honor of French ladies that in the time of peace all other countries should import into France a certain number of their honest women, and that these countries should mainly consist of England, Germany and Russia? But the European nations would in that case attempt to balance matters by demanding that France should export a certain number of her pretty women.

Morality and religion suffer so much from such calculations as this, that an honest man, in an attempt to prove the innocence of married women, finds some reason to believe that dowagers and young people are half of them involved in this general corruption, and are liars even more truly than are the celibates.

But to what conclusion does our calculation lead us? Think of our husbands, who to the disgrace of morals behave almost all of them like celibates and glory *in petto* over their secret adventures.

Why, then we believe that every married man, who is at all attached to his wife from honorable motives, can, in the words of the elder Corneille, seek a rope and a nail; *foenum habet in cornu.*

It is, however, in the bosom of these four hundred thousand honest women that we must, lantern in hand, seek for the number of the virtuous women in France! As a matter of fact, we have by our statistics of marriage so far only set down the number of those creatures with which society has really nothing to do. Is it not true that in France the honest people, the people *comme il faut*, form a total of scarcely three million individuals, namely, our one million of celibates, five hundred thousand honest women, five hundred thousand husbands, and a million of dowagers, of infants and of young girls?

Are you then astonished at the famous verse of Boileau? This verse proves that the poet had cleverly fathomed the discovery mathematically propounded to you in these tiresome meditations and that his language is by no means hyperbolical.

Nevertheless, virtuous women there certainly are:

Yes, those who have never been tempted and those who die at their first childbirth, assuming that their husbands had married them virgins;

Yes, those who are ugly as the Kaifakatadary of the Arabian Nights;

Yes, those whom Mirabeau calls "fairy cucumbers" and who are composed of atoms exactly like those of strawberry and water-lily roots. Nevertheless, we need not believe that!

Further, we acknowledge that, to the credit of our age, we meet, ever since the revival of morality and religion and during our own times, some women, here and there, so moral, so religious, so devoted to their duties, so upright, so precise, so stiff, so virtuous, so—that the devil himself dare not even look at them; they are guarded on all sides by rosaries, hours of prayer and directors. Pshaw!

We will not attempt to enumerate the women who are virtuous from stupidity, for it is acknowledged that in love all women have intellect.

In conclusion, we may remark that it is not impossible that there exist in some corner of the earth women, young, pretty and virtuous, whom the world does not suspect.

But you must not give the name of virtuous woman to her who, in her struggle against an involuntary passion, has yielded nothing to her lover whom she idolizes. She does injury in the most cruel way in which it can possibly be done to a loving husband. For what remains to him of his wife? A thing without name, a living corpse. In the very midst of delight his wife remains like the guest who has been warned by Borgia that certain meats were poisoned; he felt no hunger, he ate sparingly or pretended to eat. He longed for the meat which he had abandoned for that provided by the terrible cardinal, and sighed for the moment when the feast was over and he could leave the table.

What is the result which these reflections on the feminine virtue lead to? Here they are; but the last two maxims have been given us by an eclectic philosopher of the eighteenth century.

XVIII.

A virtuous woman has in her heart one fibre less or one fibre more than other women; she is either stupid or sublime.

XIX.

The virtue of women is perhaps a question of temperament.

XX.

The most virtuous women have in them something which is never chaste.

XXI.

"That a man of intellect has doubts about his mistress is conceivable, but about his wife!—that would be too stupid."

XXII.

"Men would be insufferably unhappy if in the presence of women they thought the least bit in the world of that which they know by heart."

The number of those rare women who, like the Virgins of the Parable, have kept their lamps lighted, will always appear very small in the eyes of the defenders of virtue and fine feeling; but we must needs exclude it from the total sum of honest women, and this subtraction, consoling as it is, will increase the danger which threatens husbands, will intensify the scandal of their married life, and involve, more or less, the reputation of all other lawful spouses.

What husband will be able to sleep peacefully beside his young and beautiful wife while he knows that three celibates, at least, are on the watch; that if they have not already encroached upon his little property, they regard the bride as their destined prey, for sooner or later she will fall into their hands, either by stratagem, compulsive conquest or free choice? And it is impossible that they should fail some day or other to obtain victory!

What a startling conclusion!

On this point the purist in morality, the *collets montes* will accuse us perhaps of presenting here conclusions which are excessively despairing; they will be desirous of putting up a defence, either for the virtuous women or the celibates; but we have in reserve for them a final remark.

Increase the number of honest women and diminish the number of celibates, as much as you choose, you will always find that the result will be a larger number of gallant adventurers than of honest women; you will always find a vast multitude driven through social custom to commit three sorts of crime.

If they remain chaste, their health is injured, while they are the slaves of the most painful torture; they disappoint the sublime ends of nature, and finally die of consumption, drinking milk on the mountains of Switzerland!

If they yield to legitimate temptations, they either compromise the honest women, and on this point we re-enter on the subject of this book, or else they debase themselves by a horrible intercourse with the five hundred thousand women of whom we spoke in the third category of the first Meditation, and in this case, have still considerable chance of visiting Switzerland, drinking milk and dying there!

Have you never been struck, as we have been, by a certain error of organization in our social order, the evidence of which gives a moral certainty to our last calculations?

The average age at which a man marries is thirty years; the average age at which his passions, his most violent desires for genesial delight are developed, is twenty years. Now during the ten fairest years of his life, during the green season in which his beauty, his youth and his wit make him more dangerous to husbands than at any other epoch of his life, his finds himself without any means of satisfying legitimately that irresistible craving for love which burns in his whole nature. During this time, representing the sixth part of human life, we are obliged to admit that the sixth part or less of our total male population and the sixth part which is the most vigorous is placed in a position which is perpetually exhausting for them, and dangerous for society.

"Why don't they get married?" cries a religious woman.

But what father of good sense would wish his son to be married at twenty years of age?

Is not the danger of these precocious unions apparent at all? It would seem as if marriage was a state very much at variance with natural habitude, seeing that it requires a special ripeness of judgment in those who conform to it. All the world knows what Rousseau said: "There must always be a period of libertinage in life either in one state or another. It is an evil leaven which sooner or later ferments."

Now what mother of a family is there who would expose her daughter to the risk of this fermentation when it has not yet taken place?

On the other hand, what need is there to justify a fact under whose domination all societies exist? Are there not in every country, as we have demonstrated, a vast number of men who live as honestly as possible, without being either celibates or married men?

Cannot these men, the religious women will always ask, abide in continence like the priests?

Certainly, madame.

Nevertheless, we venture to observe that the vow of chastity is the most startling exception to the natural condition of man which society makes necessary; but continence is the great point in the priest's profession; he must be chaste, as the doctor must be insensible to physical sufferings, as the notary and the advocate insensible to the misery whose wounds are laid bare to their eyes, as the soldier to the sight of death which he meets on the field of battle. From the fact that the requirements of civilization ossify certain fibres of the heart and render callous certain membranes, we must not necessarily conclude that all men are bound to undergo this partial and exceptional death of the soul. This would be to reduce the human race to a condition of atrocious moral suicide.

But let it be granted that, in the atmosphere of a drawing-room the most Jansenistic in the world, appears a young man of twenty-eight who has scrupulously guarded his robe of innocence and is as truly virginal as the heath-cock which gourmands enjoy. Do you not see that the most austere of virtuous women would merely pay him a sarcastic compliment on his courage; the magistrate, the strictest that ever mounted a bench, would shake his head and smile, and all the ladies would hide themselves, so that he might not hear their laughter? When the heroic and exceptional young victim leaves the drawing-room, what a deluge of jokes bursts upon his innocent head? What a shower of insults! What is held to be more shameful in France than impotence, than coldness, than the absence of all passion, than simplicity?

The only king of France who would not have laughed was perhaps Louis XIII; but as for his roue of a father, he would perhaps have banished the young man, either under the accusation that he was no Frenchman or from a conviction that he was setting a dangerous example.

Strange contradiction! A young man is equally blamed if he passes life in Holy Land, to use an expression of bachelor life. Could it possibly be for the benefit of the honest women that the prefects of police, and mayors of all time have ordained that the passions of the public shall not manifest themselves until nightfall, and shall cease at eleven o'clock in the evening?

Where do you wish that our mass of celibates should sow their wild oats? And who is deceived on this point? as Figaro asks. Is it the governments or the governed? The social order is like the small boys who stop their ears at the theatre, so as not to hear the report of the firearms. Is society afraid to probe its wound or has it recognized the fact that evil is irremediable and things must be allowed to run their course? But there crops up here a question of legislation, for it is impossible to escape the material and social dilemma created by this balance of public virtue in the matter of marriage. It is not our business to solve this difficulty; but suppose for a moment that society in order to save a multitude of families, women and honest girls, found itself compelled to grant to certain licensed hearts the right of satisfying the desire of the celibates; ought not our laws then to raise up a professional body consisting of female Decii who devote themselves for the republic, and make a rampart of their bodies round the honest families? The legislators have been very wrong hitherto in disdaining to regulate the lot of courtesans.

XXIII.

The courtesan is an institution if she is a necessity.

This question bristles with so many ifs and buts that we will bequeath it for solution to our descendants; it is right that we shall leave them something to do. Moreover, its discussion is not germane to this work; for in this, more than in any other age, there is a great outburst of sensibility; at no other epoch have there been so many rules of conduct, because never before has it been so completely accepted that pleasure comes from the heart. Now, what man of sentiment is there, what celibate is there, who, in the presence of four hundred thousand young and pretty women arrayed in the splendors of fortune and the graces of wit, rich in treasures of coquetry, and lavish in the dispensing of happiness, would wish to go—? For shame!

Let us put forth for the benefit of our future legislature in clear and brief axioms the result arrived at during the last few years.

XXIV.

In the social order, inevitable abuses are laws of nature, in accordance with which mankind should frame their civil and political institutes.

XXV.

"Adultery is like a commercial failure, with this difference," says Chamfort, "that it is the innocent party who has been ruined and who bears the disgrace."

In France the laws that relate to adultery and those that relate to bankruptcy require great modifications. Are they too indulgent? Do they sin on the score of bad principles? *Caveant consules*!

Come now, courageous athlete, who have taken as your task that which is expressed in the little apostrophe which our first Meditation addresses to people who have the charge of a wife, what are you going to say about it? We hope that this rapid review of the question does not make you tremble, that you are not one of those men whose nervous fluid congeals at the sight of a precipice or a boa constrictor! Well! my friend, he who owns soil has war and toil. The men who want your gold are more numerous than those who want your wife.

After all, husbands are free to take these trifles for arithmetical estimates, or arithmetical estimates for trifles. The illusions of life are the best things in life; that which is most respectable in life is our futile credulity. Do there not exist many people whose principles are merely prejudices, and who not having the force of character to form their own ideas of happiness and virtue accept what is ready made for them by the hand of legislators? Nor do we address those Manfreds who having taken off too many garments wish to raise all the curtains, that is, in moments when they are tortured by a sort of moral spleen. By them, however, the question is boldly stated and we know the extent of the evil.

It remains that we should examine the chances and changes which each man is likely to meet in marriage, and which may weaken him in that struggle from which our champion should issue victorious.

MEDITATION V.
OF THE PREDESTINED.

Predestined means destined in advance for happiness or unhappiness. Theology has seized upon this word and employs it in relation to the happy; we give to the term a meaning which is unfortunate to our elect of which one can say in opposition to the Gospel, "Many are called, many are chosen."

Experience has demonstrated that there are certain classes of men more subject than others to certain infirmities; the Gascons are given to exaggeration and Parisians to vanity. As we see that apoplexy attacks people with short necks, or butchers are liable to carbuncle, as gout attacks the rich, health the poor, deafness kings, paralysis administrators, so it has been remarked that certain classes of husbands and their wives are more given to illegitimate passions. Thus they forestall the celibates, they form another sort of aristocracy. If any reader should be enrolled in one of these aristocratic classes he will, we hope, have sufficient presence of mind, he or at least his wife, instantly to call to mind the favorite axiom of Lhomond's Latin Grammar: "No rule without exception." A friend of the house may even recite the verse —

"Present company always excepted."

And then every one will have the right to believe, *in petto*, that he forms the exception. But our duty, the interest which we take in husbands and the keen desire which we have to preserve young and pretty women from the caprices and catastrophes which a lover brings in his train, force us to give notice to husbands that they ought to be especially on their guard.

In this recapitulation first are to be reckoned the husbands whom business, position or public office calls from their houses and detains for a definite time. It is these who are the standard-bearers of the brotherhood.

Among them, we would reckon magistrates, holding office during pleasure or for life, and obliged to remain at the Palace for the greater portion of the day; other functionaries sometimes find means to leave their office at business hours; but a judge or a public prosecutor, seated on his cushion of lilies, is bound even to die during the progress of the hearing. There is his field of battle.

It is the same with the deputies and peers who discuss the laws, of ministers who share the toils of the king, of secretaries who work with the ministers, of soldiers on campaign, and indeed with the corporal of the police patrol, as the letter of Lafleur, in the *Sentimental Journey*, plainly shows.

Next to the men who are obliged to be absent from home at certain fixed hours, come the men whom vast and serious undertakings leave not one minute for love-making; their foreheads are always wrinkled with anxiety, their conversation is generally void of merriment.

At the head of these unfortunates we must place the bankers, who toil in the acquisition of millions, whose heads are so full of calculations that the figures burst through their skulls and range themselves in columns of addition on their foreheads.

These millionaires, forgetting most of the time the sacred laws of marriage and the attention due to the tender flower which they have undertaken to cultivate, never think of watering it or of defending it from the heat and cold. They scarcely recognize the fact that the happiness of their spouses is in their keeping; if they ever do remember this, it is at table, when they see seated before them a woman in rich array, or when a coquette, fearing their brutal repulse, comes, gracious as Venus, to ask them for cash— Oh! it is then, that they recall, sometimes very vividly, the rights specified in the two hundred and thirteenth article of the civil code, and their wives are grateful to them; but like the heavy tariff which the law lays upon foreign merchandise, their wives suffer and pay the tribute, in virtue of the axiom which says: "There is no pleasure without pain."

The men of science who spend whole months in gnawing at the bone of an antediluvian monster, in calculating the laws of nature, when there is an opportunity to peer into her secrets, the Grecians and Latinists who dine on a thought of Tacitus, sup on a phrase of Thucydides, spend their life in brushing the dust from library shelves, in keeping guard over a commonplace book, or a papyrus, are all predestined. So great is their abstraction or their ecstasy, that nothing that goes on around them strikes their attention. Their unhappiness is consummated; in full light of noon they scarcely even perceive it. Oh happy men! a thousand times happy! Example: Beauzee, returning home after session at the Academy, surprises his wife with a German. "Did not I tell you, madame, that it was necessary that I shall go," cried the stranger. "My dear sir," interrupted the academician, "you ought to say that I *should* go!"

Then there come, lyre in hand, certain poets whose whole animal strength has left the ground floor and mounted to the upper story. They know better how to mount Pegasus than the beast of old Peter, they rarely marry, although they are accustomed to lavish the fury of their passions on some wandering or imaginary Chloris.

But the men whose noses are stained with snuff;

But those who, to their misfortune, have a perpetual cold in their head;

But the sailors who smoke or chew;

But those men whose dry and bilious temperament makes them always look as if they had eaten a sour apple;

But the men who in private life have certain cynical habits, ridiculous fads, and who always, in spite of everything, look unwashed;

But the husbands who have obtained the degrading name of "hen-pecked";

Finally the old men who marry young girls.

All these people are *par excellence* among the predestined.

There is a final class of the predestined whose ill-fortune is almost certain, we mean restless and irritable men, who are inclined to meddle and tyrannize, who have a great idea of domestic domination, who openly express their low ideas of women and who know no more about life than herrings about natural history. When these men marry, their homes have the appearance of a wasp whose head a schoolboy has cut off, and who dances here and there on a window pane. For this sort of predestined the present work is a sealed book. We do not write any more for those imbeciles, walking effigies, who are like the statues of a cathedral, than for those old machines of Marly which are too weak to fling water over the hedges of Versailles without being in danger of sudden collapse.

I rarely make my observations on the conjugal oddities with which the drawing-room is usually full, without recalling vividly a sight which I once enjoyed in early youth:

In 1819 I was living in a thatched cottage situated in the bosom of the delightful valley l'Isle-Adam. My hermitage neighbored on the park of Cassan, the sweetest of retreats, the most fascinating in aspect, the most attractive as a place to ramble in, the most cool and refreshing in summer, of all places created by luxury and art. This verdant country-seat owes its origin to a farmer-general of the good old times, a certain Bergeret, celebrated for his originality; who among other fantastic dandyisms adopted the habit of going to the opera, with his hair powdered in gold; he used to light up his park for his own solitary delectation and on one occasion ordered a sumptuous entertainment there, in which he alone took part. This rustic Sardanapalus returned from Italy so passionately charmed with the scenery of that beautiful country that, by a sudden freak of enthusiasm, he spent four or five millions in order to represent in his park the scenes of which he had pictures in his portfolio. The most charming contrasts of foliage, the rarest trees, long valleys, and prospects the most picturesque that could be brought from abroad, Borromean islands floating on clear eddying streams like so many rays, which concentrate their various lustres on a single point, on an Isola Bella, from which the enchanted eye takes in each detail at its leisure, or on an island in the bosom of which is a little house concealed under the drooping foliage of a century-old ash, an island fringed with irises, rose-bushes, and flowers which appears like an emerald richly set. Ah! one might rove a thousand leagues for such a place! The most sickly, the most soured, the most disgusted of our men of genius in ill health would die of satiety at the end of fifteen days, overwhelmed with the luscious sweetness of fresh life in such a spot.

The man who was quite regardless of the Eden which he thus possessed had neither wife nor children, but was attached to a large ape which he kept. A graceful turret of wood, supported by a sculptured column, served as a dwelling place for this vicious animal, who being kept chained and rarely petted by his eccentric master, oftener at Paris than in his country home, had gained a very bad reputation. I recollect seeing him once in the presence of certain ladies show almost as much insolence as if he had been a man. His master was obliged to kill him, so mischievous did he gradually become.

One morning while I was sitting under a beautiful tulip tree in flower, occupied in doing nothing but inhaling the lovely perfumes which the tall poplars kept confined within the brilliant enclosure, enjoying the silence of the groves, listening to the murmuring waters and the rustling leaves, admiring the blue gaps outlined above my head by clouds of pearly sheen and gold, wandering fancy free in dreams of my future, I heard some lout or other, who had arrived the day before from Paris, playing on a violin with the violence of a man who has nothing else to do. I would not wish for my worst enemy to hear anything so utterly in discord with the sublime harmony of nature. If the distant notes of Roland's Horn had only filled the air with life, perhaps—but a noisy fiddler like this, who undertakes to bring to you the expression of human ideas and the phraseology of music! This Amphion, who was walking up and down the dining-room, finished by taking a seat on the window-sill, exactly in front of the monkey. Perhaps he was looking for an audience. Suddenly I saw the animal quietly descend from his little dungeon, stand upon his hind feet, bow his head forward like a swimmer and fold his arms over his bosom like Spartacus in chains, or Catiline listening to Cicero. The banker, summoned by a sweet voice whose silvery tone recalled a boudoir not unknown to me, laid his violin on the window-sill and made off like a swallow who rejoins his companion by a rapid level swoop. The great monkey, whose chain was sufficiently long, approached the window and gravely took in hand the violin. I don't know whether you have ever had as I have the pleasure of seeing a monkey try to learn music, but at the present moment, when I laugh much less than I did in those careless days, I never think of that monkey without a smile; the semi-man began by grasping the instrument with his fist and by sniffing at it as if he were tasting the flavor of an apple. The snort from his nostrils probably produced a dull harmonious sound in the sonorous wood and then the orang-outang shook his head, turned over the violin, turned it back again, raised it up in the air, lowered it, held it straight out, shook it, put it to his ear, set it down, and picked it up again with a rapidity of movement peculiar to these agile creatures. He seemed to question the dumb wood with faltering sagacity and in his gestures there was something marvelous as well as infantile. At last he undertook with grotesque gestures to place the violin under his chin, while in one hand he held the neck; but like a spoiled child he soon wearied of a study which required skill not to be obtained in a moment and he twitched the strings without being able to draw forth anything but discordant sounds. He seemed annoyed, laid the violin on the window-sill and snatching up the bow he began to push it to and fro with violence, like a mason sawing a block of stone. This effort only succeeded in wearying his fastidious ears, and he took the bow with both hands and snapped it in two on the innocent instrument, source of harmony and delight. It seemed as if I saw before me a schoolboy holding under him a companion lying face downwards, while he pommeled him with a shower of blows from his fist, as if to punish him for some delinquency. The violin being now tried and condemned, the monkey sat down upon the fragments of it and amused himself with stupid joy in mixing up the yellow strings of the broken bow.

Never since that day have I been able to look upon the home of the predestined without comparing the majority of husbands to this orang-outang trying to play the violin.

Love is the most melodious of all harmonies and the sentiment of love is innate. Woman is a delightful instrument of pleasure, but it is necessary to know its trembling strings, to study the position of them, the timid keyboard, the fingering so changeful and capricious which befits it. How many monkeys—men, I mean—marry without knowing what a woman is! How many of the predestined proceed with their wives as the ape of Cassan did with his violin! They have broken the heart which they did not understand, as they might dim and disdain the amulet whose secret was unknown to them. They are children their whole life through, who leave life with empty hands after having talked about love, about pleasure, about licentiousness and virtue as slaves talk about liberty. Almost all of them married with the most profound ignorance of women and of love. They commenced by breaking in the door of a strange house and expected to be welcomed in this drawing-room. But the rudest artist knows that between him and his instrument, of wood, or of ivory, there exists a mysterious sort of friendship. He knows by experience that it takes years to establish this understanding between an inert matter and himself. He did not discover, at the first touch, the resources, the caprices, the deficiencies, the excellencies of his instrument. It did not become a living soul for him, a source of incomparable melody until he had studied for a long time; man and instrument did not come to understand each other like two friends, until both of them had been skillfully questioned and tested by frequent intercourse.

Can a man ever learn woman and know how to decipher this wondrous strain of music, by remaining through life like a seminarian in his cell? Is it possible that a man who makes it his business to think for others, to judge others, to rule others, to steal money from others, to feed, to heal, to wound others—that, in fact, any of our predestined, can spare time to study a woman? They sell their time for money, how can they give it away for happiness? Money is their god. No one can serve two masters at the same time. Is not the world, moreover, full of young women who drag along pale and weak, sickly and suffering? Some of them are the prey of feverish inflammations more or less serious, others lie under the cruel tyranny of nervous attacks more or less violent. All the husbands of these women belong to the class of the ignorant and the predestined. They have caused their own misfortune and expended as much pains in producing it as the husband artist would have bestowed in bringing to flower the late and delightful blooms of pleasure. The time which an ignorant man passes to consummate his own ruin is precisely that which a man of knowledge employs in the education of his happiness.

XXVI.

Do not begin marriage by a violation of law.

In the preceding meditations we have indicated the extent of the evil with the reckless audacity of those surgeons, who boldly induce the formation of false tissues under which a shameful wound is concealed. Public virtue, transferred to the table of our amphitheatre, has lost even its carcass under the strokes of the scalpel. Lover or husband, have you smiled, or have you trembled at this evil? Well, it is with malicious delight that we lay this huge social burden on the conscience of the predestined. Harlequin, when he tried to find out whether his horse could be accustomed to go without food, was not more ridiculous than the men who wish to find happiness in their home and yet refuse to cultivate it with all the pains which it demands. The errors of women are so many indictments of egotism, neglect and worthlessness in husbands.

Yet it is yours, reader, it pertains to you, who have often condemned in another the crime which you yourself commit, it is yours to hold the balance. One of the scales is quite loaded, take care what you are going to put in the other. Reckon up the number of predestined ones who may be found among the total number of married people, weigh them, and you will then know where the evil is seated.

Let us try to penetrate more deeply into the causes of this conjugal sickliness.

The word love, when applied to the reproduction of the species, is the most hateful blasphemy which modern manners have taught us to utter. Nature, in raising us above the beasts by the divine gift of thought, had rendered us very sensitive to bodily sensations, emotional sentiment, cravings of appetite and passions. This double nature of ours makes of man both an animal and a lover. This distinction gives the key to the social problem which we are considering.

Marriage may be considered in three ways, politically, as well as from a civil and moral point of view: as a law, as a contract and as an institution. As a law, its object is a reproduction of the species; as a contract, it relates to the transmission of property; as an institution, it is a guarantee which all men give and by which all are bound: they have father and mother, and they will have children. Marriage, therefore, ought to be the object of universal respect. Society can only take into consideration those cardinal points, which, from a social point of view, dominate the conjugal question.

Most men have no other views in marrying, than reproduction, property or children; but neither reproduction nor property nor children constitutes happiness. The command, "Increase and multiply," does not imply love. To ask of a young girl whom we have seen fourteen times in fifteen days, to give you love in the name of law, the king and justice, is an absurdity worthy of the majority of the predestined.

Love is the union between natural craving and sentiment; happiness in marriage results in perfect union of soul between a married pair. Hence it follows that in order to be happy a man must feel himself bound by certain rules of honor and delicacy. After having enjoyed the benefit of the social law which consecrates the natural craving, he must obey also the secret laws of nature by which sentiments unfold themselves. If he stakes his happiness on being himself loved, he must himself love sincerely: nothing can resist a genuine passion.

But to feel this passion is always to feel desire. Can a man always desire his wife?

Yes.

It is as absurd to deny that it is possible for a man always to love the same woman, as it would be to affirm that some famous musician needed several violins in order to execute a piece of music or compose a charming melody.

Love is the poetry of the senses. It has the destiny of all that which is great in man and of all that which proceeds from his thought. Either it is sublime, or it is not. When once it exists, it exists forever and goes on always increasing. This is the love which the ancients made the child of heaven and earth.

Literature revolves round seven situations; music expresses everything with seven notes; painting employs but seven colors; like these three arts, love perhaps founds itself on seven principles, but we leave this investigation for the next century to carry out.

If poetry, music and painting have found infinite forms of expression, pleasure should be even more diversified. For in the three arts which aid us in seeking, often with little success, truth by means of analogy, the man stands alone with his imagination, while love is the union of two bodies and of two souls. If the three principal methods upon which we rely for the expression of thought require preliminary study in those whom nature has made poets, musicians or painters, is it not obvious that, in order, to be happy, it is necessary to be initiated into the secrets of pleasure? All men experience the craving for reproduction, as all feel hunger and thirst; but all are not called to be lovers and gastronomists. Our present civilization has proved that taste is a science, and it is only certain privileged beings who have learned how to eat and drink. Pleasure considered as an art is still waiting for its physiologists. As for ourselves, we are contented with pointing out that ignorance of the principles upon which happiness is founded, is the sole cause of that misfortune which is the lot of all the predestined.

It is with the greatest timidity that we venture upon the publication of a few aphorisms which may give birth to this new art, as casts have created the science of geology; and we offer them for the meditation of philosophers, of young marrying people and of the predestined.

CATECHISM OF MARRIAGE.

XXVII.

Marriage is a science.

XXVIII.

A man ought not to marry without having studied anatomy, and dissected at least one woman.

XXIX.

The fate of the home depends on the first night.

XXX.

A woman deprived of her free will can never have the credit of making a sacrifice.

XXXI.

In love, putting aside all consideration of the soul, the heart of a woman is like a lyre which does not reveal its secret, excepting to him who is a skillful player.

XXXII.

Independently of any gesture of repulsion, there exists in the soul of all women a sentiment which tends, sooner or later, to proscribe all pleasure devoid of passionate feeling.

XXXIII.

The interest of a husband as much as his honor forbids him to indulge a pleasure which he has not had the skill to make his wife desire.

XXXIV.

Pleasure being caused by the union of sensation and sentiment, we can say without fear of contradiction that pleasures are a sort of material ideas.

XXXV.

As ideas are capable of infinite combination, it ought to be the same with pleasures.

XXXVI.

In the life of man there are no two moments of pleasure exactly alike, any more than there are two leaves of identical shape upon the same tree.

XXXVII.

If there are differences between one moment of pleasure and another, a man can always be happy with the same woman.

XXXVIII.

To seize adroitly upon the varieties of pleasure, to develop them, to impart to them a new style, an original expression, constitutes the genius of a husband.

XXXIX.

Between two beings who do not love each other this genius is licentiousness;

but the caresses over which love presides are always pure.

XL.

The married woman who is the most chaste may be also the most voluptuous.

XLI.

The most virtuous woman can be forward without knowing it.

XLII.

When two human beings are united by pleasure, all social conventionalities are put aside. This situation conceals a reef on which many vessels are wrecked. A husband is lost, if he once forgets there is a modesty which is quite independent of coverings. Conjugal love ought never either to put on or to take away the bandage of its eyes, excepting at the due season.

XLIII.

Power does not consist in striking with force or with frequency, but in striking true.

XLIV.

To call a desire into being, to nourish it, to develop it, to bring it to full growth, to excite it, to satisfy it, is a complete poem of itself.

XLV.

The progression of pleasures is from the distich to the quatrain, from the quatrain to the sonnet, from the sonnet to the ballad, from the ballad to the ode, from the ode to the cantata, from the cantata to the dithyramb. The husband who commences with dithyramb is a fool.

XLVI.

Each night ought to have its *menu*.

XLVII.

Marriage must incessantly contend with a monster which devours everything, that is, familiarity.

XLVIII.

If a man cannot distinguish the difference between the pleasures of two consecutive nights, he has married too early.

XLIX.

It is easier to be a lover than a husband, for the same reason that it is more difficult to be witty every day, than to say bright things from time to time.

L.

A husband ought never to be the first to go to sleep and the last to awaken.

LI.

The man who enters his wife's dressing-room is either a philosopher or an imbecile.

LII.

The husband who leaves nothing to desire is a lost man.

LIII.

The married woman is a slave whom one must know how to set upon a throne.

LIV.

A man must not flatter himself that he knows his wife, and is making her happy unless he sees her often at his knees.

It is to the whole ignorant troop of our predestined, of our legions of snivelers, of smokers, of snuff-takers, of old and captious men that Sterne addressed, in *Tristram Shandy*, the letter written by Walter Shandy to his brother Toby, when this last proposed to marry the widow Wadman.

These celebrated instructions which the most original of English writers has comprised in this letter, suffice with some few exceptions to complete our observations on the manner in which husbands should behave to their wives; and we offer it in its original form to the reflections of the predestined, begging that they will meditate upon it as one of the most solid masterpieces of human wit.

"MY DEAR BROTHER TOBY,

"What I am going to say to thee is upon the nature of women, and of love-making to them; and perhaps it is as well for thee—tho' not so well for me—that thou hast occasion for a letter of instructions upon that head, and that I am able to write it to thee.

"Had it been the good pleasure of Him who disposes of our lots, and thou no sufferer by the knowledge, I had been well content that thou should'st have dipped the pen this moment into the ink instead of myself; but that not being the case—Mrs. Shandy being now close beside me, preparing for bed—I have thrown together without order, and just as they have come into my mind, such hints and documents as I deem may be of use to thee; intending, in this, to give thee a token of my love; not doubting, my dear Toby, of the manner in which it will be accepted.

"In the first place, with regard to all which concerns religion in the affair—though I perceive from a glow in my cheek, that I blush as I begin to speak to thee upon the subject, as well knowing, notwithstanding thy unaffected secrecy, how few of its offices thou neglectest—yet I would remind thee of one (during the continuance of thy courtship) in a particular manner, which I would not have omitted; and that is, never to go forth upon the enterprise, whether it be in the morning or in the afternoon, without first recommending thyself to the protection of Almighty God, that He may defend thee from the evil one.

"Shave the whole top of thy crown clean once at least every four or five days, but oftener if convenient; lest in taking off thy wig before her, thro' absence of mind, she should be able to discover how much has been cut away by Time—how much by Trim.

"'Twere better to keep ideas of baldness out of her fancy.

"Always carry it in thy mind, and act upon it as a sure maxim, Toby—

"'*That women are timid.*' And 'tis well they are—else there would be no dealing with them.

"Let not thy breeches be too tight, or hang too loose about thy thighs, like the trunk-hose of our ancestors.

"A just medium prevents all conclusions.

"Whatever thou hast to say, be it more or less, forget not to utter it in a low soft tone of voice. Silence, and whatever approaches it, weaves dreams of midnight secrecy into the brain: For this cause, if thou canst help it, never throw down the tongs and poker.

"Avoid all kinds of pleasantry and facetiousness in thy discourse with her, and do whatever lies in thy power at the same time, to keep from her all books and writings which tend there to: there are some devotional tracts, which if thou canst entice her to read over, it will be well: but suffer her not to look into *Rabelais*, or *Scarron*, or *Don Quixote*.

"They are all books which excite laughter; and thou knowest, dear Toby, that there is no passion so serious as lust.

"Stick a pin in the bosom of thy shirt, before thou enterest her parlor.

"And if thou art permitted to sit upon the same sofa with her, and she gives thee occasion to lay thy hand upon hers—beware of taking it—thou canst not lay thy hand upon hers, but she will feel the temper of thine. Leave that and as many other things as thou canst, quite undetermined; by so doing, thou wilt have her curiosity on thy side; and if she is not conquered by that, and thy Asse continues still kicking, which there is great reason to suppose—thou must begin, with first losing a few ounces of blood below the ears, according to the practice of the ancient Scythians, who cured the most intemperate fits of the appetite by that means.

"*Avicenna*, after this, is for having the part anointed with the syrup of hellebore, using proper evacuations and purges—and I believe rightly. But thou must eat little or no goat's flesh, nor red deer—nor even foal's flesh by any means; and carefully abstain—that is, as much as thou canst,—from peacocks, cranes, coots, didappers and water-hens.

"As for thy drink—I need not tell thee, it must be the infusion of Vervain and the herb Hanea, of which Aelian relates such effects; but if thy stomach palls with it—discontinue it from time to time, taking cucumbers, melons, purslane, water-lilies, woodbine, and lettuce, in the stead of them.

"There is nothing further for thee, which occurs to me at present—

"Unless the breaking out of a fresh war.—So wishing everything, dear Toby, for the best,

> "I rest thy affectionate brother,
> "WALTER SHANDY."

Under the present circumstances Sterne himself would doubtless have omitted from his letter the passage about the ass; and, far from advising the predestined to be bled he would have changed the regimen of cucumbers and lettuces for one eminently substantial. He recommended the exercise of economy, in order to attain to the power of magic liberality in the moment of war, thus imitating the admirable example of the English government, which in time of peace has two hundred ships in commission, but whose shipwrights can, in time of need, furnish double that quantity when it is desirable to scour the sea and carry off a whole foreign navy.

When a man belongs to the small class of those who by a liberal education have been made masters of the domain of thought, he ought always, before marrying, to examine his physical and moral resources. To contend advantageously with the tempest which so many attractions tend to raise in the heart of his wife, a husband ought to possess, besides the science of pleasure and a fortune which saves him from sinking into any class of the predestined, robust health, exquisite tact, considerable intellect, too much good sense to make his superiority felt, excepting on fit occasions, and finally great acuteness of hearing and sight.

If he has a handsome face, a good figure, a manly air, and yet falls short of all these promises, he will sink into the class of the predestined. On the other hand, a husband who is plain in features but has a face full of expression, will find himself, if his wife once forgets his plainness, in a situation most favorable for his struggle against the genius of evil.

He will study (and this is a detail omitted from the letter of Sterne) to give no occasion for his wife's disgust. Also, he will resort moderately to the use of perfumes, which, however, always expose beauty to injurious suspicions.

He ought as carefully to study how to behave and how to pick out subjects of conversation, as if he were courting the most inconstant of women. It is for him that a philosopher has made the following reflection:

"More than one woman has been rendered unhappy for the rest of her life, has been lost and dishonored by a man whom she has ceased to love, because he took off his coat awkwardly, trimmed one of his nails crookedly, put on a stocking wrong side out, and was clumsy with a button."

One of the most important of his duties will be to conceal from his wife the real state of his fortune, so that he may satisfy her fancies and caprices as generous celibates are wont to do.

Then the most difficult thing of all, a thing to accomplish which superhuman courage is required, is to exercise the most complete control over the ass of which Sterne speaks. This ass ought to be as submissive as a serf of the thirteenth century was to his lord; to obey and be silent, advance and stop, at the slightest word.

Even when equipped with these advantages, a husband enters the lists with scarcely any hope of success. Like all the rest, he still runs the risk of becoming, for his wife, a sort of responsible editor.

"And why!" will exclaim certain good but small-minded people, whose horizon is limited to the tip of their nose, "why is it necessary to take so much pains in order to love, and why is it necessary to go to school beforehand, in order to be happy in your own home? Does the government intend to institute a professional chair of love, just as it has instituted a chair of law?"

This is our answer:

These multiplied rules, so difficult to deduce, these minute observations, these ideas which vary so as to suit different temperaments, are innate, so to speak, in the heart of those who are born for love; just as his feeling of taste and his indescribable felicity in combining ideas are natural to the soul of the poet, the painter or the musician. The men who would experience any fatigue in putting into practice the instructions given in this Meditation are naturally predestined, just as he who cannot perceive the connection which exists between two different ideas is an imbecile. As a matter of fact, love has its great men although they be unrecognized, as war has its Napoleons, poetry its Andre Cheniers and philosophy its Descartes.

This last observation contains the germ of a true answer to the question which men from time immemorial have been asking: Why are happy marriages so very rare?

This phenomenon of the moral world is rarely met with for the reason that people of genius are rarely met with. A passion which lasts is a sublime drama acted by two performers of equal talent, a drama in which sentiments form the catastrophe, where desires are incidents and the lightest thought brings a change of scene. Now how is it possible, in this herd of bimana which we call a nation, to meet, on any but rare occasions, a man and a woman who possess in the same degree the genius of love, when men of talent are so thinly sown and so rare in all other sciences, in the pursuit of which the artist needs only to understand himself, in order to attain success?

Up to the present moment, we have been confronted with making a forecast of the difficulties, to some degree physical, which two married people have to overcome, in order to be happy; but what a task would be ours if it were necessary to unfold the startling array of moral obligations which spring from their differences in character? Let us cry halt! The man who is skillful enough to guide the temperament will certainly show himself master of the soul of another.

We will suppose that our model husband fulfills the primary conditions necessary, in order that he may dispute or maintain possession of his wife, in spite of all assailants. We will admit that he is not to be reckoned in any of the numerous classes of the predestined which we have passed in review. Let us admit that he has become imbued with the spirit of all our maxims; that he has mastered the admirable science, some of whose precepts we have made known; that he has married wisely, that he knows his wife, that he is loved by her; and let us continue the enumeration of all those general causes which might aggravate the critical situation which we shall represent him as occupying for the instruction of the human race.

advance, at least by analogy, the pastimes of doves? And then her friends will marry; you will have four women to watch instead of one, four characters to divine, and you will be at the mercy of four husbands and a dozen celibates, of whose life, principles and habits you are quite ignorant, at a time when our meditations have revealed to you certain coming of a day when you will have your hands full with the people whom you married with your wife. Satan alone could have thought of placing a girl's boarding school in the middle of a large town! Madame Campan had at least the wisdom to set up her famous institution at Ecouen. This sensible precaution proved that she was no ordinary woman. There, her young ladies did not gaze upon the picture gallery of the streets, the huge and grotesque figures and the obscene words drawn by some evil-spirited pencil. They had not perpetually before their eyes the spectacle of human infirmities exhibited at every barrier in France, and treacherous book-stalls did not vomit out upon them in secret the poison of books which taught evil and set passion on fire. This wise school-mistress, moreover, could only at Ecouen preserve a young lady for you spotless and pure, if, even there, that were possible. Perhaps you hope to find no difficulty in preventing your wife from seeing her school friends? What folly! She will meet them at the ball, at the theatre, out walking and in the world at large; and how many services two friends can render each other! But we will meditate upon this new subject of alarm in its proper place and order.

Nor is this all; if your mother-in-law sent her daughter to a boarding school, do you believe that this was out of solicitude for her daughter? A girl of twelve or fifteen is a terrible Argus; and if your mother-in-law did not wish to have an Argus in her house I should be inclined to suspect that your mother-in-law belonged undoubtedly to the most shady section of our honest women. She will, therefore, prove for her daughter on every occasion either a deadly example or a dangerous adviser.

Let us stop here! — The mother-in-law requires a whole Meditation for herself.

So that, whichever way you turn, the bed of marriage, in this connection, is equally full of thorns.

Before the Revolution, several aristocratic families used to send their daughters to the convent. This example was followed by a number of people who imagined that in sending their daughters to a school where the daughters of some great noblemen were sent, they would assume the tone and manners of aristocrats. This delusion of pride was, from the first, fatal to domestic happiness; for the convents had all the disadvantages of other boarding schools. The idleness that prevailed there was more terrible. The cloister bars inflame the imagination. Solitude is a condition very favorable to the devil; and one can scarcely imagine what ravages the most ordinary phenomena of life are able to leave in the soul of these young girls, dreamy, ignorant and unoccupied.

Some of them, by reason of their having indulged idle fancies, are led into curious blunders. Others, having indulged in exaggerated ideas of married life, say to themselves, as soon as they have taken a husband, "What! Is this all?" In every way, the imperfect instruction, which is given to girls educated in common, has in it all the danger of ignorance and all the unhappiness of science.

A young girl brought up at home by her mother or by her virtuous, bigoted, amiable or cross-grained old aunt; a young girl, whose steps have never crossed the home threshold without being surrounded by chaperons, whose laborious childhood has been wearied by tasks, albeit they were profitless, to whom in short everything is a mystery, even the Seraphin puppet show, is one of those treasures which are met with, here and there in the world, like woodland flowers surrounded by brambles so thick that mortal eye cannot discern them. The man who owns a flower so sweet and pure as this, and leaves it to be cultivated by others, deserves his unhappiness a thousand times over. He is either a monster or a fool.

And if in the preceding Meditation we have succeeded in proving to you that by far the greater number of men live in the most absolute indifference to their personal honor, in the matter of marriage, is it reasonable to believe that any considerable number of them are sufficiently rich, sufficiently intellectual, sufficiently penetrating to waste, like Burchell in the *Vicar of Wakefield*, one or two years in studying and watching the girls whom they mean to make their wives, when they pay so little attention to them after conjugal possession during that period of time which the English call the honeymoon, and whose influence we shall shortly discuss?

Since, however, we have spent some time in reflecting upon this important matter, we would observe that there are many methods of choosing more or less successfully, even though the choice be promptly made.

It is, for example, beyond doubt that the probabilities will be in your favor:

I. If you have chosen a young lady whose temperament resembles that of the women of Louisiana or the Carolinas.

To obtain reliable information concerning the temperament of a young person, it is necessary to put into vigorous operation the system which Gil Blas prescribes, in dealing with chambermaids, a system employed by statesmen to discover conspiracies and to learn how the ministers have passed the night.

II. If you choose a young lady who, without being plain, does not belong to the class of pretty women.

We regard it as an infallible principle that great sweetness of disposition united in a woman with plainness that is not repulsive, form two indubitable elements of success in securing the greatest possible happiness to the home.

But would you learn the truth? Open your Rousseau; for there is not a single question of public morals whose trend he has not pointed out in advance. Read:

"Among people of fixed principles the girls are careless, the women severe; the contrary is the case among people of no principle."

To admit the truth enshrined in this profound and truthful remark is to conclude, that there would be fewer unhappy marriages if men wedded their mistresses. The education of girls requires, therefore, important modifications in France. Up to this time French laws and French manners instituted to distinguish between a misdemeanor and a crime, have encouraged crime. In reality the fault committed by a young girl is scarcely ever a misdemeanor, if you compare it with that committed by the married woman. Is there any comparison between the danger of giving liberty to girls and that of allowing it to wives? The idea of taking a young girl on trial makes more serious men think than fools laugh. The manners of Germany, of Switzerland, of England and of the United States give to young ladies such rights as in France would be considered the subversion of all morality; and yet it is certain that in these countries there are fewer unhappy marriages than in France.

LV.

"Before a woman gives herself entirely up to her lover, she ought to consider well what his love has to offer her. The gift of her esteem and confidence should necessarily precede that of her heart."

Sparkling with truth as they are, these lines probably filled with light the dungeon, in the depths of which Mirabeau wrote them; and the keen observation which they bear witness to, although prompted by the most stormy of his passions, has none the less influence even now in solving the social problem on which we are engaged. In fact, a marriage sealed under the auspices of the religious scrutiny which assumes the existence of love, and subjected to the atmosphere of that disenchantment which follows on possession, ought naturally to be the most firmly-welded of all human unions.

A woman then ought never to reproach her husband for the legal right, in virtue of which she belongs to him. She ought not to find in this compulsory submission any excuse for yielding to a lover, because some time after her marriage she has discovered in her own heart a traitor whose sophisms seduce her by asking twenty times an hour, "Wherefore, since she has been given against her will to a man whom she does not love, should she not give herself, of her own free-will, to a man whom she does love." A woman is not to be tolerated in her complaints concerning faults inseparable from human nature. She has, in advance, made trial of the tyranny which they exercise, and taken sides with the caprices which they exhibit.

A great many young girls are likely to be disappointed in their hopes of love! — But will it not be an immense advantage to them to have escaped being made the companions of men whom they would have had the right to despise?

Certain alarmists will exclaim that such an alteration in our manners would bring about a public dissoluteness which would be frightful; that the laws, and the customs which prompt the laws, could not after all authorize scandal and immorality; and if certain unavoidable abuses do exist, at least society ought not to sanction them.

It is easy to say, in reply, first of all, that the proposed system tends to prevent those abuses which have been hitherto regarded as incapable of prevention; but, the calculations of our statistics, inexact as they are, have invariably pointed out a widely prevailing social sore, and our moralists may, therefore, be accused of preferring the greater to the lesser evil, the violation of the principle on which society is constituted, to the granting of a certain liberty to girls; and dissoluteness in mothers of families, such as poisons the springs of public education and brings unhappiness upon at least four persons, to dissoluteness in a young girl, which only affects herself or at the most a child besides. Let the virtue of ten virgins be lost rather than forfeit this sanctity of morals, that crown of honor with which the mother of a family should be invested! In the picture presented by a young girl abandoned by her betrayer, there is something imposing, something indescribably sacred; here we see oaths violated, holy confidences betrayed, and on the ruins of a too facile virtue innocence sits in tears, doubting everything, because compelled to doubt the love of a father for his child. The unfortunate girl is still innocent; she may yet become a faithful wife, a tender mother, and, if the past is mantled in clouds, the future is blue as the clear sky. Shall we not find these tender tints in the gloomy pictures of loves which violate the marriage law? In the one, the woman is the victim, in the other, she is a criminal. What hope is there for the unfaithful wife? If God pardons the fault, the most exemplary life cannot efface, here below, its living consequences. If James I was the son of Rizzio, the crime of Mary lasted as long as did her mournful though royal house, and the fall of the Stuarts was the justice of God.

But in good faith, would the emancipation of girls set free such a host of dangers?

It is very easy to accuse a young person for suffering herself to be deceived, in the desire to escape, at any price, from the condition of girlhood; but such an accusation is only just in the present condition of our manners. At the present day, a young person knows nothing about seduction and its snares, she relies altogether upon her weakness, and mingling with this reliance the convenient maxims of the fashionable world, she takes as her guide while under the control of those desires which everything conspires to excite, her own deluding fancies, which prove a guide all the more treacherous, because a young girl rarely ever confides to another the secret thoughts of her first love.

If she were free, an education free from prejudices would arm her against the love of the first comer. She would, like any one else, be very much better able to meet dangers of which she knew, than perils whose extent had been concealed from her. And, moreover, is it necessary for a girl to be any the less under the watchful eye of her mother, because she is mistress of her own actions? Are we to count as nothing the modesty and the fears which nature has made so powerful in the soul of a young girl, for the very purpose of preserving her from the misfortune of submitting to a man who does not love her? Again, what girl is there so thoughtless as not to discern, that the most immoral man wishes his wife to be a woman of principle, as masters desire their servants to be perfect; and that, therefore, her virtue is the richest and the most advantageous of all possessions?

After all, what is the question before us? For what do you think we are stipulating? We are making a claim for five or six hundred thousand maidens, protected by their instinctive timidity, and by the high price at which they rate themselves; they understand how to defend themselves, just as well as they know how to sell themselves. The eighteen millions of human beings, whom we have excepted from this consideration, almost invariably contract marriages in accordance with the system which we are trying to make paramount in our system of manners; and as to the intermediary classes by which we poor bimana are separated from the men of privilege who march at the head of a nation, the number of castaway children which these classes, although in tolerably easy circumstances, consign to misery, goes on increasing since the peace, if we may believe M. Benoiston de Chateauneuf, one of the most courageous of those savants who have devoted themselves to the arid yet useful study of statistics. We may guess how deep-seated is the social hurt, for which we propound a remedy, if we reckon the number of natural children which statistics reveal, and the number of illicit adventures whose evidence in high society we are forced to suspect. But it is difficult here to make quite plain all the advantages which would result from the emancipation of young girls. When we come to observe the circumstances which attend a marriage, such as our present manners approve of, judicious minds must appreciate the value of that system of education and liberty, which we demand for young girls, in the name of reason and nature. The prejudice which we in France entertain in favor of the virginity of brides is the most silly of all those which still survive among us. The Orientals take their brides without distressing themselves about the past and lock them up in order to be more certain about the future; the French put their daughters into a sort of seraglio defended by their mothers, by prejudice, and by religious ideas, and give the most complete liberty to their wives, thus showing themselves much more solicitous about a woman's past than about her future. The point we are aiming at is to bring about a reversal of our system of manners. If we did so we should end, perhaps, by giving to faithful married life all the flavor and the piquancy which women of to-day find in acts of infidelity.

But this discussion would take us far from our subject, if it led us to examine, in all its details, the vast improvement in morals which doubtless will distinguish twentieth century France; for morals are reformed only very gradually! Is it not necessary, in order to produce the slightest change, that the most daring dreams of the past century become the most trite ideas of the present one? We have touched upon this question merely in a trifling mood, for the purposes of showing that we are not blind to its importance, and of bequeathing also to posterity the outline of a work, which they may complete. To speak more accurately there is a third work to be composed; the first concerns courtesans, while the second is the physiology of pleasure!

"When there are ten of us, we cross ourselves."

In the present state of our morals and of our imperfect civilization, a problem crops up which for the moment is insoluble, and which renders superfluous all discussion on the art of choosing a wife; we commend it, as we have done all the others, to the meditation of philosophers.

PROBLEM.

It has not yet been decided whether a wife is forced into infidelity by the impossibility of obtaining any change, or by the liberty which is allowed her in this connection.

Moreover, as in this work we pitch upon a man at the moment that he is newly married, we declare that if he has found a wife of sanguine temperament, of vivid imagination, of a nervous constitution or of an indolent character, his situation cannot fail to be extremely serious.

A man would find himself in a position of danger even more critical if his wife drank nothing but water [see the Meditation entitled *Conjugal Hygiene*]; but if she had some talent for singing, or if she were disposed to take cold easily, he should tremble all the time; for it must be remembered that women who sing are at least as passionate as women whose mucous membrane shows extreme delicacy.

Again, this danger would be aggravated still more if your wife were less than seventeen; or if, on the other hand, her general complexion were pale and dull, for this sort of woman is almost always artificial.

But we do not wish to anticipate here any description of the terrors which threaten husbands from the symptoms of unhappiness which they read in the character of their wives. This digression has already taken us too far from the subject of boarding schools, in which so many catastrophes are hatched, and from which issue so many young girls incapable of appreciating the painful sacrifices by which the honest man who does them the honor of marrying them, has obtained opulence; young girls eager for the enjoyments of luxury, ignorant of our laws, ignorant of our manners, claim with avidity the empire which their beauty yields them, and show themselves quite ready to turn away from the genuine utterances of the heart, while they readily listen to the buzzing of flattery.

This Meditation should plant in the memory of all who read it, even those who merely open the book for the sake of glancing at it or distracting their mind, an intense repugnance for young women educated in a boarding school, and if it succeeds in doing so, its services to the public will have already proved considerable.

MEDITATION VII.
OF THE HONEYMOON.

If our meditations prove that it is almost impossible for a married woman to remain virtuous in France, our enumeration of the celibates and the predestined, our remarks upon the education of girls, and our rapid survey of the difficulties which attend the choice of a wife will explain up to a certain point this national frailty. Thus, after indicating frankly the aching malady under which the social slate is laboring, we have sought for the causes in the imperfection of the laws, in the irrational condition of our manners, in the incapacity of our minds, and in the contradictions which characterize our habits. A single point still claims our observation, and that is the first onslaught of the evil we are confronting.

We reach this first question on approaching the high problems suggested by the honeymoon; and although we find here the starting point of all the phenomena of married life, it appears to us to be the brilliant link round which are clustered all our observations, our axioms, our problems, which have been scattered deliberately among the wise quips which our loquacious meditations retail. The honeymoon would seem to be, if we may use the expression, the apogee of that analysis to which we must apply ourselves, before engaging in battle our two imaginary champions.

The expression *honeymoon* is an Anglicism, which has become an idiom in all languages, so gracefully does it depict the nuptial season which is so fugitive, and during which life is nothing but sweetness and rapture; the expression survives as illusions and errors survive, for it contains the most odious of falsehoods. If this season is presented to us as a nymph crowned with fresh flowers, caressing as a siren, it is because in it is unhappiness personified and unhappiness generally comes during the indulgence of folly.

The married couple who intend to love each other during their whole life have no notion of a honeymoon; for them it has no existence, or rather its existence is perennial; they are like the immortals who do not understand death. But the consideration of this happiness is not germane to our book; and for our readers marriage is under the influence of two moons, the honeymoon and the Red-moon. This last terminates its course by a revolution, which changes it to a crescent; and when once it rises upon a home its light there is eternal.

How can the honeymoon rise upon two beings who cannot possibly love each other?

How can it set, when once it has risen?

Have all marriages their honeymoon?

Let us proceed to answer these questions in order.

It is in this connection that the admirable education which we give to girls, and the wise provisions made by the law under which men marry, bear all their fruit. Let us examine the circumstances which precede and attend those marriages which are least disastrous.

The tone of our morals develops in the young girl whom you make your wife a curiosity which is naturally excessive; but as mothers in France pique themselves on exposing their girls every day to the fire which they do not allow to scorch them, this curiosity has no limit.

Her profound ignorance of the mysteries of marriage conceals from this creature, who is as innocent as she is crafty, a clear view of the dangers by which marriage is followed; and as marriage is incessantly described to her as an epoch in which tyranny and liberty equally prevail, and in which enjoyment and supremacy are to be indulged in, her desires are intensified by all her interest in an existence as yet unfulfilled; for her to marry is to be called up from nothingness into life!

If she has a disposition for happiness, for religion, for morality, the voices of the law and of her mother have repeated to her that this happiness can only come to her from you.

Obedience if it is not virtue, is at least a necessary thing with her; for she expects everything from you. In the first place, society sanctions the slavery of a wife, but she does not conceive even the wish to be free, for she feels herself weak, timid and ignorant.

Of course she tries to please you, unless a chance error is committed, or she is seized by a repugnance which it would be unpardonable in you not to divine. She tries to please because she does not know you.

In a word, in order to complete your triumph, you take her at a moment when nature demands, often with some violence, the pleasure of which you are the dispenser. Like St. Peter you hold the keys of Paradise.

I would ask of any reasonable creature, would a demon marshal round the angel whose ruin he had vowed all the elements of disaster with more solicitude than that with which good morals conspire against the happiness of a husband? Are you not a king surrounded by flatterers?

This young girl, with all her ignorance and all her desires, committed to the mercy of a man who, even though he be in love, cannot know her shrinking and secret emotions, will submit to him with a certain sense of shame, and will be obedient and complaisant so long as her young imagination persuades her to expect the pleasure or the happiness of that morrow which never dawns.

In this unnatural situation social laws and the laws of nature are in conflict, but the young girl obediently abandons herself to it, and, from motives of self-interest, suffers in silence. Her obedience is a speculation; her complaisance is a hope; her devotion to you is a sort of vocation, of which you reap the advantage; and her silence is generosity. She will remain the victim of your caprices so long as she does not understand them; she will suffer from the limitations of your character until she has studied it; she will sacrifice herself without love, because she believed in the show of passion you made at the first moment of possession; she will no longer be silent when once she has learned the uselessness of her sacrifices.

And then the morning arrives when the inconsistencies which have prevailed in this union rise up like branches of a tree bent down for a moment under a weight which has been gradually lightened. You have mistaken for love the negative attitude of a young girl who was waiting for happiness, who flew in advance of your desires, in the hope that you would go forward in anticipation of hers, and who did not dare to complain of the secret unhappiness, for which she at first accused herself. What man could fail to be the dupe of a delusion prepared at such long range, and in which a young innocent woman is at once the accomplice and the victim? Unless you were a divine being it would be impossible for you to escape the fascination with which nature and society have surrounded you. Is not a snare set in everything which surrounds you on the outside and influences you within? For in order to be happy, is it not necessary to control the impetuous desires of your senses? Where is the powerful barrier to restrain her, raised by the light hand of a woman whom you wish to please, because you do not possess? Moreover, you have caused your troops to parade and march by, when there was no one at the window; you have discharged your fireworks whose framework alone was left, when your guest arrived to see them. Your wife, before the pledges of marriage, was like a Mohican at the Opera: the teacher becomes listless, when the savage begins to understand.

LVI.

In married life, the moment when two hearts come to understand each other is sudden as a flash of lightning, and never returns, when once it is passed.

This first entrance into life of two persons, during which a woman is encouraged by the hope of happiness, by the still fresh sentiment of her married duty, by the wish to please, by the sense of virtue which begins to be so attractive as soon as it shows love to be in harmony with duty, is called the honeymoon. How can it last long between two beings who are united for their whole life, unless they know each other perfectly? If there is one thing which ought to cause astonishment it is this, that the deplorable absurdities which our manners heap up around the nuptial couch give birth to so few hatreds! But that the life of the wise man is a calm current, and that of the prodigal a cataract; that the child, whose thoughtless hands have stripped the leaves from every rose upon his pathway, finds nothing but thorns on his return, that the man who in his wild youth has squandered a million, will never enjoy, during his life, the income of forty thousand francs, which this million would have provided—are trite commonplaces, if one thinks of the moral theory of life; but new discoveries, if we consider the conduct of most men. You may see here a true image of all honeymoons; this is their history, this is the plain fact and not the cause that underlies it.

But that men endowed with a certain power of thought by a privileged education, and accustomed to think deliberately, in order to shine in politics, literature, art, commerce or private life—that these men should all marry with the intention of being happy, of governing a wife, either by love or by force, and should all tumble into the same pitfall and should become foolish, after having enjoyed a certain happiness for a certain time,—this is certainly a problem whose solution is to be found rather in the unknown depths of the human soul, than in the quasi physical truths, on the basis of which we have hitherto attempted to explain some of these phenomena. The risky search for the secret laws, which almost all men are bound to violate without knowing it, under these circumstances, promises abundant glory for any one even though he make shipwreck in the enterprise upon which we now venture to set forth. Let us then make the attempt.

In spite of all that fools have to say about the difficulty they have had in explaining love, there are certain principles relating to it as infallible as those of geometry; but in each character these are modified according to its tendency; hence the caprices of love, which are due to the infinite number of varying temperaments. If we were permitted never to see the various effects of light without also perceiving on what they were based, many minds would refuse to believe in the movement of the sun and in its oneness. Let the blind men cry out as they like; I boast with Socrates, although I am not as wise as he was, that I know of naught save love; and I intend to attempt the formulation of some of its precepts, in order to spare married people the trouble of cudgeling their brains; they would soon reach the limit of their wit.

Now all the preceding observations may be resolved into a single proposition, which may be considered either the first or last term in this secret theory of love, whose statement would end by wearying us, if we did not bring it to a prompt conclusion. This principle is contained in the following formula:

LVII.

Between two beings susceptible of love, the duration of passion is in proportion to the original resistance of the woman, or to the obstacles which the accidents of social life put in the way of your happiness.

If you have desired your object only for one day, your love perhaps will not last more than three nights. Where must we seek for the causes of this law? I do not know. If you cast your eyes around you, you will find abundant proof of this rule; in the vegetable world the plants which take the longest time to grow are those which promise to have the longest life; in the moral order of things the works produced yesterday die to-morrow; in the physical world the womb which infringes the laws of gestation bears dead fruit. In everything, a work which is permanent has been brooded over by time for a long period. A long future requires a long past. If love is a child, passion is a man. This general law, which all men obey, to which all beings and all sentiments must submit, is precisely that which every marriage infringes, as we have plainly shown. This principle has given rise to the love tales of the Middle Ages; the Amadises, the Lancelots, the Tristans of ballad literature, whose constancy may justly be called fabulous, are allegories of the national mythology which our imitation of Greek literature nipped in the bud. These fascinating characters, outlined by the imagination of the troubadours, set their seal and sanction upon this truth.

LVIII.

We do not attach ourselves permanently to any possessions, excepting in proportion to the trouble, toil and longing which they have cost us.

All our meditations have revealed to us about the basis of the primordial law of love is comprised in the following axiom, which is at the same time the principle and the result of the law.

LIX.

In every case we receive only in proportion to what we give.

This last principle is so self-evident that we will not attempt to demonstrate it. We merely add a single observation which appears to us of some importance. The writer who said: "Everything is true, and everything is false," announced a fact which the human intellect, naturally prone to sophism, interprets as it chooses, but it really seems as though human affairs have as many facets as there are minds that contemplate them. This fact may be detailed as follows:

There cannot be found, in all creation, a single law which is not counterbalanced by a law exactly contrary to it; life in everything is maintained by the equilibrium of two opposing forces. So in the present subject, as regards love, if you give too much, you will not receive enough. The mother who shows her children her whole tenderness calls forth their ingratitude, and ingratitude is occasioned, perhaps, by the impossibility of reciprocation. The wife who loves more than she is loved must necessarily be the object of tyranny. Durable love is that which always keeps the forces of two human beings in equilibrium. Now this equilibrium may be maintained permanently; the one who loves the more ought to stop at the point of the one who loves the less. And is it not, after all the sweetest sacrifice that a loving heart can make, that love should so accommodate itself as to adjust the inequality?

What sentiment of admiration must rise in the soul of a philosopher on discovering that there is, perhaps, but one single principle in the world, as there is but one God; and that our ideas and our affections are subject to the same laws which cause the sun to rise, the flowers to bloom, the universe to teem with life!

Perhaps, we ought to seek in the metaphysics of love the reasons for the following proposition, which throws the most vivid light on the question of honeymoons and of Red-moons:

THEOREM.

Man goes from aversion to love; but if he has begun by loving, and afterwards comes to feel aversion, he never returns to love.

In certain human organisms the feelings are dwarfed, as the thought may be in certain sterile imaginations. Thus, just as some minds have the faculty of comprehending the connections existing between different things without formal deduction; and as they have the faculty of seizing upon each formula separately, without combining them, or without the power of insight, comparison and expression; so in the same way, different souls may have more or less imperfect ideas of the various sentiments. Talent in love, as in every other art, consists in the power of forming a conception combined with the power of carrying it out. The world is full of people who sing airs, but who omit the *ritornello*, who have quarters of an idea, as they have quarters of sentiment, but who can no more co-ordinate the movements of their affections than of their thoughts. In a word, they are incomplete. Unite a fine intelligence with a dwarfed intelligence and you precipitate a disaster; for it is necessary that equilibrium be preserved in everything.

We leave to the philosophers of the boudoir or to the sages of the back parlor to investigate the thousand ways in which men of different temperaments, intellects, social positions and fortunes disturb this equilibrium. Meanwhile we will proceed to examine the last cause for the setting of the honeymoon and the rising of the Red-moon.

There is in life one principle more potent than life itself. It is a movement whose celerity springs from an unknown motive power. Man is no more acquainted with the secret of this revolution than the earth is aware of that which causes her rotation. A certain something, which I gladly call the current of life, bears along our choicest thoughts, makes use of most people's will and carries us on in spite of ourselves. Thus, a man of common-sense, who never fails to pay his bills, if he is a merchant, a man who has been able to escape death, or what perhaps is more trying, sickness, by the observation of a certain easy but daily regimen, is completely and duly nailed up between the four planks of his coffin, after having said every evening: "Dear me! to-morrow I will not forget my pills!" How are we to explain this magic spell which rules all the affairs of life? Do men submit to it from a want of energy? Men who have the strongest wills are subject to it. Is it default of memory? People who possess this faculty in the highest degree yield to its fascination.

Every one can recognize the operation of this influence in the case of his neighbor, and it is one of the things which exclude the majority of husbands from the honeymoon. It is thus that the wise man, survivor of all reefs and shoals, such as we have pointed out, sometimes falls into the snares which he himself has set.

I have myself noticed that man deals with marriage and its dangers in very much the same way that he deals with wigs; and perhaps the following phases of thought concerning wigs may furnish a formula for human life in general.

FIRST EPOCH.—Is it possible that I shall ever have white hair?

SECOND EPOCH.—In any case, if I have white hair, I shall never wear a wig. Good Lord! what is more ugly than a wig?

One morning you hear a young voice, which love much oftener makes to vibrate than lulls to silence, exclaiming:

"Well, I declare! You have a white hair!"

THIRD EPOCH.—Why not wear a well-made wig which people would not notice? There is a certain merit in deceiving everybody; besides, a wig keeps you warm, prevents taking cold, etc.

FOURTH EPOCH.—The wig is so skillfully put on that you deceive every one who does not know you.

The wig takes up all your attention, and *amour-propre* makes you every morning as busy as the most skillful hairdresser.

FIFTH EPOCH.—The neglected wig. "Good heavens! How tedious it is, to have to go with bare head every evening, and to curl one's wig every morning!"

SIXTH EPOCH.—The wig allows certain white hairs to escape; it is put on awry and the observer perceives on the back of your neck a white line, which contrasts with the deep tints pushed back by the collar of your coat.

SEVENTH EPOCH.—Your wig is as scraggy as dog's tooth grass; and —excuse the expression—you are making fun of your wig.

"Sir," said one of the most powerful feminine intelligences which have condescended to enlighten me on some of the most obscure passages in my book, "what do you mean by this wig?"

"Madame," I answered, "when a man falls into a mood of indifference with regard to his wig, he is,—he is—what your husband probably is not."

"But my husband is not—" (she paused and thought for a moment). "He is not amiable; he is not—well, he is not—of an even temper; he is not—"

"Then, madame, he would doubtless be indifferent to his wig!"

We looked at each other, she with a well-assumed air of dignity, I with a suppressed smile.

"I see," said I, "that we must pay special respect to the ears of the little sex, for they are the only chaste things about them."

I assumed the attitude of a man who has something of importance to disclose, and the fair dame lowered her eyes, as if she had some reason to blush.

"Madame, in these days a minister is not hanged, as once upon a time, for saying yes or no; a Chateaubriand would scarcely torture Francoise de Foix, and we wear no longer at our side a long sword ready to avenge an insult. Now in a century when civilization has made such rapid progress, when we can learn a science in twenty-four lessons, everything must follow this race after perfection. We can no longer speak the manly, rude, coarse language of our ancestors. The age in which are fabricated such fine, such brilliant stuffs, such elegant furniture, and when are made such rich porcelains, must needs be the age of periphrase and circumlocution. We must try, therefore, to coin a new word in place of the comic expression which Moliere used; since the language of this great man, as a contemporary author has said, is too free for ladies who find gauze too thick for their garments. But people of the world know, as well as the learned, how the Greeks had an innate taste for mysteries. That poetic nation knew well how to invest with the tints of fable the antique traditions of their history. At the voice of their rhapsodists together with their poets and romancers, kings became gods and their adventures of gallantry were transformed into immortal allegories. According to M. Chompre, licentiate in law, the classic author of the *Dictionary of Mythology*, the labyrinth was 'an enclosure planted with trees and adorned with buildings arranged in such a way that when a young man once entered, he could no more find his way out.' Here and there flowery thickets were presented to his view, but in the midst of a multitude of alleys, which crossed and recrossed his path and bore the appearance of a uniform passage, among the briars, rocks and thorns, the patient found himself in combat with an animal called the Minotaur.

"Now, madame, if you will allow me the honor of calling to your mind the fact that the Minotaur was of all known beasts that which Mythology distinguishes as the most dangerous; that in order to save themselves from his ravages, the Athenians were bound to deliver to him, every single year, fifty virgins; you will perhaps escape the error of good M. Chompre, who saw in the labyrinth nothing but an English garden; and you will recognize in this ingenious fable a refined allegory, or we may better say a faithful and fearful image of the dangers of marriage. The paintings recently discovered at Herculaneum have served to confirm this opinion. And, as a matter of fact, learned men have for a long time believed, in accordance with the writings of certain authors, that the Minotaur was an animal half-man, half-bull; but the fifth panel of ancient paintings at Herculaneum represents to us this allegorical monster with a body entirely human; and, to take away all vestige of doubt, he lies crushed at the feet of Theseus. Now, my dear madame, why should we not ask Mythology to come and rescue us from that hypocrisy which is gaining ground with us and hinders us from laughing as our fathers laughed? And thus, since in the world a young lady does not very well know how to spread the veil under which an honest woman hides her behavior, in a contingency which our grandfathers would have roughly explained by a single word, you, like a crowd of beautiful but prevaricating ladies, you content yourselves with saying, 'Ah! yes, she is very amiable, but,'—but what?—'but she is often very inconsistent—.' I have for a long time tried to find out the meaning of this last word, and, above all, the figure of rhetoric by which you make it express the opposite of that which it signifies; but all my researches have been in vain. Vert-Vert used the word last, and was unfortunately addressed to the innocent nuns whose infidelities did not in any way infringe the honor of the men. When a woman is *inconsistent* the husband must be, according to me, *minotaurized*. If the minotaurized man is a fine fellow, if he enjoys a certain esteem,—and many husbands really deserve to be pitied,—then in speaking of him, you say in a pathetic voice, 'M. A—- is a very estimable man, his wife is exceedingly pretty, but they say he is not happy in his domestic relations.' Thus, madame, the estimable man who is unhappy in his domestic relations, the man who has an inconsistent wife, or the husband who is minotaurized are simply husbands as they appear in Moliere. Well, then, O goddess of modern taste, do not these expressions seem to you characterized by a transparency chaste enough for anybody?"

"Ah! mon Dieu!" she answered, laughing, "if the thing is the same, what does it matter whether it be expressed in two syllables or in a hundred?"

She bade me good-bye, with an ironical nod and disappeared, doubtless to join the countesses of my preface and all the metaphorical creatures, so often employed by romance-writers as agents for the recovery or composition of ancient manuscripts.

As for you, the more numerous and the more real creatures who read my book, if there are any among you who make common cause with my conjugal champion, I give you notice that you will not at once become unhappy in your domestic relations. A man arrives at this conjugal condition not suddenly, but insensibly and by degrees. Many husbands have even remained unfortunate in their domestic relations during their whole life and have never known it. This domestic revolution develops itself in accordance with fixed rules; for the revolutions of the honeymoon are as regular as the phases of the moon in heaven, and are the same in every married house. Have we not proved that moral nature, like physical nature, has its laws?

Your young wife will never take a lover, as we have elsewhere said, without making serious reflections. As soon as the honeymoon wanes, you will find that you have aroused in her a sentiment of pleasure which you have not satisfied; you have opened to her the book of life; and she has derived an excellent idea from the prosaic dullness which distinguishes your complacent love, of the poetry which is the natural result when souls and pleasures are in accord. Like a timid bird, just startled by the report of a gun which has ceased, she puts her head out of her nest, looks round her, and sees the world; and knowing the word of a charade which you have played, she feels instinctively the void which exists in your languishing passion. She divines that it is only with a lover that she can regain the delightful exercise of her free will in love.

You have dried the green wood in preparation for a fire.

In the situation in which both of you find yourselves, there is no woman, even the most virtuous, who would not be found worthy of a *grande passion*, who has not dreamed of it, and who does not believe that it is easily kindled, for there is always found a certain *amour-propre* ready to reinforce that conquered enemy—a jaded wife.

"If the role of an honest woman were nothing more than perilous," said an old lady to me, "I would admit that it would serve. But it is tiresome; and I have never met a virtuous woman who did not think about deceiving somebody."

And then, before any lover presents himself, a wife discusses with herself the legality of the act; she enters into a conflict with her duties, with the law, with religion and with the secret desires of a nature which knows no check-rein excepting that which she places upon herself. And then commences for you a condition of affairs totally new; then you receive the first intimation which nature, that good and indulgent mother, always gives to the creatures who are exposed to any danger. Nature has put a bell on the neck of the Minotaur, as on the tail of that frightful snake which is the terror of travelers. And then appear in your wife what we will call the first symptoms, and woe to him who does not know how to contend with them. Those who in reading our book will remember that they saw those symptoms in their own domestic life can pass to the conclusion of this work, where they will find how they may gain consolation.

The situation referred to, in which a married couple bind themselves for a longer or a shorter time, is the point from which our work starts, as it is the end at which our observations stop. A man of intelligence should know how to recognize the mysterious indications, the obscure signs and the involuntary revelation which a wife unwittingly exhibits; for the next Meditation will doubtless indicate the more evident of the manifestations to neophytes in the sublime science of marriage.

MEDITATION VIII.
OF THE FIRST SYMPTOMS.

When your wife reaches that crisis in which we have left her, you yourself are wrapped in a pleasant and unsuspicious security. You have so often seen the sun that you begin to think it is shining over everybody. You therefore give no longer that attention to the least action of your wife, which was impelled by your first outburst of passion.

This indolence prevents many husbands from perceiving the symptoms which, in their wives, herald the first storm; and this disposition of mind has resulted in the minotaurization of more husbands than have either opportunity, carriages, sofas and apartments in town.

The feeling of indifference in the presence of danger is to some degree justified by the apparent tranquillity which surrounds you. The conspiracy which is formed against you by our million of hungry celibates seems to be unanimous in its advance. Although all are enemies of each other and know each other well, a sort of instinct forces them into co-operation.

Two persons are married. The myrmidons of the Minotaur, young and old, have usually the politeness to leave the bride and bridegroom entirely to themselves at first. They look upon the husband as an artisan, whose business it is to trim, polish, cut into facets and mount the diamond, which is to pass from hand to hand in order to be admired all around. Moreover, the aspect of a young married couple much taken with each other always rejoices the heart of those among the celibates who are known as *roues*; they take good care not to disturb the excitement by which society is to be profited; they also know that heavy showers to not last long. They therefore keep quiet; they watch, and wait, with incredible vigilance, for the moment when bride and groom begin to weary of the seventh heaven.

The tact with which celibates discover the moment when the breeze begins to rise in a new home can only be compared to the indifference of those husbands for whom the Red-moon rises. There is, even in intrigue, a moment of ripeness which must be waited for. The great man is he who anticipates the outcome of certain circumstances. Men of fifty-two, whom we have represented as being so dangerous, know very well, for example, that any man who offers himself as lover to a woman and is haughtily rejected, will be received with open arms three months afterwards. But it may be truly said that in general married people in betraying their indifference towards each other show the same naivete with which they first betrayed their love. At the time when you are traversing with madame the ravishing fields of the seventh heaven—where according to their temperament, newly married people remain encamped for a longer or shorter time, as the preceding Meditation has proved—you go little or not at all into society. Happy as you are in your home, if you do go abroad, it will be for the purpose of making up a choice party and visiting the theatre, the country, etc. From the moment you the newly wedded make your appearance in the world again, you and your bride together, or separately, and are seen to be attentive to each other at balls, at parties, at all the empty amusements created to escape the void of an unsatisfied heart, the celibates discern that your wife comes there in search of distraction; her home, her husband are therefore wearisome to her.

At this point the celibate knows that half of the journey is accomplished. At this point you are on the eve of being minotaurized, and your wife is likely to become inconsistent; which means that she is on the contrary likely to prove very consistent in her conduct, that she has reasoned it out with astonishing sagacity and that you are likely very soon to smell fire. From that moment she will not in appearance fail in any of her duties, and will put on the colors of that virtue in which she is most lacking. Said Crebillon:

> "Alas!
> Is it right to be heir of the man who we slay?"

Never has she seemed more anxious to please you. She will seek, as much as possible, to allay the secret wounds which she thinks about inflicting upon your married bliss, she will do so by those little attentions which induce you to believe in the eternity of her love; hence the proverb, "Happy as a fool." But in accordance with the character of women, they either despise their own husbands from the very fact that they find no difficulty in deceiving them; or they hate them when they find themselves circumvented by them; or they fall into a condition of indifference towards them, which is a thousand times worse than hatred. In this emergency, the first thing which may be diagnosed in a woman is a decided oddness of behavior. A woman loves to be saved from herself, to escape her conscience, but without the eagerness shown in this connection by wives who are thoroughly unhappy. She dresses herself with especial care, in order, she will tell you, to flatter your *amour-propre* by drawing all eyes upon her in the midst of parties and public entertainments.

When she returns to the bosom of her stupid home you will see that, at times, she is gloomy and thoughtful, then suddenly laughing and gay as if beside herself; or assuming the serious expression of a German when he advances to the fight. Such varying moods always indicate the terrible doubt and hesitation to which we have already referred. There are women who read romances in order to feast upon the images of love cleverly depicted and always varied, of love crowned yet triumphant; or in order to familiarize themselves in thought with the perils of an intrigue.

She will profess the highest esteem for you, she will tell you that she loves you as a sister; and that such reasonable friendship is the only true, the only durable friendship, the only tie which it is the aim of marriage to establish between man and wife.

She will adroitly distinguish between the duties which are all she has to perform and the rights which she can demand to exercise.

She views with indifference, appreciated by you alone, all the details of married happiness. This sort of happiness, perhaps, has never been very agreeable to her and moreover it is always with her. She knows it well, she has analyzed it; and what slight but terrible evidence comes from these circumstances to prove to an intelligent husband that this frail creature argues and reasons, instead of being carried away on the tempest of passion.

LX.

The more a man judges the less he loves.

And now will burst forth from her those pleasantries at which you will be the first to laugh and those reflections which will startle you by their profundity; now you will see sudden changes of mood and the caprices of a mind which hesitates. At times she will exhibit extreme tenderness, as if she repented of her thoughts and her projects; sometimes she will be sullen and at cross-purposes with you; in a word, she will fulfill the *varium et mutabile femina* which we hitherto have had the folly to attribute to the feminine temperament. Diderot, in his desire to explain the mutations almost atmospheric in the behavior of women, has even gone so far as to make them the offspring of what he calls *la bete feroce*; but we never see these whims in a woman who is happy.

These symptoms, light as gossamer, resemble the clouds which scarcely break the azure surface of the sky and which they call flowers of the storm. But soon their colors take a deeper intensity.

In the midst of this solemn premeditation, which tends, as Madame de Stael says, to bring more poetry into life, some women, in whom virtuous mothers either from considerations of worldly advantage of duty or sentiment, or through sheer hypocrisy, have inculcated steadfast principles, take the overwhelming fancies by which they are assailed for suggestions of the devil; and you will see them therefore trotting regularly to mass, to midday offices, even to vespers. This false devotion exhibits itself, first of all in the shape of pretty books of devotion in a costly binding, by the aid of which these dear sinners attempt in vain to fulfill the duties imposed by religion, and long neglected for the pleasures of marriage.

Now here we will lay down a principle, and you must engrave it on your memory in letters of fire.

When a young woman suddenly takes up religious practices which she has before abandoned, this new order of life always conceals a motive highly significant, in view of her husband's happiness. In the case of at least seventy-nine women out of a hundred this return to God proves that they have been inconsistent, or that they intend to become so.

But a symptom more significant still and more decisive, and one that every husband should recognize under pain of being considered a fool, is this:

MEDITATION VI.
OF BOARDING SCHOOLS.

If you have married a young lady whose education has been carried on at a boarding school, there are thirty more obstacles to your happiness, added to all those which we have already enumerated, and you are exactly like a man who thrusts his hands into a wasp's nest.

Immediately, therefore, after the nuptial blessing has been pronounced, without allowing yourself to be imposed upon by the innocent ignorance, the frank graces and the modest countenance of your wife, you ought to ponder well and faithfully follow out the axioms and precepts which we shall develop in the second part of this book. You should even put into practice the rigors prescribed in the third part, by maintaining an active surveillance, a paternal solicitude at all hours, for the very day after your marriage, perhaps on the evening of your wedding day, there is danger in the house.

I mean to say that you should call to mind the secret and profound instruction which the pupils have acquired *de natura rerum,*—of the nature of things. Did Lapeyrouse, Cook or Captain Peary ever show so much ardor in navigating the ocean towards the Poles as the scholars of the Lycee do in approaching forbidden tracts in the ocean of pleasure? Since girls are more cunning, cleverer and more curious than boys, their secret meetings and their conversations, which all the art of their teachers cannot check, are necessarily presided over by a genius a thousand times more informal than that of college boys. What man has ever heard the moral reflections and the corrupting confidences of these young girls? They alone know the sports at which honor is lost in advance, those essays in pleasure, those promptings in voluptuousness, those imitations of bliss, which may be compared to the thefts made by greedy children from a dessert which is locked up. A girl may come forth from her boarding school a virgin, but never chaste. She will have discussed, time and time again at secret meetings, the important question of lovers, and corruption will necessarily have overcome her heart or her spirit.

Nevertheless, we will admit that your wife has not participated in these virginal delights, in these premature deviltries. Is she any better because she has never had any voice in the secret councils of grown-up girls? No! She will, in any case, have contracted a friendship with other young ladies, and our computation will be modest, if we attribute to her no more than two or three intimate friends. Are you certain that after your wife has left boarding school, her young friends have not there been admitted to those confidences, in which an attempt is made to learn in

At the time when both of you are immersed in the illusive delights of the honeymoon, your wife, as one devoted to you, would constantly carry out your will. She was happy in the power of showing the ready will, which both of you mistook for love, and she would have liked for you to have asked her to walk on the edge of the roof, and immediately, nimble as a squirrel, she would have run over the tiles. In a word, she found an ineffable delight in sacrificing to you that *ego* which made her a being distinct from yours. She had identified herself with your nature and was obedient to that vow of the heart, *Una caro.*

All this delightful promptness of an earlier day gradually faded away. Wounded to find her will counted as nothing, your wife will attempt, nevertheless, to reassert it by means of a system developed gradually, and from day to day, with increased energy.

This system is founded upon what we may call the dignity of the married woman. The first effect of this system is to mingle with your pleasures a certain reserve and a certain lukewarmness, of which you are the sole judge.

According to the greater or lesser violence of your sensual passion, you have perhaps discerned some of those twenty-two pleasures which in other times created in Greece twenty-two kinds of courtesans, devoted especially to these delicate branches of the same art. Ignorant and simple, curious and full of hope, your young wife may have taken some degrees in this science as rare as it is unknown, and which we especially commend to the attention of the future author of *Physiology of Pleasure.*

Lacking all these different kinds of pleasure, all these caprices of soul, all these arrows of love, you are reduced to the most common of love fashions, of that primitive and innocent wedding gait, the calm homage which the innocent Adam rendered to our common Mother and which doubtless suggested to the Serpent the idea of taking them in. But a symptom so complete is not frequent. Most married couples are too good Christians to follow the usages of pagan Greece, so we have ranged, among the last symptoms, the appearance in the calm nuptial couch of those shameless pleasures which spring generally from lawless passion. In their proper time and place we will treat more fully of this fascinating diagnostic; at this point, things are reduced to a listlessness and conjugal repugnance which you alone are in a condition to appreciate.

At the same time that she is ennobling by her dignity the objects of marriage, your wife will pretend that she ought to have her opinion and you yours. "In marrying," she will say, "a woman does not vow that she will abdicate the throne of reason. Are women then really slaves? Human laws can fetter the body; but the mind!—ah! God has placed it so near Himself that no human hand can touch it."

These ideas necessarily proceed either from the too liberal teachings which you have allowed her to receive, or from some reflections which you have permitted her to make. A whole Meditation has been devoted to *Home Instruction.*

Then your wife begins to say, "*My* chamber, *my* bed, *my* apartment." To many of your questions she will reply, "But, my dear, this is no business of yours!" Or: "Men have their part in the direction of the house, and women have theirs." Or, laughing at men who meddle in household affairs, she will affirm that "men do not understand some things."

The number of things which you do not understand increases day by day.

One fine morning, you will see in your little church two altars, where before you never worshiped but at one. The altar of your wife and your own altar have become distinct, and this distinction will go on increasing, always in accordance with the system founded upon the dignity of woman.

Then the following ideas will appear, and they will be inculcated in you whether you like it or not, by means of a living force very ancient in origin and little known. Steam-power, horse-power, man-power, and water-power are good inventions, but nature has provided women with a moral power, in comparison with which all other powers are nothing; we may call it *rattle-power*. This force consists in a continuance of the same sound, in an exact repetition of the same words, in a reversion, over and over again, to the same ideas, and this so unvaried, that from hearing them over and over again you will admit them, in order to be delivered from the discussion. Thus the power of the rattle will prove to you:

That you are very fortunate to have such an excellent wife;

That she has done you too much honor in marrying you;

That women often see clearer than men;

That you ought to take the advice of your wife in everything, and almost always ought to follow it;

That you ought to respect the mother of your children, to honor her and have confidence in her;

That the best way to escape being deceived, is to rely upon a wife's refinement, for according to certain old ideas which we have had the weakness to give credit, it is impossible for a man to prevent his wife from minotaurizing him;

That a lawful wife is a man's best friend;

That a woman is mistress in her own house and queen in her drawing-room, etc.

Those who wish to oppose a firm resistance to a woman's conquest, effected by means of her dignity over man's power, fall into the category of the predestined.

At first, quarrels arise which in the eye of wives give an air of tyranny to husbands. The tyranny of a husband is always a terrible excuse for inconsistency in a wife. Then, in their frivolous discussions they are enabled to prove to their families and to ours, to everybody and to ourselves, that we are in the wrong. If, for the sake of peace, or from love, you acknowledge the pretended rights of women, you yield an advantage to your wife by which she will profit eternally. A husband, like a government, ought never to acknowledge a mistake. In case you do so, your power will be outflanked by the subtle artifices of feminine dignity; then all will be lost; from that moment she will advance from concession to concession until she has driven you from her bed.

The woman being shrewd, intelligent, sarcastic and having leisure to meditate over an ironical phrase, can easily turn you into ridicule during a momentary clash of opinions. The day on which she turns you into ridicule, sees the end of your happiness. Your power has expired. A woman who has laughed at her husband cannot henceforth love him. A man should be, to the woman who is in love with him, a being full of power, of greatness, and always imposing. A family cannot exist without despotism. Think of that, ye nations!

Now the difficult course which a man has to steer in presence of such serious incidents as these, is what we may call the *haute politique* of marriage, and is the subject of the second and third parts of our book. That breviary of marital Machiavelism will teach you the manner in which you may grow to greatness within that frivolous mind, within that soul of lacework, to use Napoleon's phrase. You may learn how a man may exhibit a soul of steel, may enter upon this little domestic war without ever yielding the empire of his will, and may do so without compromising his happiness. For if you exhibit any tendency to abdication, your wife will despise you, for the sole reason that she has discovered you to be destitute of mental vigor; you are no longer a *man* to her.

But we have not yet reached the point at which are to be developed those theories and principles, by means of which a man may unite elegance of manners with severity of measures; let it suffice us, for the moment, to point out the importance of impending events and let us pursue our theme.

At this fatal epoch, you will see that she is adroitly setting up a right to go out alone.

You were at one time her god, her idol. She has now reached that height of devotion at which it is permitted to see holes in the garments of the saints.

"Oh, mon Dieu! My dear," said Madame de la Valliere to her husband, "how badly you wear your sword! M. de Richelieu has a way of making it hang straight at his side, which you ought to try to imitate; it is in much better taste."

"My dear, you could not tell me in a more tactful manner that we have been married five months!" replied the Duke, whose repartee made his fortune in the reign of Louis XV.

She will study your character in order to find weapons against you. Such a study, which love would hold in horror, reveals itself in the thousand little traps which she lays purposely to make you scold her; when a woman has no excuse for minotaurizing her husband she sets to work to make one.

She will perhaps begin dinner without waiting for you.

If you drive through the middle of the town, she will point out certain objects which escaped your notice; she will sing before you without feeling afraid; she will interrupt you, sometimes vouchsafe no reply to you, and will prove to you, in a thousand different ways, that she is enjoying at your side the use of all her faculties and exercising her private judgment.

She will try to abolish entirely your influence in the management of the house and to become sole mistress of your fortune. At first this struggle will serve as a distraction for her soul, whether it be empty or in too violent commotion; next, she will find in your opposition a new motive for ridicule. Slang expressions will not fail her, and in France we are so quickly vanquished by the ironical smile of another!

At other times headaches and nervous attacks make their appearance; but these symptoms furnish matter for a whole future Meditation. In the world she will speak of you without blushing, and will gaze at you with assurance. She will begin to blame your least actions because they are at variance with her ideas, or her secret intentions. She will take no care of what pertains to you, she will not even know whether you have all you need. You are no longer her paragon.

In imitation of Louis XIV, who carried to his mistresses the bouquets of orange blossoms which the head gardener of Versailles put on his table every morning, M. de Vivonne used almost every day to give his wife choice flowers during the early period of his marriage. One morning he found the bouquet lying on the side table without having been placed, as usual, in a vase of water.

"Oh! Oh!" said he, "if I am not a cuckold, I shall very soon be one."

You go on a journey for eight days and you receive no letters, or you receive one, three pages of which are blank.—Symptom.

You come home mounted on a valuable horse which you like very much, and between her kisses your wife shows her uneasiness about the horse and his fodder.—Symptom.

To these features of the case, you will be able to add others. We shall endeavor in the present volume always to paint things in bold fresco style and leave the miniatures to you. According to the characters concerned, the indications which we are describing, veiled under the incidents of ordinary life, are of infinite variety. One man may discover a symptom in the way a shawl is put on, while another needs to receive a fillip to his intellect, in order to notice the indifference of his mate.

Some fine spring morning, the day after a ball, or the eve of a country party, this situation reaches its last phase; your wife is listless and the happiness within her reach has no more attractions for her. Her mind, her imagination, perhaps her natural caprices call for a lover. Nevertheless, she dare not yet embark upon an intrigue whose consequences and details fill her with dread. You are still there for some purpose or other; you are a weight in the balance, although a very light one. On the other hand, the lover presents himself arrayed in all the graces of novelty and all the charms of mystery. The conflict which has arisen in the heart of your wife becomes, in presence of the enemy, more real and more full of peril than before. Very soon the more dangers and risks there are to be run, the more she burns to plunge into that delicious gulf of fear, enjoyment, anguish and delight. Her imagination kindles and sparkles, her future life rises before her eyes, colored with romantic and mysterious hues. Her soul discovers that existence has already taken its tone from this struggle which to a woman has so much solemnity in it.

All is agitation, all is fire, all is commotion within her. She lives with three times as much intensity as before, and judges the future by the present. The little pleasure which you have lavished upon her bears witness against you; for she is not excited as much by the pleasures which she has received, as by those which she is yet to enjoy; does not imagination show her that her happiness will be keener with this lover, whom the laws deny her, than with you? And then, she finds enjoyment even in her terror and terror in her enjoyment. Then she falls in love with this imminent danger, this sword of Damocles hung over her head by you yourself, thus preferring the delirious agonies of such a passion, to that conjugal inanity which is worse to her than death, to that indifference which is less a sentiment than the absence of all sentiment.

You, who must go to pay your respects to the Minister of Finance, to write memorandums at the bank, to make your reports at the Bourse, or to speak in the Chamber; you, young men, who have repeated with many others in our first Meditation the oath that you will defend your happiness in defending your wife, what can you oppose to these desires of hers which are so natural? For, with these creatures of fire, to live is to feel; the moment they cease to experience emotion they are dead. The law in virtue of which you take your position produces in her this involuntary act of minotaurism. "There is one sequel," said D'Alembert, "to the laws of movement." Well, then, where are your means of defence?— Where, indeed?

Alas! if your wife has not yet kissed the apple of the Serpent, the Serpent stands before her; you sleep, we are awake, and our book begins.

Without inquiring how many husbands, among the five hundred thousand which this book concerns, will be left with the predestined; how many have contracted unfortunate marriages; how many have made a bad beginning with their wives; and without wishing to ask if there be many or few of this numerous band who can satisfy the conditions required for struggling against the danger which is impending, we intend to expound in the second and third part of this work the methods of fighting the Minotaur and keeping intact the virtue of wives. But if fate, the devil, the celibate, opportunity, desire your ruin, in recognizing the progress of all intrigues, in joining in the battles which are fought by every home, you will possibly be able to find some consolation. Many people have such a happy disposition, that on showing to them the condition of things and explaining to them the why and the wherefore, they scratch their foreheads, rub their hands, stamp on the ground, and are satisfied.

MEDITATION IX.

EPILOGUE.

Faithful to our promise, this first part has indicated the general causes which bring all marriages to the crises which we are about to describe; and, in tracing the steps of this conjugal preamble, we have also pointed out the way in which the catastrophe is to be avoided, for we have pointed out the errors by which it is brought about.

But these first considerations would be incomplete if, after endeavoring to throw some light upon the inconsistency of our ideas, of our manners and of our laws, with regard to a question which concerns the life of almost all living beings, we did not endeavor to make plain, in a short peroration, the political causes of the infirmity which pervades all modern society. After having exposed the secret vices of marriage, would it not be an inquiry worthy of philosophers to search out the causes which have rendered it so vicious?

The system of law and of manners which so far directs women and controls marriage in France, is the outcome of ancient beliefs and traditions which are no longer in accordance with the eternal principles of reason and of justice, brought to light by the great Revolution of 1789.

Three great disturbances have agitated France; the conquest of the country by the Romans, the establishment of Christianity and the invasion of the Franks. Each of these events has left a deep impress upon the soil, upon the laws, upon the manners and upon the intellect of the nation.

Greece having one foot on Europe and the other on Asia, was influenced by her voluptuous climate in the choice of her marriage institutions; she received them from the East, where her philosophers, her legislators and her poets went to study the abstruse antiquities of Egypt and Chaldea. The absolute seclusion of women which was necessitated under the burning sun of Asia prevailed under the laws of Greece and Ionia. The women remained in confinement within the marbles of the gyneceum. The country was reduced to the condition of a city, to a narrow territory, and the courtesans who were connected with art and religion by so many ties, were sufficient to satisfy the first passions of the young men, who were few in number, since their strength was elsewhere taken up in the violent exercises of that training which was demanded of them by the military system of those heroic times.

At the beginning of her royal career Rome, having sent to Greece to seek such principles of legislation as might suit the sky of Italy, stamped upon the forehead of the married woman the brand of complete servitude. The senate understood the importance of virtue in a republic, hence the severity of manners in the excessive development of the marital and paternal power. The dependence of the woman on her husband is found inscribed on every code. The seclusion prescribed by the East becomes a duty, a moral obligation, a virtue. On these principles were raised temples to modesty and temples consecrated to the sanctity of marriage; hence, sprang the institution of censors, the law of dowries, the sumptuary laws, the respect for matrons and all the characteristics of the Roman law. Moreover, three acts of feminine violation either accomplished or attempted, produced three revolutions! And was it not a grand event, sanctioned by the decrees of the country, that these illustrious women should make their appearances on the political arena! Those noble Roman women, who were obliged to be either brides or mothers, passed their life in retirement engaged in educating the masters of the world. Rome had no courtesans because the youth of the city were engaged in eternal war. If, later on, dissoluteness appeared, it merely resulted from the despotism of emperors; and still the prejudices founded upon ancient manners were so influential that Rome never saw a woman on a stage. These facts are not put forth idly in scanning the history of marriage in France.

After the conquest of Gaul, the Romans imposed their laws upon the conquered; but they were incapable of destroying both the profound respect which our ancestors entertained for women and the ancient superstitions which made women the immediate oracles of God. The Roman laws ended by prevailing, to the exclusion of all others, in this country once known as the "land of written law," or *Gallia togata*, and their ideas of marriage penetrated more or less into the "land of customs."

But, during the conflict of laws with manners, the Franks invaded the Gauls and gave to the country the dear name of France. These warriors came from the North and brought the system of gallantry which had originated in their western regions, where the mingling of the sexes did not require in those icy climates the jealous precautions of the East. The women of that time elevated the privations of that kind of life by the exaltation of their sentiments. The drowsy minds of the day made necessary those varied forms of delicate solicitation, that versatility of address, the fancied repulse of coquetry, which belong to the system whose principles have been unfolded in our First Part, as admirably suited to the temperate clime of France.

To the East, then, belong the passion and the delirium of passion, the long brown hair, the harem, the amorous divinities, the splendor, the poetry of love and the monuments of love. — To the West, the liberty of wives, the sovereignty of their blond locks, gallantry, the fairy life of love, the secrecy of passion, the profound ecstasy of the soul, the sweet feelings of melancholy and the constancy of love.

These two systems, starting from opposite points of the globe, have come into collision in France; in France, where one part of the country, Languedoc, was attracted by Oriental traditions, while the other, Languedoil, was the native land of a creed which attributes to woman a magical power. In the Languedoil, love necessitates mystery, in the Languedoc, to see is to love.

At the height of this struggle came the triumphant entry of Christianity into France, and there it was preached by women, and there it consecrated the divinity of a woman who in the forests of Brittany, of Vendee and of Ardennes took, under the name of Notre-Dame, the place of more than one idol in the hollow of old Druidic oaks.

If the religion of Christ, which is above all things a code of morality and politics, gave a soul to all living beings, proclaimed that equality of all in the sight of God, and by such principles as these fortified the chivalric sentiments of the North, this advantage was counterbalanced by the fact, that the sovereign pontiff resided at Rome, of which seat he considered himself the lawful heir, through the universality of the Latin tongue, which became that of Europe during the Middle Ages, and through the keen interest taken by monks, writers and lawyers in establishing the ascendency of certain codes, discovered by a soldier in the sack of Amalfi.

These two principles of the servitude and the sovereignty of women retain possession of the ground, each of them defended by fresh arguments.

The Salic law, which was a legal error, was a triumph for the principle of political and civil servitude for women, but it did not diminish the power which French manners accorded them, for the enthusiasm of chivalry which prevailed in Europe supplanted the party of manners against the party of law.

And in this way was created that strange phenomenon which since that time has characterized both our national despotism and our legislation; for ever since those epochs which seemed to presage the Revolution, when the spirit of philosophy rose and reflected upon the history of the past, France has been the prey of many convulsions. Feudalism, the Crusades, the Reformation, the struggle between the monarchy and the aristocracy. Despotism and Priestcraft have so closely held the country within their clutches, that woman still remains the subject of strange counter-opinions, each springing from one of the three great movements to which we have referred. Was it possible that the woman question should be discussed and woman's political education and marriage should be ventilated when feudalism threatened the throne, when reform menaced both king and barons, and the people, between the hierarchy and the empire, were forgotten? According to a saying of Madame Necker, women, amid these great movements, were like the cotton wool put into a case of porcelain. They were counted for nothing, but without them everything would have been broken.

A married woman, then, in France presents the spectacle of a queen out at service, of a slave, at once free and a prisoner; a collision between these two principles which frequently occurred, produced odd situations by the thousand. And then, woman was physically little understood, and what was actually sickness in her, was considered a prodigy, witchcraft or monstrous turpitude. In those days these creatures, treated by the law as reckless children, and put under guardianship, were by the manners of the time deified and adored. Like the freedmen of emperors, they disposed of crowns, they decided battles, they awarded fortunes, they inspired crimes and revolutions, wonderful acts of virtue, by the mere flash of their glances, and yet they possessed nothing and were not even possessors of themselves. They were equally fortunate and unfortunate. Armed with their weakness and strong in instinct, they launched out far beyond the sphere which the law allotted them, showing themselves omnipotent for evil, but impotent for good; without merit in the virtues that were imposed upon them, without excuse in their vices; accused of ignorance and yet denied an education; neither altogether mothers nor altogether wives. Having all the time to conceal their passions, while they fostered them, they submitted to the coquetry of the Franks, while they were obliged like Roman women, to stay within the ramparts of their castles and bring up those who were to be warriors. While no system was definitely decided upon by legislation as to the position of women, their minds were left to follow their inclinations, and there are found among them as many who resemble Marion Delorme as those who resemble Cornelia; there are vices among them, but there are as many virtues. These were creatures as incomplete as the laws which governed them; they were considered by some as a being midway between man and the lower animals, as a malignant beast which the laws could not too closely fetter, and which nature had destined, with so many other things, to serve the pleasure of men; while others held woman to be an angel in exile, a source of happiness and love, the only creature who responded to the highest feelings of man, while her miseries were to be recompensed by the idolatry of every heart. How could the consistency, which was wanting in a political system, be expected in the general manners of the nation?

And so woman became what circumstances and men made her, instead of being what the climate and native institutions should have made her; sold, married against her taste, in accordance with the *Patria potestas* of the Romans, at the same time that she fell under the marital despotism which desired her seclusion, she found herself tempted to take the only reprisals which were within her power. Then she became a dissolute creature, as soon as men ceased to be intently occupied in intestine war, for the same reason that she was a virtuous woman in the midst of civil disturbances. Every educated man can fill in this outline, for we seek from movements like these the lessons and not the poetic suggestion which they yield.

The Revolution was too entirely occupied in breaking down and building up, had too many enemies, or followed perhaps too closely on the deplorable times witnessed under the regency and under Louis XV, to pay any attention to the position which women should occupy in the social order.

The remarkable men who raised the immortal monument which our codes present were almost all old-fashioned students of law deeply imbued with a spirit of Roman jurisprudence; and moreover they were not the founders of any political institutions. Sons of the Revolution, they believed, in accordance with that movement, that the law of divorce wisely restricted and the bond of dutiful submission were sufficient ameliorations of the previous marriage law. When that former order of things was remembered, the change made by the new legislation seemed immense.

At the present day the question as to which of these two principles shall triumph rests entirely in the hands of our wise legislators. The past has teaching which should bear fruit in the future. Have we lost all sense of the eloquence of fact?

The principles of the East resulted in the existence of eunuchs and seraglios; the spurious social standing of France has brought in the plague of courtesans and the more deadly plague of our marriage system; and thus, to use the language of a contemporary, the East sacrifices to paternity men and the principle of justice; France, women and modesty. Neither the East nor France has attained the goal which their institutions point to; for that is happiness. The man is not more loved by the women of a harem than the husband is sure of being in France, as the father of his children; and marrying is not worth what it costs. It is time to offer no more sacrifice to this institution, and to amass a larger sum of happiness in the social state by making our manners and our institution conformable to our climate.

Constitutional government, a happy mixture of two extreme political systems, despotism and democracy, suggests by the necessity of blending also the two principles of marriage, which so far clash together in France. The liberty which we boldly claim for young people is the only remedy for the host of evils whose source we have pointed out, by exposing the inconsistencies resulting from the bondage in which girls are kept. Let us give back to youth the indulgence of those passions, those coquetries, love and its terrors, love and its delights, and that fascinating company which followed the coming of the Franks. At this vernal season of life no fault is irreparable, and Hymen will come forth from the bosom of experiences, armed with confidence, stripped of hatred, and love in marriage will be justified, because it will have had the privilege of comparison.

In this change of manners the disgraceful plague of public prostitution will perish of itself. It is especially at the time when the man possesses the frankness and timidity of adolescence, that in his pursuit of happiness he is competent to meet and struggle with great and genuine passions of the heart. The soul is happy in making great efforts of whatever kind; provided that it can act, that it can stir and move, it makes little difference, even though it exercise its power against itself. In this observation, the truth of which everybody can see, there may be found one secret of successful legislation, of tranquillity and happiness. And then, the pursuit of learning has now become so highly developed that the most tempestuous of our coming Mirabeaus can consume his energy either in the indulgence of a passion or the study of a science. How many young people have been saved from debauchery by self-chosen labors or the persistent obstacles put in the way of a first love, a love that was pure! And what young girl does not desire to prolong the delightful childhood of sentiment, is not proud to have her nature known, and has not felt the secret tremblings of timidity, the modesty of her secret communings with herself, and wished to oppose them to the young desires of a lover inexperienced as herself! The gallantry of the Franks and the pleasures which attend it should then be the portion of youth, and then would naturally result a union of soul, of mind, of character, of habits, of temperament and of fortune, such as would produce the happy equilibrium necessary for the felicity of the married couple. This system would rest upon foundations wider and freer, if girls were subjected to a carefully calculated system of disinheritance; or if, in order to force men to choose only those who promised happiness by their virtues, their character or their talents, they married as in the United States without dowry.

In that case, the system adopted by the Romans could advantageously be applied to the married women who when they were girls used their liberty. Being exclusively engaged in the early education of their children, which is the most important of all maternal obligations, occupied in creating and maintaining the happiness of the household, so admirably described in the fourth book of *Julie*, they would be in their houses like the women of ancient Rome, living images of Providence, which reigns over all, and yet is nowhere visible. In this case, the laws covering the infidelity of the wife should be extremely severe. They should make the penalty disgrace, rather than inflict painful or coercive sentences. France has witnessed the spectacle of women riding asses for the pretended crime of magic, and many an innocent woman has died of shame. In this may be found the secret of future marriage legislation. The young girls of Miletus delivered themselves from marriage by voluntary death; the senate condemned the suicides to be dragged naked on a hurdle, and the other virgins condemned themselves for life.

Women and marriage will never be respected until we have that radical change in manners which we are now begging for. This profound thought is the ruling principle in the two finest productions of an immortal genius. *Emile* and *La Nouvelle Heloise* are nothing more than two eloquent pleas for the system. The voice there raised will resound through the ages, because it points to the real motives of true legislation, and the manners which will prevail in the future. By placing children at the breast of their mothers, Jean-Jacques rendered an immense service to the cause of virtue; but his age was too deeply gangrened with abuses to understand the lofty lessons unfolded in those two poems; it is right to add also that the philosopher was in these works overmastered by the poet, and in leaving in the heart of *Julie* after her marriage some vestiges of her first love, he was led astray by the attractiveness of a poetic situation, more touching indeed, but less useful than the truth which he wished to display.

Nevertheless, if marriage in France is an unlimited contract to which men agree with a silent understanding that they may thus give more relish to passion, more curiosity, more mystery to love, more fascination to women; if a woman is rather an ornament to the drawing-room, a fashion-plate, a portmanteau, than a being whose functions in the order politic are an essential part of the country's prosperity and the nation's glory, a creature whose endeavors in life vie in utility with those of men—I admit that all the above theory, all these long considerations sink into nothingness at the prospect of such an important destiny!——

But after having squeezed a pound of actualities in order to obtain one drop of philosophy, having paid sufficient homage to that passion for the historic, which is so dominant in our time, let us turn our glance upon the manners of the present period. Let us take the cap and bells and the coxcomb of which Rabelais once made a sceptre, and let us pursue the course of this inquiry without giving to one joke more seriousness than comports with it, and without giving to serious things the jesting tone which ill befits them.

SECOND PART
MEANS OF DEFENCE,
INTERIOR AND EXTERIOR.

"To be or not to be,
That is the question."

—Shakspeare, *Hamlet*.

MEDITATION X.
A TREATISE ON MARITAL POLICY.

When a man reaches the position in which the first part of this book sets him, we suppose that the idea of his wife being possessed by another makes his heart beat, and rekindles his passion, either by an appeal to his *amour propre*, his egotism, or his self-interest, for unless he is still on his wife's side, he must be one of the lowest of men and deserves his fate.

In this trying moment it is very difficult for a husband to avoid making mistakes; for, with regard to most men, the art of ruling a wife is even less known than that of judiciously choosing one. However, marital policy consists chiefly in the practical application of three principles which should be the soul of your conduct. The first is never to believe what a woman says; the second, always to look for the spirit without dwelling too much upon the letter of her actions; and the third, not to forget that a woman is never so garrulous as when she holds her tongue, and is never working with more energy than when she keeps quiet.

From the moment that your suspicions are aroused, you ought to be like a man mounted on a tricky horse, who always watches the ears of the beast, in fear of being thrown from the saddle.

But art consists not so much in the knowledge of principles, as in the manner of applying them; to reveal them to ignorant people is to put a razor in the hand of a monkey. Moreover, the first and most vital of your duties consists in perpetual dissimulation, an accomplishment in which most husbands are sadly lacking. In detecting the symptoms of minotaurism a little too plainly marked in the conduct of their wives, most men at once indulge in the most insulting suspicions. Their minds contract a tinge of bitterness which manifests itself in their conversation, and in their manners; and the alarm which fills their heart, like the gas flame in a glass globe, lights up their countenances so plainly, that it accounts for their conduct.

Now a woman, who has twelve hours more than you have each day to reflect and to study you, reads the suspicion written upon your face at the very moment that it arises. She will never forget this gratuitous insult. Nothing can ever remedy that. All is now said and done, and the very next day, if she has opportunity, she will join the ranks of inconsistent women.

You ought then to begin under these circumstances to affect towards your wife the same boundless confidence that you have hitherto had in her. If you begin to lull her anxieties by honeyed words, you are lost, she will not believe you; for she has her policy as you have yours. Now there is as much need for tact as for kindliness in your behavior, in order to inculcate in her, without her knowing it, a feeling of security, which will lead her to lay back her ears, and prevent you from using rein or spur at the wrong moment.

But how can we compare a horse, the frankest of all animals, to a being, the flashes of whose thought, and the movements of whose impulses render her at moments more prudent than the Servite Fra-Paolo, the most terrible adviser that the Ten at Venice ever had; more deceitful than a king; more adroit than Louis XI; more profound than Machiavelli; as sophistical as Hobbes; as acute as Voltaire; as pliant as the fiancee of Mamolin; and distrustful of no one in the whole wide world but you?

Moreover, to this dissimulation, by means of which the springs that move your conduct ought to be made as invisible as those that move the world, must be added absolute self-control. That diplomatic imperturbability, so boasted of by Talleyrand, must be the least of your qualities; his exquisite politeness and the grace of his manners must distinguish your conversation. The professor here expressly forbids you to use your whip, if you would obtain complete control over your gentle Andalusian steed.

LXI.

If a man strike his mistress it is a self-inflicted wound; but if he strike his wife it is suicide!

How can we think of a government without police, an action without force, a power without weapons? — Now this is exactly the problem which we shall try to solve in our future meditations. But first we must submit two preliminary observations. They will furnish us with two other theories concerning the application of all the mechanical means which we propose you should employ. An instance from life will refresh these arid and dry dissertations: the hearing of such a story will be like laying down a book, to work in the field.

In the year 1822, on a fine morning in the month of February, I was traversing the boulevards of Paris, from the quiet circles of the Marais to the fashionable quarters of the Chaussee-d'Antin, and I observed for the first time, not without a certain philosophic joy, the diversity of physiognomy and the varieties of costume which, from the Rue du Pas-de-la-Mule even to the Madeleine, made each portion of the boulevard a world of itself, and this whole zone of Paris, a grand panorama of manners. Having at that time no idea of what the world was, and little thinking that one day I should have the audacity to set myself up as a legislator on marriage, I was going to take lunch at the house of a college friend, who was perhaps too early in life afflicted with a wife and two children. My former professor of mathematics lived at a short distance from the house of my college friend, and I promised myself the pleasure of a visit to this worthy mathematician before indulging my appetite for the dainties of friendship. I accordingly made my way to the heart of a study, where everything was covered with a dust which bore witness to the lofty abstraction of the scholar. But a surprise was in store for me there. I perceived a pretty woman seated on the arm of an easy chair, as if mounted on an English horse; her face took on the look of conventional surprise worn by mistresses of the house towards those they do not know, but she did not disguise the expression of annoyance which, at my appearance, clouded her countenance with the thought that I was aware how ill-timed was my presence. My master, doubtless absorbed in an equation, had not yet raised his head; I therefore waved my right hand towards the young lady, like a fish moving his fin, and on tiptoe I retired with a mysterious smile which might be translated "I will not be the one to prevent him committing an act of infidelity to Urania." She nodded her head with one of those sudden gestures whose graceful vivacity is not to be translated into words.

"My good friend, don't go away," cried the geometrician. "This is my wife!"

I bowed for the second time!—Oh, Coulon! Why wert thou not present to applaud the only one of thy pupils who understood from that moment the expression, "anacreontic," as applied to a bow?—The effect must have been very overwhelming; for Madame the Professoress, as the Germans say, rose hurriedly as if to go, making me a slight bow which seemed to say: "Adorable!——" Her husband stopped her, saying:

"Don't go, my child, this is one of my pupils."

The young woman bent her head towards the scholar as a bird perched on a bough stretches its neck to pick up a seed.

"It is not possible," said the husband, heaving a sigh, "and I am going to prove it to you by A plus B."

"Let us drop that, sir, I beg you," she answered, pointing with a wink to me.

If it had been a problem in algebra, my master would have understood this look, but it was Chinese to him, and so he went on.

"Look here, child, I constitute you judge in the matter; our income is ten thousand francs."

At these words I retired to the door, as if I were seized with a wild desire to examine the framed drawings which had attracted my attention. My discretion was rewarded by an eloquent glance. Alas! she did not know that in Fortunio I could have played the part of Sharp-Ears, who heard the truffles growing.

"In accordance with the principles of general economy," said my master, "no one ought to spend in rent and servant's wages more than two-tenths of his income; now our apartment and our attendance cost altogether a hundred louis. I give you twelve hundred francs to dress with" [in saying this he emphasized every syllable]. "Your food," he went on, takes up four thousand francs, our children demand at lest twenty-five louis; I take for myself only eight hundred francs; washing, fuel and light mount up to about a thousand francs; so that there does not remain, as you see, more than six hundred francs for unforeseen expenses. In order to buy the cross of diamonds, we must draw a thousand crowns from our capital, and if once we take that course, my little darling, there is no reason why we should not leave Paris which you love so much, and at once take up our residence in the country, in order to retrench. Children and household expenses will increase fast enough! Come, try to be reasonable!"

"I suppose I must," she said, "but you will be the only husband in Paris who has not given a New Year's gift to his wife."

And she stole away like a school-boy who goes to finish an imposed duty. My master made a gesture of relief. When he saw the door close he rubbed his hands, he talked of the war in Spain; and I went my way to the Rue de Provence, little knowing that I had received the first installment of a great lesson in marriage, any more than I dreamt of the conquest of Constantinople by General Diebitsch. I arrived at my host's house at the very moment they were sitting down to luncheon, after having waited for me the half hour demanded by usage. It was, I believe, as she opened a *pate de foie gras* that my pretty hostess said to her husband, with a determined air:

"Alexander, if you were really nice you would give me that pair of ear-rings that we saw at Fossin's."

"You shall have them," cheerfully replied my friend, drawing from his pocketbook three notes of a thousand francs, the sight of which made his wife's eyes sparkle. "I can no more resist the pleasure of offering them to you," he added, "than you can that of accepting them. This is the anniversary of the day I first saw you, and the diamonds will perhaps make you remember it! — —"

"You bad man!" said she, with a winning smile.

She poked two fingers into her bodice, and pulling out a bouquet of violets she threw them with childlike contempt into the face of my friend. Alexander gave her the price of the jewels, crying out:

"I had seen the flowers!"

I shall never forget the lively gesture and the eager joy with which, like a cat which lays its spotted paw upon a mouse, the little woman seized the three bank notes; she rolled them up blushing with pleasure, and put them in the place of the violets which before had perfumed her bosom. I could not help thinking about my old mathematical master. I did not then see any difference between him and his pupil, than that which exists between a frugal man and a prodigal, little thinking that he of the two who seemed to calculate the better, actually calculated the worse. The luncheon went off merrily. Very soon, seated in a little drawing-room newly decorated, before a cheerful fire which gave warmth and made our hearts expand as in spring time, I felt compelled to make this loving couple a guest's compliments on the furnishing of their little bower.

"It is a pity that all this costs so dear," said my friend, "but it is right that the nest be worthy of the bird; but why the devil do you compliment me upon curtains which are not paid for? — You make me remember, just at the time I am digesting lunch, that I still owe two thousand francs to a Turk of an upholsterer."

At these words the mistress of the house made a mental inventory of the pretty room with her eyes, and the radiancy of her face changed to thoughtfulness. Alexander took me by the hand and led me to the recess of a bay window.

"Do you happen," he said in a low voice, "to have a thousand crowns to lend me? I have only twelve thousand francs income, and this year—"

"Alexander," cried the dear creature, interrupting her husband, while, rushing up, she offered him the three banknotes, "I see now that it is a piece of folly—"

"What do you mean?" answered he, "keep your money."

"But, my love, I am ruining you! I ought to know that you love me so much, that I ought not to tell you all that I wish for."

"Keep it, my darling, it is your lawful property—nonsense, I shall gamble this winter and get all that back again!"

"Gamble!" cried she, with an expression of horror. "Alexander, take back these notes! Come, sir, I wish you to do so."

"No, no," replied my friend, repulsing the white and delicious little hand. "Are you not going on Thursday to a ball of Madame de B——-?"

"I will think about what you asked of me," said I to my comrade.

I went away bowing to his wife, but I saw plainly after that scene that my anacreontic salutation did not produce much effect upon her.

"He must be mad," thought I as I went away, "to talk of a thousand crowns to a law student."

Five days later I found myself at the house of Madame de B——-, whose balls were becoming fashionable. In the midst of the quadrilles I saw the wife of my friend and that of the mathematician. Madame Alexander wore a charming dress; some flowers and white muslin were all that composed it. She wore a little cross *a la Jeannette*, hanging by a black velvet ribbon which set off the whiteness of her scented skin; long pears of gold decorated her ears. On the neck of Madame the Professoress sparkled a superb cross of diamonds.

"How funny that is," said I to a personage who had not yet studied the world's ledger, nor deciphered the heart of a single woman.

That personage was myself. If I had then the desire to dance with those fair women, it was simply because I knew a secret which emboldened my timidity.

"So after all, madame, you have your cross?" I said to her first.

"Well, I fairly won it!" she replied, with a smile hard to describe.

"How is this! no ear-rings?" I remarked to the wife of my friend.

"Ah!" she replied, "I have enjoyed possession of them during a whole luncheon time, but you see that I have ended by converting Alexander."

"He allowed himself to be easily convinced?"

She answered with a look of triumph.

Eight years afterwards, this scene suddenly rose to my memory, though I had long since forgotten it, and in the light of the candles I distinctly discerned the moral of it. Yes, a woman has a horror of being convinced of anything; when you try to persuade her she immediately submits to being led astray and continues to play the role which nature gave her. In her view, to allow herself to be won over is to grant a favor, but exact arguments irritate and confound her; in order to guide her you must employ the power which she herself so frequently employs and which lies in an appeal to sensibility. It is therefore in his wife, and not in himself, that a husband can find the instruments of his despotism; as diamond cuts diamond so must the woman be made to tyrannize over herself. To know how to offer the ear-rings in such a way that they will be returned, is a secret whose application embraces the slightest details of life. And now let us pass to the second observation.

"He who can manage property of one toman, can manage one of an hundred thousand," says an Indian proverb; and I, for my part, will enlarge upon this Asiatic adage and declare, that he who can govern one woman can govern a nation, and indeed there is very much similarity between these two governments. Must not the policy of husbands be very nearly the same as the policy of kings? Do not we see kings trying to amuse the people in order to deprive them of their liberty; throwing food at their heads for one day, in order to make them forget the misery of a whole year; preaching to them not to steal and at the same time stripping them of everything; and saying to them: "It seems to me that if I were the people I should be virtuous"? It is from England that we obtain the precedent which husbands should adopt in their houses. Those who have eyes ought to see that when the government is running smoothly the Whigs are rarely in power. A long Tory ministry has always succeeded an ephemeral Liberal cabinet. The orators of a national party resemble the rats which wear their teeth away in gnawing the rotten panel; they close up the hole as soon as they smell the nuts and the lard locked up in the royal cupboard. The woman is the Whig of our government. Occupying the situation in which we have left her she might naturally aspire to the conquest of more than one privilege. Shut your eyes to the intrigues, allow her to waste her strength in mounting half the steps of your throne; and when she is on the point of touching your sceptre, fling her back to the ground, quite gently and with infinite grace, saying to her: "Bravo!" and leaving her to expect success in the hereafter. The craftiness of this manoeuvre will prove a fine support to you in the employment of any means which it may please you to choose from your arsenal, for the object of subduing your wife.

Such are the general principles which a husband should put into practice, if he wishes to escape mistakes in ruling his little kingdom. Nevertheless, in spite of what was decided by the minority at the council of Macon (Montesquieu, who had perhaps foreseen the coming of constitutional government has remarked, I forget in what part of his writings, that good sense in public assemblies is always found on the side of the minority), we discern in a woman a soul and a body, and we commence by investigating the means to gain control of her moral nature. The exercise of thought, whatever people may say, is more noble than the exercise of bodily organs, and we give precedence to science over cookery and to intellectual training over hygiene.

MEDITATION XI.

INSTRUCTION IN THE HOME.

Whether wives should or should not be put under instruction—such is the question before us. Of all those which we have discussed this is the only one which has two extremes and admits of no compromise. Knowledge and ignorance, such are the two irreconcilable terms of this problem. Between these two abysses we seem to see Louis XVIII reckoning up the felicities of the eighteenth century, and the unhappiness of the nineteenth. Seated in the centre of the seesaw, which he knew so well how to balance by his own weight, he contemplates at one end of it the fanatic ignorance of a lay brother, the apathy of a serf, the shining armor on the horses of a banneret; he thinks he hears the cry, "France and Montjoie-Saint-Denis!" But he turns round, he smiles as he sees the haughty look of a manufacturer, who is captain in the national guard; the elegant carriage of a stock broker; the simple costume of a peer of France turned journalist and sending his son to the Polytechnique; then he notices the costly stuffs, the newspapers, the steam engines; and he drinks his coffee from a cup of Sevres, at the bottom of which still glitters the "N" surmounted by a crown.

"Away with civilization! Away with thought!"—That is your cry. You ought to hold in horror the education of women for the reason so well realized in Spain, that it is easier to govern a nation of idiots than a nation of scholars. A nation degraded is happy: if she has not the sentiment of liberty, neither has she the storms and disturbances which it begets; she lives as polyps live; she can be cut up into two or three pieces and each piece is still a nation, complete and living, and ready to be governed by the first blind man who arms himself with the pastoral staff.

What is it that produces this wonderful characteristic of humanity? Ignorance; ignorance is the sole support of despotism, which lives on darkness and silence. Now happiness in the domestic establishment as in a political state is a negative happiness. The affection of a people for a king, in an absolute monarchy, is perhaps less contrary to nature than the fidelity of a wife towards her husband, when love between them no longer exists. Now we know that, in your house, love at this moment has one foot on the window-sill. It is necessary for you, therefore, to put into practice that salutary rigor by which M. de Metternich prolongs his *statu quo*; but we would advise you to do so with more tact and with still more tenderness; for your wife is more crafty than all the Germans put together, and as voluptuous as the Italians.

You should, therefore, try to put off as long as possible the fatal moment when your wife asks you for a book. This will be easy. You will first of all pronounce in a tone of disdain the phrase "Blue stocking;" and, on her request being repeated, you will tell her what ridicule attaches, among the neighbors, to pedantic women.

You will then repeat to her, very frequently, that the most lovable and the wittiest women in the world are found at Paris, where women never read;

That women are like people of quality who, according to Mascarillo, know everything without having learned anything; that a woman while she is dancing, or while she is playing cards, without even having the appearance of listening, ought to know how to pick up from the conversation of talented men the ready-made phrases out of which fools manufacture their wit at Paris;

That in this country decisive judgments on men and affairs are passed round from hand to hand; and that the little cutting phrase with which a woman criticises an author, demolishes a work, or heaps contempt on a picture, has more power in the world than a court decision;

That women are beautiful mirrors, which naturally reflect the most brilliant ideas;

That natural wit is everything, and the best education is gained rather from what we learn in the world than by what we read in books;

That, above all, reading ends in making the eyes dull, etc.

To think of leaving a woman at liberty to read the books which her character of mind may prompt her to choose! This is to drop a spark in a powder magazine; it is worse than that, it is to teach your wife to separate herself from you; to live in an imaginary world, in a Paradise. For what do women read? Works of passion, the *Confessions* of Rousseau, romances, and all those compositions which work most powerfully on their sensibility. They like neither argument nor the ripe fruits of knowledge. Now have you ever considered the results which follow these poetical readings?

Romances, and indeed all works of imagination, paint sentiments and events with colors of a very different brilliancy from those presented by nature. The fascination of such works springs less from the desire which each author feels to show his skill in putting forth choice and delicate ideas than from the mysterious working of the human intellect. It is characteristic of man to purify and refine everything that he lays up in the treasury of his thoughts. What human faces, what monuments of the dead are not made more beautiful than actual nature in the artistic representation? The soul of the reader assists in this conspiracy against the truth, either by means of the profound silence which it enjoys in reading or by the fire of mental conception with which it is agitated or by the clearness with which imagery is reflected in the mirror of the understanding. Who has not seen on reading the *Confessions* of Jean-Jacques, that Madame de Warens is described as much prettier than she ever was in actual life? It might almost be said that our souls dwell with delight upon the figures which they had met in a former existence, under fairer skies; that they accept the creations of another soul only as wings on which they may soar into space; features the most delicate they bring

birds, to make herbals, to water little Bengal rose-bushes, to fill in worsted work, or to put on collars. Moreover, if a little girl in her tenth year has more refinement than a boy of twenty, she is timid and awkward. She is frightened at a spider, chatters nonsense, thinks of dress, talks about the fashions and has not the courage to be either a watchful mother or a chaste wife.

Notice what progress she had made; she has been shown how to paint roses, and to embroider ties in such a way as to earn eight sous a day. She has learned the history of France in *Ragois* and chronology in the *Tables du Citoyen Chantreau*, and her young imagination has been set free in the realm of geography; all without any aim, excepting that of keeping away all that might be dangerous to her heart; but at the same time her mother and her teachers repeat with unwearied voice the lesson, that the whole science of a woman lies in knowing how to arrange the fig leaf which our Mother Eve wore. "She does not hear for fifteen years," says Diderot, "anything else but 'my daughter, your fig leaf is on badly; my daughter, your fig leaf is on well; my daughter, would it not look better so?'"

Keep your wife then within this fine and noble circle of knowledge. If by chance your wife wishes to have a library, buy for her Florian, Malte-Brun, *The Cabinet des Fees*, *The Arabian Nights*, Redoute's *Roses*, *The Customs of China*, *The Pigeons*, by Madame Knip, the great work on Egypt, etc. Carry out, in short, the clever suggestion of that princess who, when she was told of a riot occasioned by the dearness of bread, said, "Why don't they eat cake?"

Perhaps, one evening, your wife will reproach you for being sullen and not speaking to her; perhaps she will say that you are ridiculous, when you have just made a pun; but this is one of the slight annoyances incident to our system; and, moreover, what does it matter to you that the education of women in France is the most pleasant of absurdities, and that your marital obscurantism has brought a doll to your arms? As you have not sufficient courage to undertake a fairer task, would it not be better to lead your wife along the beaten track of married life in safety, than to run the risk of making her scale the steep precipices of love? She is likely to be a mother: you must not exactly expect to have Gracchi for sons, but to be really *pater quem nuptiae demonstrant*; now, in order to aid you in reaching this consummation, we must make this book an arsenal from which each one, in accordance with his wife's character and his own, may choose weapons fit to employ against the terrible genius of evil, which is always ready to rise up in the soul of a wife; and since it may fairly be considered that the ignorant are the most cruel opponents of feminine education, this Meditation will serve as a breviary for the majority of husbands.

If a woman has received a man's education, she possesses in very truth the most brilliant and most fertile sources of happiness both to herself and to her husband; but this kind of woman is as rare as happiness itself; and if you do not possess her for your wife, your best course is to confine the one you do possess, for the sake of your common felicity, to the region of ideas she was born in, for you must not forget that one moment of pride in her might destroy you, by setting on the throne a slave who would immediately be tempted to abuse her power.

After all, by following the system prescribed in this Meditation, a man of superiority will be relieved from the necessity of putting his thoughts into small change, when he wishes to be understood by his wife, if indeed this man of superiority has been guilty of the folly of marrying one of those poor creatures who cannot understand him, instead of choosing for his wife a young girl whose mind and heart he has tested and studied for a considerable time.

Our aim in this last matrimonial observation has not been to advise all men of superiority to seek for women of superiority and we do not wish each one to expound our principles after the manner of Madame de Stael, who attempted in the most indelicate manner to effect a union between herself and Napoleon. These two beings would have been very unhappy in their domestic life; and Josephine was a wife accomplished in a very different sense from this virago of the nineteenth century.

And, indeed, when we praise those undiscoverable girls so happily educated by chance, so well endowed by nature, whose delicate souls endure so well the rude contact of the great soul of him we call *a man*, we mean to speak of those rare and noble creatures of whom Goethe has given us a model in his Claire of *Egmont*; we are thinking of those women who seek no other glory than that of playing their part well; who adapt themselves with amazing pliancy to the will and pleasure of those whom nature has given them for masters; soaring at one time into the boundless sphere of their thought and in turn stooping to the simple task of amusing them as if they were children; understanding well the inconsistencies of masculine and violent souls, understanding also their slightest word, their most puzzling looks; happy in silence, happy also in the midst of loquacity; and well aware that the pleasures, the ideas and the moral instincts of a Lord Byron cannot be those of a bonnet-maker. But we must stop; this fair picture has led us too far from our subject; we are treating of marriage and not of love.

MEDITATION XII.
THE HYGIENE OF MARRIAGE.

The aim of this Meditation is to call to your attention a new method of defence, by which you may reduce the will of your new wife to a condition of utter and abject submission. This is brought about by the reaction upon her moral nature of physical changes, and the wise lowering of her physical condition by a diet skillfully controlled.

This great and philosophical question of conjugal medicine will doubtless be regarded favorably by all who are gouty, are impotent, or suffer from catarrh; and by that legion of old men whose dullness we have quickened by our article on the predestined. But it principally concerns those husbands who have courage enough to enter into those paths of machiavelism, such as would not have been unworthy of that great king of France who endeavored to secure the happiness of the nation at the expense of certain noble heads. Here, the subject is the same. The amputation or the weakening of certain members is always to the advantage of the whole body.

Do you think seriously that a celibate who has been subject to a diet consisting of the herb hanea, of cucumbers, of purslane and the applications of leeches to his ears, as recommended by Sterne, would be able to carry by storm the honor of your wife? Suppose that a diplomat had been clever enough to affix a permanent linen plaster to the head of Napoleon, or to purge him every morning: Do you think that Napoleon, Napoleon the Great, would ever have conquered Italy? Was Napoleon, during his campaign in Russia, a prey to the most horrible pangs of dysuria, or was he not? That is one of the questions which has weighed upon the minds of the whole world. Is it not certain that cooling applications, douches, baths, etc., produce great changes in more or less acute affections of the brain? In the middle of the heat of July when each one of your pores slowly filters out and returns to the devouring atmosphere the glasses of iced lemonade which you have drunk at a single draught, have you ever felt the flame of courage, the vigor of thought, the complete energy which rendered existence light and sweet to you some months before?

No, no; the iron most closely cemented into the hardest stone will raise and throw apart the most durable monument, by reason of the secret influence exercised by the slow and invisible variations of heat and cold, which vex the atmosphere. In the first place, let us be sure that if atmospheric mediums have an influence over man, there is still a stronger reason for believing that man, in turn, influences the imagination of his kind, by the more or less vigor with which he projects his will and thus produces a veritable atmosphere around him.

It is in this fact that the power of the actor's talent lies, as well as that of poetry and of fanaticism; for the former is the eloquence of words, as the latter is the eloquence of actions; and in this lies the foundation of a science, so far in its infancy.

This will, so potent in one man against another, this nervous and fluid force, eminently mobile and transmittable, is itself subject to the changing condition of our organization, and there are many circumstances which make this frail organism of ours to vary. At this point, our metaphysical observation shall stop and we will enter into an analysis of the circumstances which develop the will of man and impart to it a grater degree of strength or weakness.

Do not believe, however, that it is our aim to induce you to put cataplasms on the honor of your wife, to lock her up in a sweating house, or to seal her up like a letter; no. We will not even attempt to teach you the magnetic theory which would give you the power to make your will triumph in the soul of your wife; there is not a single husband who would accept the happiness of an eternal love at the price of this perpetual strain laid upon his animal forces. But we shall attempt to expound a powerful system of hygiene, which will enable you to put out the flame when your chimney takes fire. The elegant women of Paris and the provinces (and these elegant women form a very distinguished class among the honest women) have plenty of means of attaining the object which we propose, without rummaging in the arsenal of medicine for the four cold specifics, the water-lily and the thousand inventions worthy only of witches. We will leave to Aelian his herb hanea and to Sterne the purslane and cucumber which indicate too plainly his antiphlogistic purpose.

You should let your wife recline all day long on soft armchairs, in which she sinks into a veritable bath of eiderdown or feathers; you should encourage in every way that does no violence to your conscience, the inclination which women have to breathe no other air but the scented atmosphere of a chamber seldom opened, where daylight can scarcely enter through the soft, transparent curtains.

You will obtain marvelous results from this system, after having previously experienced the shock of her excitement; but if you are strong enough to support this momentary transport of your wife you will soon see her artificial energy die away. In general, women love to live fast, but, after their tempest of passion, return to that condition of tranquillity which insures the happiness of a husband.

Jean-Jacques, through the instrumentality of his enchanting Julie, must have proved to your wife that it was infinitely becoming to refrain from affronting her delicate stomach and her refined palate by making chyle out of coarse lumps of beef, and enormous collops of mutton. Is there anything purer in the world than those interesting vegetables, always fresh and scentless, those tinted fruits, that coffee, that fragrant chocolate, those oranges, the golden apples of Atalanta, the dates of Arabia and the biscuits of Brussels, a wholesome and elegant food which produces satisfactory results, at the same time that it imparts to a woman an air of mysterious originality? By the regimen which she chooses she becomes quite celebrated in her immediate circle, just as she would be by a singular toilet, a benevolent action or a *bon mot*. Pythagoras must needs have cast his spell over her, and become as much petted by her as a poodle or an ape.

Never commit the imprudence of certain men who, for the sake of putting on the appearance of wit, controvert the feminine dictum, *that the figure is preserved by meagre diet*. Women on such a diet never grow fat, that is clear and positive; do you stick to that.

Praise the skill with which some women, renowned for their beauty, have been able to preserve it by bathing themselves in milk, several times a day, or in water compounded of substances likely to render the skin softer and to lower the nervous tension.

Advise her above all things to refrain from washing herself in cold water; because water warm or tepid is the proper thing for all kinds of ablutions.

Let Broussais be your idol. At the least indisposition of your wife, and on the slightest pretext, order the application of leeches; do not even shrink from applying from time to time a few dozen on yourself, in order to establish the system of that celebrated doctor in your household. You will constantly be called upon from your position as husband to discover that your wife is too ruddy; try even sometimes to bring the blood to her head, in order to have the right to introduce into the house at certain intervals a squad of leeches.

Your wife ought to drink water, lightly tinged with a Burgundy wine agreeable to her taste, but destitute of any tonic properties; every other kind of wine would be bad for her. Never allow her to drink water alone; if you do, you are lost.

"Impetuous fluid! As soon as you press against the floodgates of the brain, how quickly do they yield to your power! Then Curiosity comes swimming by, making signs to her companions to follow; they plunge into the current. Imagination sits dreaming on the bank. She follows the torrent with her eyes and transforms the fragments of straw and reed into masts and bowsprit. And scarcely has the transformation taken place, before Desire, holding in one hand her skirt drawn up even to her knees, appears, sees the vessel and takes possession of it. O ye drinkers of water, it is by means of that magic spring that you have so often turned and turned again the world at your will, throwing beneath your feet the weak, trampling on his neck, and sometimes changing even the form and aspect of nature!"

If by this system of inaction, in combination with our system of diet, you fail to obtain satisfactory results, throw yourself with might and main into another system, which we will explain to you.

Man has a certain degree of energy given to him. Such and such a man or woman stands to another as ten is to thirty, as one to five; and there is a certain degree of energy which no one of us ever exceeds. The quantity of energy, or will-power, which each of us possesses diffuses itself like sound; it is sometimes weak, sometimes strong; it modifies itself according to the octaves to which it mounts. This force is unique, and although it may be dissipated in desire, in passion, in toils of intellect or in bodily exertion, it turns towards the object to which man directs it. A boxer expends it in blows of the fist, the baker in kneading his bread, the poet in the enthusiasm which consumes and demands an enormous quantity of it; it passes to the feet of the dancer; in fact, every one diffuses it at will, and may I see the Minotaur tranquilly seated this very evening upon my bed, if you do not know as well as I do how he expends it. Almost all men spend in necessary toils, or in the anguish of direful passions, this fine sum of energy and of will, with which nature has endowed them; but our honest women are all the prey to the caprices and the struggles of this power which knows not what to do with itself. If, in the case of your wife, this energy has not been subdued by the prescribed dietary regimen, subject her to some form of activity which will constantly increase in violence. Find some means by which her sum of force which inconveniences you may be carried off, by some occupation which shall entirely absorb her strength. Without setting your wife to work the crank of a machine, there are a thousand ways of tiring her out under the load of constant work.

In leaving it to you to find means for carrying out our design—and these means vary with circumstances—we would point out that dancing is one of the very best abysses in which love may bury itself. This point having been very well treated by a contemporary, we will give him here an opportunity of speaking his mind:

"The poor victim who is the admiration of an enchanted audience pays dear for her success. What result can possibly follow on exertions so ill-proportioned to the resources of the delicate sex? The muscles of the body, disproportionately wearied, are forced to their full power of exertion. The nervous forces, intended to feed the fire of passions, and the labor of the brain, are diverted from their course. The failure of desire, the wish for rest, the exclusive craving for substantial food, all point to a nature impoverished, more anxious to recruit than to enjoy. Moreover, a denizen of the side scenes said to me one day, 'Whoever has lived with dancers has lived with sheep; for in their exhaustion they can think of nothing but strong food.' Believe me, then, the love which a ballet girl inspires is very delusive; in her we find, under an appearance of an artificial springtime, a soil which is cold as well as greedy, and senses which are utterly dulled. The Calabrian doctors prescribed the dance as a remedy for the hysteric affections which are common among the women of their country; and the Arabs use a somewhat similar recipe for the highbred mares, whose too lively temperament hinders their fecundity. 'Dull as a dancer' is a familiar proverb at the theatre. In fact, the best brains of Europe are convinced that dancing brings with it a result eminently cooling.

"In support of this it may be necessary to add other observations. The life of shepherds gives birth to irregular loves. The morals of weavers were horribly decried in Greece. The Italians have given birth to a proverb concerning the lubricity of lame women. The Spanish, in whose veins are found many mixtures of African incontinence, have expressed their sentiments in a maxim which is familiar with them: *Muger y gallina pierna quebrantada* [it is good that a woman and a hen have one broken leg]. The profound sagacity of the Orientals in the art of pleasure is altogether expressed by this ordinance of the caliph Hakim, founder of the Druses, who forbade, under pain of death, the making in his kingdom of any shoes for women. It seems that over the whole globe the tempests of the heart wait only to break out after the limbs are at rest!"

What an admirable manoeuvre it would be to make a wife dance, and to feed her on vegetables!

Do not believe that these observations, which are as true as they are wittily stated, contradict in any way the system which we have previously prescribed; by the latter, as by the former, we succeed in producing in a woman that needed listlessness, which is the pledge of repose and tranquility. By the latter you leave a door open, that the enemy may flee; by the former, you slay him.

Now at this point it seems to us that we hear timorous people and those of narrow views rising up against our idea of hygiene in the name of morality and sentiment.

"Is not woman endowed with a soul? Has she not feelings as we have? What right has any one, without regard to her pain, her ideas, or her requirements, to hammer her out, as a cheap metal, out of which a workman fashions a candlestick or an extinguisher? Is it because the poor creatures are already so feeble and miserable that a brute claims the power to torture them, merely at the dictate of his own fancies, which may be more or less just? And, if by this weakening or heating system of yours, which draws out, softens, hardens the fibres, you cause frightful and cruel sickness, if you bring to the tomb a woman who is dear to you; if, if,—"

This is our answer:

Have you never noticed into how many different shapes harlequin and columbine change their little white hats? They turn and twist them so well that they become, one after another, a spinning-top, a boat, a wine-glass, a half-moon, a cap, a basket, a fish, a whip, a dagger, a baby, and a man's head.

This is an exact image of the despotism with which you ought to shape and reshape your wife.

The wife is a piece of property, acquired by contract; she is part of your furniture, for possession is nine-tenths of the law; in fact, the woman is not, to speak correctly, anything but an adjunct to the man; therefore abridge, cut, file this article as you choose; she is in every sense yours. Take no notice at all of her murmurs, of her cries, of her sufferings; nature has ordained her for your use, that she may bear everything—children, griefs, blows and pains from man.

Don't accuse yourself of harshness. In the codes of all the nations which are called civilized, man has written the laws which govern the destiny of women in these cruel terms: *Vae victis!* Woe to the conquered!

Finally, think upon this last observation, the most weighty, perhaps, of all that we have made up to this time: if you, her husband, do not break under the scourge of your will this weak and charming reed, there will be a celibate, capricious and despotic, ready to bring her under a yoke more cruel still; and she will have to endure two tyrannies instead of one. Under all considerations, therefore, humanity demands that you should follow the system of our hygiene.

MEDITATION XIII.
OF PERSONAL MEASURES.

Perhaps the preceding Meditations will prove more likely to develop general principles of conduct, than to repel force by force. They furnish, however, the pharmacopoeia of medicine and not the practice of medicine. Now consider the personal means which nature has put into your hands for self-defence; for Providence has forgotten no one; if to the sepia (that fish of the Adriatic) has been given the black dye by which he produces a cloud in which he disappears from his enemy, you should believe that a husband has not been left without a weapon; and now the time has come for you to draw yours.

You ought to have stipulated before you married that your wife should nurse her own children; in this case, as long as she is occupied in bearing children or in nursing them you will avoid the danger from one or two quarters. The wife who is engaged in bringing into the world and nursing a baby has not really the time to bother with a lover, not to speak of the fact that before and after her confinement she cannot show herself in the world. In short, how can the most bold of the distinguished women who are the subject of this work show herself under these circumstances in public? O Lord Byron, thou didst not wish to see women even eat!

Six months after her confinement, and when the child is on the eve of being weaned, a woman just begins to feel that she can enjoy her restoration and her liberty.

If your wife has not nursed her first child, you have too much sense not to notice this circumstance, and not to make her desire to nurse her next one. You will read to her the *Emile* of Jean-Jacques; you will fill her imagination with a sense of motherly duties; you will excite her moral feelings, etc.: in a word, you are either a fool or a man of sense; and in the first case, even after reading this book, you will always be minotaurized; while in the second, you will understand how to take a hint.

This first expedient is in reality your own personal business. It will give you a great advantage in carrying out all the other methods.

Since Alcibiades cut the ears and the tail of his dog, in order to do a service to Pericles, who had on his hands a sort of Spanish war, as well as an Ouvrard contract affair, such as was then attracting the notice of the Athenians, there is not a single minister who has not endeavored to cut the ears of some dog or other.

So in medicine, when inflammation takes place at some vital point of the system, counter-irritation is brought about at some other point, by means of blisters, scarifications and cupping.

Another method consists in blistering your wife, or giving her, with a mental needle, a prod whose violence is such as to make a diversion in your favor.

A man of considerable mental resources had made his honeymoon last for about four years; the moon began to wane, and he saw appearing the fatal hollow in its circle. His wife was exactly in that state of mind which we attributed at the close of our first part to every honest woman; she had taken a fancy to a worthless fellow who was both insignificant in appearance and ugly; the only thing in his favor was, he was not her own husband. At this juncture, her husband meditated the cutting of some dog's tail, in order to renew, if possible, his lease of happiness. His wife had conducted herself with such tact, that it would have been very embarrassing to forbid her lover the house, for she had discovered some slight tie of relationship between them. The danger became, day by day, more imminent. The scent of the Minotaur was all around. One evening the husband felt himself plunged into a mood of deep vexation so acute as to be apparent to his wife. His wife had begun to show him more kindness than she had ever exhibited, even during the honeymoon; and hence question after question racked his mind. On her part a dead silence reigned. The anxious questionings of his mind were redoubled; his suspicions burst forth, and he was seized with forebodings of future calamity! Now, on this occasion, he deftly applied a Japanese blister, which burned as fiercely as an *auto-da-fe* of the year 1600. At first his wife employed a thousand stratagems to discover whether the annoyance of her husband was caused by the presence of her lover; it was her first intrigue and she displayed a thousand artifices in it. Her imagination was aroused; it was no longer taken up with her lover; had she not better, first of all, probe her husband's secret?

One evening the husband, moved by the desire to confide in his loving helpmeet all his troubles, informed her that their whole fortune was lost. They would have to give up their carriage, their box at the theatre, balls, parties, even Paris itself; perhaps, by living on their estate in the country a year or two, they might retrieve all! Appealing to the imagination of his wife, he told her how he pitied her for her attachment to a man who was indeed deeply in love with her, but was now without fortune; he tore his hair, and his wife was compelled in honor to be deeply moved; then in this first excitement of their conjugal disturbance he took her off to his estate. Then followed scarifications, mustard plaster upon mustard plaster, and the tails of fresh dogs were cut: he caused a Gothic wing to be built to the chateau; madame altered the park ten time over in order to have fountains and lakes and variations in the grounds; finally, the husband in the midst of her labors did not forget his own, which consisted in providing her with interesting reading, and launching upon her delicate attentions, etc. Notice, he never informed his wife of the trick he had played on her; and if his fortune was recuperated, it was directly after the building of the wing, and the expenditure of enormous sums in making water-courses; but he assured her that the lake provided a water-power by which mills might be run, etc.

Now, there was a conjugal blister well conceived, for this husband neither neglected to rear his family nor to invite to his house neighbors who were tiresome, stupid or old; and if he spent the winter in Paris, he flung his wife into the vortex of balls and races, so that she had not a minute to give to lovers, who are usually the fruit of a vacant life.

Journeys to Italy, Switzerland or Greece, sudden complaints which require a visit to the waters, and the most distant waters, are pretty good blisters. In fact, a man of sense should know how to manufacture a thousand of them.

Let us continue our examination of such personal methods.

And here we would have you observe that we are reasoning upon a hypothesis, without which this book will be unintelligible to you; namely, we suppose that your honeymoon has lasted for a respectable time and that the lady that you married was not a widow, but a maid; on the opposite supposition, it is at least in accordance with French manners to think that your wife married you merely for the purpose of becoming inconsistent.

From the moment when the struggle between virtue and inconsistency begins in your home, the whole question rests upon the constant and involuntary comparison which your wife is instituting between you and her lover.

And here you may find still another mode of defence, entirely personal, seldom employed by husbands, but the men of superiority will not fear to attempt it. It is to belittle the lover without letting your wife suspect your intention. You ought to be able to bring it about so that she will say to herself some evening while she is putting her hair in curl-papers, "My husband is superior to him."

In order to succeed, and you ought to be able to succeed, since you have the immense advantage over the lover in knowing the character of your wife, and how she is most easily wounded, you should, with all the tact of a diplomat, lead this lover to do silly things and cause him to annoy her, without his being aware of it.

In the first place, this lover, as usual, will seek your friendship, or you will have friends in common; then, either through the instrumentality of these friends or by insinuations adroitly but treacherously made, you will lead him astray on essential points; and, with a little cleverness, you will succeed in finding your wife ready to deny herself to her lover when he calls, without either she or he being able to tell the reason. Thus you will have created in the bosom of your home a comedy in five acts, in which you play, to your profit, the brilliant role of Figaro or Almaviva; and for some months you will amuse yourself so much the more, because your *amour-propre*, your vanity, your all, were at stake.

I had the good fortune in my youth to win the confidence of an old *emigre* who gave me those rudiments of education which are generally obtained by young people from women. This friend, whose memory will always be dear to me, taught me by his example to put into practice those diplomatic stratagems which require tact as well as grace.

The Comte de Noce had returned from Coblenz at a time when it was dangerous for the nobility to be found in France. No one had such courage and such kindness, such craft and such recklessness as this aristocrat. Although he was sixty years old he had married a woman of twenty-five, being compelled to this act of folly by soft-heartedness; for he thus delivered this poor child from the despotism of a capricious mother. "Would you like to be my widow?" this amiable old gentleman had said to Mademoiselle de Pontivy, but his heart was too affectionate not to become more attached to his wife than a sensible man ought to be. As in his youth he had been under the influence of several among the cleverest women in the court of Louis XV, he thought he would have no difficulty in keeping his wife from any entanglement. What man excepting him have I ever seen, who could put into successful practice the teachings which I am endeavoring to give to husbands! What charm could he impart to life by his delightful manners and fascinating conversation!—His wife never knew until after his death what she then learned from me, namely, that he had the gout. He had wisely retired to a home in the hollow of a valley, close to a forest. God only knows what rambles he used to take with his wife!—His good star decreed that Mademoiselle de Pontivy should possess an excellent heart and should manifest in a high degree that exquisite refinement, that sensitive modesty which renders beautiful the plainest girl in the world. All of a sudden, one of his nephews, a good-looking military man, who had escaped from the disasters of Moscow, returned to his uncle's house, as much for the sake of learning how far he had to fear his cousins, as heirs, as in the hope of laying siege to his aunt. His black hair, his moustache, the easy small-talk of the staff officer, a certain freedom which was elegant as well as trifling, his bright eyes, contrasted favorably with the faded graces of his uncle. I arrived at the precise moment when the young countess was teaching her newly found relation to play backgammon. The proverb says that "women never learn this game excepting from their lovers, and vice versa." Now, during a certain game, M. de Noce had surprised his wife and the viscount in the act of exchanging one of those looks which are full of mingled innocence, fear, and desire. In the evening he proposed to us a hunting-party, and we agreed. I never saw him so gay and so eager as he appeared on the following morning, in spite of the twinges of gout which heralded an approaching attack. The devil himself could not have been better able to keep up a conversation on trifling subjects than he was. He had formerly been a musketeer in the Grays and had known Sophie Arnoud. This explains all. The conversation after a time became so exceedingly free among us three, that I hope God may forgive me for it!

"I would never have believed that my uncle was such a dashing blade?" said the nephew.

We made a halt, and while we were sitting on the edge of a green forest clearing, the count led us on to discourse about women just as Brantome and Aloysia might have done.

"You fellows are very happy under the present government!—the women of the time are well mannered" (in order to appreciate the exclamation of the old gentleman, the reader should have heard the atrocious stories which the captain had been relating). "And this," he went on, "is one of the advantages resulting from the Revolution. The present system gives very much more charm and mystery to passion. In former times women were easy; ah! indeed, you would not believe what skill it required, what daring, to wake up those worn-out hearts; we were always on the *qui vive*. But yet in those days a man became celebrated for a broad joke, well put, or for a lucky piece of insolence. That is what women love, and it will always be the best method of succeeding with them!"

These last words were uttered in a tone of profound contempt; he stopped, and began to play with the hammer of his gun as if to disguise his deep feeling.

"But nonsense," he went on, "my day is over! A man ought to have the body as well as the imagination young. Why did I marry? What is most treacherous in girls educated by mothers who lived in that brilliant era of gallantry, is that they put on an air of frankness, of reserve; they look as if butter would not melt in their mouths, and those who know them well feel that they would swallow anything!"

He rose, lifted his gun with a gesture of rage, and dashing it to the ground thrust it far up the butt in the moist sod.

"It would seem as if my dear aunt were fond of a little fun," said the officer to me in a low voice.

"Or of denouements that do not come off!" I added.

The nephew tightened his cravat, adjusted his collar and gave a jump like a Calabrian goat. We returned to the chateau at about two in the afternoon. The count kept me with him until dinner-time, under the pretext of looking for some medals, of which he had spoken during our return home. The dinner was dull. The countess treated her nephew with stiff and cold politeness. When we entered the drawing-room the count said to his wife:

"Are you going to play backgammon? — We will leave you."

The young countess made no reply. She gazed at the fire, as if she had not heard. Her husband took some steps towards the door, inviting me by the wave of his hand to follow him. At the sound of his footsteps, his wife quickly turned her head.

"Why do you leave us?" said she, "you will have all tomorrow to show your friend the reverse of the medals."

The count remained. Without paying any attention to the awkwardness which had succeeded the former military aplomb of his nephew, the count exercised during the whole evening his full powers as a charming conversationalist. I had never before seen him so brilliant or so gracious. We spoke a great deal about women. The witticisms of our host were marked by the most exquisite refinement. He made me forget that his hair was white, for he showed the brilliancy which belonged to a youthful heart, a gaiety which effaces the wrinkles from the cheek and melts the snow of wintry age.

The next day the nephew went away. Even after the death of M. de Noce, I tried to profit by the intimacy of those familiar conversations in which women are sometimes caught off their guard to sound her, but I could never learn what impertinence the viscount had exhibited towards his aunt. His insolence must have been excessive, for since that time Madame de Noce has refused to see her nephew, and up to the present moment never hears him named without a slight movement of her eyebrows. I did not at once guess the end at which the Comte de Noce aimed, in inviting us to go shooting; but I discovered later that he had played a pretty bold game.

Nevertheless, if you happen at last, like M. de Noce, to carry off a decisive victory, do not forget to put into practice at once the system of blisters; and do not for a moment imagine that such *tours de force* are to be repeated with safety. If that is the way you use your talents, you will end by losing caste in your wife's estimation; for she will demand of you, reasonably enough, double what you would give her, and the time will come when you declare bankruptcy. The human soul in its desires follows a sort of arithmetical progression, the end and origin of which are equally unknown. Just as the opium-eater must constantly increase his doses in order to obtain the same result, so our mind, imperious as it is weak, desires that feeling, ideas and objects should go on ever increasing in size and in intensity. Hence the necessity of cleverly distributing the interest in a dramatic work, and of graduating doses in medicine. Thus you see, if you always resort to the employment of means like these, that you must accommodate such daring measures to many circumstances, and success will always depend upon the motives to which you appeal.

And finally, have you influence, powerful friends, an important post? The last means I shall suggest cuts to the root of the evil. Would you have the power to send your wife's lover off by securing his promotion, or his change of residence by an exchange, if he is a military man? You cut off by this means all communication between them; later on we will show you how to do it; for *sublata causa tollitur effectus,*—Latin words which may be freely translated "there is no effect without a cause."

Nevertheless, you feel that your wife may easily choose another lover; but in addition to these preliminary expedients, you will always have a blister ready, in order to gain time, and calculate how you may bring the affair to an end by fresh devices.

Study how to combine the system of blisters with the mimic wiles of Carlin, the immortal Carlin of the *Comedie-Italienne* who always held and amused an audience for whole hours, by uttering the same words, varied only by the art of pantomime and pronounced with a thousand inflections of different tone,—"The queen said to the king!" Imitate Carlin, discover some method of always keeping your wife in check, so as not to be checkmated yourself. Take a degree among constitutional ministers, a degree in the art of making promises. Habituate yourself to show at seasonable times the punchinello which makes children run after you without knowing the distance they run. We are all children, and women are all inclined through their curiosity to spend their time in pursuit of a will-o'-the-wisp. The flame is brilliant and quickly vanishes, but is not the imagination at hand to act as your ally? Finally, study the happy art of being near her and yet not being near her; of seizing the opportunity which will yield you pre-eminence in her mind without ever crushing her with a sense of your superiority, or even of her own happiness. If the ignorance in which you have kept her does not altogether destroy her intellect, you must remain in such relations with her that each of you will still desire the company of the other.

MEDITATION XIV.
OF APARTMENTS.

The preceding methods and systems are in a way purely moral; they share the nobility of the soul, there is nothing repulsive in them; but now we must proceed to consider precautions *a la Bartholo*. Do not give way to timidity. There is a marital courage, as there is a civil and military courage, as there is the courage of the National Guard.

What is the first course of a young girl after having purchased a parrot? Is it not to fasten it up in a pretty cage, from which it cannot get out without permission?

You may learn your duty from this child.

Everything that pertains to the arrangement of your house and of your apartments should be planned so as not to give your wife any advantage, in case she has decided to deliver you to the Minotaur; half of all actual mischances are brought about by the deplorable facilities which the apartments furnish.

Before everything else determine to have for your porter a *single man* entirely devoted to your person. This is a treasure easily to be found. What husband is there throughout the world who has not either a foster-father or some old servant, upon whose knees he has been dandled! There ought to exist by means of your management, a hatred like that of Artreus and Thyestes between your wife and this Nestor —guardian of your gate. This gate is the Alpha and Omega of an intrigue. May not all intrigues in love be confined in these words —entering and leaving?

Your house will be of no use to you if it does not stand between a court and a garden, and so constructed as to be detached from all other buildings. You must abolish all recesses in your apartments. A cupboard, if it contain but six pots of preserves, should be walled in. You are preparing yourself for war, and the first thought of a general is to cut his enemy off from supplies. Moreover, all the walls must be smooth, in order to present to the eye lines which may be taken in at a glance, and permit the immediate recognition of the least strange object. If you consult the remains of antique monuments you will see that the beauty of Greek and Roman apartments sprang principally from the purity of their lines, the clear sweep of their walls and scantiness of furniture. The Greeks would have smiled in pity, if they had seen the gaps which our closets make in our drawing-rooms.

This magnificent system of defence should above all be put in active operation in the apartment of your wife; never let her curtain her bed in such a way that one can walk round it amid a maze of hangings; be inexorable in the matter of connecting passages, and let her chamber be at the bottom of your reception-rooms, so as to show at a glance those who come and go.

The Marriage of Figaro will no doubt have taught you to put your wife's chamber at a great height from the ground. All celibates are Cherubins.

Your means, doubtless, will permit your wife to have a dressing-room, a bathroom, and a room for her chambermaid. Think then on Susanne, and never commit the fault of arranging this little room below that of madame's, but place it always above, and do not shrink from disfiguring your mansion by hideous divisions in the windows.

If, by ill luck, you see that this dangerous apartment communicates with that of your wife by a back staircase, earnestly consult your architect; let his genius exhaust itself in rendering this dangerous staircase as innocent as the primitive garret ladder; we conjure you let not this staircase have appended to it any treacherous lurking-place; its stiff and angular steps must not be arranged with that tempting curve which Faublas and Justine found so useful when they waited for the exit of the Marquis de B— —-. Architects nowadays make such staircases as are absolutely preferable to ottomans. Restore rather the virtuous garret steps of our ancestors.

Concerning the chimneys in the apartment of madame, you must take care to place in the flue, five feet from the ground, an iron grill, even though it be necessary to put up a fresh one every time the chimney is swept. If your wife laughs at this precaution, suggest to her the number of murders that have been committed by means of chimneys. Almost all women are afraid of robbers. The bed is one of those important pieces of furniture whose structure will demand long consideration. Everything concerning it is of vital importance. The following is the result of long experience in the construction of beds. Give to this piece of furniture a form so original that it may be looked upon without disgust, in the midst of changes of fashion which succeed so rapidly in rendering antiquated the creations of former decorators, for it is essential that your wife be unable to change, at pleasure, this theatre of married happiness. The base should be plain and massive and admit of no treacherous interval between it and the floor; and bear in mind always that the Donna Julia of Byron hid Don Juan under her pillow. But it would be ridiculous to treat lightly so delicate a subject.

LXII.

The bed is the whole of marriage.

Moreover, we must not delay to direct your attention to this wonderful creation of human genius, an invention which claims our recognition much more than ships, firearms, matches, wheeled carriages, steam engines of all kinds, more than even barrels and bottles. In the first place, a little thought will convince us that this is all true of the bed; but when we begin to think that it is our second father, that the most tranquil and most agitated half of our existence is spent under its protecting canopy, words fail in eulogizing it. (See Meditation XVII, entitled "Theory of the Bed.")

When the war, of which we shall speak in our third part, breaks out between you and madame, you will always have plenty of ingenious excuses for rummaging in the drawers and escritoires; for if your wife is trying to hide from you some statue of her adoration, it is your interest to know where she has hidden it. A gyneceum, constructed on the method described, will enable you to calculate at a glance, whether there is present in it two pounds of silk more than usual. Should a single closet be constructed there, you are a lost man! Above all, accustom your wife, during the honeymoon, to bestow especial pains in the neatness of her apartment; let nothing put off that. If you do not habituate her to be minutely particular in this respect, if the same objects are not always found in the same places, she will allow things to become so untidy, that you will not be able to see that there are two pounds of silk more or less in her room.

The curtains of your apartments ought to be of a stuff which is quite transparent, and you ought to contract the habit in the evenings of walking outside so that madame may see you come right up to the window just out of absent-mindedness. In a word, with regard to windows, let the sills be so narrow that even a sack of flour cannot be set up on them.

If the apartment of your wife can be arranged on these principles, you will be in perfect safety, even if there are niches enough there to contain all the saints of Paradise. You will be able, every evening, with the assistance of your porter, to strike the balance between the entrances and exits of visitors; and, in order to obtain accurate results, there is nothing to prevent your teaching him to keep a book of visitors, in double entry.

If you have a garden, cultivate a taste for dogs, and always keep at large one of these incorruptible guardians under your windows; you will thus gain the respect of the Minotaur, especially if you accustom your four-footed friend to take nothing substantial excepting from the hand of your porter, so that hard-hearted celibates may not succeed in poisoning him.

But all these precautions must be taken as a natural thing so that they may not arouse suspicions. If husbands are so imprudent as to neglect precautions from the moment they are married, they ought at once to sell their house and buy another one, or, under the pretext of repairs, alter their present house in the way prescribed.

You will without scruple banish from your apartment all sofas, ottomans, lounges, sedan chairs and the like. In the first place, this is the kind of furniture that adorns the homes of grocers, where they are universally found, as they are in those of barbers; but they are essentially the furniture of perdition; I can never see them without alarm. It has always seemed to me that there the devil himself is lurking with his horns and cloven foot.

After all, nothing is so dangerous as a chair, and it is extremely unfortunate that women cannot be shut up within the four walls of a bare room! What husband is there, who on sitting down on a rickety chair is not always forced to believe that this chair has received some of the lessons taught by the *Sofa* of Crebillion junior? But happily we have arranged your apartment on such a system of prevention that nothing so fatal can happen, or, at any rate, not without your contributory negligence.

One fault which you must contract, and which you must never correct, will consist in a sort of heedless curiosity, which will make you examine unceasingly all the boxes, and turn upside down the contents of all dressing-cases and work-baskets. You must proceed to this domiciliary visit in a humorous mood, and gracefully, so that each time you will obtain pardon by exciting the amusement of your wife.

You must always manifest a most profound astonishment on noticing any piece of furniture freshly upholstered in her well-appointed apartment. You must immediately make her explain to you the advantages of the change; and then you must ransack your mind to discover whether there be not some underhand motive in the transaction.

This is by no means all. You have too much sense to forget that your pretty parrot will remain in her cage only so long as that cage is beautiful. The least accessory of her apartment ought, therefore, to breathe elegance and taste. The general appearance should always present a simple, at the same time a charming picture. You must constantly renew the hangings and muslin curtains. The freshness of the decorations is too essential to permit of economy on this point. It is the fresh chickweed each morning carefully put into the cage of their birds, that makes their pets believe it is the verdure of the meadows. An apartment of this character is then the *ultima ratio* of husbands; a wife has nothing to say when everything is lavished on her.

Husbands who are condemned to live in rented apartments find themselves in the most terrible situation possible. What happy or what fatal influence cannot the porter exercise upon their lot?

Is not their home flanked on either side by other houses? It is true that by placing the apartment of their wives on one side of the house the danger is lessened by one-half; but are they not obliged to learn by heart and to ponder the age, the condition, the fortune, the character, the habits of the tenants of the next house and even to know their friends and relations?

A husband will never take lodgings on the ground floor.

Every man, however, can apply in his apartments the precautionary methods which we have suggested to the owner of a house, and thus the tenant will have this advantage over the owner, that the apartment, which is less spacious than the house, is more easily guarded.

MEDITATION XV.
OF THE CUSTOM HOUSE.

"But no, madame, no—"

"Yes, for there is such inconvenience in the arrangement."

"Do you think, madame, that we wish, as at the frontier, to watch the visits of persons who cross the threshold of your apartments, or furtively leave them, in order to see whether they bring to you articles of contraband? That would not be proper; and there is nothing odious in our proceeding, any more than there is anything of a fiscal character; do not be alarmed."

The Custom House of the marriage state is, of all the expedients prescribed in this second part, that which perhaps demands the most tact and the most skill as well as the most knowledge acquired *a priori*, that is to say before marriage. In order to carry it out, a husband ought to have made a profound study of Lavater's book, and to be imbued with all his principles; to have accustomed his eye to judge and to apprehend with the most astonishing promptitude, the slightest physical expressions by which a man reveals his thoughts.

Lavater's *Physiognomy* originated a veritable science, which has won a place in human investigation. If at first some doubts, some jokes greeted the appearance of this book, since then the celebrated Doctor Gall is come with his noble theory of the skull and has completed the system of the Swiss savant, and given stability to his fine and luminous observations. People of talent, diplomats, women, all those who are numbered among the choice and fervent disciples of these two celebrated men, have often had occasion to recognize many other evident signs, by which the course of human thought is indicated. The habits of the body, the handwriting, the sound of the voice, have often betrayed the woman who is in love, the diplomat who is attempting to deceive, the clever administrator, or the sovereign who is compelled to distinguish at a glance love, treason or merit hitherto unknown. The man whose soul operates with energy is like a poor glowworm, which without knowing it irradiates light from every pore. He moves in a brilliant sphere where each effort makes a burning light and outlines his actions with long streamers of fire.

These, then, are all the elements of knowledge which you should possess, for the conjugal custom house insists simply in being able by a rapid but searching examination to know the moral and physical condition of all who enter or leave your house—all, that is, who have seen or intend to see your wife. A husband is, like a spider, set at the centre of an invisible net, and receives a shock from the to perfection by making them their own; and the most poetic expression which appears in the imagery of an author brings forth still more ethereal imagery in the mind of a reader. To read is to join with the writer in a creative act. The mystery of the transubstantiation of ideas, originates perhaps in the instinctive consciousness that we have of a vocation loftier than our present destiny. Or, is it based on the lost tradition of a former life? What must that life have been, if this slight residuum of memory offers us such volumes of delight?

Moreover, in reading plays and romances, woman, a creature much more susceptible than we are to excitement, experiences the most violent transport. She creates for herself an ideal existence beside which all reality grows pale; she at once attempts to realize this voluptuous life, to take to herself the magic which she sees in it. And, without knowing it, she passes from spirit to letter and from soul to sense.

And would you be simple enough to believe that the manners, the sentiments of a man like you, who usually dress and undress before your wife, can counterbalance the influence of these books and outshine the glory of their fictitious lovers, in whose garments the fair reader sees neither hole nor stain?—Poor fool! too late, alas! for her happiness and for yours, your wife will find out that the *heroes* of poetry are as rare in real life as the *Apollos* of sculpture!

Very many husbands will find themselves embarrassed in trying to prevent their wives from reading, yet there are certain people who allege that reading has this advantage, that men know what their wives are about when they have a book in hand. In the first place you will see, in the next Meditation, what a tendency the sedentary life has to make a woman quarrelsome; but have you never met those beings without poetry, who succeed in petrifying their unhappy companions by reducing life to its most mechanical elements? Study great men in their conversation and learn by heart the admirable arguments by which they condemn poetry and the pleasures of imagination.

But if, after all your efforts, your wife persists in wishing to read, put at her disposal at once all possible books from the A B C of her little boy to *Rene*, a book more dangerous to you when in her hands than *Therese Philosophe*. You might create in her an utter disgust for reading by giving her tedious books; and plunge her into utter idiocy with *Marie Alacoque, The Brosse de Penitence*, or with the chansons which were so fashionable in the time of Louis XV; but later on you will find, in the present volume, the means of so thoroughly employing your wife's time, that any kind of reading will be quite out of the question.

And first of all, consider the immense resources which the education of women has prepared for you in your efforts to turn your wife from her fleeting taste for science. Just see with what admirable stupidity girls lend themselves to reap the benefit of the education which is imposed upon them in France; we give them in charge to nursery maids, to companions, to governesses who teach them twenty tricks of coquetry and false modesty, for every single noble and true idea which they impart to them. Girls are brought up as slaves, and are accustomed to the idea that they are sent into the world to imitate their grandmothers, to breed canary least fool of a fly who touches it, and from a distance, hears, judges and sees what is either his prey or his enemy.

Thus you must obtain means to examine the celibate who rings at your door under two circumstances which are quite distinct, namely, when he is about to enter and when he is inside.

At the moment of entering how many things does he utter without even opening his mouth!

It may be by a slight wave of his hand, or by his plunging his fingers many times into his hair, he sticks up or smoothes down his characteristic bang.

Or he hums a French or an Italian air, merry or sad, in a voice which may be either tenor, contralto, soprano or baritone.

Perhaps he takes care to see that the ends of his necktie are properly adjusted.

Or he smoothes down the ruffles or front of his shirt or evening-dress.

Or he tries to find out by a questioning and furtive glance whether his wig, blonde or brown, curled or plain, is in its natural position.

Perhaps he looks at his nails to see whether they are clean and duly cut.

Perhaps with a hand which is either white or untidy, well-gloved or otherwise, he twirls his moustache, or his whiskers, or picks his teeth with a little tortoise-shell toothpick.

Or by slow and repeated movements he tries to place his chin exactly over the centre of his necktie.

Or perhaps he crosses one foot over the other, putting his hands in his pockets.

Or perhaps he gives a twist to his shoe, and looks at it as if he thought, "Now, there's a foot that is not badly formed."

Or according as he has come on foot or in a carriage, he rubs off or he does not rub off the slight patches of mud which soil his shoes.

Or perhaps he remains as motionless as a Dutchman smoking his pipe.

Or perhaps he fixes his eyes on the door and looks like a soul escaped from Purgatory and waiting for Saint Peter with the keys.

Perhaps he hesitates to pull the bell; perhaps he seizes it negligently, precipitately, familiarly, or like a man who is quite sure of himself.

Perhaps he pulls it timidly, producing a faint tinkle which is lost in the silence of the apartments, as the first bell of matins in winter-time, in a convent of Minims; or perhaps after having rung with energy, he rings again impatient that the footman has not heard him.

Perhaps he exhales a delicate scent, as he chews a pastille.

Perhaps with a solemn air he takes a pinch of snuff, brushing off with care the grains that might mar the whiteness of his linen.

Perhaps he looks around like a man estimating the value of the staircase lamp, the balustrade, the carpet, as if he were a furniture dealer or a contractor.

Perhaps this celibate seems a young or an old man, is cold or hot, arrives slowly, with an expression of sadness or merriment, etc.

You see that here, at the very foot of your staircase, you are met by an astonishing mass of things to observe.

The light pencil-strokes, with which we have tried to outline this figure, will suggest to you what is in reality a moral kaleidoscope with millions of variations. And yet we have not even attempted to bring any woman on to the threshold which reveals so much; for in that case our remarks, already considerable in number, would have been countless and light as the grains of sand on the seashore.

For as a matter of fact, when he stands before the shut door, a man believes that he is quite alone; and he would have no hesitation in beginning a silent monologue, a dreamy soliloquy, in which he revealed his desires, his intentions, his personal qualities, his faults, his virtues, etc.; for undoubtedly a man on a stoop is exactly like a young girl of fifteen at confession, the evening before her first communion.

Do you want any proof of this? Notice the sudden change of face and manner in this celibate from the very moment he steps within the house. No machinist in the Opera, no change in the temperature in the clouds or in the sun can more suddenly transform the appearance of a theatre, the effect of the atmosphere, or the scenery of the heavens.

On reaching the first plank of your antechamber, instead of betraying with so much innocence the myriad thoughts which were suggested to you on the steps, the celibate has not a single glance to which you could attach any significance. The mask of social convention wraps with its thick veil his whole bearing; but a clever husband must already have divined at a single look the object of his visit, and he reads the soul of the new arrival as if it were a printed book.

The manner in which he approaches your wife, in which he addresses her, looks at her, greets her and retires—there are volumes of observations, more or less trifling, to be made on these subjects.

The tone of his voice, his bearing, his awkwardness, it may be his smile, even his gloom, his avoidance of your eye,—all are significant, all ought to be studied, but without apparent attention. You ought to conceal the most disagreeable discovery you may make by an easy manner and remarks such as are ready at hand to a man of society. As we are unable to detail the minutiae of this subject we leave them entirely to the sagacity of the reader, who must by this time have perceived the drift of our investigation, as well as the extent of this science which begins at the analysis of glances and ends in the direction of such movements as contempt may inspire in a great toe hidden under the satin of a lady's slipper or the leather of a man's boot.

But the exit!—for we must allow for occasions where you have omitted your rigid scrutiny at the threshold of the doorway, and in that case the exit becomes of vital importance, and all the more so because this fresh study of the celibate ought to be made on the same lines, but from an opposite point of view, from that which we have already outlined.

In the exit the situation assumes a special gravity; for then is the moment in which the enemy has crossed all the intrenchments within which he was subject to our examination and has escaped into the street! At this point a man of understanding when he sees a visitor passing under the *porte-cochere* should be able to divine the import of the whole visit. The indications are indeed fewer in number, but how distinct is their character! The denouement has arrived and the man instantly betrays the importance of it by the frankest expression of happiness, pain or joy.

These revelations are therefore easy to apprehend; they appear in the glance cast either at the building or at the windows of the apartment; in a slow or loitering gait, in the rubbing of hands, on the part of a fool, in the bounding gait of a coxcomb, or the involuntary arrest of his footsteps, which marks the man who is deeply moved; in a word, you see upon the stoop certain questions as clearly proposed to you as if a provincial academy had offered a hundred crowns for an essay; but in the exit you behold the solution of these questions clearly and precisely given to you. Our task would be far above the power of human intelligence if it consisted in enumerating the different ways by which men betray their feelings, the discernment of such things is purely a matter of tact and sentiment.

If strangers are the subject of these principles of observation, you have a still stronger reason for submitting your wife to the formal safeguards which we have outlined.

A married man should make a profound study of his wife's countenance. Such a study is easy, it is even involuntary and continuous. For him the pretty face of his wife must needs contain no mysteries, he knows how her feelings are depicted there and with what expression she shuns the fire of his glance.

The slightest movement of the lips, the faintest contraction of the nostrils, scarcely perceptible changes in the expression of the eye, an altered voice, and those indescribable shades of feeling which pass over her features, or the light which sometimes bursts forth from them, are intelligible language to you.

The whole woman nature stands before you; all look at her, but none can interpret her thoughts. But for you, the eye is more or less dimmed, wide-opened or closed; the lid twitches, the eyebrow moves; a wrinkle, which vanishes as quickly as a ripple on the ocean, furrows her brow for one moment; the lip tightens, it is slightly curved or it is wreathed with animation—for you the woman has spoken.

If in those puzzling moments in which a woman tries dissimulation in presence of her husband, you have the spirit of a sphinx in seeing through her, you will plainly observe that your custom-house restrictions are mere child's play to her.

When she comes home or goes out, when in a word she believes she is alone, your wife will exhibit all the imprudence of a jackdaw and will tell her secret aloud to herself; moreover, by her sudden change of expression the moment she notices you (and despite the rapidity of this change, you will not fail to have observed the expression she wore behind your back) you may read her soul as if you were reading a book of Plain Song. Moreover, your wife will often find herself just on the point of indulging in soliloquies, and on such occasions her husband may recognize the secret feelings of his wife.

Is there a man as heedless of love's mysteries as not to have admired, over and over again, the light, mincing, even bewitching gait of a woman who flies on her way to keep an assignation? She glides through the crowd, like a snake through the grass. The costumes and stuffs of the latest fashion spread out their dazzling attractions in the shop windows without claiming her attention; on, on she goes like the faithful animal who follows the invisible tracks of his master; she is deaf to all compliments, blind to all glances, insensible even to the light touch of the crowd, which is inevitable amid the circulation of Parisian humanity. Oh, how deeply she feels the value of a minute! Her gait, her toilet, the expression of her face, involve her in a thousand indiscretions, but oh, what a ravishing picture she presents to the idler, and what an ominous page for the eye of a husband to read, is the face of this woman when she returns from the secret place of rendezvous in which her heart ever dwells! Her happiness is impressed even on the unmistakable disarray of her hair, the mass of whose wavy tresses has not received from the broken comb of the celibate that radiant lustre, that elegant and well-proportioned adjustment which only the practiced hand of her maid can give. And what charming ease appears in her gait! How is it possible to describe the emotion which adds such rich tints to her complexion! — which robs her eyes of all their assurance and gives to them an expression of mingled melancholy and delight, of shame which is yet blended with pride!

These observations, stolen from our Meditation, *Of the Last Symptoms*, and which are really suggested by the situation of a woman who tries to conceal everything, may enable you to divine by analogy the rich crop of observation which is left for you to harvest when your wife arrives home, or when, without having committed the great crime she innocently lets out the secrets of her thoughts. For our own part we never see a landing without wishing to set up there a mariner's card and a weather-cock.

As the means to be employed for constructing a sort of domestic observatory depend altogether on places and circumstances, we must leave to the address of a jealous husband the execution of the methods suggested in this Meditation.

MEDITATION XVI.
THE CHARTER OF MARRIAGE.

I acknowledge that I really know of but one house in Paris which is managed in accordance with the system unfolded in the two preceding Meditations. But I ought to add, also, that I have built up my system on the example of that house. The admirable fortress I allude to belonged to a young councillor of state, who was mad with love and jealousy.

As soon as he learned that there existed a man who was exclusively occupied in bringing to perfection the institution of marriage in France, he had the generosity to open the doors of his mansion to me and to show me his gyneceum. I admired the profound genius which so cleverly disguised the precautions of almost oriental jealousy under the elegance of furniture, beauty of carpets and brightness of painted decorations. I agreed with him that it was impossible for his wife to render his home a scene of treachery.

"Sir," said I, to this Othello of the council of state who did not seem to me peculiarly strong in the *haute politique* of marriage, "I have no doubt that the viscountess is delighted to live in this little Paradise; she ought indeed to take prodigious pleasure in it, especially if you are here often. But the time will come when she will have had enough of it; for, my dear sir, we grow tired of everything, even of the sublime. What will you do then, when madame, failing to find in all your inventions their primitive charm, shall open her mouth in a yawn, and perhaps make a request with a view to the exercise of two rights, both of which are indispensable to her happiness: individual liberty, that is, the privilege of going and coming according to the caprice of her will; and the liberty of the press, that is, the privilege of writing and receiving letters without fear of your censure?"

Scarcely had I said these words when the Vicomte de V——- grasped my arm tightly and cried:

"Yes, such is the ingratitude of woman! If there is any thing more ungrateful than a king, it is a nation; but, sir, woman is more ungrateful than either of them. A married woman treats us as the citizens of a constitutional monarchy treat their king; every measure has been taken to give these citizens a life of prosperity in a prosperous country; the government has taken all the pains in the world with its gendarmes, its churches, its ministry and all the paraphernalia of its military forces, to prevent the people from dying of hunger, to light the cities by gas at the expense of the citizens, to give warmth to every one by means of the sun which shines at the forty-fifth degree of latitude, and to forbid every one, excepting the tax-gatherers, to ask for money; it has labored hard to give to all the main roads a more or less substantial pavement—but none of these advantages of our fair Utopia is appreciated! The citizens want something else. They are not ashamed to demand the right of traveling over the roads at their own will, and of being informed where that money given to the tax-gatherers goes. And, finally, the monarch will soon be obliged, if we pay any attention to the chatter of certain scribblers, to give to every individual a share in the throne or to adopt certain revolutionary ideas, which are mere Punch and Judy shows for the public, manipulated by a band of self-styled patriots, riff-raff, always ready to sell their conscience for a million francs, for an honest woman, or for a ducal coronet."

"But, monsieur," I said, interrupting him, "while I perfectly agree with you on this last point, the question remains, how will you escape giving an answer to the just demands of your wife?"

"Sir" he replied, "I shall do—I shall answer as the government answers, that is, those governments which are not so stupid as the opposition would make out to their constituents. I shall begin by solemnly interdicting any arrangement, by virtue of which my wife will be declared entirely free. I fully recognize her right to go wherever it seems good to her, to write to whom she chooses, and to receive letters, the contents of which I do not know. My wife shall have all the rights that belong to an English Parliament; I shall let her talk as much as she likes, discuss and propose strong and energetic measures, but without the power to put them into execution, and then after that—well, we shall see!"

"By St. Joseph!" said I to myself, "Here is a man who understands the science of marriage as well as I myself do. And then, you will see, sir," I answered aloud, in order to obtain from him the fullest revelation of his experience; "you will see, some fine morning, that you are as big a fool as the next man."

"Sir," he gravely replied, "allow me to finish what I was saying. Here is what the great politicians call a theory, but in practice they can make that theory vanish in smoke; and ministers possess in a greater degree than even the lawyers of Normandy, the art of making fact yield to fancy. M. de Metternich and M. de Pilat, men of the highest authority, have been for a long time asking each other whether Europe is in its right senses, whether it is dreaming, whether it knows whither it is going, whether it has ever exercised its reason, a thing impossible on the part of the masses, of nations and of women. M. de Metternich and M. de Pilat are terrified to see this age carried away by a passion for constitutions, as the preceding age was by the passion for philosophy, as that of Luther was for a reform of abuses in the Roman religion; for it truly seems as if different generations of men were like those conspirators whose actions are directed to the same end, as soon as the watchword has been given them. But their alarm is a mistake, and it is on this point alone that I condemn them, for they are right in their wish to enjoy power without permitting the middle class to come on a fixed day from the depth of each of their six kingdoms, to torment them. How could men of such remarkable talent fail to divine that the constitutional comedy has in it a moral of profound meaning, and to see that it is the very best policy to give the age a bone to exercise its teeth upon! I think exactly as they do on the subject of sovereignty. A power is a moral being as much interested as a man is in self-preservation. This sentiment of self-preservation is under the control of an essential principle which may be expressed in three words—*to lose nothing*. But in order to lose nothing, a power must grow or remain indefinite, for a power which remains stationary is nullified. If it retrogrades, it is under the control of something else, and loses its independent existence. I am quite as well aware, as are those gentlemen, in what a false position an unlimited power puts itself by making concessions; it allows to another power whose essence is to expand a place within its own sphere of activity. One of them will necessarily nullify the other, for every existing thing aims at the greatest possible development of its own forces. A power, therefore, never makes concessions which it does not afterwards seek to retract. This struggle between two powers is the basis on which stands the balance of government, whose elasticity so mistakenly alarmed the patriarch of Austrian diplomacy, for comparing comedy with comedy the least perilous and the most advantageous administration is found in the seesaw system of the English and of the French politics. These two countries have said to the people, 'You are free;' and the people have been satisfied; they enter the government like the zeros which give value to the unit. But if the people wish to take an active part in the government, immediately they are treated, like Sancho Panza, on that occasion when the squire, having become sovereign over an island on terra firma, made an attempt at dinner to eat the viands set before him.

"Now we ought to parody this admirable scene in the management of our homes. Thus, my wife has a perfect right to go out, provided she tell me where she is going, how she is going, what is the business she is engaged in when she is out and at what hour she will return. Instead of demanding this information with the brutality of the police, who will doubtless some day become perfect, I take pains to speak to her in the most gracious terms. On my lips, in my eyes, in my whole countenance, an expression plays, which indicates both curiosity and indifference, seriousness and pleasantry, harshness and tenderness. These little conjugal scenes are so full of vivacity, of tact and address that it is a pleasure to take part in them. The very day on which I took from the head of my wife the wreath of orange blossoms which she wore, I understood that we were playing at a royal coronation—the first scene in a comic pantomime!—I have my gendarmes!—I have my guard royal!—I have my attorney general—that I do!" he continued enthusiastically. "Do you think that I would allow madame to go anywhere on foot unaccompanied by a lackey in livery? Is not that the best style? Not to count the pleasure she takes in saying to everybody, 'I have my people here.' It has always been a conservative principle of mine that my times of exercise should coincide with those of my wife, and for two years I have proved to her that I take an ever fresh pleasure in giving her my arm. If the weather is not suitable for walking, I try to teach her how to drive with success a frisky horse; but I swear to you that I undertake this in such a manner that she does not learn very quickly!—If either by chance, or prompted by a deliberate wish, she takes measures to escape without a passport, that is to say, alone in the carriage, have I not a driver, a footman, a groom? My wife, therefore, go where she will, takes with her a complete *Santa Hermandad*, and I am perfectly easy in mind—But, my dear sir, there is abundance of means by which to annul the charter of marriage by our manner of fulfilling it! I have remarked that the manners of high society induce a habit of idleness which absorbs half of the life of a woman without permitting her to feel that she is alive. For my part, I have formed the project of dexterously leading my wife along, up to her fortieth year, without letting her think of adultery, just as poor Musson used to amuse himself in leading some simple fellow from the Rue Saint-Denis to Pierrefitte without letting him think that he had left the shadows of St. Lew's tower."

"How is it," I said, interrupting him, "that you have hit upon those admirable methods of deception which I was intending to describe in a Meditation entitled *The Act of Putting Death into Life!* Alas! I thought I was the first man to discover that science. The epigrammatic title was suggested to me by an account which a young doctor gave me of an excellent composition of Crabbe, as yet unpublished. In this work, the English poet has introduced a fantastic being called *Life in Death*. This personage crosses the oceans of the world in pursuit of a living skeleton called *Death in Life*—I recollect at the time very few people, among the guests of a certain elegant translator of English poetry, understood the mystic meaning of a fable as true as it was fanciful. Myself alone, perhaps, as I sat buried in silence, thought of the whole generations which as they were hurried along by life, passed on their way without living. Before my eyes rose faces of women by the million, by the myriad, all dead, all disappointed and shedding tears of despair, as they looked back upon the lost moments of their ignorant youth. In the distance I saw a playful Meditation rise to birth, I heard the satanic laughter which ran through it, and now you doubtless are about to kill it.—But come, tell me in confidence what means you have discovered by which to assist a woman to squander the swift moments during which her beauty is at its full flower and her desires at their full strength.—Perhaps you have some stratagems, some clever devices, to describe to me—"

The viscount began to laugh at this literary disappointment of mine, and he said to me, with a self-satisfied air:

"My wife, like all the young people of our happy century, has been accustomed, for three or four consecutive years, to press her fingers on the keys of a piano, a long-suffering instrument. She has hammered out Beethoven, warbled the airs of Rossini and run through the exercises of Crammer. I had already taken pains to convince her of the excellence of music; to attain this end, I have applauded her, I have listened without yawning to the most tiresome sonatas in the world, and I have at last consented to give her a box at the Bouffons. I have thus gained three quiet evenings out of the seven which God has created in the week. I am the mainstay of the music shops. At Paris there are drawing-rooms which exactly resemble the musical snuff-boxes of Germany. They are a sort of continuous orchestra to which I regularly go in search of that surfeit of harmony which my wife calls a concert. But most part of the time my wife keeps herself buried in her music-books—"

"But, my dear sir, do you not recognize the danger that lies in cultivating in a woman a taste for singing, and allowing her to yield to all the excitements of a sedentary life? It is only less dangerous to make her feed on mutton and drink cold water."

"My wife never eats anything but the white meat of poultry, and I always take care that a ball shall come after a concert and a reception after an Opera! I have also succeeded in making her lie down between one and two in the day. Ah! my dear sir, the benefits of this nap are incalculable! In the first place each necessary pleasure is accorded as a favor, and I am considered to be constantly carrying out my wife's wishes. And then I lead her to imagine, without saying a single word, that she is being constantly amused every day from six o'clock in the evening, the time of our dinner and of her toilet, until eleven o'clock in the morning, the time when we get up."

"Ah! sir, how grateful you ought to be for a life which is so completely filled up!"

"I have scarcely more than three dangerous hours a day to pass; but she has, of course, sonatas to practice and airs to go over, and there are always rides in the Bois de Boulogne, carriages to try, visits to pay, etc. But this is not all. The fairest ornament of a woman is the most exquisite cleanliness. A woman cannot be too particular in this respect, and no pains she takes can be laughed at. Now her toilet has also suggested to me a method of thus consuming the best hours of the day in bathing."

"How lucky I am in finding a listener like you!" I cried; "truly, sir, you could waste for her four hours a day, if only you were willing to teach her an art quite unknown to the most fastidious of our modern fine ladies. Why don't you enumerate to the viscountess the astonishing precautions manifest in the Oriental luxury of the Roman dames? Give her the names of the slaves merely employed for the bath in Poppea's palace: the *unctores*, the *fricatores*, the *alipilarili*, the *dropacistae*, the *paratiltriae*, the *picatrices*, the *tracatrices*, the swan whiteners, and all the rest. —Talk to her about this multitude of slaves whose names are given by Mirabeau in his *Erotika Biblion*. If she tries to secure the services of all these people you will have the fine times of quietness, not to speak of the personal satisfaction which will redound to you yourself from the introduction into your house of the system invented by these illustrious Romans, whose hair, artistically arranged, was deluged with perfumes, whose smallest vein seemed to have acquired fresh blood from the myrrh, the lint, the perfume, the douches, the flowers of the bath, all of which were enjoyed to the strains of voluptuous music."

"Ah! sir," continued the husband, who was warming to his subject, "can I not find also admirable pretexts in my solicitude for her heath? Her health, so dear and precious to me, forces me to forbid her going out in bad weather, and thus I gain a quarter of the year. And I have also introduced the charming custom of kissing when either of us goes out, this parting kiss being accompanied with the words, 'My sweet angel, I am going out.' Finally, I have taken measures for the future to make my wife as truly a prisoner in the house as the conscript in his sentry box! For I have inspired her with an incredible enthusiasm for the sacred duties of maternity."

"You do it by opposing her?" I asked.

"You have guessed it," he answered, laughing. "I have maintained to her that it is impossible for a woman of the world to discharge her duties towards society, to manage her household, to devote herself to fashion, as well as to the wishes of her husband, whom she loves, and, at the same time, to rear children. She then avers that, after the example of Cato, who wished to see how the nurse changed the swaddling bands of the infant Pompey, she would never leave to others the least of the services required in shaping the susceptible minds and tender bodies of these little creatures whose education begins in the cradle. You understand, sir, that my conjugal diplomacy would not be of much service to me unless, after having put my wife in solitary confinement, I did not also employ a certain harmless machiavelism, which consists in begging her to do whatever she likes, and asking her advice in every circumstance and on every contingency. As this delusive liberty has entirely deceived a creature so high-minded as she is, I have taken pains to stop at no sacrifice which would convince Madame de V———- that she is the freest woman in Paris; and, in order to attain this end, I take care not to commit those gross political blunders into which our ministers so often fall."

"I can see you," said I, "when you wish to cheat your wife out of some right granted her by the charter, I can see you putting on a mild and deliberate air, hiding your dagger under a bouquet of roses, and as you plunge it cautiously into her heart, saying to her with a friendly voice, 'My darling, does it hurt?' and she, like those on whose toes you tread in a crowd, will probably reply, 'Not in the least.'"

He could not restrain a laugh and said:

"Won't my wife be astonished at the Last Judgment?"

"I scarcely know," I replied, "whether you or she will be most astonished."

The jealous man frowned, but his face resumed its calmness as I added:

"I am truly grateful, sir, to the chance which has given me the pleasure of your acquaintance. Without the assistance of your remarks I should have been less successful than you have been in developing certain ideas which we possess in common. I beg of you that you will give me leave to publish this conversation. Statements which you and I find pregnant with high political conceptions, others perhaps will think characterized by more or less cutting irony, and I shall pass for a clever fellow in the eyes of both parties."

While I thus tried to express my thanks to the viscount (the first husband after my heart that I had met with), he took me once more through his apartments, where everything seemed to be beyond criticism.

I was about to take leave of him, when opening the door of a little boudoir he showed me a room with an air which seemed to say, "Is there any way by which the least irregularity should occur without my seeing it?"

I replied to this silent interrogation by an inclination of the head, such as guests make to their Amphytrion when they taste some exceptionally choice dish.

"My whole system," he said to me in a whisper, "was suggested to me by three words which my father heard Napoleon pronounce at a crowded council of state, when divorce was the subject of conversation. 'Adultery,' he exclaimed, 'is merely a matter of opportunity!' See, then, I have changed these accessories of crime, so that they become spies," added the councillor, pointing out to me a divan covered with tea-colored cashmere, the cushions of which were slightly pressed. "Notice that impression,—I learn from it that my wife has had a headache, and has been reclining there."

We stepped toward the divan, and saw the word FOOL lightly traced upon the fatal cushion, by four

> Things that I know not, plucked by lover's hand
> From Cypris' orchard, where the fairy band
> Are dancing, once by nobles thought to be
> Worthy an order of new chivalry,
> A brotherhood, wherein, with script of gold,
> More mortal men than gods should be enrolled.

"Nobody in my house has black hair!" said the husband, growing pale.

I hurried away, for I was seized with an irresistible fit of laughter, which I could not easily overcome.

"That man has met his judgment day!" I said to myself; "all the barriers by which he has surrounded her have only been instrumental in adding to the intensity of her pleasures!"

This idea saddened me. The adventure destroyed from summit to foundation three of my most important Meditations, and the catholic infallibility of my book was assailed in its most essential point. I would gladly have paid to establish the fidelity of the Viscountess V——- a sum as great as very many people would have offered to secure her surrender. But alas! my money will now be kept by me.

Three days afterwards I met the councillor in the foyer of the Italiens. As soon as he saw me he rushed up. Impelled by a sort of modesty I tried to avoid him, but grasping my arm: "Ah! I have just passed three cruel days," he whispered in my ear. "Fortunately my wife is as innocent as perhaps a new-born babe—"

"You have already told me that the viscountess was extremely ingenious," I said, with unfeeling gaiety.

"Oh!" he said, "I gladly take a joke this evening; for this morning I had irrefragable proofs of my wife's fidelity. I had risen very early to finish a piece of work for which I had been rushed, and in looking absently in my garden, I suddenly saw the *valet de chambre* of a general, whose house is next to mine, climbing over the wall. My wife's maid, poking her head from the vestibule, was stroking my dog and covering the retreat of the gallant. I took my opera glass and examined the intruder—his hair was jet black!—Ah! never have I seen a Christian face that gave me more delight! And you may well believe that during the day all my perplexities vanished. So, my dear sir," he continued, "if you marry, let your dog loose and put broken bottles over the top of your walls."

"And did the viscountess perceive your distress during these three days?

"Do you take me for a child?" he said, shrugging his shoulders. "I have never been so merry in all my life as I have been since we met."

"You are a great man unrecognized," I cried, "and you are not—"

He did not permit me to conclude; for he had disappeared on seeing one of his friends who approached as if to greet the viscountess.

Now what can we add that would not be a tedious paraphrase of the lessons suggested by this conversation? All is included in it, either as seed or fruit. Nevertheless, you see, O husband! that your happiness hangs on a hair.

MEDITATION XVII.
THE THEORY OF THE BED.

It was about seven o'clock in the evening. They were seated upon the academic armchairs, which made a semi-circle round a huge hearth, on which a coal fire was burning fitfully—symbol of the burning subject of their important deliberations. It was easy to guess, on seeing the grave but earnest faces of all the members of this assembly, that they were called upon to pronounce sentence upon the life, the fortunes and the happiness of people like themselves. They had no commission excepting that of their conscience, and they gathered there as the assessors of an ancient and mysterious tribunal; but they represented interests much more important than those of kings or of peoples; they spoke in the name of the passions and on behalf of the happiness of the numberless generations which should succeed them.

The grandson of the celebrated Boulle was seated before a round table on which were placed the criminal exhibits which had been collected with remarkable intelligence. I, the insignificant secretary of the meeting, occupied a place at this desk, where it was my office to take down a report of the meeting.

"Gentlemen," said an old man, "the first question upon which we have to deliberate is found clearly stated in the following passage of a letter. The letter was written to the Princess of Wales, Caroline of Anspach, by the widow of the Duke of Orleans, brother of Louis XIV, mother of the Regent: 'The Queen of Spain has a method of making her husband say exactly what she wishes. The king is a religious man; he believes that he will be damned if he touched any woman but his wife, and still this excellent prince is of a very amorous temperament. Thus the queen obtains her every wish. She has placed castors on her husband's bed. If he refuses her anything, she pushes the bed away. If he grants her request, the beds stand side by side, and she admits him into hers. And so the king is highly delighted, since he likes — —-' I will not go any further, gentlemen, for the virtuous frankness of the German princess might in this assembly be charged with immorality."

Should wise husbands adopt these beds on castors? This is the problem which we have to solve.

The unanimity of the vote left no doubt about the opinion of the assembly. I was ordered to inscribe in the records, that if two married people slept on two separate beds in the same room the beds ought not to be set on castors.

"With this proviso," put in one of the members, "that the present decision should have no bearing on any subsequent ruling upon the best arrangement of the beds of married people."

The president passed to me a choicely bound volume, in which was contained the original edition, published in 1788, of the letters of Charlotte Elizabeth de Baviere, widow of the Duke of Orleans, the only brother of Louis XIV, and, while I was transcribing the passage already quoted, he said:

"But, gentlemen, you must all have received at your houses the notification in which the second question is stated."

"I rise to make an observation," exclaimed the youngest of the jealous husbands there assembled.

The president took his seat with a gesture of assent.

"Gentlemen," said the young husband, "are we quite prepared to deliberate upon so grave a question as that which is presented by the universally bad arrangement of the beds? Is there not here a much wider question than that of mere cabinet-making to decide? For my own part I see in it a question which concerns that of universal human intellect. The mysteries of conception, gentlemen, are still enveloped in a darkness which modern science has but partially dissipated. We do not know how far external circumstances influence the microscopic beings whose discovery is due to the unwearied patience of Hill, Baker, Joblot, Eichorn, Gleichen, Spallanzani, and especially of Muller, and last of all of M. Bory de Saint Vincent. The imperfections of the bed opens up a musical question of the highest importance, and for my part I declare I shall write to Italy to obtain clear information as to the manner in which beds are generally arranged. We do not know whether there are in the Italian bed numerous curtain rods, screws and castors, or whether the construction of beds is in this country more faulty than everywhere else, or whether the dryness of timber in Italy, due to the influence of the sun, does not *ab ovo* produce the harmony, the sense of which is to so large an extent innate in Italians. For these reasons I move that we adjourn."

"What!" cried a gentleman from the West, impatiently rising to his feet, "are we here to dilate upon the advancement of music? What we have to consider first of all is manners, and the moral question is paramount in this discussion."

"Nevertheless," remarked one of the most influential members of the council, "the suggestion of the former speaker is not in my opinion to be passed by. In the last century, gentlemen, Sterne, one of the writers most philosophically delightful and most delightfully philosophic, complained of the carelessness with which human beings were procreated; 'Shame!' he cried 'that he who copies the divine physiognomy of man receives crowns and applause, but he who achieves the masterpiece, the prototype of mimic art, feels that like virtue he must be his own reward.'

"Ought we not to feel more interest in the improvement of the human race than in that of horses? Gentlemen, I passed through a little town of Orleanais where the whole population consisted of hunchbacks, of glum and gloomy people, veritable children of sorrow, and the remark of the former speaker caused me to recollect that all the beds were in a very bad condition and the bedchambers presented nothing to the eyes of the married couple but what was hideous and revolting. Ah! gentlemen, how is it possible that our minds should be in an ideal state, when instead of the music of angels flying here and there in the bosom of that heaven to which we have attained, our ears are assailed by the most detestable, the most angry, the most piercing of human cries and lamentations? We are perhaps indebted for the fine geniuses who have honored humanity to beds which are solidly constructed; and the turbulent population which caused the French Revolution were conceived perhaps upon a multitude of tottering couches, with twisted and unstable legs; while the Orientals, who are such a beautiful race, have a unique method of making their beds. I vote for the adjournment."

And the gentleman sat down.

A man belonging to the sect of Methodists arose. "Why should we change the subject of debate? We are not dealing here with the improvement of the race nor with the perfecting of the work. We must not lose sight of the interests of the jealous husband and the principles on which moral soundness is based. Don't you know that the noise of which you complain seems more terrible to the wife uncertain of her crime, than the trumpet of the Last Judgment? Can you forget that a suit for infidelity could never be won by a husband excepting through this conjugal noise? I will undertake, gentlemen, to refer to the divorces of Lord Abergavenny, of Viscount Bolingbroke, of the late Queen Caroline, of Eliza Draper, of Madame Harris, in fact, of all those who are mentioned in the twenty volumes published by—." (The secretary did not distinctly hear the name of the English publisher.)

The motion to adjourn was carried. The youngest member proposed to make up a purse for the author producing the best dissertation addressed to the society upon a subject which Sterne considered of such importance; but at the end of the seance eighteen shillings was the total sum found in the hat of the president.

The above debate of the society, which had recently been formed in London for the improvement of manners and of marriage and which Lord Byron scoffed at, was transmitted to us by the kindness of W. Hawkins, Esq., cousin-german of the famous Captain Clutterbuck. The extract may serve to solve any difficulties which may occur in the theory of bed construction.

But the author of the book considers that the English society has given too much importance to this preliminary question. There exists in fact quite as many reasons for being a *Rossinist* as for being a *Solidist* in the matter of beds, and the author acknowledges that it is either beneath or above him to solve this difficulty. He thinks with Laurence Sterne that it is a disgrace to European civilization that there exist so few physiological observations on callipedy, and he refuses to state the results of his Meditations on this subject, because it would be difficult to formulate them in terms of prudery, and they would be but little understood, and misinterpreted. Such reserve produces an hiatus in this part of the book; but the author has the pleasant satisfaction of leaving a fourth work to be accomplished by the next century, to which he bequeaths the legacy of all that he has not accomplished, a negative munificence which may well be followed by all those who may be troubled by an overplus of ideas.

The theory of the bed presents questions much more important than those put forth by our neighbors with regard to castors and the murmurs of criminal conversation.

We know only three ways in which a bed (in the general sense of this term) may be arranged among civilized nations, and particularly among the privileged classes to whom this book is addressed. These three ways are as follows:

1. TWIN BEDS.

2. SEPARATE ROOMS.

3. ONE BED FOR BOTH.

Before applying ourselves to the examination of these three methods of living together, which must necessarily have different influences upon the happiness of husbands and wives, we must take a rapid survey of the practical object served by the bed and the part it plays in the political economy of human existence.

The most incontrovertible principle which can be laid down in this matter is, *that the bed was made to sleep upon.*

It would be easy to prove that the practice of sleeping together was established between married people but recently, in comparison with the antiquity of marriage.

By what reasonings has man arrived at that point in which he brought in vogue a practice so fatal to happiness, to health, even to *amour-propre*? Here we have a subject which it would be curious to investigate.

If you knew one of your rivals who had discovered a method of placing you in a position of extreme absurdity before the eyes of those who were dearest to you— for instance, while you had your mouth crooked like that of a theatrical mask, or while your eloquent lips, like the copper faucet of a scanty fountain, dripped pure water—you would probably stab him. This rival is sleep. Is there a man in the world who knows how he appears to others, and what he does when he is asleep?

In sleep we are living corpses, we are the prey of an unknown power which seizes us in spite of ourselves, and shows itself in the oddest shapes; some have a sleep which is intellectual, while the sleep of others is mere stupor.

There are some people who slumber with their mouths open in the silliest fashion.

There are others who snore loud enough to make the timbers shake.

Most people look like the impish devils that Michael Angelo sculptured, putting out their tongues in silent mockery of the passers-by.

The only person I know of in the world who sleeps with a noble air is Agamemnon, whom Guerin has represented lying on his bed at the moment when Clytemnestra, urged by Egisthus, advances to slay him. Moreover, I have always had an ambition to hold myself on my pillow as the king of kings Agamemnon holds himself, from the day that I was seized with dread of being seen during sleep by any other eyes than those of Providence. In the same way, too, from the day I heard my old nurse snorting in her sleep "like a whale," to use a slang expression, I have added a petition to the special litany which I address to Saint-Honore, my patron saint, to the effect that he would save me from indulging in this sort of eloquence.

When a man wakes up in the morning, his drowsy face grotesquely surmounted by the folds of a silk handkerchief which falls over his left temple like a police cap, he is certainly a laughable object, and it is difficult to recognize in him the glorious spouse, celebrated in the strophes of Rousseau; but, nevertheless, there is a certain gleam of life to illume the stupidity of a countenance half dead—and if you artists wish to make fine sketches, you should travel on the stage-coach and, when the postilion wakes up the postmaster, just examine the physiognomies of the departmental clerks! But, were you a hundred times as pleasant to look upon as are these bureaucratic physiognomies, at least, while you have your mouth shut, your eyes are open, and you have some expression in your countenance. Do you know how you looked an hour before you awoke, or during the first hour of your sleep, when you were neither a man nor an animal, but merely a thing, subject to the dominion of those dreams which issue from the gate of horn? But this is a secret between your wife and God.

Is it for the purpose of insinuating the imbecility of slumber that the Romans decorated the heads of their beds with the head of an ass? We leave to the gentlemen who form the academy of inscriptions the elucidation of this point.

Assuredly, the first man who took it into his head, at the inspiration of the devil, not to leave his wife, even while she was asleep, should know how to sleep in the very best style; but do not forget to reckon among the sciences necessary to a man on setting up an establishment, the art of sleeping with elegance. Moreover, we will place here as a corollary to Axiom XXV of our Marriage Catechism the two following aphorisms:

A husband should sleep as lightly as a watch-dog, so as never to be caught with his eyes shut.

A man should accustom himself from childhood to go to bed bareheaded.

Certain poets discern in modesty, in the alleged mysteries of love, some reason why the married couple should share the same bed; but the fact must be recognized that if primitive men sought the shade of caverns, the mossy couch of deep ravines, the flinty roof of grottoes to protect his pleasure, it was because the delight of love left him without defence against his enemies. No, it is not more natural to lay two heads upon the same pillow, than it is reasonable to tie a strip of muslin round the neck. Civilization is come. It has shut up a million of men within an area of four square leagues; it has stalled them in streets, houses, apartments, rooms, and chambers eight feet square; after a time it will make them shut up one upon another like the tubes of a telescope.

From this cause and from many others, such as thrift, fear, and ill-concealed jealousy, has sprung the custom of the sleeping together of the married couple; and this custom has given rise to punctuality and simultaneity in rising and retiring.

And here you find the most capricious thing in the world, the feeling most pre-eminently fickle, the thing which is worthless without its own spontaneous inspiration, which takes all its charm from the suddenness of its desires, which owes its attractions to the genuineness of its outbursts—this thing we call love, subjugated to a monastic rule, to that law of geometry which belongs to the Board of Longitude!

If I were a father I should hate the child, who, punctual as the clock, had every morning and evening an explosion of tenderness and wished me good-day and good-evening, because he was ordered to do so. It is in this way that all that is generous and spontaneous in human sentiment becomes strangled at its birth. You may judge from this what love means when it is bound to a fixed hour!

Only the Author of everything can make the sun rise and set, morn and eve, with a pomp invariably brilliant and always new, and no one here below, if we may be permitted to use the hyperbole of Jean-Baptiste Rousseau, can play the role of the sun.

From these preliminary observations, we conclude that it is not natural for two to lie under the canopy in the same bed;

That a man is almost always ridiculous when he is asleep;

And that this constant living together threatens the husband with inevitable dangers.

We are going to try, therefore, to find out a method which will bring our customs in harmony with the laws of nature, and to combine custom and nature in a way that will enable a husband to find in the mahogany of his bed a useful ally, and an aid in defending himself.

1. TWIN BEDS.

If the most brilliant, the best-looking, the cleverest of husbands wishes to find himself minotaurized just as the first year of his married life ends, he will infallibly attain that end if he is unwise enough to place two beds side by side, under the voluptuous dome of the same alcove.

The argument in support of this may be briefly stated. The following are its main lines:

The first husband who invented the twin beds was doubtless an obstetrician, who feared that in the involuntary struggles of some dream he might kick the child borne by his wife.

But no, he was rather some predestined one who distrusted his power of checking a snore.

Perhaps it was some young man who, fearing the excess of his own tenderness, found himself always lying at the edge of the bed and in danger of tumbling off, or so near to a charming wife that he disturbed her slumber.

But may it not have been some Maintenon who received the suggestion from her confessor, or, more probably, some ambitious woman who wished to rule her husband? Or, more undoubtedly, some pretty little Pompadour overcome by that Parisian infirmity so pleasantly described by M. de Maurepas in that quatrain which cost him his protracted disgrace and certainly contributed to the disasters of Louis XVI's reign:

> "Iris, we love those features sweet,
> Your graces all are fresh and free;
> And flowerets spring beneath your feet,
> Where naught, alas! but flowers are seen."

But why should it not have been a philosopher who dreaded the disenchantment which a woman would experience at the sight of a man asleep? And such a one would always roll himself up in a coverlet and keep his head bare.

Unknown author of this Jesuitical method, whoever thou art, in the devil's name, we hail thee as a brother! Thou hast been the cause of many disasters. Thy work has the character of all half measures; it is satisfactory in no respect, and shares the bad points of the two other methods without yielding the advantages of either. How can the man of the nineteenth century, how can this creature so supremely intelligent, who has displayed a power well-nigh supernatural, who has employed the resources of his genius in concealing the machinery of his life, in deifying his necessary cravings in order that he might not despise them, going so far as to wrest from Chinese leaves, from Egyptian beans, from seeds of Mexico, their perfume, their treasure, their soul; going so far as to chisel the diamond, chase the silver, melt the gold ore, paint the clay and woo every art that may serve to decorate and to dignify the bowl from which he feeds!—how can this king, after having hidden under folds of muslin covered with diamonds, studded with rubies, and buried under linen, under folds of cotton, under the rich hues of silk, under the fairy patterns of lace, the partner of his wretchedness, how can he induce her to make shipwreck in the midst of all this luxury on the decks of two beds. What advantage is it that we have made the whole universe subserve our existence, our delusions, the poesy of our life? What good is it to have instituted law, morals and religion, if the invention of an upholsterer [for probably it was an upholsterer who invented the twin beds] robs our love of all its illusions, strips it bare of the majestic company of its delights and gives it in their stead nothing but what is ugliest and most odious? For this is the whole history of the two bed system.

LXIII.

That it shall appear either sublime or grotesque are the alternatives to which we have reduced a desire.

If it be shared, our love is sublime; but should you sleep in twin beds, your love will always be grotesque. The absurdities which this half separation occasions may be comprised in either one of two situations, which will give us occasion to reveal the causes of very many marital misfortunes.

Midnight is approaching as a young woman is putting on her curl papers and yawning as she did so. I do not know whether her melancholy proceeded from a headache, seated in the right or left lobe of her brain, or whether she was passing through one of those seasons of weariness during which all things appear black to us; but to see her negligently putting up her hair for the night, to see her languidly raising her leg to take off her garter, it seemed to me that she would prefer to be drowned rather than to be denied the relief of plunging her draggled life into the slumber that might restore it. At this instant, I know not to what degree from the North Pole she stands, whether at Spitzberg or in Greenland. Cold and indifferent she goes to bed thinking, as Mistress Walter Shandy might have thought, that the morrow would be a day of sickness, that her husband is coming home very late, that the beaten eggs which she has just eaten were not sufficiently sweetened, that she owes more than five hundred francs to her dressmaker; in fine, thinking about everything which you may suppose would occupy the mind of a tired woman. In the meanwhile arrives her great lout of a husband, who, after some business meeting, has drunk punch, with a consequent elation. He takes off his boots, leaves his stockings on a lounge, his bootjack lies before the fireplace; and wrapping his head up in a red silk handkerchief, without giving himself the trouble to tuck in the corners, he fires off at his wife certain interjectory phrases, those little marital endearments, which form almost the whole conversation at those twilight hours, where drowsy reason is no longer shining in this mechanism of ours. "What, in bed already! It was devilish cold this evening! Why don't you speak, my pet? You've already rolled yourself up in bed, then! Ah! you are in the dumps and pretend to be asleep!" These exclamations are mingled with yawns; and after numberless little incidents which according to the usage of each home vary this preface of the night, our friend flings himself into his own bed with a heavy thud.

Alas! before a woman who is cold, how mad a man must appear when desire renders him alternately angry and tender, insolent and abject, biting as an epigram and soothing as a madrigal; when he enacts with more or less sprightliness the scene where, in *Venice Preserved*, the genius of Orway has represented the senator Antonio, repeating a hundred times over at the feet of Aquilina: "Aquilina, Quilina, Lina, Aqui, Nacki!" without winning from her aught save the stroke of her whip, inasmuch as he has undertaken to fawn upon her like a dog. In the eyes of every woman, even of a lawful wife, the more a man shows eager passion under these circumstances, the more silly he appears. He is odious when he commands, he is minotaurized if he abuses his power. On this point I would remind you of certain aphorisms in the marriage catechism from which you will see that you are violating its most sacred precepts. Whether a woman yields, or does not yield, this institution of twin beds gives to marriage such an element of roughness and nakedness that the most chaste wife and the most intelligent husband are led to immodesty.

This scene, which is enacted in a thousand ways and which may originate in a thousand different incidents, has a sequel in that other situation which, while it is less pleasant, is far more terrible.

One evening when I was talking about these serious matters with the late Comte de Noce, of whom I have already had occasion to speak, a tall white-haired old man, his intimate friend, whose name I will not give, because he is still alive, looked at us with a somewhat melancholy air. We guessed that he was about to relate some tale of scandal, and we accordingly watched him, somewhat as the stenographer of the *Moniteur* might watch, as he mounted the tribune, a minister whose speech had already been written out for the reporter. The story-teller on this occasion was an old marquis, whose fortune, together with his wife and children, had perished in the disasters of the Revolution. The marchioness had been one of the most inconsistent women of the past generation; the marquis accordingly was not wanting in observations on feminine human nature. Having reached an age in which he saw nothing before him but the gulf of the grave, he spoke about himself as if the subject of his talk were Mark Antony or Cleopatra.

"My young friend"—he did me the honor to address me, for it was I who made the last remark in this discussion—"your reflections make me think of a certain evening, in the course of which one of my friends conducted himself in such a manner as to lose forever the respect of his wife. Now, in those days a woman could take vengeance with marvelous facility—for it was always a word and a blow. The married couple I speak of were particular in sleeping on separate beds, with their head under the arch of the same alcove. They came home one night from a brilliant ball given by the Comte de Mercy, ambassador of the emperor. The husband had lost a considerable sum at play, so he was completely absorbed in thought. He had to pay a debt, the next day, of six thousand crowns!—and you will recollect, Noce, that a hundred crowns couldn't be made up from scraping together the resources of ten such musketeers. The young woman, as generally happens under such circumstances, was in a gale of high spirits. 'Give to the marquis,' she said to a *valet de chambre*, 'all that he requires for his toilet.' In those days people dressed for the night. These extraordinary words did not rouse the husband from his mood of abstraction, and then madame, assisted by her maid, began to indulge in a thousand coquetries. 'Was my appearance to your taste this evening?' 'You are always to my taste,' answered the marquis, continuing to stride up and down the room. 'You are very gloomy! Come and talk to me, you frowning lover,' said she, placing herself before him in the most seductive negligee. But you can have no idea of the enchantments of the marchioness unless you had known her. Ah! you have seen her, Noce!" he said with a mocking smile. "Finally, in spite of all her allurements and beauty, the marchioness was lost sight of amid thoughts of the six thousand crowns which this fool of a husband could not get out of his head, and she went to bed all alone. But women always have one resource left; so that the moment that the good husband made as though he would get into his bed, the marchioness cried, 'Oh, how cold I am!' 'So am I,' he replied. 'How is it that the servants have not warmed our beds?'—And then I rang."

The Comte de Noce could not help laughing, and the old marquis, quite put out of countenance, stopped short.

Not to divine the desire of a wife, to snore while she lies awake, to be in Siberia when she is in the tropics, these are the slighter disadvantages of twin beds. What risks will not a passionate woman run when she becomes aware that her husband is a heavy sleeper?

I am indebted to Beyle for an Italian anecdote, to which his dry and sarcastic manner lent an infinite charm, as he told me this tale of feminine hardihood.

Ludovico had his palace at one end of the town of Milan; at the other was that of the Countess of Pernetti. At midnight, on a certain occasion, Ludovico resolved, at the peril of his life, to make a rash expedition for the sake of gazing for one second on the face he adored, and accordingly appeared as if by magic in the palace of his well-beloved. He reached the nuptial chamber. Elisa Pernetti, whose heart most probably shared the desire of her lover, heard the sound of his footsteps and divined his intention. She saw through the walls of her chamber a countenance glowing with love. She rose from her marriage bed, light as a shadow she glided to the threshold of her door, with a look she embraced him, she seized his hand, she made a sign to him, she drew him in.

"But he will kill you!" said he.

"Perhaps so."

But all this amounts to nothing. Let us grant that most husbands sleep lightly. Let us grant that they sleep without snoring, and that they always discern the degree of latitude at which their wives are to be found. Moreover, all the reasons which we have given why twin beds should be condemned, let us consider but dust in the balance. But, after all, a final consideration would make us also proscribe the use of beds ranged within the limits of the same alcove.

To a man placed in the position of a husband, there are circumstances which have led us to consider the nuptial couch as an actual means of defence. For it is only in bed that a man can tell whether his wife's love is increasing or decreasing. It is the conjugal barometer. Now to sleep in twin beds is to wish for ignorance. You will understand, when we come to treat of *civil war* (See Part Third) of what extreme usefulness a bed is and how many secrets a wife reveals in bed, without knowing it.

Do not therefore allow yourself to be led astray by the specious good nature of such an institution as that of twin beds.

It is the silliest, the most treacherous, the most dangerous in the world. Shame and anathema to him who conceived it!

But in proportion as this method is pernicious in the case of young married people, it is salutary and advantageous for those who have reached the twentieth year of married life. Husband and wife can then most conveniently indulge their duets of snoring. It will, moreover, be more convenient for their various maladies, whether rheumatism, obstinate gout, or even the taking of a pinch of snuff; and the cough or the snore will not in any respect prove a greater hindrance than it is found to be in any other arrangement.

We have not thought it necessary to mention the exceptional cases which authorize a husband to resort to twin beds. However, the opinion of Bonaparte was that when once there had taken place an interchange of life and breath (such are his words), nothing, not even sickness, should separate married people. This point is so delicate that it is not possible here to treat it methodically.

Certain narrow minds will object that there are certain patriarchal families whose legislation of love is inflexible in the matter of two beds and an alcove, and that, by this arrangement, they have been happy from generation to generation. But, the only answer that the author vouchsafes to this is that he knows a great many respectable people who pass their lives in watching games of billiards.

2. SEPARATE ROOMS.

There cannot be found in Europe a hundred husbands of each nation sufficiently versed in the science of marriage, or if you like, of life, to be able to dwell in an apartment separate from that of their wives.

The power of putting this system into practice shows the highest degree of intellectual and masculine force.

The married couple who dwell in separate apartments have become either divorced, or have attained to the discovery of happiness. They either abominate or adore each other. We will not undertake to detail here the admirable precepts which may be deduced from this theory whose end is to make constancy and fidelity easy and delightful. It may be sufficient to declare that by this system alone two married people can realize the dream of many noble souls. This will be understood by all the faithful.

As for the profane, their curious questionings will be sufficiently answered by the remark that the object of this institution is to give happiness to one woman. Which among them will be willing to deprive general society of any share in the talents with which they think themselves endowed, to the advantage of one woman? Nevertheless, the rendering of his mistress happy gives any one the fairest title to glory which can be earned in this valley of Jehosaphat, since, according to Genesis, Eve was not satisfied even with a terrestrial Paradise. She desired to taste the forbidden fruit, the eternal emblem of adultery.

But there is an insurmountable reason why we should refrain from developing this brilliant theory. It would cause a digression from the main theme of our work. In the situation which we have supposed to be that of a married establishment, a man who is sufficiently unwise to sleep apart from his wife deserves no pity for the disaster which he himself invites.

Let us then resume our subject. Every man is not strong enough to undertake to occupy an apartment separate from that of his wife; although any man might derive as much good as evil from the difficulties which exist in using but one bed.

We now proceed to solve the difficulties which superficial minds may detect in this method, for which our predilection is manifest.

But this paragraph, which is in some sort a silent one, inasmuch as we leave it to the commentaries which will be made in more than one home, may serve as a pedestal for the imposing figure of Lycurgus, that ancient legislator, to whom the Greeks are indebted for their profoundest thoughts on the subject of marriage. May his system be understood by future generations! And if modern manners are too much given to softness to adopt his system in its entirety, they may at least be imbued with the robust spirit of this admirable code.

3. ONE BED FOR BOTH.

On a night in December, Frederick the Great looked up at the sky, whose stars were twinkling with that clear and living light which presages heavy frost, and he exclaimed, "This weather will result in a great many soldiers to Prussia."

The king expressed here, by a single phrase, the principal disadvantage which results from the constant living together of married people. Although it may be permitted to Napoleon and to Frederick to estimate the value of a woman more or less according to the number of her children, yet a husband of talent ought, according to the maxims of the thirteenth Meditation, to consider child-begetting merely as a means of defence, and it is for him to know to what extent it may take place.

The observation leads into mysteries from which the physiological Muse recoils. She has been quite willing to enter the nuptial chambers while they are occupied, but she is a virgin and a prude, and there are occasions on which she retires. For, since it is at this passage in my book that the Muse is inclined to put her white hands before her eyes so as to see nothing, like the young girl looking through the interstices of her tapering fingers, she will take advantage of this attack of modesty, to administer a reprimand to our manners. In England the nuptial chamber is a sacred place. The married couple alone have the privilege of entering it, and more than one lady, we are told, makes her bed herself. Of all the crazes which reign beyond the sea, why should the only one which we despise be precisely that, whose grace and mystery ought undoubtedly to meet the approval of all tender souls on this continent? Refined women condemn the immodesty with which strangers are introduced into the sanctuary of marriage. As for us, who have energetically anathematized women who walk abroad at the time when they expect soon to be confined, our opinion cannot be doubted. If we wish the celibate to respect marriage, married people ought to have some regard for the inflammability of bachelors.

To sleep every night with one's wife may seem, we confess, an act of the most insolent folly.

Many husbands are inclined to ask how a man, who desires to bring marriage to perfection, dare prescribe to a husband a rule of conduct which would be fatal in a lover.

Nevertheless, such is the decision of a doctor of arts and sciences conjugal.

In the first place, without making a resolution never to sleep by himself, this is the only course left to a husband, since we have demonstrated the dangers of the preceding systems. We must now try to prove that this last method yields more advantage and less disadvantage than the two preceding methods, that is, so far as relates to the critical position in which a conjugal establishment stands.

Our observations on the twin beds ought to have taught husbands that they should always be strung into the same degree of fervor as that which prevails in the harmonious organization of their wives. Now it seems to us that this perfect equality in feelings would naturally be created under the white Aegis, which spreads over both of them its protecting sheet; this at the outset is an immense advantage, and really nothing is easier to verify at any moment than the degree of love and expansion which a woman reaches when the same pillow receives the heads of both spouses.

Man [we speak now of the species] walks about with a memorandum always totalized, which shows distinctly and without error the amount of passion which he carries within him. This mysterious gynometer is traced in the hollow of the hand, for the hand is really that one of our members which bears the impress most plainly of our characters. Chirology is a fifth work which I bequeath to my successors, for I am contented here to make known but the elements of this interesting science.

The hand is the essential organ of touch. Touch is the sense which very nearly takes the place of all the others, and which alone is indispensable. Since the hand alone can carry out all that a man desires, it is to an extent action itself. The sum total of our vitality passes through it; and men of powerful intellects are usually remarkable for their shapely hands, perfection in that respect being a distinguishing trait of their high calling.

Jesus Christ performed all His miracles by the imposition of hands. The hand is the channel through which life passes. It reveals to the physician all the mysteries of our organism. It exhales more than any other part of our bodies the nervous fluid, or that unknown substance, which for want of another term we style *will*. The eye can discover the mood of our soul but the hand betrays at the same time the secrets of the body and those of the soul. We can acquire the faculty of imposing silence on our eyes, on our lips, on our brows, and on our forehead; but the hand never dissembles and nothing in our features can be compared to the richness of its expression. The heat and cold which it feels in such delicate degrees often escape the notice of other senses in thoughtless people; but a man knows how to distinguish them, however little time he may have bestowed in studying the anatomy of sentiments and the affairs of human life. Thus the hand has a thousand ways of becoming dry, moist, hot, cold, soft, rough, unctuous. The hand palpitates, becomes supple, grows hard and again is softened. In fine it presents a phenomenon which is inexplicable so that one is tempted to call it the incarnation of thought. It causes the despair of the sculptor and the painter when they wish to express the changing labyrinth of its mysterious lineaments. To stretch out your hand to a man is to save him, it serves as a ratification of the sentiments we express. The sorcerers of every age have tried to read our future destines in those lines which have nothing fanciful in them, but absolutely correspond with the principles of each one's life and character. When she charges a man with want of tact, which is merely touch, a woman condemns him without hope. We use the expressions, the "Hand of Justice," the "Hand of God;" and a *coup de main* means a bold undertaking.

To understand and recognize the hidden feelings by the atmospheric variations of the hand, which a woman almost always yields without distrust, is a study less unfruitful and surer than that of physiognomy.

In this way you will be able, if you acquire this science, to wield vast power, and to find a clue which will guide you through the labyrinth of the most impenetrable heart. This will render your living together free from very many mistakes, and, at the same time, rich in the acquisition of many a treasure.

Buffon and certain physiologists affirm that our members are more completely exhausted by desire than by the most keen enjoyments. And really, does not desire constitute of itself a sort of intuitive possession? Does it not stand in the same relation to visible action, as those incidents in our mental life, in which we take part in a dream, stand to the incidents of our actual life? This energetic apprehension of things, does it not call into being an internal emotion more powerful than that of the external action? If our gestures are only the accomplishment of things already enacted by our thought, you may easily calculate how desire frequently entertained must necessarily consume the vital fluids. But the passions which are no more than the aggregation of desires, do they not furrow with the wrinkle of their lightning the faces of the ambitious, of gamblers, for instance, and do they not wear out their bodies with marvelous swiftness?

These observations, therefore, necessarily contain the germs of a mysterious system equally favored by Plato and by Epicurus; we will leave it for you to meditate upon, enveloped as it is in the veil which enshrouds Egyptian statues.

But the greatest mistake that a man commits is to believe that love can belong only to those fugitive moments which, according to the magnificent expression of Bossuet, are like to the nails scattered over a wall: to the eye they appear numerous; but when they are collected they make but a handful.

Love consists almost always in conversation. There are few things inexhaustible in a lover: goodness, gracefulness and delicacy. To feel everything, to divine everything, to anticipate everything; to reproach without bringing affliction upon a tender heart; to make a present without pride; to double the value of a certain action by the way in which it is done; to flatter rather by actions than by words; to make oneself understood rather than to produce a vivid impression; to touch without striking; to make a look and the sound of the voice produce the effect of a caress; never to produce embarrassment; to amuse without offending good taste; always to touch the heart; to speak to the soul—this is all that women ask. They will abandon all the delights of all the nights of Messalina, if only they may live with a being who will yield them those caresses of the soul, for which they are so eager, and which cost nothing to men if only they have a little consideration.

This outline comprises a great portion of such secrets as belong to the nuptial couch. There are perhaps some witty people who may take this long definition of politeness for a description of love, while in any case it is no more than a recommendation to treat your wife as you would treat the minister on whose good-will depends your promotion to the post you covet.

I hear numberless voices crying out that this book is a special advocate for women and neglects the cause of men;

That the majority of women are unworthy of these delicate attentions and would abuse them;

That there are women given to licentiousness who would not lend themselves to very much of what they would call mystification;

That women are nothing but vanity and think of nothing but dress;

That they have notions which are truly unreasonable;

That they are very often annoyed by an attention;

That they are fools, they understand nothing, are worth nothing, etc.

In answer to all these clamors we will write here the following phrases, which, placed between two spaces, will perhaps have the air of a thought, to quote an expression of Beaumarchais.

LXIV.

A wife is to her husband just what her husband has made her.

The reasons why the single bed must triumph over the other two methods of organizing the nuptial couch are as follows: In the single couch we have a faithful interpreter to translate with profound truthfulness the sentiments of a woman, to render her a spy over herself, to keep her at the height of her amorous temperature, never to leave her, to have the power of hearing her breathe in slumber, and thus to avoid all the nonsense which is the ruin of so many marriages.

As it is impossible to receive benefits without paying for them, you are bound to learn how to sleep gracefully, to preserve your dignity under the silk handkerchief that wraps your head, to be polite, to see that your slumber is light, not to cough too much, and to imitate those modern authors who write more prefaces than books.

MEDITATION XVIII.
OF MARITAL REVOLUTIONS.

The time always comes in which nations and women even the most stupid perceive that their innocence is being abused. The cleverest policy may for a long time proceed in a course of deceit; but it would be very happy for men if they could carry on their deceit to an infinite period; a vast amount of bloodshed would then be avoided, both in nations and in families.

Nevertheless, we hope that the means of defence put forth in the preceding Meditations will be sufficient to deliver a certain number of husbands from the clutches of the Minotaur! You must agree with the doctor that many a love blindly entered upon perishes under the treatment of hygiene or dies away, thanks to marital policy. Yes [what a consoling mistake!] many a lover will be driven away by personal efforts, many a husband will learn how to conceal under an impenetrable veil the machinery of his machiavelism, and many a man will have better success than the old philosopher who cried: *Nolo coronari!*

But we are here compelled to acknowledge a mournful truth. Despotism has its moments of secure tranquillity. Her reign seems like the hour which precedes the tempest, and whose silence enables the traveler, stretched upon the faded grass, to hear at a mile's distance, the song of the cicada. Some fine morning an honest woman, who will be imitated by a great portion of our own women, discerns with an eagle eye the clever manoeuvres which have rendered her the victim of an infernal policy. She is at first quite furious at having for so long a time preserved her virtue. At what age, in what day, does this terrible revolution occur? This question of chronology depends entirely upon the genius of each husband; for it is not the vocation of all to put in practice with the same talent the precepts of our conjugal gospel.

"A man must have very little love," the mystified wife will exclaim, "to enter upon such calculations as these! What! From the first day I have been to him perpetually an object of suspicion! It is monstrous, even a woman would be incapable of such artful and cruel treachery!"

This is the question. Each husband will be able to understand the variations of this complaint which will be made in accordance with the character of the young Fury, of whom he has made a companion.

A woman by no means loses her head under these circumstances; she holds her tongue and dissembles. Her vengeance will be concealed. Only you will have some symptoms of hesitation to contend with on the arrival of the crisis, which we presume you to have reached on the expiration of the honeymoon; but you will also have to contend against a resolution. She has determined to revenge herself. From that day, so far as regards you, her mask, like her heart, has turned to bronze. Formerly you were an object of indifference to her; you are becoming by degrees absolutely insupportable. The Civil War commences only at the moment in which, like the drop of water which makes the full glass overflow, some incident, whose more or less importance we find difficulty in determining, has rendered you odious. The lapse of time which intervenes between this last hour, the limit of your good understanding, and the day when your wife becomes cognizant of your artifices, is nevertheless quite sufficient to permit you to institute a series of defensive operations, which we will now explain.

Up to this time you have protected your honor solely by the exertion of a power entirely occult. Hereafter the wheels of your conjugal machinery must be set going in sight of every one. In this case, if you would prevent a crime you must strike a blow. You have begun by negotiating, you must end by mounting your horse, sabre in hand, like a Parisian gendarme. You must make your horse prance, you must brandish your sabre, you must shout strenuously, and you must endeavor to calm the revolt without wounding anybody.

Just as the author has found a means of passing from occult methods to methods that are patent, so it is necessary for the husband to justify the sudden change in his tactics; for in marriage, as in literature, art consists entirely in the gracefulness of the transitions. This is of the highest importance for you. What a frightful position you will occupy if your wife has reason to complain of your conduct at the moment, which is, perhaps, the most critical of your whole married life!

You must therefore find some means or other to justify the secret tyranny of your initial policy; some means which still prepare the mind of your wife for the severe measures which you are about to take; some means which so far from forfeiting her esteem will conciliate her; some means which will gain her pardon, which will restore some little of that charm of yours, by which you won her love before your marriage.

"But what policy is it that demands this course of action? Is there such a policy?"

Certainly there is.

But what address, what tact, what histrionic art must a husband possess in order to display the mimic wealth of that treasure which we are about to reveal to him! In order to counterfeit the passion whose fire is to make you a new man in the presence of your wife, you will require all the cunning of Talma.

This passion is JEALOUSY.

"My husband is jealous. He has been so from the beginning of our marriage. He has concealed this feeling from me by his usual refined delicacy. Does he love me still? I am going to do as I like with him!"

Such are the discoveries which a woman is bound to make, one after another, in accordance with the charming scenes of the comedy which you are enacting for your amusement; and a man of the world must be an actual fool, if he fails in making a woman believe that which flatters her.

With what perfection of hypocrisy must you arrange, step by step, your hypocritical behavior so as to rouse the curiosity of your wife, to engage her in a new study, and to lead her astray among the labyrinths of your thought!

Ye sublime actors! Do ye divine the diplomatic reticence, the gestures of artifice, the veiled words, the looks of doubtful meaning which some evening may induce your wife to attempt the capture of your secret thoughts?

Ah! to laugh in your sleeve while you are exhibiting the fierceness of a tiger; neither to lie nor to tell the truth; to comprehend the capricious mood of a woman, and yet to make her believe that she controls you, while you intend to bind her with a collar of iron! O comedy that has no audience, which yet is played by one heart before another heart and where both of you applaud because both of you think that you have obtained success!

She it is who will tell you that you are jealous, who will point out to you that she knows you better than you know yourself, who will prove to you the uselessness of your artifices and who perhaps will defy you. She triumphs in the excited consciousness of the superiority which she thinks she possesses over you; you of course are ennobled in her eyes; for she finds your conduct quite natural. The only thing she feels is that your want of confidence was useless; if she wished to betray, who could hinder her?

Then, some evening, you will burst into a passion, and, as some trifle affords you a pretext, you will make a scene, in the course of which your anger will make you divulge the secret of your distress. And here comes in the promulgation of our new code.

Have no fear that a woman is going to trouble herself about this. She needs your jealousy, she rather likes your severity. This comes from the fact that in the first place she finds there a justification for her own conduct; and then she finds immense satisfaction in playing before other people the part of a victim. What delightful expressions of sympathy will she receive! Afterwards she will use this as a weapon against you, in the expectation thereby of leading you into a pitfall.

She sees in your conduct the source of a thousand more pleasures in her future treachery, and her imagination smiles at all the barricades with which you surround her, for will she not have the delight of surmounting them all?

Women understand better than we do the art of analyzing the two human feelings, which alternately form their weapons of attack, or the weapons of which they are victims. They have the instinct of love, because it is their whole life, and of jealousy, because it is almost the only means by which they can control us. Within them jealousy is a genuine sentiment and springs from the instinct of self-preservation; it is vital to their life or death. But with men this feeling is absolutely absurd when it does not subserve some further end.

To entertain feelings of jealousy towards the woman you love, is to start from a position founded on vicious reasoning. We are loved, or we are not loved; if a man entertains jealousy under either of these circumstances, it is a feeling absolutely unprofitable to him; jealousy may be explained as fear, fear in love. But to doubt one's wife is to doubt one's self.

To be jealous is to exhibit, at once, the height of egotism, the error of *amour-propre*, the vexation of morbid vanity. Women rather encourage this ridiculous feeling, because by means of it they can obtain cashmere shawls, silver toilet sets, diamonds, which for them mark the high thermometer mark of their power. Moreover, unless you appear blinded by jealousy, your wife will not keep on her guard; for there is no pitfall which she does not distrust, excepting that which she makes for herself.

Thus the wife becomes the easy dupe of a husband who is clever enough to give to the inevitable revolution, which comes sooner or later, the advantageous results we have indicated.

You must import into your establishment that remarkable phenomenon whose existence is demonstrated in the asymptotes of geometry. Your wife will always try to minotaurize you without being successful. Like those knots which are never so tight as when one tries to loosen them, she will struggle to the advantage of your power over her, while she believes that she is struggling for her independence.

The highest degree of good play on the part of a prince lies in persuading his people that he goes to war for them, while all the time he is causing them to be killed for his throne.

But many husbands will find a preliminary difficulty in executing this plan of campaign. If your wife is a woman of profound dissimulation, the question is, what signs will indicate to her the motives of your long mystification?

It will be seen that our Meditation on the Custom House, as well as that on the Bed, has already revealed certain means of discerning the thought of a woman; but we make no pretence in this book of exhaustively stating the resources of human wit, which are immeasurable. Now here is a proof of this. On the day of the Saturnalia the Romans discovered more features in the character of their slaves, in ten minutes, than they would have found out during the rest of the year! You ought therefore to ordain Saturnalia in your establishment, and to imitate Gessler, who, when he saw William Tell shoot the apple off his son's head, was forced to remark, "Here is a man whom I must get rid of, for he could not miss his aim if he wished to kill me."

You understand, then, that if your wife wishes to drink Roussillon wine, to eat mutton chops, to go out at all hours and to read the encyclopaedia, you are bound to take her very seriously. In the first place, she will begin to distrust you against her own wish, on seeing that your behaviour towards her is quite contrary to your previous proceedings. She will suppose that you have some ulterior motive in this change of policy, and therefore all the liberty that you give her will make her so anxious that she cannot enjoy it. As regards the misfortunes that this change may bring, the future will provide for them. In a revolution the primary principle is to exercise a control over the evil which cannot be prevented and to attract the lightning by rods which shall lead it to the earth.

And now the last act of the comedy is in preparation.

The lover who, from the day when the feeblest of all first symptoms shows itself in your wife until the moment when the marital revolution takes place, has jumped upon the stage, either as a material creature or as a being of the imagination—the LOVER, summoned by a sign from her, now declares: "Here I am!"

MEDITATION XIX.
OF THE LOVER.

We offer the following maxims for your consideration:

We should despair of the human race if these maxims had been made before 1830; but they set forth in so clear a manner the agreements and difficulties which distinguish you, your wife and a lover; they so brilliantly describe what your policy should be, and demonstrate to you so accurately the strength of the enemy, that the teacher has put his *amour-propre* aside, and if by chance you find here a single new thought, send it to the devil, who suggested this work.

LXV.

To speak of love is to make love.

LXVI.

In a lover the coarsest desire always shows itself as a burst of honest admiration.

LXVII.

A lover has all the good points and all the bad points which are lacking in a husband.

LXVIII.

A lover not only gives life to everything, he makes one forget life; the husband does not give life to anything.

LXIX.

All the affected airs of sensibility which a woman puts on invariably deceive a lover; and on occasions when a husband shrugs his shoulders, a lover is in ecstasies.

LXX.

A lover betrays by his manner alone the degree of intimacy in which he stands to a married woman.

LXXI.

A woman does not always know why she is in love. It is rarely that a man falls in love without some selfish purpose. A husband should discover this secret motive of egotism, for it will be to him the lever of Archimedes.

LXXII.

A clever husband never betrays his supposition that his wife has a lover.

LXXIII.

The lover submits to all the caprices of a woman; and as a man is never vile while he lies in the arms of his mistress, he will take the means to please her that a husband would recoil from.

LXXIV.

A lover teaches a wife all that her husband has concealed from her.

LXXV.

All the sensations which a woman yields to her lover, she gives in exchange; they return to her always intensified; they are as rich in what they give as in what they receive. This is the kind of commerce in which almost all husbands end by being bankrupt.

LXXVI.

A lover speaks of nothing to a woman but that which exalts her; while a husband, although he may be a loving one, can never refrain from giving advice which always has the appearance of reprimand.

LXXVII.

A lover always starts from his mistress to himself; with a husband the contrary is the case.

LXXVIII.

A lover always has a desire to appear amiable. There is in this sentiment an element of exaggeration which leads to ridicule; study how to take advantage of this.

LXXIX.

When a crime has been committed the magistrate who investigates the case knows [excepting in the case of a released convict who commits murder in jail] that there are not more than five persons to whom he can attribute the act. He starts from this premise a series of conjectures. The husband should reason like the judge; there are only three people in society whom he can suspect when seeking the lover of his wife.

LXXX.

A lover is never in the wrong.

LXXXI.

The lover of a married woman says to her: "Madame, you have need of rest. You have to give an example of virtue to your children. You have sworn to make your husband happy, and although he has some faults—he has fewer than I have— he is worthy of your esteem. Nevertheless you have sacrificed everything for me. Do not let a single murmur escape you; for regret is an offence which I think worthy of a severer penalty than the law decrees against infidelity. As a reward for these sacrifices, I will bring you as much pleasure as pain." And the incredible part about it is, that the lover triumphs. The form which his speech takes carries it. He says but one phrase: "I love you." A lover is a herald who proclaims either the merit, the beauty, or the wit of a woman. What does a husband proclaim?

To sum up all, the love which a married woman inspires, or that which she gives back, is the least creditable sentiment in the world; in her it is boundless vanity; in her lover it is selfish egotism. The lover of a married woman contracts so many obligations, that scarcely three men in a century are met with who are capable of discharging them. He ought to dedicate his whole life to his mistress, but he always ends by deserting her; both parties are aware of this, and, from the beginning of social life, the one has always been sublime in self-sacrifice, the other an ingrate. The infatuation of love always rouses the pity of the judges who pass sentence on it. But where do you find such love genuine and constant? What power must a husband possess to struggle successfully against a man who casts over a woman a spell strong enough to make her submit to such misfortunes!

We think, then, as a general rule, a husband, if he knows how to use the means of defence which we have outlined, can lead his wife up to her twenty-seventh year, not without her having chosen a lover, but without her having committed the great crime. Here and there we meet with men endowed with deep marital genius, who can keep their wives, body and soul to themselves alone up to their thirtieth or thirty-fifth year; but these exceptions cause a sort of scandal and alarm. The phenomenon scarcely ever is met with excepting in the country, where life is transparent and people live in glass houses and the husband wields immense power. The miraculous assistance which men and things thus give to a husband always vanishes in the midst of a city whose population reaches to two hundred and fifty thousand.

It would therefore almost appear to be demonstrated that thirty is the age of virtue. At that critical period, a woman becomes so difficult to guard, that in order successfully to enchain her within the conjugal Paradise, resort must be had to those last means of defence which remain to be described, and which we will reveal in the *Essay on Police*, the *Art of Returning Home*, and *Catastrophes*.

MEDITATION XX.

ESSAY ON POLICE.

The police of marriage consist of all those means which are given you by law, manners, force, and stratagem for preventing your wife in her attempt to accomplish those three acts which in some sort make up the life of love: writing, seeing and speaking.

The police combine in greater or less proportion the means of defence put forth in the preceding Meditations. Instinct alone can teach in what proportions and on what occasions these compounded elements are to be employed. The whole system is elastic; a clever husband will easily discern how it must be bent, stretched or retrenched. By the aid of the police a man can guide his wife to her fortieth year pure from any fault.

We will divide this treatise on Police into five captions:

1. OF MOUSE-TRAPS.

2. OF CORRESPONDENCE.

3. OF SPIES.

4. THE INDEX.

5.OF THE BUDGET.

1. OF MOUSE-TRAPS.

In spite of the grave crisis which the husband has reached, we do not suppose that the lover has completely acquired the freedom of the city in the marital establishment. Many husbands often suspect that their wives have a lover, and yet they do not know upon which of the five or six chosen ones of whom we have spoken their suspicions ought to fall. This hesitation doubtless springs from some moral infirmity, to whose assistance the professor must come.

Fouche had in Paris three or four houses resorted to by people of the highest distinction; the mistresses of these dwellings were devoted to him. This devotion cost a great deal of money to the state. The minister used to call these gatherings, of which nobody at the time had any suspicion, his *mouse-traps*. More than one arrest was made at the end of the ball at which the most brilliant people of Paris had been made accomplices of this oratorian.

The act of offering some fragments of roasted nuts, in order to see your wife put her white hand in the trap, is certainly exceedingly delicate, for a woman is certain to be on her guard; nevertheless, we reckon upon at least three kinds of mouse-traps: *The Irresistible, The Fallacious,* and that which is *Touch and Go.*

The Irresistible.

Suppose two husbands, we will call them A and B, wish to discover who are the lovers of their wives. We will put the husband A at the centre of a table loaded with the finest pyramids of fruit, of crystals, of candies and of liqueurs, and the husband B shall be at whatever point of this brilliant circle you may please to suppose. The champagne has gone round, every eye is sparkling and every tongue is wagging.

HUSBAND A. (peeling a chestnut)—Well, as for me, I admire literary people, but from a distance. I find them intolerable; in conversation they are despotic; I do not know what displeases me more, their faults or their good qualities. In short (he swallows his chestnut), people of genius are like tonics—you like, but you must use them temperately.

WIFE B. (who has listened attentively)—But, M. A., you are very exacting (with an arch smile); it seems to me that dull people have as many faults as people of talent, with this difference perhaps, that the former have nothing to atone for them!

HUSBAND A. (irritably)—You will agree at least, madame, that they are not very amiable to you.

WIFE B. (with vivacity)—Who told you so?

HUSBAND A. (smiling)—Don't they overwhelm you all the time with their superiority? Vanity so dominates their souls that between you and them the effort is reciprocal—

THE MISTRESS OF THE HOUSE. (aside to Wife A)—You well deserved it, my dear. (Wife A shrugs her shoulders.)

HUSBAND A. (still continuing)—Then the habit they have of combining ideas which reveal to them the mechanism of feeling! For them love is purely physical and every one knows that they do not shine.

WIFE B. (biting her lips, interrupting him)—It seems to me, sir, that we are the sole judges in this matter. I can well understand why men of the world do not like men of letters! But it is easier to criticise than to imitate them.

HUSBAND A. (disdainfully)—Oh, madame, men of the world can assail the authors of the present time without being accused of envy. There is many a gentleman of the drawing-room, who if he undertook to write—

WIFE B. (with warmth)—Unfortunately for you, sir, certain friends of yours in the Chamber have written romances; have you been able to read them?—But really, in these days, in order to attain the least originality, you must undertake historic research, you must—

HUSBAND B. (making no answer to the lady next him and speaking aside) —Oh! Oh! Can it be that it is M. de L———, author of the *Dreams of a Young Girl,* whom my wife is in love with?—That is singular; I thought that it was Doctor M— —-. But stay! (Aloud.) Do you know, my dear, that you are right in what you say? (All laugh.) Really, I should prefer to have always artists and men of letters in my drawing-room—(aside) when we begin to receive!—rather than to see there other professional men. In any case artists speak of things about which every one is enthusiastic, for who is there who does not believe in good taste? But judges, lawyers, and, above all, doctors—Heavens! I confess that to hear them constantly speaking about lawsuits and diseases, those two human ills—

WIFE A. (sitting next to Husband B, speaking at the same time)—What is that you are saying, my friend? You are quite mistaken. In these days nobody wishes to wear a professional manner; doctors, since you have mentioned doctors, try to avoid speaking of professional matters. They talk politics, discuss the fashions and the theatres, they tell anecdotes, they write books better than professional authors do; there is a vast difference between the doctors of to-day and those of Moliere—

HUSBAND A. (aside)—Whew! Is it possible my wife is in love with Dr. M— —- ? That would be odd. (Aloud.) That is quite possible, my dear, but I would not give a sick dog in charge of a physician who writes.

WIFE A. (interrupting her husband)—I know people who have five or six offices, yet the government has the greatest confidence in them; anyway, it is odd that you should speak in this way, you who were one of Dr. M— —-'s great cases—

HUSBAND A. (aside)—There can be no doubt of it!

The Fallacious.

A HUSBAND. (as he reaches home)—My dear, we are invited by Madame de Fischtaminel to a concert which she is giving next Tuesday. I reckoned on going there, as I wanted to speak with a young cousin of the minister who was among the singers; but he is gone to Frouville to see his aunt. What do you propose doing?

HIS WIFE.—These concerts tire me to death!—You have to sit nailed to your chair whole hours without saying a word.—Besides, you know quite well that we dine with my mother on that day, and it is impossible to miss paying her a visit.

HER HUSBAND. (carelessly)—Ah! that is true.

(Three days afterwards.)

THE HUSBAND. (as he goes to bed)—What do you think, my darling? To-morrow I will leave you at your mother's, for the count has returned from Frouville and will be at Madame de Fischtaminel's concert.

HIS WIFE. (vivaciously)—But why should you go alone? You know how I adore music!

The Touch and Go Mouse-Trap.

THE WIFE.—Why did you go away so early this evening?

THE HUSBAND. (mysteriously)—Ah! It is a sad business, and all the more so because I don't know how I can settle it.

THE WIFE.—What is it all about, Adolph? You are a wretch if you do not tell me what you are going to do!

THE HUSBAND.—My dear, that ass of a Prosper Magnan is fighting a duel with M. de Fontanges, on account of an Opera singer.—But what is the matter with you?

THE WIFE.—Nothing.—It is very warm in this room and I don't know what ails me, for the whole day I have been suffering from sudden flushing of the face.

THE HUSBAND. (aside)—She is in love with M. de Fontanges. (Aloud.) Celestine! (He shouts out still louder.) Celestine! Come quick, madame is ill!

You will understand that a clever husband will discover a thousand ways of setting these three kinds of traps.

2. OF CORRESPONDENCE.

To write a letter, and to have it posted; to get an answer, to read it and burn it; there we have correspondence stated in the simplest terms.

Yet consider what immense resources are given by civilization, by our manners and by our love to the women who wish to conceal these material actions from the scrutiny of a husband.

The inexorable box which keeps its mouth open to all comers receives its epistolary provender from all hands.

There is also the fatal invention of the General Delivery. A lover finds in the world a hundred charitable persons, male and female, who, for a slight consideration, will slip the billets-doux into the amorous and intelligent hand of his fair mistress.

A correspondence is a variable as Proteus. There are sympathetic inks. A young celibate has told us in confidence that he has written a letter on the fly-leaf of a new book, which, when the husband asked for it of the bookseller, reached the hands of his mistress, who had been prepared the evening before for this charming article.

A woman in love, who fears her husband's jealousy, will write and read billets-doux during the time consecrated to those mysterious occupations during which the most tyrannical husband must leave her alone.

Moreover, all lovers have the art of arranging a special code of signals, whose arbitrary import it is difficult to understand. At a ball, a flower placed in some odd way in the hair; at the theatre, a pocket handkerchief unfolded on the front of the box; rubbing the nose, wearing a belt of a particular color, putting the hat on one side, wearing one dress oftener than another, singing a certain song in a concert or touching certain notes on the piano; fixing the eyes on a point agreed; everything, in fact, from the hurdy-gurdy which passes your windows and goes away if you open the shutter, to the newspaper announcement of a horse for sale—all may be reckoned as correspondence.

How many times, in short, will a wife craftily ask her husband to do such and such commission for her, to go to such and such a shop or house, having previously informed her lover that your presence at such or such a place means yes or no?

On this point the professor acknowledges with shame that there is no possible means of preventing correspondence between lovers. But a little machiavelism on the part of the husband will be much more likely to remedy the difficulty than any coercive measures.

An agreement, which should be kept sacred between married people, is their solemn oath that they will respect each other's sealed letters. Clever is the husband who makes this pledge on his wedding-day and is able to keep it conscientiously.

In giving your wife unrestrained liberty to write and to receive letters, you will be enabled to discern the moment she begins to correspond with a lover.

But suppose your wife distrusts you and covers with impenetrable clouds the means she takes to conceal from you her correspondence. Is it not then time to display that intellectual power with which we armed you in our Meditation entitled *Of the Custom House*? The man who does not see when his wife writes to her lover, and when she receives an answer, is a failure as a husband.

The proposed study which you ought to bestow upon the movements, the actions, the gestures, the looks of your wife, will be perhaps troublesome and wearying, but it will not last long; the only point is to discover when your wife and her lover correspond and in what way.

We cannot believe that a husband, even of moderate intelligence, will fail to see through this feminine manoeuvre, when once he suspects its existence.

Meanwhile, you can judge from a single incident what means of police and of restraint remain to you in the event of such a correspondence.

A young lawyer, whose ardent passion exemplified certain of the principles dwelt upon in this important part of our work, had married a young person whose love for him was but slight; yet this circumstance he looked upon as an exceedingly happy one; but at the end of his first year of marriage he perceived that his dear Anna [for Anna was her name] had fallen in love with the head clerk of a stock-broker.

Adolph was a young man of about twenty-five, handsome in face and as fond of amusement as any other celibate. He was frugal, discreet, possessed of an excellent heart, rode well, talked well, had fine black hair always curled, and dressed with taste. In short, he would have done honor and credit to a duchess. The advocate was ugly, short, stumpy, square-shouldered, mean-looking, and, moreover, a husband. Anna, tall and pretty, had almond eyes, white skin and refined features. She was all love; and passion lighted up her glance with a bewitching expression. While her family was poor, Maitre Lebrun had an income of twelve thousand francs. That explains all.

One evening Lebrun got home looking extremely chop-fallen. He went into his study to work; but he soon came back shivering to his wife, for he had caught a fever and hurriedly went to bed. There he lay groaning and lamenting for his clients and especially for a poor widow whose fortune he was to save the very next day by effecting a compromise. An appointment had been made with certain business men and he was quite incapable of keeping it. After having slept for a quarter of an hour, he begged his wife in a feeble voice to write to one of his intimate friends, asking him to take his (Lebrun's) place next day at the conference. He dictated a long letter and followed with his eye the space taken up on the paper by his phrases. When he came to begin the second page of the last sheet, the advocate set out to describe to his confrere the joy which his client would feel on the signing of the compromise, and the fatal page began with these words:

"My good friend, go for Heaven's sake to Madame Vernon's at once; you are expected with impatience there; she lives at No. 7 Rue de Sentier. Pardon my brevity; but I count on your admirable good sense to guess what I am unable to explain.

"Tout a vous,"

"Give me the letter," said the lawyer, "that I may see whether it is correct before signing it."

The unfortunate wife, who had been taken off her guard by this letter, which bristled with the most barbarous terms of legal science, gave up the letter. As soon as Lebrun got possession of the wily script he began to complain, to twist himself about, as if in pain, and to demand one little attention after another of his wife. Madame left the room for two minutes during which the advocate leaped from his bed, folded a piece of paper in the form of a letter and hid the missive written by his wife. When Anna returned, the clever husband seized the blank paper, made her address it to the friend of his, to whom the letter which he had taken out was written, and the poor creature handed the blank letter to his servant. Lebrun seemed to grow gradually calmer; he slept or pretended to do so, and the next morning he still affected to feel strange pains. Two days afterwards he tore off the first leaf of the letter and put an "e" to the word *tout* in the phrase "tout a vous."[2] He folded mysteriously the paper which contained the innocent forgery, sealed it, left his bedroom and called the maid, saying to her:

"Madame begs that you will take this to the house of M. Adolph; now, be quick about it."

He saw the chambermaid leave the house and soon afterwards he, on a plea of business, went out, hurried to Rue de Sentier, to the address indicated, and awaited the arrival of his rival at the house of a friend who was in the secret of his stratagem. The lover, intoxicated with happiness, rushed to the place and inquired for Madame de Vernon; he was admitted and found himself face to face with Maitre Lebrun, who showed a countenance pale but chill, and gazed at him with tranquil but implacable glance.

"Sir," he said in a tone of emotion to the young clerk, whose heart palpitated with terror, "you are in love with my wife, and you are trying to please her; I scarcely know how to treat you in return for this, because in your place and at your age I should have done exactly the same. But Anna is in despair; you have

[2] Thus giving a feminine ending to the signature, and lending the impression that the note emanated from the wife personally—J.W.M.

disturbed her happiness, and her heart is filled with the torments of hell. More-over, she has told me all, a quarrel soon followed by a reconciliation forced her to write the letter which you have received, and she has sent me here in her place. I will not tell you, sir, that by persisting in your plan of seduction you will cause the misery of her you love, that you will forfeit her my esteem, and eventually your own; that your crime will be stamped on the future by causing perhaps sorrow to my children. I will not even speak to you of the bitterness you will infuse into my life;—unfortunately these are commonplaces! But I declare to you, sir, that the first step you take in this direction will be the signal for a crime; for I will not trust the risk of a duel in order to stab you to the heart!"

And the eyes of the lawyer flashed ominously.

"Now, sir," he went on in a gentler voice, "you are young, you have a gener-ous heart. Make a sacrifice for the future happiness of her you love; leave her and never see her again. And if you must needs be a member of my family, I have a young aunt who is yet unsettled in life; she is charming, clever and rich. Make her acquaintance, and leave a virtuous woman undisturbed."

This mixture of raillery and intimidation, together with the unwavering glance and deep voice of the husband, produced a remarkable impression on the lover. He remained for a moment utterly confused, like people overcome with passion and deprived of all presence of mind by a sudden shock. If Anna has since then had any lovers [which is a pure hypothesis] Adolph certainly is not one of them.

This occurrence may help you to understand that correspondence is a dou-ble-edged weapon which is of as much advantage for the defence of the husband as for the inconsistency of the wife. You should therefore encourage correspon-dence for the same reason that the prefect of police takes special care that the street lamps of Paris are kept lighted.

3. OF SPIES.

To come so low as to beg servants to reveal secrets to you, and to fall lower still by paying for a revelation, is not a crime; it is perhaps not even a dastardly act, but it is certainly a piece of folly; for nothing will ever guarantee to you the honesty of a servant who betrays her mistress, and you can never feel certain whether she is operating in your interest or in that of your wife. This point therefore may be looked upon as beyond controversy.

Nature, that good and tender parent, has set round about the mother of a fam-ily the most reliable and the most sagacious of spies, the most truthful and at the same time the most discreet in the world. They are silent and yet they speak, they see everything and appear to see nothing.

One day I met a friend of mine on the boulevard. He invited me to dinner, and we went to his house. Dinner had been already served, and the mistress of the house was helping her two daughters to plates of soup.

"I see here my first symptoms," I said to myself.

We sat down. The first word of the husband, who spoke without thinking, and for the sake of talking, was the question:

"Has any one been here to-day?"

"Not a soul," replied his wife, without lifting her eyes.

I shall never forget the quickness with which the two daughters looked up to their mother. The elder girl, aged eight, had something especially peculiar in her glance. There was at the same time revelation and mystery, curiosity and silence, astonishment and apathy in that look. If there was anything that could be compared to the speed with which the light of candor flashed from their eyes, it was the prudent reserve with which both of them closed down, like shutters, the folds of their white eyelids.

Ye sweet and charming creatures, who from the age of nine even to the age of marriage too often are the torment of a mother even when she is not a coquette, is it by the privilege of your years or the instinct of your nature that your young ears catch the faint sound of a man's voice through walls and doors, that your eyes are awake to everything, and that your young spirit busies itself in divining all, even the meaning of a word spoken in the air, even the meaning of your mother's slightest gesture?

There is something of gratitude, something in fact instinctive, in the predilection of fathers for their daughters and mothers for their sons.

But the act of setting spies which are in some way inanimate is mere dotage, and nothing is easier than to find a better plan than that of the beadle, who took it into his head to put egg-shells in his bed, and who obtained no other sympathy from his confederate than the words, "You are not very successful in breaking them."

The Marshal de Saxe did not give much consolation to his Popeliniere when they discovered in company that famous revolving chimney, invented by the Duc de Richelieu.

"That is the finest piece of horn work that I have ever seen!" cried the victor of Fontenoy.

Let us hope that your espionage will not give you so troublesome a lesson. Such misfortunes are the fruits of the civil war and we do not live in that age.

4. THE INDEX.

The Pope puts books only on the Index; you will mark with a stigma of reprobation men and things.

It is forbidden to madame to go into a bath except in her own house.

It is forbidden to madame to receive into her house him whom you suspect of being her lover, and all those who are the accomplices of their love.

It is forbidden to madame to take a walk without you.

But the peculiarities which in each household originate from the diversity of characters, the numberless incidents of passion, and the habits of the married people give to this black book so many variations, the lines in it are multiplied or erased with such rapidity that a friend of the author has called this Index *The History of Changes in the Marital Church.*

There are only two things which can be controlled or prescribed in accordance with definite rules; the first is the country, the second is the promenade.

A husband ought never to take his wife to the country nor permit her to go there. Have a country home if you like, live there, entertain there nobody excepting ladies or old men, but never leave your wife alone there. But to take her, for even half a day, to the house of another man is to show yourself as stupid as an ostrich.

To keep guard over a wife in the country is a task most difficult of accomplishment. Do you think that you will be able to be in the thickets, to climb the trees, to follow the tracks of a lover over the grass trodden down at night, but straightened by the dew in the morning and refreshed by the rays of the sun? Can you keep your eye on every opening in the fence of the park? Oh! the country and the Spring! These are the two right arms of the celibate.

When a woman reaches the crisis at which we suppose her to be, a husband ought to remain in town till the declaration of war, or to resolve on devoting himself to all the delights of a cruel espionage.

With regard to the promenade: Does madame wish to go to parties, to the theatre, to the Bois de Boulogne, to purchase her dresses, to find out what is the fashion? Madame shall go, shall see everything in the respectable company of her lord and master.

If she take advantage of the moment when a business appointment, which you cannot fail to keep, detains you, in order to obtain your tacit permission to some meditated expedition; if in order to obtain that permission she displays all the witcheries of those cajoleries in which women excel and whose powerful influence you ought already to have known, well, well, the professor implores you to allow her to win you over, while at the same time you sell dear the boon she asks; and above all convince this creature, whose soul is at once as changeable as water and as firm as steel, that it is impossible for you from the importance of your work to leave your study.

But as soon as your wife has set foot upon the street, if she goes on foot, don't give her time to make fifty steps; follow and track her in such a way that you will not be noticed.

It is possible that there exist certain Werthers whose refined and delicate souls recoil from this inquisition. But this is not more blamable than that of a landed proprietor who rises at night and looks through the windows for the purpose of keeping watch over the peaches on his *espaliers.* You will probably by this course of action obtain, before the crime is committed, exact information with regard to the apartments which so many lovers rent in the city under fictitious names. If it happens [which God forbid!] that your wife enters a house suspected by you, try to find out if the place has several exits.

Should your wife take a hack, what have you to fear? Is there not a prefect of police, to whom all husbands ought to decree a crown of solid gold, and has he not set up a little shed or bench where there is a register, an incorruptible guardian of public morality? And does he not know all the comings and goings of these Parisian gondolas?

One of the vital principles of our police will consist in always following your wife to the furnishers of your house, if she is accustomed to visit them. You will carefully find out whether there is any intimacy between her and her draper, her dressmaker or her milliner, etc. In this case you will apply the rules of the conjugal Custom House, and draw your own conclusions.

If in your absence your wife, having gone out against your will, tells you that she had been to such a place, to such a shop, go there yourself the next day and try to find out whether she has spoken the truth.

But passion will dictate to you, even better than the Meditation, the various resources of conjugal tyranny, and we will here cut short these tiresome instructions.

5. OF THE BUDGET.

In outlining the portrait of a sane and sound husband (See *Meditation on the Predestined*), we urgently advise that he should conceal from his wife the real amount of his income.

In relying upon this as the foundation stone of our financial system we hope to do something towards discounting the opinion, so very generally held, that a man ought not to give the handling of his income to his wife. This principle is one of the many popular errors and is one of the chief causes of misunderstanding in the domestic establishment.

But let us, in the first place, deal with the question of heart, before we proceed to that of money.

To draw up a little civil list for your wife and for the requirements of the house and to pay her money as if it were a contribution, in twelve equal portions month by month, has something in it that is a little mean and close, and cannot be agreeable to any but sordid and mistrustful souls. By acting in this way you prepare for yourself innumerable annoyances.

I could wish that during the first year of your mellifluous union, scenes more or less delightful, pleasantries uttered in good taste, pretty purses and caresses might accompany and might decorate the handing over of this monthly gift; but the time will come when the self-will of your wife or some unforeseen expenditure will compel her to ask a loan of the Chamber; I presume that you will always grant her the bill of indemnity, as our unfaithful deputies never fail to do. They pay, but they grumble; you must pay and at the same time compliment her. I hope it will be so.

But in the crisis which we have reached, the provisions of the annual budget can never prove sufficient. There must be an increase of fichus, of bonnets, of frocks; there is an expense which cannot be calculated beforehand demanded by the meetings, by the diplomatic messengers, by the ways and means of love, even while the receipts remain the same as usual. Then must commence in your establishment a course of education the most odious, and the most dreadful which a woman can undergo. I know but few noble and generous souls who value, more than millions, purity of heart, frankness of soul, and who would a thousand times more readily pardon a passion than a lie, whose instinctive delicacy has divined the existence of this plague of the soul, the lowest step in human degradation.

Under these circumstances there occur in the domestic establishment the most delightful scenes of love. It is then that a woman becomes utterly pliant and like to the most brilliant of all the strings of a harp, when thrown before the fire; she rolls round you, she clasps you, she holds you tight; she defers to all your caprices; never was her conversation so full of tenderness; she lavishes her endearments upon you, or rather she sells them to you; she at last becomes lower than a chorus girl, for she prostitutes herself to her husband. In her sweetest kisses there is money; in all her words there is money. In playing this part her heart becomes like lead towards you. The most polished, the most treacherous usurer never weighs so completely with a single glance the future value in bullion of a son of a family who may sign a note to him, than your wife appraises one of your desires as she leaps from branch to branch like an escaping squirrel, in order to increase the sum of money she may demand by increasing the appetite which she rouses in you. You must not expect to get scot-free from such seductions. Nature has given boundless gifts of coquetry to a woman, the usages of society have increased them tenfold by its fashions, its dresses, its embroideries and its tippets.

"If I ever marry," one of the most honorable generals of our ancient army used to say, "I won't put a sou among the wedding presents—"

"What will you put there then, general?" asked a young girl.

"The key of my safe."

The young girl made a curtsey of approbation. She moved her little head with a quiver like that of the magnetic needle; raised her chin slightly as if she would have said:

"I would gladly marry the general in spite of his forty-five years."

But with regard to money, what interest can you expect your wife to take in a machine in which she is looked upon as a mere bookkeeper?

Now look at the other system.

In surrendering to your wife, with an avowal of absolute confidence in her, two-thirds of your fortune and letting her as mistress control the conjugal administration, you win from her an esteem which nothing can destroy, for confidence and high-mindedness find powerful echoes in the heart of a woman. Madame will be loaded with a responsibility which will often raise a barrier against extravagances, all the stronger because it is she herself who has created it in her heart. You yourself have made a portion of the work, and you may be sure that from henceforth your wife will never perhaps dishonor herself.

Moreover, by seeking in this way a method of defence, consider what admirable aids are offered to you by this plan of finances.

You will have in your house an exact estimate of the morality of your wife, just as the quotations of the Bourse give you a just estimate of the degree of confidence possessed by the government.

And doubtless, during the first years of your married life, your wife will take pride in giving you every luxury and satisfaction which your money can afford.

She will keep a good table, she will renew the furniture, and the carriages; she will always keep in her drawer a sum of money sacred to her well-beloved and ready for his needs. But of course, in the actual circumstances of life, the drawer will be very often empty and monsieur will spend a great deal too much. The economies ordered by the Chamber never weigh heavily upon the clerks whose income is twelve hundred francs; and you will be the clerk at twelve hundred francs in your own house. You will laugh in your sleeve, because you will have saved, capitalized, invested one-third of your income during a long time, like Louis XV, who kept for himself a little separate treasury, "against a rainy day," he used to say.

Thus, if your wife speaks of economy, her discourse will be equal to the varying quotations of the money-market. You will be able to divine the whole progress of the lover by these financial fluctuations, and you will have avoided all difficulties. *E sempre bene.*

If your wife fails to appreciate the excessive confidence, and dissipates in one day a large proportion of your fortune, in the first place it is not probable that this prodigality will amount to one-third of the revenue which you have been saving for ten years; moreover you will learn, from the Meditation on *Catastrophes*, that in the very crisis produced by the follies of your wife, you will have brilliant opportunities of slaying the Minotaur.

But the secret of the treasure which has been amassed by your thoughtfulness need never be known till after your death; and if you have found it necessary to draw upon it, in order to assist your wife, you must always let it be thought that you have won at play, or made a loan from a friend.

These are the true principles which should govern the conjugal budget.

The police of marriage has its martyrology. We will cite but one instance which will make plain how necessary it is for husbands who resort to severe measures to keep watch over themselves as well as over their wives.

An old miser who lived at T——-, a pleasure resort if there ever was one, had married a young and pretty woman, and he was so wrapped up in her and so jealous that love triumphed over avarice; he actually gave up trade in order to guard his wife more closely, but his only real change was that his covetousness took another form. I acknowledge that I owe the greater portion of the observations contained in this essay, which still is doubtless incomplete, to the person who made a study of this remarkable marital phenomenon, to portray which, one single detail will be amply sufficient. When he used to go to the country, this husband never went to bed without secretly raking over the pathways of his park, and he had a special rake for the sand of his terraces. He had made a close study of the foot-prints made by the different members of his household; and early in the morning he used to go and identify the tracks that had been made there.

"All this is old forest land," he used to say to the person I have referred to, as he showed him over the park; "for nothing can be seen through the brushwood."

His wife fell in love with one of the most charming young men of the town. This passion had continued for nine years bright and fresh in the hearts of the two lovers, whose sole avowal had been a look exchanged in a crowded ball-room; and while they danced together their trembling hands revealed through the scented gloves the depth of their love. From that day they had both of them taken great delight on those trifles which happy lovers never disdain. One day the young man led his only confidant, with a mysterious air, into a chamber where he kept under glass globes upon his table, with more care than he would have bestowed upon the finest jewels in the world, the flowers that, in the excitement of the dance, had fallen from the hair of his mistress, and the finery which had been caught in the trees which she had brushed through in the park. He also preserved there the narrow footprint left upon the clay soil by the lady's step.

"I could hear," said this confidant to me afterwards, "the violent and repressed palpitations of his heart sounding in the silence which we preserved before the treasures of this museum of love. I raised my eyes to the ceiling, as if to breathe to heaven the sentiment which I dared not utter. 'Poor humanity!' I thought. 'Madame de — —- told me that one evening at a ball you had been found nearly fainting in her card-room?' I remarked to him.

"'I can well believe it,' said he casting down his flashing glance, 'I had kissed her arm!—But,' he added as he pressed my hand and shot at me a glance that pierced my heart, 'her husband at that time had the gout which threatened to attack his stomach.'"

Some time afterwards, the old man recovered and seemed to take a new lease of life; but in the midst of his convalescence he took to his bed one morning and died suddenly. There were such evident symptoms of poisoning in the condition of the dead man that the officers of justice were appealed to, and the two lovers were arrested. Then was enacted at the court of assizes the most heartrending scene that ever stirred the emotions of the jury. At the preliminary examination, each of the two lovers without hesitation confessed to the crime, and with one thought each of them was solely bent on saving, the one her lover, the other his mistress. There were two found guilty, where justice was looking for but a single culprit. The trial was entirely taken up with the flat contradictions which each of them, carried away by the fury of devoted love, gave to the admissions of the other. There they were united for the first time, but on the criminals' bench with a gendarme seated between them. They were found guilty by the unanimous verdict of a weeping jury. No one among those who had the barbarous courage to witness their conveyance to the scaffold can mention them to-day without a shudder. Religion had won for them a repentance for their crime, but could not induce them to abjure their love. The scaffold was their nuptial bed, and there they slept together in the long night of death.

MEDITATION XXI.

THE ART OF RETURNING HOME.

Finding himself incapable of controlling the boiling transports of his anxiety, many a husband makes the mistake of coming home and rushing into the presence of his wife, with the object of triumphing over her weakness, like those bulls of Spain, which, stung by the red *banderillo*, disembowel with furious horns horses, matadors, picadors, toreadors and their attendants.

But oh! to enter with a tender gentle mien, like Mascarillo, who expects a beating and becomes merry as a lark when he finds his master in a good humor! Well—that is the mark of a wise man!—

"Yes, my darling, I know that in my absence you could have behaved badly! Another in your place would have turned the house topsy-turvy, but you have only broken a pane of glass! God bless you for your considerateness. Go on in the same way and you will earn my eternal gratitude."

Such are the ideas which ought to be expressed by your face and bearing, but perhaps all the while you say to yourself:

"Probably he has been here!"

Always to bring home a pleasant face, is a rule which admits of no exception.

But the art of never leaving your house without returning when the police have revealed to you a conspiracy—to know how to return at the right time—this is the lesson which is hard to learn. In this matter everything depends upon tact and penetration. The actual events of life always transcend anything that is imaginable.

The manner of coming home is to be regulated in accordance with a number of circumstances. For example:

Lord Catesby was a man of remarkable strength. It happened one day that he was returning from a fox hunt, to which he had doubtless promised to go, with some ulterior view, for he rode towards the fence of his park at a point where, he said, he saw an extremely fine horse. As he had a passion for horses, he drew near to examine this one close at hand, There he caught sight of Lady Catesby, to whose rescue it was certainly time to go, if he were in the slightest degree jealous for his own honor. He rushed upon the gentleman he saw there, and seizing him by the belt he hurled him over the fence on to the road side.

"Remember, sir," he said calmly, "it rests with me to decide whether it well be necessary to address you hereafter and ask for satisfaction on this spot."

"Very well, my lord; but would you have the goodness to throw over my horse also?"

But the phlegmatic nobleman had already taken the arm of his wife as he gravely said:

"I blame you very much, my dear creature, for not having told me that I was to love you for two. Hereafter every other day I shall love you for the gentleman yonder, and all other days for myself."

This adventure is regarded in England as one of the best returns home that were ever known. It is true it consisted in uniting, with singular felicity, eloquence of deed to that of word.

But the art of re-entering your home, principles of which are nothing else but natural deductions from the system of politeness and dissimulation which have been commended in preceding Meditations, is after all merely to be studied in preparation for the conjugal catastrophes which we will now consider.

MEDITATION XXII.

OF CATASTROPHES.

The word *Catastrophe* is a term of literature which signifies the final climax of a play.

To bring about a catastrophe in the drama which you are playing is a method of defence which is as easy to undertake as it is certain to succeed. In advising to employ it, we would not conceal from you its perils.

The conjugal catastrophe may be compared to one of those high fevers which either carry off a predisposed subject or completely restore his health. Thus, when the catastrophe succeeds, it keeps a woman for years in the prudent realms of virtue.

Moreover, this method is the last of all those which science has been able to discover up to this present moment.

The massacre of St. Bartholomew, the Sicilian Vespers, the death of Lucretia, the two embarkations of Napoleon at Frejus are examples of political catastrophe. It will not be in your power to act on such a large scale; nevertheless, within their own area, your dramatic climaxes in conjugal life will not be less effective than these.

But since the art of creating a situation and of transforming it, by the introduction of natural incidents, constitutes genius; since the return to virtue of a woman, whose foot has already left some tracks upon the sweet and gilded sand which mark the pathway of vice, is the most difficult to bring about of all denouements, and since genius neither knows it nor teaches it, the practitioner in conjugal laws feels compelled to confess at the outset that he is incapable of reducing to definite principles a science which is as changeable as circumstances, as delusive as opportunity, and as indefinable as instinct.

If we may use an expression which neither Diderot, d'Alembert nor Voltaire, in spite of every effort, have been able to engraft on our language, a conjugal catastrophe *se subodore* is scented from afar; so that our only course will be to sketch out imperfectly certain conjugal situations of an analogous kind, thus imitating the philosopher of ancient time who, seeking in vain to explain motion, walked forward in his attempt to comprehend laws which were incomprehensible.

A husband, in accordance with the principles comprised in our Meditation on *Police*, will expressly forbid his wife to receive the visits of a celibate whom he suspects of being her lover, and whom she has promised never again to see. Some minor scenes of the domestic interior we leave for matrimonial imaginations to conjure up; a husband can delineate them much better than we can; he will betake himself in thought back to those days when delightful longings invited sincere confidences and when the workings of his policy put into motion certain adroitly handled machinery.

Let us suppose, in order to make more interesting the natural scene to which I refer, that you who read are a husband, whose carefully organized police has made the discovery that your wife, profiting by the hours devoted by you to a ministerial banquet, to which she probably procured you an invitation, received at your house M. A— —z.

Here we find all the conditions necessary to bring about the finest possible of conjugal catastrophes.

You return home just in time to find your arrival has coincided with that of M. A— —z, for we would not advise you to have the interval between acts too long. But in what mood should you enter? Certainly not in accordance with the rules of the previous Meditation. In a rage then? Still less should you do that. You should come in with good-natured carelessness, like an absent-minded man who has forgotten his purse, the statement which he has drawn up for the minister, his pocket-handkerchief or his snuff-box.

In that case you will either catch two lovers together, or your wife, forewarned by the maid, will have hidden the celibate.

Now let us consider these two unique situations.

But first of all we will observe that husbands ought always to be in a position to strike terror in their homes and ought long before to make preparations for the matrimonial second of September.

Thus a husband, from the moment that his wife has caused him to perceive certain *first symptoms*, should never fail to give, time after time, his personal opinion on the course of conduct to be pursued by a husband in a great matrimonial crisis.

"As for me," you should say, "I should have no hesitation in killing the man I caught at my wife's feet."

With regard to the discussion that you will thus give rise to, you will be led on to aver that the law ought to have given to the husband, as it did in ancient Rome, the right of life and death over his children, so that he could slay those who were spurious.

These ferocious opinions, which really do not bind you to anything, will impress your wife with salutary terror; you will enumerate them lightly, even laughingly—and say to her, "Certainly, my dear, I would kill you right gladly. Would you like to be murdered by me?"

A woman cannot help fearing that this pleasantry may some day become a very serious matter, for in these crimes of impulse there is a certain proof of love; and then women who know better than any one else how to say true things laughingly at times suspect their husbands of this feminine trick.

When a husband surprises his wife engaged in even innocent conversation with her lover, his face still calm, should produce the effect mythologically attributed to the celebrated Gorgon.

In order to produce a favorable catastrophe at this juncture, you must act in accordance with the character of your wife, either play a pathetic scene a la Diderot, or resort to irony like Cicero, or rush to your pistols loaded with a blank charge, or even fire them off, if you think that a serious row is indispensable.

A skillful husband may often gain a great advantage from a scene of unexaggerated sentimentality. He enters, he sees the lover and transfixes him with a glance. As soon as the celibate retires, he falls at the feet of his wife, he declaims a long speech, in which among other phrases there occurs this:

"Why, my dear Caroline, I have never been able to love you as I should!"

He weeps, and she weeps, and this tearful catastrophe leaves nothing to be desired.

We would explain, apropos of the second method by which the catastrophe may be brought about, what should be the motives which lead a husband to vary this scene, in accordance with the greater or less degree of strength which his wife's character possesses.

Let us pursue this subject.

If by good luck it happens that your wife has put her lover in a place of concealment, the catastrophe will be very much more successful.

Even if the apartment is not arranged according to the principles prescribed in the Meditation, you will easily discern the place into which the celibate has vanished, although he be not, like Lord Byron's Don Juan, bundled up under the cushion of a divan. If by chance your apartment is in disorder, you ought to have sufficient discernment to know that there is only one place in which a man could bestow himself. Finally, if by some devilish inspiration he has made himself so small that he has squeezed into some unimaginable lurking-place (for we may expect anything from a celibate), well, either your wife cannot help casting a glance towards this mysterious spot, or she will pretend to look in an exactly opposite direction, and then nothing is easier for a husband than to set a mouse-trap for his wife.

The hiding-place being discovered, you must walk straight up to the lover. You must meet him face to face!

And now you must endeavor to produce a fine effect. With your face turned three-quarters towards him, you must raise your head with an air of superiority. This attitude will enhance immensely the effect which you aim at producing.

The most essential thing to do at this moment, is to overwhelm the celibate by some crushing phrase which you have been manufacturing all the time; when you have thus floored him, you will coldly show him the door. You will be very polite, but as relentless as the executioner's axe, and as impassive as the law. This freezing contempt will already probably have produced a revolution in the mind of your wife. There must be no shouts, no gesticulations, no excitement. "Men of high social rank," says a young English author, "never behave like their inferiors, who cannot lose a fork without sounding the alarm throughout the whole neighborhood."

When the celibate has gone, you will find yourself alone with your wife, and then is the time when you must subjugate her forever.

You should therefore stand before her, putting on an air whose affected calmness betrays the profoundest emotion; then you must choose from among the following topics, which we have rhetorically amplified, and which are most congenial to your feelings: "Madame," you must say, "I will speak to you neither of your vows, nor of my love; for you have too much sense and I have too much pride to make it possible that I should overwhelm you with those execrations, which all husbands have a right to utter under these circumstances; for the least of the mistakes that I should make, if I did so, is that I would be fully justified. I will not now, even if I could, indulge either in wrath or resentment. It is not I who have been outraged; for I have too much heart to be frightened by that public opinion which almost always treats with ridicule and condemnation a husband whose wife has misbehaved. When I examine my life, I see nothing there that makes this treachery deserved by me, as it is deserved by many others. I still love you. I have never been false, I will not say to my duty, for I have found nothing onerous in adoring you, but not even to those welcome obligations which sincere feeling imposes upon us both. You have had all my confidence and you have also had the administration of my fortune. I have refused you nothing. And now this is the first time that I have turned to you a face, I will not say stern, but which is yet reproachful. But let us drop this subject, for it is of no use for me to defend myself at a moment when you have proved to me with such energy that there is something lacking in me, and that I am not intended by nature to accomplish the difficult task of rendering you happy. But I would ask you, as a friend speaking to a friend, how could you have the heart to imperil at the same time the lives of three human creatures: that of the mother of my children, who will always be sacred to me; that of the head of the family; and finally of him—who loves—[she perhaps at these words will throw herself at your feet; you must not permit her to do so; she is unworthy of kneeling there]. For you no longer love me, Eliza. Well, my poor child [you must not call her *my poor child* excepting when the crime has not been committed]—why deceive ourselves? Why do you not answer me? If love is extinguished between a married couple, cannot friendship and confidence still survive? Are we not two companions united in making the same journey? Can it be said that during the journey the one must never hold out his hand to the other to raise up a comrade or to prevent a comrade's fall? But I have perhaps said too much and I am wounding your pride—Eliza! Eliza!"

Now what the deuce would you expect a woman to answer? Why a catastrophe naturally follows, without a single word.

In a hundred women there may be found at least a good half dozen of feeble creatures who under this violent shock return to their husbands never perhaps again to leave them, like scorched cats that dread the fire. But this scene is a veritable alexipharmaca, the doses of which should be measured out by prudent hands.

For certain women of delicate nerves, whose souls are soft and timid, it would be sufficient to point out the lurking-place where the lover lies, and say: "M. A——z is there!" [at this point shrug your shoulders]. "How can you thus run the risk of causing the death of two worthy people? I am going out; let him escape and do not let this happen again."

But there are women whose hearts, too violently strained in these terrible catastrophes, fail them and they die; others whose blood undergoes a change, and they fall a prey to serious maladies; others actually go out of their minds. These are examples of women who take poison or die suddenly—and we do not suppose that you wish the death of the sinner.

Nevertheless, the most beautiful and impressionable of all the queens of France, the charming and unfortunate Mary Stuart, after having seen Rizzio murdered almost in her arms, fell in love, nevertheless, with the Earl of Bothwell; but she was a queen and queens are abnormal in disposition.

We will suppose, then, that the woman whose portrait adorns our first Meditation is a little Mary Stuart, and we will hasten to raise the curtain for the fifth act in this grand drama entitled *Marriage*.

A conjugal catastrophe may burst out anywhere, and a thousand incidents which we cannot describe may give it birth. Sometimes it is a handkerchief, as in *Othello*; or a pair of slippers, as in *Don Juan*; sometimes it is the mistake of your wife, who cries out—"Dear Alphonse!" instead of "Dear Adolph!" Sometimes a husband, finding out that his wife is in debt, will go and call on her chief creditor, and will take her some morning to his house, as if by chance, in order to bring about a catastrophe. "Monsieur Josse, you are a jeweler and you sell your jewels with a readiness which is not equaled by the readiness of your debtors to pay for them. The countess owes you thirty thousand francs. If you wish to be paid to-morrow [tradesmen should always be visited at the end of the month] come to her at noon; her husband will be in the chamber. Do not attend to any sign which she may make to impose silence upon you—speak out boldly. I will pay all."

So that the catastrophe in the science of marriage is what figures are in arithmetic.

All the principles of higher conjugal philosophy, on which are based the means of defence outlined in this second part of our book, are derived from the nature of human sentiments, and we have found them in different places in the great book of the world. Just as persons of intellect instinctively apply the laws of taste whose principles they would find difficulty in formulating, so we have seen numberless people of deep feeling employing with singular felicity the precepts which we are about to unfold, yet none of them consciously acted on a definite system. The sentiments which this situation inspired only revealed to them incomplete fragments of a vast system; just as the scientific men of the sixteenth century found that their imperfect microscopes did not enable them to see all the living organisms, whose existence had yet been proved to them by the logic of their patient genius.

We hope that the observations already made in this book, and in those which follow, will be of a nature to destroy the opinion which frivolous men maintain, namely that marriage is a sinecure. According to our view, a husband who gives way to ennui is a heretic, and more than that, he is a man who lives quite out of sympathy with the marriage state, of whose importance he has no conception. In this connection, these Meditations perhaps will reveal to very many ignorant men the mysteries of a world before which they stand with open eyes, yet without seeing it.

We hope, moreover, that these principles when well applied will produce many conversions, and that among the pages that separate this second part from that entitled *Civil War* many tears will be shed and many vows of repentance breathed.

Yes, among the four hundred thousand honest women whom we have so carefully sifted out from all the European nations, we indulge the belief that there are a certain number, say three hundred thousand, who will be sufficiently self-willed, charming, adorable, and bellicose to raise the standard of *Civil War*.

To arms then, to arms!

THIRD PART
RELATING TO CIVIL WAR.

"Lovely as the seraphs of Klopstock,
Terrible as the devils of Milton."

—DIDEROT.

MEDITATION XXIII.
OF MANIFESTOES.

The Preliminary precepts, by which science has been enabled at this point to put weapons into the hand of a husband, are few in number; it is not of so much importance to know whether he will be vanquished, as to examine whether he can offer any resistance in the conflict.

Meanwhile, we will set up here certain beacons to light up the arena where a husband is soon to find himself, in alliance with religion and law, engaged single-handed in a contest with his wife, who is supported by her native craft and the whole usages of society as her allies.

LXXXII.

Anything may be expected and anything may be supposed of a woman who is in love.

LXXXIII.

The actions of a woman who intends to deceive her husband are almost always the result of study, but never dictated by reason.

LXXXIV.

The greater number of women advance like the fleas, by erratic leaps and bounds, They owe their escape to the height or depth of their first ideas, and any interruption of their plans rather favors their execution. But they operate only within a narrow area which it is easy for the husband to make still narrower; and if he keeps cool he will end by extinguishing this piece of living saltpetre.

LXXXV.

A husband should never allow himself to address a single disparaging remark to his wife, in presence of a third party.

LXXXVI.

The moment a wife decides to break her marriage vow she reckons her husband as everything or nothing. All defensive operations must start from this proposition.

LXXXVII.

The life of a woman is either of the head, of the heart, or of passion. When a woman reaches the age to form an estimate of life, her husband ought to find out whether the primary cause of her intended infidelity proceeds from vanity, from sentiment or from temperament. Temperament may be remedied like disease; sentiment is something in which the husband may find great opportunities of success; but vanity is incurable. A woman whose life is of the head may be a terrible scourge. She combines the faults of a passionate woman with those of the tender-hearted woman, without having their palliations. She is destitute alike of pity, love, virtue or sex.

LXXXVIII.

A woman whose life is of the head will strive to inspire her husband with indifference; the woman whose life is of the heart, with hatred; the passionate woman, with disgust.

LXXXIX.

A husband never loses anything by appearing to believe in the fidelity of his wife, by preserving an air of patience and by keeping silence. Silence especially troubles a woman amazingly.

XC.

To show himself aware of the passion of his wife is the mark of a fool; but to affect ignorance of all proves that a man has sense, and this is in fact the only attitude to take. We are taught, moreover, that everybody in France is sensible.

XCI.

The rock most to be avoided is ridicule.—"At least, let us be affectionate in public," ought to be the maxim of a married establishment. For both the married couple to lose honor, esteem, consideration, respect and all that is worth living for in society, is to become a nonentity.

These axioms relate to the contest alone. As for the catastrophe, others will be needed for that.

We have called this crisis *Civil War* for two reasons; never was a war more really intestine and at the same time so polite as this war. But in what point and in what manner does this fatal war break out? You do not believe that your wife will call out regiments and sound the trumpet, do you? She will, perhaps, have a commanding officer, but that is all. And this feeble army corps will be sufficient to destroy the peace of your establishment.

"You forbid me to see the people that I like!" is an exordium which has served for a manifesto in most homes. This phrase, with all the ideas that are concomitant, is oftenest employed by vain and artificial women.

The most usual manifesto is that which is proclaimed in the conjugal bed, the principal theatre of war. This subject will be treated in detail in the Meditation entitled: *Of Various Weapons*, in the paragraph, *Of Modesty in its Connection with Marriage*.

Certain women of a lymphatic temperament will pretend to have the spleen and will even feign death, if they can only gain thereby the benefit of a secret divorce.

But most of them owe their independence to the execution of a plan, whose effect upon the majority of husbands is unfailing and whose perfidies we will now reveal.

One of the greatest of human errors springs from the belief that our honor and our reputation are founded upon our actions, or result from the approbation which the general conscience bestows upon on conduct. A man who lives in the world is born to be a slave to public opinion. Now a private man in France has less opportunity of influencing the world than his wife, although he has ample occasion for ridiculing it. Women possess to a marvelous degree the art of giving color by specious arguments to the recriminations in which they indulge. They never set up any defence, excepting when they are in the wrong, and in this proceeding they are pre-eminent, knowing how to oppose arguments by precedents, proofs by assertions, and thus they very often obtain victory in minor matters of detail. They see and know with admirable penetration, when one of them presents to another a weapon which she herself is forbidden to whet. It is thus that they sometimes lose a husband without intending it. They apply the match and long afterwards are terror-stricken at the conflagration.

As a general thing, all women league themselves against a married man who is accused of tyranny; for a secret tie unites them all, as it unites all priests of the same religion. They hate each other, yet shield each other. You can never gain over more than one of them; and yet this act of seduction would be a triumph for your wife.

You are, therefore, outlawed from the feminine kingdom. You see ironical smiles on every lip, you meet an epigram in every answer. These clever creatures force their daggers and amuse themselves by sculpturing the handle before dealing you a graceful blow.

The treacherous art of reservation, the tricks of silence, the malice of suppositions, the pretended good nature of an inquiry, all these arts are employed against you. A man who undertakes to subjugate his wife is an example too dangerous to escape destruction from them, for will not his conduct call up against them the satire of every husband? Moreover, all of them will attack you, either by bitter witticisms, or by serious arguments, or by the hackneyed maxims of gallantry. A swarm of celibates will support all their sallies and you will be assailed and persecuted as an original, a tyrant, a bad bed-fellow, an eccentric man, a man not to be trusted.

Your wife will defend you like the bear in the fable of La Fontaine; she will throw paving stones at your head to drive away the flies that alight on it. She will tell you in the evening all the things that have been said about you, and will ask an explanation of acts which you never committed, and of words which you never said. She professes to have justified you for faults of which you are innocent; she has boasted of a liberty which she does not possess, in order to clear you of the wrong which you have done in denying that liberty. The deafening rattle which your wife shakes will follow you everywhere with its obtrusive din. Your darling will stun you, will torture you, meanwhile arming herself by making you feel only the thorns of married life. She will greet you with a radiant smile in public, and will be sullen at home. She will be dull when you are merry, and will make you detest her merriment when you are moody. Your two faces will present a perpetual contrast.

Very few men have sufficient force of mind not to succumb to this preliminary comedy, which is always cleverly played, and resembles the *hourra* raised by the Cossacks, as they advance to battle. Many husbands become irritated and fall into irreparable mistakes. Others abandon their wives. And, indeed, even those of superior intelligence do not know how to get hold of the enchanted ring, by which to dispel this feminine phantasmagoria.

Two-thirds of such women are enabled to win their independence by this single manoeuvre, which is no more than a review of their forces. In this case the war is soon ended.

But a strong man who courageously keeps cool throughout this first assault will find much amusement in laying bare to his wife, in a light and bantering way, the secret feelings which make her thus behave, in following her step by step through the labyrinth which she treads, and telling her in answer to her every remark, that she is false to herself, while he preserves throughout a tone of pleasantry and never becomes excited.

Meanwhile war is declared, and if her husband has not been dazzled by these first fireworks, a woman has yet many other resources for securing her triumph; and these it is the purpose of the following Meditations to discover.

MEDITATION XXIV.
PRINCIPLES OF STRATEGY.

The Archduke Charles published a very fine treatise on military under the title *Principles of Strategy in Relation to the Campaigns of 1796*. These principles seem somewhat to resemble poetic canons prepared for poems already published. In these days we are become very much more energetic, we invent rules to suit works and works to suit rules. But of what use were ancient principles of military art in presence of the impetuous genius of Napoleon? If, to-day, however, we reduce to a system the lessons taught by this great captain whose new tactics have destroyed the ancient ones, what future guarantee do we possess that another Napoleon will not yet be born? Books on military art meet, with few exceptions, the fate of ancient works on Chemistry and Physics. Everything is subject to change, either constant or periodic.

This, in a few words, is the history of our work.

So long as we have been dealing with a woman who is inert or lapped in slumber, nothing has been easier than to weave the meshes with which we have bound her; but the moment she wakes up and begins to struggle, all is confusion and complication. If a husband would make an effort to recall the principles of the system which we have just described in order to involve his wife in the nets which our second part has set for her, he would resemble Wurmser, Mack and Beaulieu arranging their halts and their marches while Napoleon nimbly turns their flank, and makes use of their own tactics to destroy them.

This is just what your wife will do.

How is it possible to get at the truth when each of you conceals it under the same lie, each setting the same trap for the other? And whose will be the victory when each of you is caught in a similar snare?

"My dear, I have to go out; I have to pay a visit to Madame So and So. I have ordered the carriage. Would you like to come with me? Come, be good, and go with your wife."

You say to yourself:

"She would be nicely caught if I consented! She asks me only to be refused."

Then you reply to her:

"Just at the moment I have some business with Monsieur Blank, for he has to give a report in a business matter which deeply concerns us both, and I must absolutely see him. Then I must go to the Minister of Finance. So your arrangement will suit us both."

"Very well, dearest, go and dress yourself, while Celine finishes dressing me; but don't keep me waiting."

"I am ready now, love," you cry out, at the end of ten minutes, as you stand shaved and dressed.

But all is changed. A letter has arrived; madame is not well; her dress fits badly; the dressmaker has come; if it is not the dressmaker it is your mother. Ninety-nine out of a hundred husbands will leave the house satisfied, believing that their wives are well guarded, when, as a matter of fact, the wives have gotten rid of them.

A lawful wife who from her husband cannot escape, who is not distressed by pecuniary anxiety, and who in order to give employment to a vacant mind, examines night and day the changing tableaux of each day's experience, soon discovers the mistake she has made in falling into a trap or allowing herself to be surprised by a catastrophe; she will then endeavor to turn all these weapons against you.

There is a man in society, the sight of whom is strangely annoying to your wife; she can tolerate neither his tone, his manners nor his way of regarding things. Everything connected with him is revolting to her; she is persecuted by him, he is odious to her; she hopes that no one will tell him this. It seems almost as if she were attempting to oppose you; for this man is one for whom you have the highest esteem. You like his disposition because he flatters you; and thus your wife presumes that your esteem for him results from flattered vanity. When you give a ball, an evening party or a concert, there is almost a discussion on this subject, and madame picks a quarrel with you, because you are compelling her to see people who are not agreeable to her.

"At least, sir, I shall never have to reproach myself with omitting to warn you. That man will yet cause you trouble. You should put some confidence in women when they pass sentence on the character of a man. And permit me to tell you that this baron, for whom you have such a predilection, is a very dangerous person, and you are doing very wrong to bring him to your house. And this is the way you behave; you absolutely force me to see one whom I cannot tolerate, and if I ask you to invite Monsieur A — —-, you refuse to do so, because you think that I like to have him with me! I admit that he talks well, that he is kind and amiable; but you are more to me than he can ever be."

These rude outlines of feminine tactics, which are emphasized by insincere gestures, by looks of feigned ingenuousness, by artful intonations of the voice and even by the snare of cunning silence, are characteristic to some degree of their whole conduct.

There are few husbands who in such circumstances as these do not form the idea of setting a mouse-trap; they welcome as their guests both Monsieur A — —- and the imaginary baron who represents the person whom their wives abhor, and they do so in the hope of discovering a lover in the celibate who is apparently beloved.

Oh yes, I have often met in the world young men who were absolutely star-
lings in love and complete dupes of a friendship which women pretended to show
them, women who felt themselves obliged to make a diversion and to apply a blis-
ter to their husbands as their husbands had previously done to them! These poor
innocents pass their time in running errands, in engaging boxes at the theatre, in
riding in the Bois de Boulogne by the carriages of their pretended mistresses; they
are publicly credited with possessing women whose hands they have not even
kissed. Vanity prevents them from contradicting these flattering rumors, and like
the young priests who celebrate masses without a Host, they enjoy a mere show
passion, and are veritable supernumeraries of love.

Under these circumstances sometimes a husband on returning home asks the
porter: "Has no one been here?"—"M. le Baron came past at two o'clock to see
monsieur; but as he found no one was in but madame he went away; but Monsieur
A——- is with her now."

You reach the drawing-room, you see there a young celibate, sprightly, scent-
ed, wearing a fine necktie, in short a perfect dandy. He is a man who holds you
in high esteem; when he comes to your house your wife listens furtively for his
footsteps; at a ball she always dances with him. If you forbid her to see him, she
makes a great outcry and it is not till many years afterwards [see Meditation on
Las Symptoms] that you see the innocence of Monsieur A——- and the culpability
of the baron.

We have observed and noted as one of the cleverest manoeuvres, that of a
young woman who, carried away by an irresistible passion, exhibited a bitter ha-
tred to the man she did not love, but lavished upon her lover secret intimations of
her love. The moment that her husband was persuaded that she loved the *Cicisbeo*
and hated the *Patito*, she arranged that she and the *Patito* should be found in a
situation whose compromising character she had calculated in advance, and her
husband and the execrated celibate were thus induced to believe that her love and
her aversion were equally insincere. When she had brought her husband into the
condition of perplexity, she managed that a passionate letter should fall into his
hands. One evening in the midst of the admirable catastrophe which she had thus
brought to a climax, madame threw herself at her husband's feet, wet them with
her tears, and thus concluded the climax to her own satisfaction.

"I esteem and honor you profoundly," she cried, "for keeping your own coun-
sel as you have done. I am in love! Is this a sentiment which is easy for me to re-
press? But what I can do is to confess the fact to you; to implore you to protect me
from myself, to save me from my own folly. Be my master and be a stern master to
me; take me away from this place, remove me from what has caused all this trou-
ble, console me; I will forget him, I desire to do so. I do not wish to betray you. I
humbly ask your pardon for the treachery love has suggested to me. Yes, I confess
to you that the love which I pretended to have for my cousin was a snare set to
deceive you. I love him with the love of friendship and no more.—Oh! forgive me!
I can love no one but"—her voice was choked in passionate sobs—"Oh! let us go

away, let us leave Paris!"

She began to weep; her hair was disheveled, her dress in disarray; it was midnight, and her husband forgave her. From henceforth, the cousin made his appearance without risk, and the Minotaur devoured one victim more.

What instructions can we give for contending with such adversaries as these? Their heads contain all the diplomacy of the congress of Vienna; they have as much power when they are caught as when they escape. What man has a mind supple enough to lay aside brute force and strength and follow his wife through such mazes as these?

To make a false plea every moment, in order to elicit the truth, a true plea in order to unmask falsehood; to charge the battery when least expected, and to spike your gun at the very moment of firing it; to scale the mountain with the enemy, in order to descend to the plain again five minutes later; to accompany the foe in windings as rapid, as obscure as those of a plover on the breezes; to obey when obedience is necessary, and to oppose when resistance is inertial; to traverse the whole scale of hypotheses as a young artist with one stroke runs from the lowest to the highest note of his piano; to divine at last the secret purpose on which a woman is bent; to fear her caresses and to seek rather to find out what are the thoughts that suggested them and the pleasure which she derived from them — this is mere child's pay for the man of intellect and for those lucid and searching imaginations which possess the gift of doing and thinking at the same time. But there are a vast number of husbands who are terrified at the mere idea of putting in practice these principles in their dealings with a woman.

Such men as these prefer passing their lives in making huge efforts to become second-class chess-players, or to pocket adroitly a ball in billiards.

Some of them will tell you that they are incapable of keeping their minds on such a constant strain and breaking up the habits of their life. In that case the woman triumphs. She recognizes that in mind and energy she is her husband's superior, although the superiority may be but temporary; and yet there rises in her a feeling of contempt for the head of the house.

If many man fail to be masters in their own house this is not from lack of willingness, but of talent. As for those who are ready to undergo the toils of this terrible duel, it is quite true that they must needs possess great moral force.

And really, as soon as it is necessary to display all the resources of this secret strategy, it is often useless to attempt setting any traps for these satanic creatures. Once women arrive at a point when they willfully deceive, their countenances become as inscrutable as vacancy. Here is an example which came within my own experience.

A very young, very pretty, and very clever coquette of Paris had not yet risen. Seated by her bed was one of her dearest friends. A letter arrived from another, a very impetuous fellow, to whom she had allowed the right of speaking to her like a master. The letter was in pencil and ran as follows:

"I understand that Monsieur C— —- is with you at this moment. I am waiting for him to blow his brains out."

Madame D— —- calmly continued the conversation with Monsieur C— —-. She asked him to hand her a little writing desk of red leather which stood on the table, and he brought it to her.

"Thanks, my dear," she said to him; "go on talking, I am listening to you."

C— —- talked away and she replied, all the while writing the following note:

"As soon as you become jealous of C— —- you two can blow out each other's brains at your pleasure. As for you, you may die; but brains —you haven't any brains to blow out."

"My dear friend," she said to C— —-, "I beg you will light this candle. Good, you are charming. And now be kind enough to leave me and let me get up, and give this letter to Monsieur d'H— —-, who is waiting at the door."

All this was said with admirable coolness. The tones and intonations of her voice, the expression of her face showed no emotion. Her audacity was crowned with complete success. On receiving the answer from the hand of Monsieur C— —-, Monsieur d'H— —- felt his wrath subside. He was troubled with only one thing and that was how to disguise his inclination to laugh.

The more torch-light one flings into the immense cavern which we are now trying to illuminate, the more profound it appears. It is a bottomless abyss. It appears to us that our task will be accomplished more agreeably and more instructively if we show the principles of strategy put into practice in the case of a woman, when she has reached a high degree of vicious accomplishment. An example suggests more maxims and reveals the existence of more methods than all possible theories.

One day at the end of a dinner given to certain intimate friends by Prince Lebrun, the guests, heated by champagne, were discussing the inexhaustible subject of feminine artifice. The recent adventure which was credited to the Countess R. D. S. J. D. A— —-, apropos of a necklace, was the subject first broached. A highly esteemed artist, a gifted friend of the emperor, was vigorously maintaining the opinion, which seemed somewhat unmanly, that it was forbidden to a man to resist successfully the webs woven by a woman.

"It is my happy experience," he said, "that to them nothing is sacred."

The ladies protested.

"But I can cite an instance in point."

"It is an exception!"

"Let us hear the story," said a young lady.

"Yes, tell it to us," cried all the guests.

The prudent old gentleman cast his eyes around, and, after having formed his conclusions as to the age of the ladies, smiled and said:

"Since we are all experienced in life, I consent to relate the adventure."

Dead silence followed, and the narrator read the following from a little book which he had taken from his pocket:

I was head over ears in love with the Comtesse de — —-. I was twenty and I was ingenuous. She deceived me. I was angry; she threw me over. I was ingenuous, I repeat, and I was grieved to lose her. I was twenty; she forgave me. And as I was twenty, as I was always ingenuous, always deceived, but never again thrown over by her, I believed myself to have been the best beloved of lovers, consequently the happiest of men. The countess had a friend, Madame de T— —-, who seemed to have some designs on me, but without compromising her dignity; for she was scrupulous and respected the proprieties. One day while I was waiting for the countess in her Opera box, I heard my name called from a contiguous box. It was Madame de T— —-.

"What," she said, "already here? Is this fidelity or merely a want of something to do? Won't you come to me?"

Her voice and her manner had a meaning in them, but I was far from inclined at that moment to indulge in a romance.

"Have you any plans for this evening?" she said to me. "Don't make any! If I cheer your tedious solitude you ought to be devoted to me. Don't ask any questions, but obey. Call my servants."

I answered with a bow and on being requested to leave the Opera box, I obeyed.

"Go to this gentleman's house," she said to the lackey. "Say he will not be home till to-morrow."

She made a sign to him, he went to her, she whispered in his ear, and he left us. The Opera began. I tried to venture on a few words, but she silenced me; some one might be listening. The first act ended, the lackey brought back a note, and told her that everything was ready. Then she smiled, asked for my hand, took me off, put me in her carriage, and I started on my journey quite ignorant of my destination. Every inquiry I made was answered by a peal of laughter. If I had not been aware that this was a woman of great passion, that she had long loved the Marquis de V— —-, that she must have known I was aware of it, I should have believed myself in good luck; but she knew the condition of my heart, and the Comtesse de — —-. I therefore rejected all presumptuous ideas and bided my time. At the first stop, a change of horses was supplied with the swiftness of lightning and we started afresh. The matter was becoming serious. I asked with some insistency, where this joke was to end.

"Where?" she said, laughing. "In the pleasantest place in the world, but can't you guess? I'll give you a thousand chances. Give it up, for you will never guess. We are going to my husband's house. Do you know him?"

"Not in the least."

"So much the better, I thought you didn't. But I hope you will like him. We have lately become reconciled. Negotiations went on for six months; and we have been writing to one another for a month. I think it is very kind of me to go and look him up."

"It certainly is, but what am I going to do there? What good will I be in this reconciliation?"

"Ah, that is my business. You are young, amiable, unconventional; you suit me and will save me from the tediousness of a tete-a-tete."

"But it seems odd to me, to choose the day or the night of a reconciliation to make us acquainted; the awkwardness of the first interview, the figure all three of us will cut,—I don't see anything particularly pleasant in that."

"I have taken possession of you for my own amusement!" she said with an imperious air, "so please don't preach."

I saw she was decided, so surrendered myself to circumstances. I began to laugh at my predicament and we became exceedingly merry. We again changed horses. The mysterious torch of night lit up a sky of extreme clearness and shed around a delightful twilight. We were approaching the spot where our tete-a-tete must end. She pointed out to me at intervals the beauty of the landscape, the tranquillity of the night, the all-pervading silence of nature. In order to admire these things in company as it was natural we should, we turned to the same window and our faces touched for a moment. In a sudden shock she seized my hand, and by a chance which seemed to me extraordinary, for the stone over which our carriage had bounded could not have been very large, I found Madame de T——- in my arms. I do not know what we were trying to see; what I am sure of is that the objects before our eyes began in spite of the full moon to grow misty, when suddenly I was released from her weight, and she sank into the back cushions of the carriage.

"Your object," she said, rousing herself from a deep reverie, "is possibly to convince me of the imprudence of this proceeding. Judge, therefore, of my embarrassment!"

"My object!" I replied, "what object can I have with regard to you? What a delusion! You look very far ahead; but of course the sudden surprise or turn of chance may excuse anything."

"You have counted, then, upon that chance, it seems to me?"

We had reached our destination, and before we were aware of it, we had entered the court of the chateau. The whole place was brightly lit up. Everything wore a festal air, excepting the face of its master, who at the sight of me seemed anything but delighted. He came forward and expressed in somewhat hesitating terms the tenderness proper to the occasion of a reconciliation. I understood later on that this reconciliation was absolutely necessary from family reasons. I was presented to him and was coldly greeted. He extended his hand to his wife, and I followed the two, thinking of my part in the past, in the present and in the future. I passed through apartments decorated with exquisite taste. The master in this respect had gone beyond all the ordinary refinement of luxury, in the hope of reanimating, by the influence of voluptuous imagery, a physical nature that was dead. Not knowing what to say, I took refuge in expressions of admiration. The goddess of the temple, who was quite ready to do the honors, accepted my compliments.

"You have not seen anything," she said. "I must take you to the apartments of my husband."

"Madame, five years ago I caused them to be pulled down."

"Oh! Indeed!" said she.

At the dinner, what must she do but offer the master some fish, on which he said to her:

"Madame, I have been living on milk for the last three years."

"Oh! Indeed!" she said again.

Can any one imagine three human beings as astonished as we were to find ourselves gathered together? The husband looked at me with a supercilious air, and I paid him back with a look of audacity.

Madame de T——- smiled at me and was charming to me; Monsieur de T——- accepted me as a necessary evil. Never in all my life have I taken part in a dinner which was so odd as that. The dinner ended, I thought that we would go to bed early—that is, I thought that Monsieur de T——- would. As we entered the drawing-room:

"I appreciate, madame," said he, "your precaution in bringing this gentleman with you. You judged rightly that I should be but poor company for the evening, and you have done well, for I am going to retire."

Then turning to me, he added in a tone of profound sarcasm:

"You will please to pardon me, and obtain also pardon from madame."

He left us. My reflections? Well, the reflections of a twelvemonth were then comprised in those of a minute. When we were left alone, Madame de T——- and I, we looked at each other so curiously that, in order to break through the awkwardness, she proposed that we should take a turn on the terrace while we waited, as she said, until the servants had supped.

It was a superb night. It was scarcely possible to discern surrounding objects, they seemed to be covered with a veil, that imagination might be permitted to take a loftier flight. The gardens, terraced on the side of a mountain, sloped down, platform after platform, to the banks of the Seine, and the eye took in the many windings of the stream covered with islets green and picturesque. These variations in the landscape made up a thousand pictures which gave to the spot, naturally charming, a thousand novel features. We walked along the most extensive of these terraces, which was covered with a thick umbrage of trees. She had recovered from the effects of her husband's persiflage, and as we walked along she gave me her confidence. Confidence begets confidence, and as I told her mine, all she said to me became more intimate and more interesting. Madame de T——- at first gave me her arm; but soon this arm became interlaced in mine, I know not how, but in some way almost lifted her up and prevented her from touching the ground. The position was agreeable, but became at last fatiguing. We had been walking for a long time and we still had much to say to each other. A bank of turf appeared and she sat down without withdrawing her arm. And in this position we began to sound the praises of mutual confidence, its charms and its delights.

"Ah!" she said to me, "who can enjoy it more than we and with less cause of fear? I know well the tie that binds you to another, and therefore have nothing to fear."

Perhaps she wished to be contradicted. But I answered not a word. We were then mutually persuaded that it was possible for us to be friends without fear of going further.

"But I was afraid, however," I said, "that that sudden jolt in the carriage and the surprising consequences may have frightened you."

"Oh, I am not so easily alarmed!"

"I fear it has left a little cloud on your mind?"

"What must I do to reassure you?"

"Give me the kiss here which chance—"

"I will gladly do so; for if I do not, your vanity will lead you to think that I fear you."

I took the kiss.

It is with kisses as with confidences, the first leads to another. They are multiplied, they interrupt conversation, they take its place; they scarce leave time for a sigh to escape. Silence followed. We could hear it, for silence may be heard. We rose without a word and began to walk again.

"We must go in," said she, "for the air of the river is icy, and it is not worth while—"

"I think to go in would be more dangerous," I answered.

"Perhaps so! Never mind, we will go in."

"Why, is this out of consideration for me? You wish doubtless to save me from the impressions which I may receive from such a walk as this —the consequences which may result. Is it for me—for me only—?"

"You are modest," she said smiling, "and you credit me with singular consideration."

"Do you think so? Well, since you take it in this way, we will go in; I demand it."

A stupid proposition, when made by two people who are forcing themselves to say something utterly different from what they think.

Then she compelled me to take the path that led back to the chateau. I do not know, at least I did not then know, whether this course was one which she forced upon herself, whether it was the result of a vigorous resolution, or whether she shared my disappointment in seeing an incident which had begun so well thus suddenly brought to a close but by a mutual instinct our steps slackened and we pursued our way gloomily dissatisfied the one with the other and with ourselves. We knew not the why and the wherefore of what we were doing. Neither of us had the right to demand or even to ask anything. We had neither of us any ground for uttering a reproach. O that we had got up a quarrel! But how could I pick one with her? Meanwhile we drew nearer and nearer, thinking how we might evade the duty which we had so awkwardly imposed upon ourselves. We reached the door, when Madame de T— —- said to me:

"I am angry with you! After the confidences I have given you, not to give me a single one! You have not said a word about the countess. And yet it is so delightful to speak of the one we love! I should have listened with such interest! It was the very best I could do after I had taken you away from her!"

"Cannot I reproach you with the same thing?" I said, interrupting her, "and if instead of making me a witness to this singular reconciliation in which I play so odd a part, you had spoken to me of the marquis—"

"Stop," she said, "little as you know of women, you are aware that their confidences must be waited for, not asked. But to return to yourself. Are you very happy with my friend? Ah! I fear the contrary—"

"Why, madame, should everything that the public amuses itself by saying claim our belief?"

"You need not dissemble. The countess makes less a mystery of things than you do. Women of her stamp do not keep the secrets of their loves and of their lovers, especially when you are prompted by discretion to conceal her triumph. I am far from accusing her of coquetry; but a prude has as much vanity as a coquette.— Come, tell me frankly, have you not cause of complaint against her?"

"But, madame, the air is really too icy for us to stay here. Would you like to go in?" said I with a smile.

"Do you find it so?—That is singular. The air is quite warm."

She had taken my arm again, and we continued to walk, although I did not know the direction which we took. All that she had hinted at concerning the lover of the countess, concerning my mistress, together with this journey, the incident which took place in the carriage, our conversation on the grassy bank, the time of night, the moonlight—all made me feel anxious. I was at the same time carried along by vanity, by desire, and so distracted by thought, that I was too excited perhaps to take notice of all that I was experiencing. And, while I was overwhelmed with these mingled feelings, she continued talking to me of the countess, and my silence confirmed the truth of all that she chose to say about her. Nevertheless, certain passages in her talk recalled me to myself.

"What an exquisite creature she is!" she was saying. "How graceful! On her lips the utterances of treachery sound like witticism; an act of infidelity seems the prompting of reason, a sacrifice to propriety; while she is never reckless, she is always lovable; she is seldom tender and never sincere; amorous by nature, prudish on principle; sprightly, prudent, dexterous though utterly thoughtless, varied as Proteus in her moods, but charming as the Graces in her manner; she attracts but she eludes. What a number of parts I have seen her play! *Entre nous*, what a number of dupes hang round her! What fun she has made of the baron, what a life she has led the marquis! When she took you, it was merely for the purpose of throwing the two rivals off the scent; they were on the point of a rupture; for she had played with them too long, and they had had time to see through her. But she brought you on the scene. Their attention was called to you, she led them to redouble their pursuit, she was in despair over you, she pitied you, she consoled you— Ah! how happy is a clever woman when in such a game as this she professes to stake nothing of her own! But yet, is this true happiness?"

This last phrase, accompanied by a significant sigh, was a master-stroke. I felt as if a bandage had fallen from my eyes, without seeing who had put it there. My mistress appeared to me the falsest of women, and I believed that I held now the only sensible creature in the world. Then I sighed without knowing why. She seemed grieved at having given me pain and at having in her excitement drawn a picture, the truth of which might be open to suspicion, since it was the work of a woman. I do not know how I answered; for without realizing the drift of all I heard, I set out with her on the high road of sentiment, and we mounted to such lofty heights of feeling that it was impossible to guess what would be the end of our journey. It was fortunate that we also took the path towards a pavilion which she pointed out to me at the end of the terrace, a pavilion, the witness of many sweet moments. She described to me the furnishing of it. What a pity that she had not the key! As she spoke we reached the pavilion and found that it was open. The clearness of the moonlight outside did not penetrate, but darkness has many charms. We trembled as we went in. It was a sanctuary. Might it not be the sanctuary of love? We drew near a sofa and sat down, and there we remained a moment listening to our heart-beats. The last ray of the moon carried away the last scruple. The hand which repelled me felt my heart beat. She struggled to get away, but fell back overcome with tenderness. We talked together through that silence in the language of thought. Nothing is more rapturous than these mute conversations. Madame de T— —- took refuge in my arms, hid her head in my bosom, sighed and then grew calm under my caresses. She grew melancholy, she was consoled, and she asked of love all that love had robbed her of. The sound of the river broke the silence of night with a gentle murmur, which seemed in harmony with the beating of our hearts. Such was the darkness of the place it was scarcely possible to discern objects; but through the transparent crepe of a fair summer's night, the queen of that lovely place seemed to me adorable.

"Oh!" she said to me with an angelic voice, "let us leave this dangerous spot. Resistance here is beyond our strength."

She drew me away and we left the pavilion with regret.

"Ah! how happy is she!" cried Madame de T— —-.

"Whom do you mean?" I asked.

"Did I speak?" said she with a look of alarm.

And then we reached the grassy bank, and stopped there involuntarily. "What a distance there is," she said to me, "between this place and the pavilion!"

"Yes indeed," said I. "But must this bank be always ominous? Is there a regret?

Is there—?"

I do not know by what magic it took place; but at this point the conversation changed and became less serious. She ventured even to speak playfully of the pleasures of love, to eliminate from them all moral considerations, to reduce them to their simplest elements, and to prove that the favors of lovers were mere pleasure, that there were no pledges—philosophically speaking—excepting those which were given to the world, when we allowed it to penetrate our secrets and joined it in the acts of indiscretion.

"How mild is the night," she said, "which we have by chance picked out! Well, if there are reasons, as I suppose there are, which compel us to part to-morrow, our happiness, ignored as it is by all nature, will not leave us any ties to dissolve. There will, perhaps, be some regrets, the pleasant memory of which will give us reparation; and then there will be a mutual understanding, without all the delays, the fuss and the tyranny of legal proceedings. We are such machines—and I blush to avow it—that in place of all the shrinkings that tormented me before this scene took place, I was half inclined to embrace the boldness of these principles, and I felt already disposed to indulge in the love of liberty.

"This beautiful night," she continued, "this lovely scenery at this moment have taken on fresh charms. O let us never forget this pavilion! The chateau," she added smilingly, "contains a still more charming place, but I dare not show you anything; you are like a child, who wishes to touch everything and breaks everything that he touches."

Moved by a sentiment of curiosity I protested that I was a very good child. She changed the subject.

"This night," she said, "would be for me without a regret if I were not vexed with myself for what I said to you about the countess. Not that I wish to find fault with you. Novelty attracts me. You have found me amiable, I should like to believe in your good faith. But the dominion of habit takes a long time to break through and I have not learned the secret of doing this—By the bye, what do you think of my husband?"

"Well, he is rather cross, but I suppose he could not be otherwise to me."

"Oh, that is true, but his way of life isn't pleasant, and he could not see you here with indifference. He might be suspicious even of our friendship."

"Oh! he is so already."

"Confess that he has cause. Therefore you must not prolong this visit; he might take it amiss. As soon as any one arrives—" and she added with a smile, "some one is going to arrive—you must go. You have to keep up appearance, you know. Remember his manner when he left us to-night."

I was tempted to interpret this adventure as a trap, but as she noticed the impression made by her words, she added:

"Oh, he was very much gayer when he was superintending the arrangement of the cabinet I told you about. That was before my marriage. This passage leads to my apartment. Alas! it testifies to the cunning artifices to which Monsieur de T——- has resorted in protecting his love for me."

"How pleasant it would be," I said to her, keenly excited by the curiosity she had roused in me, "to take vengeance in this spot for the insults which your charms have suffered, and to seek to make restitution for the pleasures of which you have been robbed."

She doubtless thought this remark in good taste, but she said: "You promised to be good!"

* * * * *

I threw a veil over the follies which every age will pardon to youth, on the ground of so many balked desires and bitter memories. In the morning, scarcely raising her liquid eyes, Madame de T——-, fairer than ever, said to me:

"Now will you ever love the countess as much as you do me?"

I was about to answer when her maid, her confidante, appeared saying:

"You must go. It is broad daylight, eleven o'clock, and the chateau is already awake."

All had vanished like a dream! I found myself wandering through the corridors before I had recovered my senses. How could I regain my apartment, not knowing where it was? Any mistake might bring about an exposure. I resolved on a morning walk. The coolness of the fresh air gradually tranquilized my imagination and brought me back to the world of reality; and now instead of a world of enchantment I saw myself in my soul, and my thoughts were no longer disturbed but followed each other in connected order; in fact, I breathed once more. I was, above all things, anxious to learn what I was to her so lately left—I who knew that she had been desperately in love with the Marquis de V——-. Could she have broken with him? Had she taken me to be his successor, or only to punish him? What a night! What an adventure! Yes, and what a delightful woman! While I floated on the waves of these thoughts, I heard a sound near at hand. I raised my eyes, I rubbed them, I could not believe my senses. Can you guess who it was? The Marquis de V——-!

"You did not expect to see me so early, did you?" he said. "How has it all gone off?"

"Did you know that I was here?" I asked in utter amazement.

"Oh, yes, I received word just as you left Paris. Have you played your part well? Did not the husband think your visit ridiculous? Was he put out? When are you going to take leave? You had better go, I have made every provision for you. I have brought you a good carriage. It is at your service. This is the way I requite you, my dear friend. You may rely on me in the future, for a man is grateful for such services as yours."

These last words gave me the key to the whole mystery, and I saw how I stood.

"But why should you have come so soon?" I asked him; "it would have been more prudent to have waited a few days."

"I foresaw that; and it is only chance that has brought me here. I am supposed to be on my way back from a neighboring country house. But has not Madame de T——- taken you into her secret? I am surprised at her want of confidence, after all you have done for us."

"My dear friend," I replied, "she doubtless had her reasons. Perhaps I did not play my part very well."

"Has everything been very pleasant? Tell me the particulars; come, tell me."

"Now wait a moment. I did not know that this was to be a comedy; and although Madame de T——- gave me a part in the play—"

"It wasn't a very nice one."

"Do not worry yourself; there are no bad parts for good actors."

"I understand, you acquitted yourself well."

"Admirably."

"And Madame de T——-?"

"Is adorable."

"To think of being able to win such a woman!" said he, stopping short in our walk, and looking triumphantly at me. "Oh, what pains I have taken with her! And I have at last brought her to a point where she is perhaps the only woman in Paris on whose fidelity a man may infallibly count!"

"You have succeeded—?"

"Yes; in that lies my special talent. Her inconstancy was mere frivolity, unrestrained imagination. It was necessary to change that disposition of hers, but you have no idea of her attachment to me. But really, is she not charming?"

"I quite agree with you."

"And yet *entre nous* I recognize one fault in her. Nature in giving her everything, has denied her that flame divine which puts the crown on all other endowments; while she rouses in others the ardor of passion, she feels none herself, she is a thing of marble."

"I am compelled to believe you, for I have had no opportunity of judging, but do you think that you know that woman as well as if you were her husband? It is possible to be deceived. If I had not dined yesterday with the veritable—I should take you—"

"By the way, has he been good?"

"Oh, I was received like a dog!"

"I understand. Let us go in, let us look for Madame de T——-. She must be up by this time."

"But should we not out of decency begin with the husband?" I said to him.

"You are right. Let us go to your room, I wish to put on a little powder. But tell me, did he really take you for her lover?"

"You may judge by the way he receives me; but let us go at once to his apartment."

I wished to avoid having to lead him to an apartment whose whereabouts I did not know; but by chance we found it. The door was open and there I saw my *valet de chambre* asleep on an armchair. A candle was going out on a table beside him. He drowsily offered a night robe to the marquis. I was on pins and needles; but the marquis was in a mood to be easily deceived, took the man for a mere sleepy-head, and made a joke of the matter. We passed on to the apartment of Monsieur de T———-. There was no misunderstanding the reception which he accorded me, and the welcome, the compliments which he addressed to the marquis, whom he almost forced to stay. He wished to take him to madame in order that she might insist on his staying. As for me, I received no such invitation. I was reminded that my health was delicate, the country was damp, fever was in the air, and I seemed so depressed that the chateau would prove too gloomy for me. The marquis offered me his chaise and I accepted it. The husband seemed delighted and we were all satisfied. But I could not refuse myself the pleasure of seeing Madame de T———- once more. My impatience was wonderful. My friend conceived no suspicions from the late sleep of his mistress.

"Isn't this fine?" he said to me as we followed Monsieur de T———-. "He couldn't have spoken more kindly if she had dictated his words. He is a fine fellow. I am not in the least annoyed by this reconciliation; they will make a good home together, and you will agree with me, that he could not have chosen a wife better able to do the honors."

"Certainly," I replied.

"However pleasant the adventure has been," he went on with an air of mystery, "you must be off! I will let Madame de T———- understand that her secret will be well kept."

"On that point, my friend, she perhaps counts more on me than on you; for you see her sleep is not disturbed by the matter."

"Oh! I quite agree that there is no one like you for putting a woman to sleep."

"Yes, and a husband too, and if necessary a lover, my dear friend."

At last Monsieur de T———- was admitted to his wife's apartment, and there we were all summoned.

"I trembled," said Madame de T———- to me, "for fear you would go before I awoke, and I thank you for saving me the annoyance which that would have caused me."

"Madame," I said, and she must have perceived the feeling that was in my tones—"I come to say good-bye."

She looked at me and at the marquis with an air of disquietude; but the self-satisfied, knowing look of her lover reassured her. She laughed in her sleeve with me as if she would console me as well as she could, without lowering herself in my eyes.

"He has played his part well," the marquis said to her in a low voice, pointing to me, "and my gratitude—"

"Let us drop the subject," interrupted Madame de T——-; "you may be sure that I am well aware of all I owe him."

At last Monsieur de T——-, with a sarcastic remark, dismissed me; my friend threw the dust in his eyes by making fun of me; and I paid back both of them by expressing my admiration for Madame de T——-, who made fools of us all without forfeiting her dignity. I took myself off; but Madame de T——- followed me, pretending to have a commission to give me.

"Adieu, monsieur!" she said, "I am indebted to you for the very great pleasure you have given me; but I have paid you back with a beautiful dream," and she looked at me with an expression of subtle meaning. "But adieu, and forever! You have plucked a solitary flower, blossoming in its loveliness, which no man—"

She stopped and her thought evaporated in a sigh; but she checked the rising flood of sensibility and smiled significantly.

"The countess loves you," she said. "If I have robbed her of some transports, I give you back to her less ignorant than before. Adieu! Do not make mischief between my friend and me."

She wrung my hand and left me.

More than once the ladies who had mislaid their fans blushed as they listened to the old gentleman, whose brilliant elocution won their indulgence for certain details which we have suppressed, as too erotic for the present age; nevertheless, we may believe that each lady complimented him in private; for some time afterwards he gave to each of them, as also to the masculine guests, a copy of this charming story, twenty-five copies of which were printed by Pierre Didot. It is from copy No. 24 that the author has transcribed this tale, hitherto unpublished, and, strange to say, attributed to Dorat. It has the merit of yielding important lessons for husbands, while at the same time it gives the celibates a delightful picture of morals in the last century.

MEDITATION XXV.

OF ALLIES.

Of all the miseries that civil war can bring upon a country the greatest lies in the appeal which one of the contestants always ends by making to some foreign government.

Unhappily we are compelled to confess that all women make this great mistake, for the lover is only the first of their soldiers. It may be a member of their family or at least a distant cousin. This Meditation, then, is intended to answer the inquiry, what assistance can each of the different powers which influence human life give to your wife? or better than that, what artifices will she resort to to arm them against you?

Two beings united by marriage are subject to the laws of religion and society; to those of private life, and, from considerations of health, to those of medicine. We will therefore divide this important Meditation into six paragraphs:

1. OF RELIGIONS AND OF CONFESSION; CONSIDERED IN THEIR CONNECTION WITH MARRIAGE.

2. OF THE MOTHER-IN-LAW.

3. OF BOARDING SCHOOL FRIENDS AND INTIMATE FRIENDS.

4. OF THE LOVER'S ALLIES.

5. OF THE MAID.

6. OF THE DOCTOR.

1. OF RELIGIONS AND OF CONFESSION; CONSIDERED IN THEIR CONNECTION WITH MARRIAGE.

La Bruyere has very wittily said, "It is too much for a husband to have ranged against him both devotion and gallantry; a woman ought to choose but one of them for her ally."

The author thinks that La Bruyere is mistaken.

2. OF THE MOTHER-IN-LAW.

Up to the age of thirty the face of a woman is a book written in a foreign tongue, which one may still translate in spite of all the *feminisms* of the idiom; but on passing her fortieth year a woman becomes an insoluble riddle; and if any one can see through an old woman, it is another old woman.

Some diplomats have attempted on more than one occasion the diabolical task of gaining over the dowagers who opposed their machinations; but if they have ever succeeded it was only after making enormous concessions to them; for diplomats are practiced people and we do not think that you can employ their recipe in dealing with your mother-in-law. She will be the first aid-de-camp of her daughter, for if the mother did not take her daughter's side, it would be one of those monstrous and unnatural exceptions, which unhappily for husbands are extremely rare.

When a man is so happy as to possess a mother-in-law who is well-preserved, he may easily keep her in check for a certain time, although he may not know any young celibate brave enough to assail her. But generally husbands who have the slightest conjugal genius will find a way of pitting their own mother against that of their wife, and in that case they will naturally neutralize each other's power.

To be able to keep a mother-in-law in the country while he lives in Paris, and vice versa, is a piece of good fortune which a husband too rarely meets with.

What of making mischief between the mother and the daughter?—That may be possible; but in order to accomplish such an enterprise he must have the metallic heart of Richelieu, who made a son and a mother deadly enemies to each other. However, the jealousy of a husband who forbids his wife to pray to male saints and wishes her to address only female saints, would allow her liberty to see her mother.

Many sons-in-law take an extreme course which settles everything, which consists in living on bad terms with their mothers-in-law. This unfriendliness would be very adroit policy, if it did not inevitably result in drawing tighter the ties that unite mother and daughter. These are about all the means which you have for resisting maternal influence in your home. As for the services which your wife can claim from her mother, they are immense; and the assistance which she may derive from the neutrality of her mother is not less powerful. But on this point everything passes out of the domain of science, for all is veiled in secrecy. The reinforcements which a mother brings up in support of a daughter are so varied in nature, they depend so much on circumstances, that it would be folly to attempt even a nomenclature for them. Yet you may write out among the most valuable precepts of this conjugal gospel, the following maxims.

A husband should never let his wife visit her mother unattended.

A husband ought to study all the reasons why all the celibates under forty who form her habitual society are so closely united by ties of friendship to his mother-in-law; for, if a daughter rarely falls in love with the lover of her mother, her mother has always a weak spot for her daughter's lover.

3. OF BOARDING SCHOOL FRIENDS AND INTIMATE FRIENDS.

Louise de L——-, daughter of an officer killed at Wagram, had been the object of Napoleon's special protection. She left Ecouen to marry a commissary general, the Baron de V——-, who is very rich.

Louise was eighteen and the baron forty. She was ordinary in face and her complexion could not be called white, but she had a charming figure, good eyes, a small foot, a pretty hand, good taste and abundant intelligence. The baron, worn out by the fatigues of war and still more by the excesses of a stormy youth, had one of those faces upon which the Republic, the Directory, the Consulate and the Empire seemed to have set their impress.

He became so deeply in love with his wife, that he asked and obtained from the Emperor a post at Paris, in order that he might be enabled to watch over his treasure. He was as jealous as Count Almaviva, still more from vanity than from love. The young orphan had married her husband from necessity, and, flattered by the ascendancy she wielded over a man much older than herself, waited upon his wishes and his needs; but her delicacy was offended from the first days of their marriage by the habits and ideas of a man whose manners were tinged with republican license. He was a predestined.

I do not know exactly how long the baron made his honeymoon last, nor when war was declared in his household; but I believe it happened in 1816, at a very brilliant ball given by Monsieur D——-, a commissariat officer, that the commissary general, who had been promoted head of the department, admired the beautiful Madame B——-, the wife of a banker, and looked at her much more amorously than a married man should have allowed himself to do.

At two o'clock in the morning it happened that the banker, tired of waiting any longer, went home leaving his wife at the ball.

"We are going to take you home to your house," said the baroness to Madame B——-. "Monsieur de V——-, offer your arm to Emilie!"

And now the baron is seated in his carriage next to a woman who, during the whole evening, had been offered and had refused a thousand attentions, and from whom he had hoped in vain to win a single look. There she was, in all the lustre of her youth and beauty, displaying the whitest shoulders and the most ravishing lines of beauty. Her face, which still reflected the pleasures of the evening, seemed to vie with the brilliancy of her satin gown; her eyes to rival the blaze of her diamonds; and her skin to cope with the soft whiteness of the marabouts which tied in her hair, set off the ebon tresses and the ringlets dangling from her headdress. Her tender voice would stir the chords of the most insensible hearts; in a word, so powerfully did she wake up love in the human breast that Robert d'Abrissel himself would perhaps have yielded to her.

The baron glanced at his wife, who, overcome with fatigue, had sunk to sleep in a corner of the carriage. He compared, in spite of himself, the toilette of Louise and that of Emilie. Now on occasions of this kind the presence of a wife is singularly calculated to sharpen the unquenchable desires of a forbidden love. Moreover, the glances of the baron, directed alternately to his wife and to her friend, were easy to interpret, and Madame B——- interpreted them.

"Poor Louise," she said, "she is overtired. Going out does not suit her, her tastes are so simple. At Ecouen she was always reading—"

"And you, what used you to do?"

"I, sir? Oh, I thought about nothing but acting comely. It was my passion!"

"But why do you so rarely visit Madame de V——-? We have a country house at Saint-Prix, where we could have a comedy acted, in a little theatre which I have built there."

"If I have not visited Madame de V——-, whose fault is it?" she replied. "You are so jealous that you will not allow her either to visit her friends or to receive them."

"I jealous!" cried Monsieur de V——-, "after four years of marriage, and after having had three children!"

"Hush," said Emilie, striking the fingers of the baron with her fan, "Louise is not asleep!"

The carriage stopped, and the baron offered his hand to his wife's fair friend and helped her to get out.

"I hope," said Madame B——-, "that you will not prevent Louise from coming to the ball which I am giving this week."

The baron made her a respectful bow.

This ball was a triumph of Madame B——-'s and the ruin of the husband of Louise; for he became desperately enamored of Emilie, to whom he would have sacrificed a hundred lawful wives.

Some months after that evening on which the baron gained some hopes of succeeding with his wife's friend, he found himself one morning at the house of Madame B——-, when the maid came to announce the Baroness de V——-.

"Ah!" cried Emilie, "if Louise were to see you with me at such an hour as this, she would be capable of compromising me. Go into that closet and don't make the least noise."

The husband, caught like a mouse in a trap, concealed himself in the closet.

"Good-day, my dear!" said the two women, kissing each other.

"Why are you come so early?" asked Emilie.

"Oh! my dear, cannot you guess? I came to have an understanding with you!"

"What, a duel?"

"Precisely, my dear. I am not like you, not I! I love my husband and am jealous of him. You! you are beautiful, charming, you have the right to be a coquette, you can very well make fun of B——-, to whom your virtue seems to be of little importance. But as you have plenty of lovers in society, I beg you that you will leave me my husband. He is always at your house, and he certainly would not come unless you were the attraction."

"What a very pretty jacket you have on."

"Do you think so? My maid made it."

"Then I shall get Anastasia to take a lesson from Flore—"

"So, then, my dear, I count on your friendship to refrain from bringing trouble in my house."

"But, my child, I do not know how you can conceive that I should fall in love with your husband; he is coarse and fat as a deputy of the centre. He is short and ugly—Ah! I will allow that he is generous, but that is all you can say for him, and this is a quality which is all in all only to opera girls; so that you can understand, my dear, that if I were choosing a lover, as you seem to suppose I am, I wouldn't choose an old man like your baron. If I have given him any hopes, if I have received him, it was certainly for the purpose of amusing myself, and of giving you liberty; for I believed you had a weakness for young Rostanges."

"I?" exclaimed Louise, "God preserve me from it, my dear; he is the most intolerable coxcomb in the world. No, I assure you, I love my husband! You may laugh as you choose; it is true. I know it may seem ridiculous, but consider, he has made my fortune, he is no miser, and he is everything to me, for it has been my unhappy lot to be left an orphan. Now even if I did not love him, I ought to try to preserve his esteem. Have I a family who will some day give me shelter?"

"Come, my darling, let us speak no more about it," said Emilie, interrupting her friend, "for it tires me to death."

After a few trifling remarks the baroness left.

"How is this, monsieur?" cried Madame B———-, opening the door of the closet where the baron was frozen with cold, for this incident took place in winter; "how is this? Aren't you ashamed of yourself for not adoring a little wife who is so interesting? Don't speak to me of love; you may idolize me, as you say you do, for a certain time, but you will never love me as you love Louise. I can see that in your heart I shall never outweigh the interest inspired by a virtuous wife, children, and a family circle. I should one day be deserted and become the object of your bitter reflections. You would coldly say of me 'I have had that woman!' That phrase I have heard pronounced by men with the most insulting indifference. You see, monsieur, that I reason in cold blood, and that I do not love you, because you never would be able to love me."

"What must I do then to convince you of my love?" cried the baron, fixing his gaze on the young woman.

She had never appeared to him so ravishingly beautiful as at that moment, when her soft voice poured forth a torrent of words whose sternness was belied by the grace of her gestures, by the pose of her head and by her coquettish attitude.

"Oh, when I see Louise in possession of a lover," she replied, "when I know that I am taking nothing away from her, and that she has nothing to regret in losing your affection; when I am quite sure that you love her no longer, and have obtained certain proof of your indifference towards her—Oh, then I may listen to you!—These words must seem odious to you," she continued in an earnest voice; "and so indeed they are, but do not think that they have been pronounced by me. I am the rigorous mathematician who makes his deductions from a preliminary proposition. You are married, and do you deliberately set about making love to some one else? I should be mad to give any encouragement to a man who cannot be mine eternally."

"Demon!" exclaimed the husband. "Yes, you are a demon, and not a woman!"

"Come now, you are really amusing!" said the young woman as she seized the bell-rope.

"Oh! no, Emilie," continued the lover of forty, in a calmer voice. "Do not ring; stop, forgive me! I will sacrifice everything for you."

"But I do not promise you anything!" she answered quickly with a laugh.

"My God! How you make me suffer!" he exclaimed.

"Well, and have not you in your life caused the unhappiness of more than one person?" she asked. "Remember all the tears which have been shed through you and for you! Oh, your passion does not inspire me with the least pity. If you do not wish to make me laugh, make me share your feelings."

"Adieu, madame, there is a certain clemency in your sternness. I appreciate the lesson you have taught me. Yes, I have many faults to expiate."

"Well then, go and repent of them," she said with a mocking smile; "in making Louise happy you will perform the rudest penance in your power."

They parted. But the love of the baron was too violent to allow of Madame B——-'s harshness failing to accomplish her end, namely, the separation of the married couple.

At the end of some months the Baron de V——- and his wife lived apart, though they lived in the same mansion. The baroness was the object of universal pity, for in public she always did justice to her husband and her resignation seemed wonderful. The most prudish women of society found nothing to blame in the friendship which united Louise to the young Rostanges. And all was laid to the charge of Monsieur de V——-'s folly.

When this last had made all the sacrifices that a man could make for Madame B——-, his perfidious mistress started for the waters of Mount Dore, for Switzerland and for Italy, on the pretext of seeking the restoration of her health.

The baron died of inflammation of the liver, being attended during his sickness by the most touching ministrations which his wife could lavish upon him; and judging from the grief which he manifested at having deserted her, he seemed never to have suspected her participation in the plan which had been his ruin.

This anecdote, which we have chosen from a thousand others, exemplifies the services which two women can render each other.

From the words—"Let me have the pleasure of bringing my husband" up to the conception of the drama, whose denouement was inflammation of the liver, every female perfidy was assembled to work out the end. Certain incidents will, of course, be met with which diversify more or less the typical example which we have given, but the march of the drama is almost always the same. Moreover a husband ought always to distrust the woman friends of his wife. The subtle artifices of these lying creatures rarely fail of their effect, for they are seconded by two enemies, who always keep close to a man—and these are vanity and desire.

4. OF THE LOVER'S ALLIES.

The man who hastens to tell another man that he has dropped a thousand franc bill from his pocket-book, or even that the handkerchief is coming out of his pocket, would think it a mean thing to warn him that some one was carrying off his wife. There is certainly something extremely odd in this moral inconsistency, but after all it admits of explanation. Since the law cannot exercise any interference with matrimonial rights, the citizens have even less right to constitute themselves a conjugal police; and when one restores a thousand franc bill to him who has lost it, he acts under a certain kind of obligation, founded on the principle which says, "Do unto others as ye would they should do unto you!"

But by what reasoning can justification be found for the help which one celibate never asks in vain, but always receives from another celibate in deceiving a husband, and how shall we qualify the rendering of such help? A man who is incapable of assisting a gendarme in discovering an assassin, has no scruple in taking a husband to a theatre, to a concert or even to a questionable house, in order to help a comrade, whom he would not hesitate to kill in a duel to-morrow, in keeping an assignation, the result of which is to introduce into a family a spurious child, and to rob two brothers of a portion of their fortune by giving them a co-heir whom they never perhaps would otherwise have had; or to effect the misery of three human beings. We must confess that integrity is a very rare virtue, and, very often, the man that thinks he has most actually has least. Families have been divided by feuds, and brothers have been murdered, which events would never have taken place if some friend had refused to perform what passes to the world as a harmless trick.

It is impossible for a man to be without some hobby or other, and all of us are devoted either to hunting, fishing, gambling, music, money, or good eating. Well, your ruling passion will always be an accomplice in the snare which a lover sets for you, the invisible hand of this passion will direct your friends, or his, whether they consent or not, to play a part in the little drama when they want to take you away from home, or to induce you to leave your wife to the mercy of another. A lover will spend two whole months, if necessary, in planning the construction of the mouse-trap.

I have seen the most cunning men on earth thus taken in.

There was a certain retired lawyer of Normandy. He lived in the little town of B——-, where a regiment of the chasseurs of Cantal were garrisoned. A fascinating officer of this regiment had fallen in love with the wife of this pettifogger, and the regiment was leaving before the two lovers had been able to enjoy the least privacy. It was the fourth military man over whom the lawyer had triumphed. As he left the dinner-table one evening, about six o'clock, the husband took a walk on the terrace of his garden from which he could see the whole country side. The officers arrived at this moment to take leave of him. Suddenly the flame of a conflagration burst forth on the horizon. "Heavens! La Daudiniere is on fire!" exclaimed the major. He was an old simple-minded soldier, who had dined at home. Every one mounted horse. The young wife smiled as she found herself alone, for her lover, hidden in the coppice, had said to her, "It is a straw stack on fire!" The flank of the husband was turned with all the more facility in that a fine courser was provided for him by the captain, and with a delicacy very rare in the cavalry, the lover actually sacrificed a few moments of his happiness in order to catch up with the cavalcade, and return in company with the husband.

Marriage is a veritable duel, in which persistent watchfulness is required in order to triumph over an adversary; for, if you are unlucky enough to turn your head, the sword of the celibate will pierce you through and through.

5. OF THE MAID.

The prettiest waiting-maid I have ever seen is that of Madame V——y, a lady who to-day plays at Paris a brilliant part among the most fashionable women, and passes for a wife who keeps on excellent terms with her husband. Mademoiselle Celestine is a person whose points of beauty are so numerous that, in order to describe her, it would be necessary to translate the thirty verses which we are told form an inscription in the seraglio of the Grand Turk and contain each of them an excellent description of one of the thirty beauties of women.

"You show a great deal of vanity in keeping near you such an accomplished creature," said a lady to the mistress of the house.

"Ah! my dear, some day perhaps you will find yourself jealous of me in possessing Celestine."

"She must be endowed with very rare qualities, I suppose? She perhaps dresses you well?"

"Oh, no, very badly!"

"She sews well?"

"She never touches her needle."

"She is faithful?"

"She is one of those whose fidelity costs more than the most cunning dishonesty."

"You astonish me, my dear; she is then your foster-sister?"

"Not at all; she is positively good for nothing, but she is more useful to me than any other member of my household. If she remains with me ten years, I have promised her twenty thousand francs. It will be money well earned, and I shall not forget to give it!" said the young woman, nodding her head with a meaning gesture.

At last the questioner of Madame V——y understood.

When a woman has no friend of her own sex intimate enough to assist her in proving false to marital love, her maid is a last resource which seldom fails in bringing about the desired result.

Oh! after ten years of marriage to find under his roof, and to see all the time, a young girl of from sixteen to eighteen, fresh, dressed with taste, the treasures of whose beauty seem to breathe defiance, whose frank bearing is irresistibly attractive, whose downcast eyes seem to fear you, whose timid glance tempts you, and for whom the conjugal bed has no secrets, for she is at once a virgin and an experienced woman! How can a man remain cold, like St. Anthony, before such powerful sorcery, and have the courage to remain faithful to the good principles represented by a scornful wife, whose face is always stern, whose manners are always snappish, and who frequently refuses to be caressed? What husband is stoical enough to resist such fires, such frosts? There, where you see a new harvest of pleasure, the young innocent sees an income, and your wife her liberty. It is a little family compact, which is signed in the interest of good will.

In this case, your wife acts with regard to marriage as young fashionables do with regard to their country. If they are drawn for the army, they buy a man to carry the musket, to die in their place and to spare them the hardships of military life.

In compromises of this sort there is not a single woman who does not know how to put her husband in the wrong. I have noticed that, by a supreme stroke of diplomacy, the majority of wives do not admit their maids into the secret of the part which they give them to play. They trust to nature, and assume an affected superiority over the lover and his mistress.

These secret perfidies of women explain to a great degree the odd features of married life which are to be observed in the world; and I have heard women discuss, with profound sagacity, the dangers which are inherent in this terrible method of attack, and it is necessary to know thoroughly both the husband and the creature to whom he is to be abandoned, in order to make successful use of her. Many a woman, in this connection, has been the victim of her own calculations.

Moreover, the more impetuous and passionate a husband shows himself, the less will a woman dare to employ this expedient; but a husband caught in this snare will never have anything to say to his stern better-half, when the maid, giving evidence of the fault she has committed, is sent into the country with an infant and a dowry.

6. OF THE DOCTOR.

The doctor is one of the most potent auxiliaries of an honest woman, when she wishes to acquire a friendly divorce from her husband. The services that the doctor renders, most of the time without knowing it, to a woman, are of such importance that there does not exist a single house in France where the doctor is chosen by any one but the wife.

All doctors know what great influence women have on their reputation; thus we meet with few doctors who do not study to please the ladies. When a man of talent has become celebrated it is true that he does not lend himself to the crafty conspiracies which women hatch; but without knowing it he becomes involved in them.

I suppose that a husband taught by the adventures of his own youth makes up his mind to pick out a doctor for his wife, from the first days of his marriage. So long as his feminine adversary fails to conceive the assistance that she may derive from this ally, she will submit in silence; but later on, if all her allurements fail to win over the man chosen by her husband, she will take a more favorable opportunity to give her husband her confidence, in the following remarkable manner.

"I don't like the way in which the doctor feels my pulse!"

And of course the doctor is dropped.

Thus it happens that either a woman chooses her doctor, wins over the man who has been imposed upon her, or procures his dismissal. But this contest is very rare; the majority of young men who marry are acquainted with none but beardless doctors whom they have no anxiety to procure for their wives, and almost always the Esculapius of the household is chosen by the feminine power. Thus it happens that some fine morning the doctor, when he leaves the chamber of madame, who has been in bed for a fortnight, is induced by her to say to you:

"I do not say that the condition of madame presents any serious symptoms; but this constant drowsiness, this general listlessness, and her natural tendency to a spinal affection demand great care. Her lymph is inspissated. She wants a change of air. She ought to be sent either to the waters of Bareges or to the waters of Plombieres."

"All right, doctor."

You allow your wife to go to Plombieres; but she goes there because Captain Charles is quartered in the Vosges. She returns in capital health and the waters of Plombieres have done wonders for her. She has written to you every day, she has lavished upon you from a distance every possible caress. The danger of a spinal affection has utterly disappeared.

There is extant a little pamphlet, whose publication was prompted doubtless by hate. It was published in Holland, and it contains some very curious details of the manner in which Madame de Maintenon entered into an understanding with Fagon, for the purposes of controlling Louis XIV. Well, some morning your doctor will threaten you, as Fagon threatened his master, with a fit of apoplexy, if you do not diet yourself. This witty work of satire, doubtless the production of some courtier, entitled "Madame de Saint Tron," has been interpreted by the modern author who has become proverbial as "the young doctor." But his delightful sketch is very much superior to the work whose title I cite for the benefit of the book-lovers, and we have great pleasure in acknowledging that the work of our clever contemporary has prevented us, out of regard for the glory of the seventeenth century, from publishing the fragment of the old pamphlet.

Very frequently a doctor becomes duped by the judicious manoeuvres of a young and delicate wife, and comes to you with the announcement:

"Sir, I would not wish to alarm madame with regard to her condition; but I will advise you, if you value her health, to keep her in perfect tranquillity. The irritation at this moment seems to threaten the chest, and we must gain control of it; there is need of rest for her, perfect rest; the least agitation might change the seat of the malady. At this crisis, the prospect of bearing a child would be fatal to her."

"But, doctor—"

"Ah, yes! I know that!"

He laughs and leaves the house.

Like the rod of Moses, the doctor's mandate makes and unmakes generations. The doctor will restore you to your marriage bed with the same arguments that he used in debarring you. He treats your wife for complaints which she has not, in order to cure her of those which she has, and all the while you have no idea of it; for the scientific jargon of doctors can only be compared to the layers in which they envelop their pills.

An honest woman in her chamber with the doctor is like a minister sure of a majority; she has it in her power to make a horse, or a carriage, according to her good pleasure and her taste; she will send you away or receive you, as she likes. Sometimes she will pretend to be ill in order to have a chamber separate from yours; sometimes she will surround herself with all the paraphernalia of an invalid; she will have an old woman for a nurse, regiments of vials and of bottles, and, environed by these ramparts, will defy you by her invalid airs. She will talk to you in such a depressing way of the electuaries and of the soothing draughts which she has taken, of the agues which she has had, of her plasters and cataplasms, that she will fill you with disgust at these sickly details, if all the time these sham sufferings are not intended to serve as engines by means of which, eventually, a successful attack may be made on that singular abstraction known as *your honor*.

In this way your wife will be able to fortify herself at every point of contact which you possess with the world, with society and with life. Thus everything will take arms against you, and you will be alone among all these enemies. But suppose that it is your unprecedented privilege to possess a wife who is without religious connections, without parents or intimate friends; that you have penetration enough to see through all the tricks by which your wife's lover tries to entrap you; that you still have sufficient love for your fair enemy to resist all the Martons of the earth; that, in fact, you have for your doctor a man who is so celebrated that he has no time to listen to the maunderings of your wife; or that if your Esculapius is madame's vassal, you demand a consultation, and an incorruptible doctor intervenes every time the favorite doctor prescribes a remedy that disquiets you; even in that case, your prospects will scarcely be more brilliant. In fact, even if you do not succumb to this invasion of allies, you must not forget that, so far, your adversary has not, so to speak, struck the decisive blow. If you hold out still longer, your wife, having flung round you thread upon thread, as a spider spins his web, an invisible net, will resort to the arms which nature has given her, which civilization has perfected, and which will be treated of in the next Meditation.

MEDITATION XXVI.
OF DIFFERENT WEAPONS.

A weapon is anything which is used for the purpose of wounding. From this point of view, some sentiments prove to be the most cruel weapons which man can employ against his fellow man. The genius of Schiller, lucid as it was comprehensive, seems to have revealed all the phenomena which certain ideas bring to light in the human organization by their keen and penetrating action. A man may be put to death by a thought. Such is the moral of those heartrending scenes, when in *The Brigands* the poet shows a young man, with the aid of certain ideas, making such powerful assaults on the heart of an old man, that he ends by causing the latter's death. The time is not far distant when science will be able to observe the complicated mechanism of our thoughts and to apprehend the transmission of our feelings. Some developer of the occult sciences will prove that our intellectual organization constitutes nothing more than a kind of interior man, who projects himself with less violence than the exterior man, and that the struggle which may take place between two such powers as these, although invisible to our feeble eyes, is not a less mortal struggle than that in which our external man compels us to engage.

But these considerations belong to a different department of study from that in which we are now engaged; these subjects we intend to deal with in a future publication; some of our friends are already acquainted with one of the most important,—that, namely, entitled "THE PATHOLOGY OF SOCIAL LIFE, *or Meditations mathematical, physical, chemical and transcendental on the manifestations of thought, taken under all the forms which are produced by the state of society, whether by living, marriage, conduct, veterinary medicine, or by speech and action, etc.,*" in which all these great questions are fully discussed. The aim of this brief metaphysical observation is only to remind you that the higher classes of society reason too well to admit of their being attacked by any other than intellectual arms.

Although it is true that tender and delicate souls are found enveloped in a body of metallic hardness, at the same time there are souls of bronze enveloped in bodies so supple and capricious that their grace attracts the friendship of others, and their beauty calls for a caress. But if you flatter the exterior man with your hand, the *Homo duplex*, the interior man, to use an expression of Buffon, immediately rouses himself and rends you with his keen points of contact.

This description of a special class of human creatures, which we hope you will not run up against during your earthly journey, presents a picture of what your wife may be to you. Every one of the sentiments which nature has endowed your heart with, in their gentlest form, will become a dagger in the hand of your wife. You will be stabbed every moment, and you will necessarily succumb; for your love will flow like blood from every wound.

This is the last struggle, but for her it also means victory.

In order to carry out the distinction which we think we have established among three sorts of feminine temperament, we will divide this Meditation into three parts, under the following titles:

1. OF HEADACHES.

2. OF NERVOUS AFFECTATIONS.

3. OF MODESTY, IN ITS CONNECTION WITH MARRIAGE.

1. OF HEADACHES.

Women are constantly the dupes or the victims of excessive sensibility; but we have already demonstrated that with the greater number of them this delicacy of soul must needs, almost without their knowing it, receive many rude blows, from the very fact of their marriage. (See Meditations entitled *The Predestined* and *Of the Honeymoon*.) Most of the means of defence instinctively employed by husbands are nothing but traps set for the liveliness of feminine affections.

Now the moment comes when the wife, during the Civil War, traces by a single act of thought the history of her moral life, and is irritated on perceiving the prodigious way in which you have taken advantage of her sensibility. It is very rarely that women, moved either by an innate feeling for revenge, which they themselves can never explain, or by their instinct of domination, fail to discover that this quality in their natural machinery, when brought into play against the man, is inferior to no other instrument for obtaining ascendancy over him.

With admirable cleverness, they proceed to find out what chords in the hearts of their husbands are most easily touched; and when once they discover this secret, they eagerly proceed to put it into practice; then, like a child with a mechanical toy, whose spring excites their curiosity, they go on employing it, carelessly calling into play the movements of the instrument, and satisfied simply with their success in doing so. If they kill you, they will mourn over you with the best grace in the world, as the most virtuous, the most excellent, the most sensible of men.

In this way your wife will first arm herself with that generous sentiment which leads us to respect those who are in pain. The man most disposed to quarrel with a woman full of life and health becomes helpless before a woman who is weak and feeble. If your wife has not attained the end of her secret designs, by means of those various methods already described, she will quickly seize this all-powerful weapon. In virtue of this new strategic method, you will see the young girl, so strong in life and beauty, whom you had wedded in her flower, metamorphosing herself into a pale and sickly woman.

Now headache is an affection which affords infinite resources to a woman.

This malady, which is the easiest of all to feign, for it is destitute of any apparent symptom, merely obliges her to say: "I have a headache." A woman trifles with you and there is no one in the world who can contradict her skull, whose impenetrable bones defy touch or ocular test. Moreover, headache is, in our opinion, the queen of maladies, the pleasantest and the most terrible weapon employed by wives against their husbands. There are some coarse and violent men who have been taught the tricks of women by their mistresses, in the happy hours of their celibacy, and so flatter themselves that they are never to be caught by this vulgar trap. But all their efforts, all their arguments end by being vanquished before the magic of these words: "I have a headache." If a husband complains, or ventures on a reproach, if he tries to resist the power of this *Il buondo cani* of marriage, he is lost.

Imagine a young woman, voluptuously lying on a divan, her head softly supported by a cushion, one hand hanging down; on a small table close at hand is her glass of lime-water. Now place by her side a burly husband. He has made five or six turns round the room; but each time he has turned on his heels to begin his walk all over again, the little invalid has made a slight movement of her eyebrows in a vain attempt to remind him that the slightest noise fatigues her. At last he musters all his courage and utters a protest against her pretended malady, in the bold phrase:

"And have you really a headache?"

At these words the young woman slightly raises her languid head, lifts an arm, which feebly falls back again upon her divan, raises her eyes to the ceiling, raises all that she has power to raise; then darting at you a leaden glance, she says in a voice of remarkable feebleness:

"Oh! What can be the matter with me? I suffer the agonies of death! And this is all the comfort you give me! Ah! you men, it is plainly seen that nature has not given you the task of bringing children into the world. What egoists and tyrants you are! You take us in all the beauty of our youth, fresh, rosy, with tapering waist, and then all is well! When your pleasures have ruined the blooming gifts which we received from nature, you never forgive us for having forfeited them to you! That was all understood. You will allow us to have neither the virtues nor the sufferings of our condition. You must needs have children, and we pass many nights in taking care of them. But child-bearing has ruined our health, and left behind the germs of serious maladies.—Oh, what pain I suffer! There are few women who are not subject to headaches; but your wife must be an exception. You even laugh at our sufferings; that is generosity!—please don't walk about —I should not have expected this of you!—Stop the clock; the click of the pendulum rings in my head. Thanks! Oh, what an unfortunate creature I am! Have you a scent-bottle with you? Yes, oh! for pity's sake, allow me to suffer in peace, and go away; for this scent splits my head!"

What can you say in reply? Do you not hear within you a voice which cries, "And what if she is actually suffering?" Moreover, almost all husbands evacuate the field of battle very quietly, while their wives watch them from the corner of their eyes, marching off on tip-toe and closing the door quietly on the chamber henceforth to be considered sacred by them.

Such is the headache, true or false, which is patronized at your home. Then the headache begins to play a regular role in the bosom of your family. It is a theme on which a woman can play many admirable variations. She sets it forth in every key. With the aid of the headache alone a wife can make a husband desperate. A headache seizes madame when she chooses, where she chooses, and as much as she chooses. There are headaches of five days, of ten minutes, periodic or intermittent headaches.

You sometimes find your wife in bed, in pain, helpless, and the blinds of her room are closed. The headache has imposed silence on every one, from the regions of the porter's lodge, where he is cutting wood, even to the garret of your groom, from which he is throwing down innocent bundles of straw. Believing in this headache, you leave the house, but on your return you find that madame has decamped! Soon madame returns, fresh and ruddy:

"The doctor came," she says, "and advised me to take exercise, and I find myself much better!"

Another day you wish to enter madame's room.

"Oh, sir," says the maid, showing the most profound astonishment, "madame has her usual headache, and I have never seen her in such pain! The doctor has been sent for."

"You are a happy man," said Marshal Augereau to General R— —-, "to have such a pretty wife!"

"To have!" replied the other. "If I have my wife ten days in the year, that is about all. These confounded women have always either the headache or some other thing!"

The headache in France takes the place of the sandals, which, in Spain, the Confessor leaves at the door of the chamber in which he is with his penitent.

If your wife, foreseeing some hostile intentions on your part, wishes to make herself as inviolable as the charter, she immediately gets up a little headache performance. She goes to bed in a most deliberate fashion, she utters shrieks which rend the heart of the hearer. She goes gracefully through a series of gesticulations so cleverly executed that you might think her a professional contortionist. Now what man is there so inconsiderate as to dare to speak to a suffering woman about desires which, in him, prove the most perfect health? Politeness alone demands of him perfect silence. A woman knows under these circumstances that by means of this all-powerful headache, she can at her will paste on her bed the placard which sends back home the amateurs who have been allured by the announcement of the Comedie Francaise, when they read the words: "Closed through the sudden indisposition of Mademoiselle Mars."

O headache, protectress of love, tariff of married life, buckler against which all married desires expire! O mighty headache! Can it be possible that lovers have never sung thy praises, personified thee, or raised thee to the skies? O magic headache, O delusive headache, blest be the brain that first invented thee! Shame on the doctor who shall find out thy preventive! Yes, thou art the only ill that women bless, doubtless through gratitude for the good things thou dispensest to them, O deceitful headache! O magic headache!

2. OF NERVOUS AFFECTATIONS.

There is, however, a power which is superior even to that of the headache; and we must avow to the glory of France, that this power is one of the most recent which has been won by Parisian genius. As in the case with all the most useful discoveries of art and science, no one knows to whose intellect it is due. Only, it is certain that it was towards the middle of the last century that "Vapors" made their first appearance in France. Thus while Papin was applying the force of vaporized water in mechanical problems, a French woman, whose name unhappily is unknown, had the glory of endowing her sex with the faculty of vaporizing their fluids. Very soon the prodigious influence obtained by vapors was extended to the nerves; it was thus in passing from fibre to fibre that the science of neurology was born. This admirable science has since then led such men as Philips and other clever physiologists to the discovery of the nervous fluid in its circulation; they are now perhaps on the eve of identifying its organs, and the secret of its origin and of its evaporation. And thus, thanks to certain quackeries of this kind, we may be enabled some day to penetrate the mysteries of that unknown power which we have already called more than once in the present book, the *Will*. But do not let us trespass on the territory of medical philosophy. Let us consider the nerves and the vapors solely in their connection with marriage.

Victims of Neurosis (a pathological term under which are comprised all affections of the nervous system) suffer in two ways, as far as married women are concerned; for our physiology has the loftiest disdain for medical classifications. Thus we recognize only:

1. CLASSIC NEUROSIS.

2. ROMANTIC NEUROSIS.

The classic affection has something bellicose and excitable on it. Those who thus suffer are as violent in their antics as pythonesses, as frantic as *monads*, as excited as *bacchantes*; it is a revival of antiquity, pure and simple.

The romantic sufferers are mild and plaintive as the ballads sung amid the mists of Scotland. They are pallid as young girls carried to their bier by the dance or by love; they are eminently elegiac and they breathe all the melancholy of the North.

That woman with black hair, with piercing eye, with high color, with dry lips and a powerful hand, will become excited and convulsive; she represents the genius of classic neurosis; while a young blonde woman, with white skin, is the genius of romantic neurosis; to one belongs the empire gained by nerves, to the other the empire gained by vapors.

Very frequently a husband, when he comes home, finds his wife in tears.

"What is the matter, my darling?"

"It is nothing."

"But you are in tears!"

"I weep without knowing why. I am quite sad! I saw faces in the clouds, and those faces never appear to me except on the eve of some disaster—I think I must be going to die."

Then she talks to you in a low voice of her dead father, of her dead uncle, of her dead grandfather, of her dead cousin. She invokes all these mournful shades, she feels as if she had all their sicknesses, she is attacked with all the pains they felt, she feels her heart palpitate with excessive violence, she feels her spleen swelling. You say to yourself, with a self-satisfied air:

"I know exactly what this is all about!"

And then you try to soothe her; but you find her a woman who yawns like an open box, who complains of her chest, who begins to weep anew, who implores you to leave her to her melancholy and her mournful memories. She talks to you about her last wishes, follows her own funeral, is buried, plants over her tomb the green canopy of a weeping willow, and at the very time when you would like to raise a joyful epithalamium, you find an epitaph to greet you all in black. Your wish to console her melts away in the cloud of Ixion.

There are women of undoubted fidelity who in this way extort from their feeling husbands cashmere shawls, diamonds, the payment of their debts, or the rent of a box at the theatre; but almost always vapors are employed as decisive weapons in Civil War.

On the plea of her spinal affection or of her weak chest, a woman takes pains to seek out some distraction or other; you see her dressing herself in soft fabrics like an invalid with all the symptoms of spleen; she never goes out because an intimate friend, her mother or her sister, has tried to tear her away from that divan which monopolizes her and on which she spends her life in improvising elegies. Madame is going to spend a fortnight in the country because the doctor orders it. In short, she goes where she likes and does what she likes. Is it possible that there can be a husband so brutal as to oppose such desires, by hindering a wife from going to seek a cure for her cruel sufferings? For it has been established after many long discussions that in the nerves originate the most fearful torture.

But it is especially in bed that vapors play their part. There when a woman has not a headache she has her vapors; and when she has neither vapors nor headache, she is under the protection of the girdle of Venus, which, as you know, is a myth.

Among the women who fight with you the battle of vapors, are some more blonde, more delicate, more full of feeling than others, and who possess the gift of tears. How admirably do they know how to weep! They weep when they like, as they like and as much as they like. They organize a system of offensive warfare which consists of manifesting sublime resignation, and they gain victories which are all the more brilliant, inasmuch as they remain all the time in excellent health.

Does a husband, irritated beyond all measure, at last express his wishes to them? They regard him with an air of submission, bow their heads and keep silence. This pantomime almost always puts a husband to rout. In conjugal struggles of this kind, a man prefers a woman should speak and defend herself, for then he may show elation or annoyance; but as for these women, not a word. Their silence distresses you and you experience a sort of remorse, like the murderer who, when he finds his victim offers no resistance, trembles with redoubled fear. He would prefer to slay him in self-defence. You return to the subject. As you draw near, your wife wipes away her tears and hides her handkerchief, so as to let you see that she has been weeping. You are melted, you implore your little Caroline to speak, your sensibility has been touched and you forget everything; then she sobs while she speaks, and speaks while she sobs. This is a sort of machine eloquence; she deafens you with her tears, with her words which come jerked out in confusion; it is the clapper and torrent of a mill.

French women and especially Parisians possess in a marvelous degree the secret by which such scenes are enacted, and to these scenes their voices, their sex, their toilet, their manner give a wonderful charm. How often do the tears upon the cheeks of these adorable actresses give way to a piquant smile, when they see their husbands hasten to break the silk lace, the weak fastening of their corsets, or to restore the comb which holds together the tresses of their hair and the bunch of golden ringlets always on the point of falling down?

But how all these tricks of modernity pale before the genius of antiquity, before nervous attacks which are violent, before the Pyrrhic dance of married life! Oh! how many hopes for a lover are there in the vivacity of those convulsive movements, in the fire of those glances, in the strength of those limbs, beautiful even in contortion! It is then that a woman is carried away like an impetuous wind, darts forth like the flames of a conflagration, exhibits a movement like a billow which glides over the white pebbles. She is overcome with excess of love, she sees the future, she is the seer who prophesies, but above all, she sees the present moment and tramples on her husband, and impresses him with a sort of terror.

The sight of his wife flinging off vigorous men as if they were so many feathers, is often enough to deter a man from ever striving to wrong her. He will be like the child who, having pulled the trigger of some terrific engine, has ever afterwards an incredible respect for the smallest spring. I have known a man, gentle and amiable in his ways, whose eyes were fixed upon those of his wife, exactly as if he had been put into a lion's cage, and some one had said to him that he must not irritate the beast, if he would escape with his life.

Nervous attacks of this kind are very fatiguing and become every day more rare. Romanticism, however, has maintained its ground.

Sometimes, we meet with phlegmatic husbands, those men whose love is long enduring, because they store up their emotions, whose genius gets the upper hand of these headaches and nervous attacks; but these sublime creatures are rare. Faithful disciples of the blessed St. Thomas, who wished to put his finger into the wound, they are endowed with an incredulity worthy of an atheist. Imperturbable in the midst of all these fraudulent headaches and all these traps set by neurosis, they concentrate their attention on the comedy which is being played before them, they examine the actress, they search for one of the springs that sets her going; and when they have discovered the mechanism of this display, they arm themselves by giving a slight impulse to the puppet-valve, and thus easily assure themselves either of the reality of the disease or the artifices of these conjugal mummeries.

But if by study which is almost superhuman in its intensity a husband escapes all the artifices which lawless and untamable love suggests to women, he will beyond doubt be overcome by the employment of a terrible weapon, the last which a woman would resort to, for she never destroys with her own hands her empire over her husband without some sort of repugnance. But this is a poisoned weapon as powerful as the fatal knife of the executioner. This reflection brings us to the last paragraph of the present Meditation.

3. OF MODESTY, IN ITS CONNECTION WITH MARRIAGE.

Before taking up the subject of modesty, it may perhaps be necessary to inquire whether there is such a thing. Is it anything in a woman but well understood coquetry? Is it anything but a sentiment that claims the right, on a woman's part, to dispose of her own body as she chooses, as one may well believe, when we consider that half the women in the world go almost naked? Is it anything but a social chimera, as Diderot supposed, reminding us that this sentiment always gives way before sickness and before misery?

Justice may be done to all these questions.

An ingenious author has recently put forth the view that men are much more modest than women. He supports this contention by a great mass of surgical experiences; but, in order that his conclusions merit our attention, it would be necessary that for a certain time men were subjected to treatment by women surgeons.

The opinion of Diderot is of still less weight.

To deny the existence of modesty, because it disappears during those crises in which almost all human sentiments are annihilated, is as unreasonable as to deny that life exists because death sooner or later comes.

Let us grant, then, that one sex has as much modesty as the other, and let us inquire in what modesty consists.

Rousseau makes modesty the outcome of all those coquetries which females display before males. This opinion appears to us equally mistaken.

The writers of the eighteenth century have doubtless rendered immense services to society; but their philosophy, based as it is upon sensualism, has never penetrated any deeper than the human epidermis. They have only considered the exterior universe; and so they have retarded, for some time, the moral development of man and the progress of science which will always draw its first principles from the Gospel, principles hereafter to be best understood by the fervent disciples of the Son of Man.

The study of thought's mysteries, the discovery of those organs which belong to the human soul, the geometry of its forces, the phenomena of its active power, the appreciation of the faculty by which we seem to have an independent power of bodily movement, so as to transport ourselves whither we will and to see without the aid of bodily organs, —in a word the laws of thought's dynamic and those of its physical influence,—these things will fall to the lot of the next century, as their portion in the treasury of human sciences. And perhaps we, of the present time, are merely occupied in quarrying the enormous blocks which later on some mighty genius will employ in the building of a glorious edifice.

Thus the error of Rousseau is simply the error of his age. He explains modesty by the relations of different human beings to each other instead of explaining it by the moral relations of each one with himself. Modesty is no more susceptible of analysis than conscience; and this perhaps is another way of saying that modesty is the conscience of the body; for while conscience directs our sentiments and the least movement of our thoughts towards the good, modesty presides over external movements. The actions which clash with our interests and thus disobey the laws of conscience wound us more than any other; and if they are repeated call forth our hatred. It is the same with acts which violate modesty in their relations to love, which is nothing but the expression of our whole sensibility. If extreme modesty is one of the conditions on which the reality of marriage is based, as we have tried to prove [See *Conjugal Catechism, Meditation IV.*], it is evident that immodesty will destroy it. But this position, which would require long deductions for the acceptance of the physiologist, women generally apply, as it were, mechanically; for society, which exaggerates everything for the benefit of the exterior man, develops this sentiment of women from childhood, and around it are grouped almost every other sentiment. Moreover, the moment that this boundless veil, which takes away the natural brutality from the least gesture, is dragged down, woman disappears. Heart, mind, love, grace, all are in ruins. In a situation where the virginal innocence of a daughter of Tahiti is most brilliant, the European becomes detestable. In this lies the last weapon which a wife seizes, in order to escape from the sentiment which her husband still fosters towards her. She is powerful because she had made herself loathsome; and this woman, who would count it as the greatest misfortune that her lover should be permitted to see the slightest mystery of her toilette, is delighted to exhibit herself to her husband in the most disadvantageous situation that can possibly be imagined.

It is by means of this rigorous system that she will try to banish you from the conjugal bed. Mrs. Shandy may be taken to mean us harm in bidding the father of Tristram wind up the clock; so long as your wife is not blamed for the pleasure she takes in interrupting you by the most imperative questions. Where there formerly was movement and life is now lethargy and death. An act of love becomes a transaction long discussed and almost, as it were, settled by notarial seal. But we have in another place shown that we never refuse to seize upon the comic element in a matrimonial crisis, although here we may be permitted to disdain the diversion which the muse of Verville and of Marshall have found in the treachery of feminine manoeuvres, the insulting audacity of their talk, amid the cold-blooded cynicism which they exhibit in certain situations. It is too sad to laugh at, and too funny to mourn over. When a woman resorts to such extreme measures, worlds at once separate her from her husband. Nevertheless, there are some women to whom Heaven has given the gift of being charming under all circumstances, who know how to put a certain witty and comic grace into these performances, and who have such smooth tongues, to use the expression of Sully, that they obtain forgiveness for their caprices and their mockeries, and never estrange the hearts of their husbands.

What soul is so robust, what man so violently in love as to persist in his passion, after ten years of marriage, in presence of a wife who loves him no longer, who gives him proofs of this every moment, who repulses him, who deliberately shows herself bitter, caustic, sickly and capricious, and who will abjure her vows of elegance and cleanliness, rather than not see her husband turn away from her; in presence of a wife who will stake the success of her schemes upon the horror caused by her indecency?

All this, my dear sir, is so much more horrible because—

XCII.

LOVERS IGNORE MODESTY.

We have now arrived at the last infernal circle in the Divine Comedy of Marriage. We are at the very bottom of Hell. There is something inexpressibly terrible in the situation of a married woman at the moment when unlawful love turns her away from her duties as mother and wife. As Diderot has very well put it, "infidelity in a woman is like unbelief in a priest, the last extreme of human failure; for her it is the greatest of social crimes, since it implies in her every other crime besides, and indeed either a wife profanes her lawless love by continuing to belong to her husband, or she breaks all the ties which attach her to her family, by giving herself over altogether to her lover. She ought to choose between the two courses, for her sole possible excuse lies in the intensity of her love."

She lives then between the claims of two obligations. It is a dilemma; she will work either the unhappiness of her lover, if he is sincere in his passion, or that of her husband, if she is still beloved by him.

It is to this frightful dilemma of feminine life that all the strange inconsistencies of women's conduct is to be attributed. In this lies the origin of all their lies, all their perfidies; here is the secret of all their mysteries. It is something to make one shudder. Moreover, even as simply based upon cold-blooded calculations, the conduct of a woman who accepts the unhappiness which attends virtue and scorns the bliss which is bought by crime, is a hundred times more reasonable. Nevertheless, almost all women will risk suffering in the future and ages of anguish for the ecstasy of one half hour. If the human feeling of self-preservation, if the fear of death does not check them, how fruitless must be the laws which send them for two years to the Madelonnettes? O sublime infamy! And when one comes to think that he for whom these sacrifices are to be made is one of our brethren, a gentleman to whom we would not trust our fortune, if we had one, a man who buttons his coat just as all of us do, it is enough to make one burst into a roar of laughter so loud, that starting from the Luxembourg it would pass over the whole of Paris and startle an ass browsing in the pasture at Montmartre.

It will perhaps appear extraordinary that in speaking of marriage we have touched upon so many subjects; but marriage is not only the whole of human life, it is the whole of two human lives. Now just as the addition of a figure to the drawing of a lottery multiplies the chances a hundredfold, so one single life united to another life multiplies by a startling progression the risks of human life, which are in any case so manifold.

II.

A woman is at a ball, one of her friends comes up to her and says:

"Your husband has much wit."

"You find it so?"

III.

Your wife discovers that it is time to send your boy to a boarding school, with whom, a little time ago, she was never going to part.

IV.

*In Lord Abergavenny's suit for divorce, the *valet de chambre* deposed that "the countess had such a detestation of all that belonged to my lord that he had very often seen her burning the scraps of paper which he had touched in her room."

V.

If an indolent woman becomes energetic, if a woman who formerly hated study learns a foreign language; in short, every appearance of a complete change in character is a decisive symptom.

VI.

The woman who is happy in her affections does not go much into the world.

VII.

The woman who has a lover becomes very indulgent in judging others.

VIII.

*A husband gives to his wife a hundred crowns a month for dress; and, taking everything into account, she spends at least five hundred francs without being a sou in debt; the husband is robbed every night with a high hand by escalade, but without burglarious breaking in.

IX.

*A married couple slept in the same bed; madame was always sick. Now they sleep apart, she has no more headache, and her health becomes more brilliant than ever; an alarming symptom!

X.

A woman who was a sloven suddenly develops extreme nicety in her attire. There is a Minotaur at hand!

XI.

"Ah! my dear, I know no greater torment than not to be understood."

"Yes, my dear, but when one is—"

"Oh, that scarcely ever happens."

"I agree with you that it very seldom does. Ah! it is great happiness, but there are not two people in the world who are able to understand you."

XII.

*The day when a wife behaves nicely to her husband—all is over.

XIII.

I asked her: "Where have you been, Jeanne?"

"I have been to your friend's to get your plate that you left there."

"Ah, indeed! everything is still mine," I said. The following year I repeated the question under similar circumstances.

"I have been to bring back our plate."

"Well, well, part of the things are still mine," I said. But after that, when I questioned her, she spoke very differently.

"You wish to know everything, like great people, and you have only three shirts. I went to get my plate from my friend's house, where I had stopped."

"I see," I said, "nothing is left me."

XIV.

Do not trust a woman who talks of her virtue.

XV.

Some one said to the Duchess of Chaulnes, whose life was despaired of:

"The Duke of Chaulnes would like to see you once more."

"Is he there?"

"Yes."

"Let him wait; he shall come in with the sacraments." This minotauric anecdote has been published by Chamfort, but we quote it here as typical.

XVI.

*Some women try to persuade their husbands that they have duties to perform towards certain persons.

"I am sure that you ought to pay a visit to such and such a man. . . . We cannot avoid asking such and such a man to dinner."

XVII.

"Come, my son, hold yourself straight: try to acquire good manners! Watch such and such a man! See how he walks! Notice the way in which he dresses."

XVIII.

When a woman utters the name of a man but twice a day, there is perhaps some uncertainty about her feelings toward him—but if thrice? —Oh! oh!

XIX.

When a woman goes home with a man who is neither a lawyer nor a minister, to the door of his apartment, she is very imprudent.

XX.

It is a terrible day when a husband fails to explain to himself the motive of some action of his wife.

XXI.

*The woman who allows herself to be found out deserves her fate.

What should be the conduct of a husband, when he recognizes a last symptom which leaves no doubt as to the infidelity of his wife? There are only two courses open; that of resignation or that of vengeance; there is no third course. If vengeance is decided upon, it should be complete.

The husband who does not separate himself forever from his wife is a veritable simpleton. If a wife and husband think themselves fit for that union of friendship which exists between men, it is odious in the husband to make his wife feel his superiority over her.

Here are some anecdotes, most of them as yet unpublished, which indicate pretty plainly, in my opinion, the different shades of conduct to be observed by a husband in like case.

M. de Roquemont slept once a month in the chamber of his wife, and he used to say, as he went away:

"I wash my hands of anything that may happen."

There is something disgusting in that remark, and perhaps something profound in its suggestion of conjugal policy.

A diplomat, when he saw his wife's lover enter, left his study and, going to his wife's chamber, said to the two:

"I hope you will at least refrain from fighting."

This was good humor.

M. de Boufflers was asked what he would do if on returning after a long absence he found his wife with child?

"I would order my night dress and slippers to be taken to her room."

This was magnanimity.

"Madame, if this man ill treats you when you are alone, it is your own fault; but I will not permit him to behave ill towards you in my presence, for this is to fail in politeness in me."

This was nobility.

The sublime is reached in this connection when the square cap of the judge is placed by the magistrate at the foot of the bed wherein the two culprits are asleep.

There are some fine ways of taking vengeance. Mirabeau has admirably described in one of the books he wrote to make a living the mournful resignation of that Italian lady who was condemned by her husband to perish with him in the Maremma.

LAST AXIOMS.

XCIII.

It is no act of vengeance to surprise a wife and her lover and to kill them locked in each other's arms; it is a great favor to them both.

XCIV

A husband will be best avenged by his wife's lover.

MEDITATION XXVIII.
OF COMPENSATIONS.

The marital catastrophe which a certain number of husbands cannot avoid, almost always forms the closing scene of the drama. At that point all around you is tranquil. Your resignation, if you are resigned, has the power of awakening keen remorse in the soul of your wife and of her lover; for their happiness teaches them the depth of the wound they have inflicted upon you. You are, you may be sure, a third element in all their pleasures. The principle of kindliness and goodness which lies at the foundation of the human soul, is not so easily repressed as people think; moreover the two people who are causing you tortures are precisely those for whom you wish the most good.

In the conversations so sweetly familiar which link together the pleasures of love, and form in some way to lovers the caresses of thought, your wife often says to your rival:

"Well, I assure you, Auguste, that in any case I should like to see my poor husband happy; for at bottom he is good; if he were not my husband, but were only my brother, there are so many things I would do to please him! He loves me, and—his friendship is irksome to me."

"Yes, he is a fine fellow!"

Then you become an object of respect to the celibate, who would yield to you all the indemnity possible for the wrong he has done you; but he is repelled by the disdainful pride which gives a tone to your whole conversation, and is stamped upon your face.

So that actually, during the first moments of the Minotaur's arrival, a man is like an actor who feels awkward in a theatre where he is not accustomed to appear. It is very difficult to bear the affront with dignity; but though generosity is rare, a model husband is sometimes found to possess it.

Eventually you are little by little won over by the charming way in which your wife makes herself agreeable to you. Madame assumes a tone of friendship which she never henceforth abandons. The pleasant atmosphere of your home is one of the chief compensations which renders the Minotaur less odious to a husband. But as it is natural to man to habituate himself to the hardest conditions, in spite of the sentiment of outraged nobility which nothing can change, you are gradually induced by a fascination whose power is constantly around you, to accept the little amenities of your position.

Suppose that conjugal misfortune has fallen upon an epicure. He naturally demands the consolations which suit his taste. His sense of pleasure takes refuge in other gratifications, and forms other habits. You shape your life in accordance with the enjoyment of other sensations.

One day, returning from your government office, after lingering for a long time before the rich and tasteful book shop of Chevet, hovering in suspense between the hundred francs of expense, and the joys of a Strasbourg *pate de fois gras*, you are struck dumb on finding this *pate* proudly installed on the sideboard of your dining-room. Is this the vision offered by some gastronomic mirage? In this doubting mood you approach with firm step, for a *pate* is a living creature, and seem to neigh as you scent afar off the truffles whose perfumes escape through the gilded enclosure. You stoop over it two distinct times; all the nerve centres of your palate have a soul; you taste the delights of a genuine feast, etc.; and during this ecstasy a feeling of remorse seizes upon you, and you go to your wife's room.

"Really, my dear girl, we have not means which warrant our buying *pates*."

"But it costs us nothing!"

"Oh! ho!"

"Yes, it is M. Achille's brother who sent it to him."

You catch sight of M. Achille in a corner. The celibate greets you, he is radiant on seeing that you have accepted the *pate*. You look at your wife, who blushes; you stroke your beard a few times; and, as you express no thanks, the two lovers divine your acceptance of the compensation.

A sudden change in the ministry takes place. A husband, who is Councillor of State, trembles for fear of being wiped from the roll, when the night before he had been made director-general; all the ministers are opposed to him and he has turned Constitutionalist. Foreseeing his disgrace he has betaken himself to Auteuil, in search of consolation from an old friend who quotes Horace and Tibullus to him. On returning home he sees the table laid as if to receive the most influential men of the assembly.

"In truth, madame," he says with acrimony as he enters his wife's room, where she is finishing her toilette, "you seem to have lost your habitual tact. This is a nice time to be giving dinner parties! Twenty persons will soon learn—"

"That you are director-general!" she cries, showing him a royal despatch.

He is thunderstruck. He takes the letter, he turns it now one way, now another; he opens it. He sits down and spreads it out.

"I well know," he says, "that justice would be rendered me under whatever ministers I served."

"Yes, my dear! But M. Villeplaine has answered for you with his life, and his eminence the Cardinal de — —- of whom he is the—"

"M. de Villeplaine?"

This is such a munificent recompense, that the husband adds with the smile of a director-general:

"Why, deuce take it, my dear, this is your doing!"

"Ah! don't thank me for it; Adolphe did it from personal attachment to you."

On a certain evening a poor husband was kept at home by a pouring rain, or tired, perhaps, of going to spend his evening in play, at the cafe, or in the world, and sick of all this he felt himself carried away by an impulse to follow his wife to the conjugal chamber. There he sank into an arm-chair and like any sultan awaited his coffee, as if he would say:

"Well, after all, she is my wife!"

The fair siren herself prepares the favorite draught; she strains it with special care, sweetens it, tastes it, and hands it to him; then, with a smile, she ventures like a submissive odalisque to make a joke, with a view to smoothing the wrinkles on the brow of her lord and master. Up to that moment he had thought his wife stupid; but on hearing a sally as witty as that which even you would cajole with, madame, he raises his head in the way peculiar to dogs who are hunting the hare.

"Where the devil did she get that—but it's a random shot!" he says to himself.

From the pinnacle of his own greatness he makes a piquant repartee. Madame retorts, the conversation becomes as lively as it is interesting, and this husband, a very superior man, is quite astonished to discover the wit of his wife, in other respects, an accomplished woman; the right word occurs to her with wonderful readiness; her tact and keenness enable her to meet an innuendo with charming originality. She is no longer the same woman. She notices the effect she produces upon her husband, and both to avenge herself for his neglect and to win his admiration for the lover from whom she has received, so to speak, the treasures of her intellect, she exerts herself, and becomes actually dazzling. The husband, better able than any one else to appreciate a species of compensation which may have some influence on his future, is led to think that the passions of women are really necessary to their mental culture.

But how shall we treat those compensations which are most pleasing to husbands?

Between the moment when the last symptoms appear, and the epoch of conjugal peace, which we will not stop to discuss, almost a dozen years have elapsed. During this interval and before the married couple sign the treaty which, by means of a sincere reconciliation of the feminine subject with her lawful lord, consecrates their little matrimonial restoration, in order to close in, as Louis XVIII said, the gulf of revolutions, it is seldom that the honest woman has but one lover. Anarchy has its inevitable phases. The stormy domination of tribunes is supplanted by that of the sword and the pen, for few loves are met with whose constancy outlives ten years. Therefore, since our calculations prove that an honest woman has merely paid strictly her physiological or diabolical dues by rendering but three men happy, it is probable that she has set foot in more than one region of love. Sometimes it may happen that in an interregnum of love too long protracted, the wife, whether from whim, temptation or the desire of novelty, undertakes to seduce her own husband.

Imagine charming Mme. de T— —-, the heroine of our Meditation of *Strategy*, saying with a fascinating smile:

"I never before found you so agreeable!"

By flattery after flattery, she tempts, she rouses curiosity, she soothes, she rouses in you the faintest spark of desire, she carries you away with her, and makes you proud of yourself. Then the right of indemnifications for her husband comes. On this occasion the wife confounds the imagination of her husband. Like cosmopolitan travelers she tells tales of all the countries which she had traversed. She intersperses her conversation with words borrowed from several languages. The passionate imagery of the Orient, the unique emphasis of Spanish phraseology, all meet and jostle one another. She opens out the treasures of her notebook with all the mysteries of coquetry, she is delightful, you never saw her thus before! With that remarkable art which women alone possess of making their own everything that has been told them, she blends all shades and variations of character so as to create a manner peculiarly her own. You received from the hands of Hymen only one woman, awkward and innocent; the celibate returns you a dozen of them. A joyful and rapturous husband sees his bed invaded by the giddy and wanton courtesans, of whom we spoke in the Meditation on *The First Symptoms*. These goddesses come in groups, they smile and sport under the graceful muslin curtains of the nuptial bed. The Phoenician girl flings to you her garlands, gently sways herself to and fro; the Chalcidian woman overcomes you by the witchery of her fine and snowy feet; the Unelmane comes and speaking the dialect of fair Ionia reveals the treasures of happiness unknown before, and in the study of which she makes you experience but a single sensation.

Filled with regret at having disdained so many charms, and frequently tired of finding too often as much perfidiousness in priestesses of Venus as in honest women, the husband sometimes hurries on by his gallantry the hour of reconciliation desired of worthy people. The aftermath of bliss is gathered even with greater pleasure, perhaps, than the first crop. The Minotaur took your gold, he makes restoration in diamonds. And really now seems the time to state a fact of the utmost importance. A man may have a wife without possessing her. Like most husbands you had hitherto received nothing from yours, and the powerful intervention of the celibate was needed to make your union complete. How shall we give a name to this miracle, perhaps the only one wrought upon a patient during his absence? Alas, my brothers, we did not make Nature!

But how many other compensations, not less precious, are there, by which the noble and generous soul of the young celibate may many a time purchase his pardon! I recollect witnessing one of the most magnificent acts of reparation which a lover should perform toward the husband he is minotaurizing.

One warm evening in the summer of 1817, I saw entering one of the rooms of Tortoni one of the two hundred young men whom we confidently style our friends; he was in the full bloom of his modesty. A lovely woman, dressed in perfect taste, and who had consented to enter one of the cool parlors devoted to people of fashion, had stepped from an elegant carriage which had stopped on the boulevard, and was approaching on foot along the sidewalk. My young friend, the celibate, then appeared and offered his arm to his queen, while the husband followed holding by the hand two little boys, beautiful as cupids. The two lovers, more nimble than the father of the family, reached in advance of him one of the small rooms pointed out by the attendant. In crossing the vestibule the husband knocked up against some dandy, who claimed that he had been jostled. Then arose a quarrel, whose seriousness was betrayed by the sharp tones of the altercation. The moment the dandy was about to make a gesture unworthy of a self-respecting man, the celibate intervened, seized the dandy by the arm, caught him off his guard, overcame and threw him to the ground; it was magnificent. He had done the very thing the aggressor was meditating, as he exclaimed:

"Monsieur!"

This "Monsieur" was one of the finest things I have ever heard. It was as if the young celibate had said: "This father of a family belongs to me; as I have carried off his honor, it is mine to defend him. I know my duty, I am his substitute and will fight for him." The young woman behaved superbly! Pale, and bewildered, she took the arm of her husband, who continued his objurgations; without a word she led him away to the carriage, together with her children. She was one of those women of the aristocracy, who also know how to retain their dignity and self-control in the midst of violent emotions.

"O Monsieur Adolphe!" cried the young lady as she saw her friend with an air of gayety take his seat in the carriage.

"It is nothing, madame, he is one of my friends; we have shaken hands."

Nevertheless, the next morning, the courageous celibate received a sword thrust which nearly proved fatal, and confined him six months to his bed. The attentions of the married couple were lavished upon him. What numerous compensations do we see here! Some years afterwards, an old uncle of the husband, whose opinions did not fit in with those of the young friend of the house, and who nursed a grudge against him on account of some political discussion, undertook to have him driven from the house. The old fellow went so far as to tell his nephew to choose between being his heir and sending away the presumptuous celibate. It was then that the worthy stockbroker said to his uncle:

"Ah, you must never think, uncle, that you will succeed in making me ungrateful! But if I tell him to do so this young man will let himself be killed for you. He has saved my credit, he would go through fire and water for me, he has relieved me of my wife, he has brought me clients, he has procured for me almost all the business in the Villele loans—I owe my life to him, he is the father of my children; I can never forget all this."

In this case the compensations may be looked upon as complete; but unfortunately there are compensations of all kinds. There are those which must be considered negative, deluding, and those which are both in one.

I knew a husband of advanced years who was possessed by the demon of gambling. Almost every evening his wife's lover came and played with him. The celibate gave him a liberal share of the pleasures which come from games of hazard, and knew how to lose to him a certain number of francs every month; but madame used to give them to him, and the compensation was a deluding one.

You are a peer of France, and you have no offspring but daughters. Your wife is brought to bed of a boy! The compensation is negative.

The child who is to save your name from oblivion is like his mother. The duchess persuades you that the child is yours. The negative compensation becomes deluding.

Here is one of the most charming compensations known. One morning the Prince de Ligne meets his wife's lover and rushes up to him, laughing wildly:

"My friend," he says to him, "I cuckolded you, last night!"

If some husbands attain to conjugal peace by quiet methods, and carry so gracefully the imaginary ensigns of matrimonial pre-eminence, their philosophy is doubtless based on the *comfortabilisme* of accepting certain compensations, a *comfortabilisme* which indifferent men cannot imagine. As years roll by the married couple reach the last stage in that artificial existence to which their union has condemned them.

MEDITATION XXIX.

OF CONJUGAL PEACE.

My imagination has followed marriage through all the phases of its fantastic life in so fraternal a spirit, that I seem to have grown old with the house I made my home so early in life at the commencement of this work.

After experiencing in thought the ardor of man's first passion; and outlining, in however imperfect a way, the principal incidents of married life; after struggling against so many wives that did not belong to me, exhausting myself in conflict with so many personages called up from nothingness, and joining so many battles, I feel an intellectual lassitude, which makes me see everything in life hang, as it were, in mournful crape. I seem to have a catarrh, to look at everything through green spectacles, I feel as if my hands trembled, as if I must needs employ the second half of my existence and of my book in apologizing for the follies of the first half.

I see myself surrounded by tall children of whom I am not the father, and seated beside a wife I never married. I think I can feel wrinkles furrowing my brow. The fire before which I am placed crackles, as if in derision, the room is ancient in its furniture; I shudder with sudden fright as I lay my hand upon my heart, and ask myself: "Is that, too, withered?"

I am like an old attorney, unswayed by any sentiment whatever. I never accept any statement unless it be confirmed, according to the poetic maxim of Lord Byron, by the testimony of at least two false witnesses. No face can delude me. I am melancholy and overcast with gloom. I know the world and it has no more illusions for me. My closest friends have proved traitors. My wife and myself exchange glances of profound meaning and the slightest word either of us utters is a dagger which pierces the heart of the other through and through. I stagnate in a dreary calm. This then is the tranquillity of old age! The old man possesses in himself the cemetery which shall soon possess him. He is growing accustomed to the chill of the tomb. Man, according to philosophers, dies in detail; at the same time he may be said even to cheat death; for that which his withered hand has laid hold upon, can it be called life?

Oh, to die young and throbbing with life! 'Tis a destiny enviable indeed! For is not this, as a delightful poet has said, "to take away with one all one's illusions, to be buried like an Eastern king, with all one's jewels and treasures, with all that makes the fortune of humanity!"

How many thank-offerings ought we to make to the kind and beneficent spirit that breathes in all things here below! Indeed, the care which nature takes to strip us piece by piece of our raiment, to unclothe the soul by enfeebling gradually our hearing, sight, and sense of touch, in making slower the circulation of our blood, and congealing our humors so as to make us as insensible to the approach of death as we were to the beginnings of life, this maternal care which she lavishes on our frail tabernacle of clay, she also exhibits in regard to the emotions of man, and to the double existence which is created by conjugal love. She first sends us Confidence, which with extended hand and open heart says to us: "Behold, I am thine forever!" Lukewarmness follows, walking with languid tread, turning aside her blonde face with a yawn, like a young widow obliged to listen to the minister of state who is ready to sign for her a pension warrant. Then Indifference comes; she stretches herself on the divan, taking no care to draw down the skirts of her robe which Desire but now lifted so chastely and so eagerly. She casts a glance upon the nuptial bed, with modesty and without shamelessness; and, if she longs for anything, it is for the green fruit that calls up again to life the dulled papillae with which her blase palate is bestrewn. Finally the philosophical Experience of Life presents herself, with careworn and disdainful brow, pointing with her finger to the results, and not the causes of life's incidents; to the tranquil victory, not to the tempestuous combat. She reckons up the arrearages, with farmers, and calculates the dowry of a child. She materializes everything. By a touch of her wand, life becomes solid and springless; of yore, all was fluid, now it is crystallized into rock. Delight no longer exists for our hearts, it has received its sentence, 'twas but mere sensation, a passing paroxysm. What the soul desires to-day is a condition of fixity; and happiness alone is permanent, and consists in absolute tranquillity, in the regularity with which eating and sleeping succeed each other, and the sluggish organs perform their functions.

"This is horrible!" I cried; "I am young and full of life! Perish all the books in the world rather than my illusions should perish!"

I left my laboratory and plunged into the whirl of Paris. As I saw the fairest faces glide by before me, I felt that I was not old. The first young woman who appeared before me, lovely in face and form and dressed to perfection, with one glance of fire made all the sorcery whose spells I had voluntarily submitted to vanish into thin air. Scarcely had I walked three steps in the Tuileries gardens, the place which I had chosen as my destination, before I saw the prototype of the matrimonial situation which has last been described in this book. Had I desired to characterize, to idealize, to personify marriage, as I conceived it to be, it would have been impossible for the Creator himself to have produced so complete a symbol of it as I then saw before me.

Imagine a woman of fifty, dressed in a jacket of reddish brown merino, holding in her left hand a green cord, which was tied to the collar of an English terrier, and with her right arm linked with that of a man in knee-breeches and silk stockings, whose hat had its brim whimsically turned up, while snow-white tufts of hair like pigeon plumes rose at its sides. A slender queue, thin as a quill, tossed about on the back of his sallow neck, which was thick, as far as it could be seen above the turned down collar of a threadbare coat. This couple assumed the stately tread of an ambassador; and the husband, who was at least seventy, stopped complaisantly every time the terrier began to gambol. I hastened to pass this living impersonation of my Meditation, and was surprised to the last degree to recognize the Marquis de T— —-, friend of the Comte de Noce, who had owed me for a long time the end of the interrupted story which I related in the *Theory of the Bed*. [See Meditation XVII.]

"I have the honor to present to you the Marquise de T— —-," he said to me.

I made a low bow to a lady whose face was pale and wrinkled; her forehead was surmounted by a toupee, whose flattened ringlets, ranged around it, deceived no one, but only emphasized, instead of concealing, the wrinkles by which it was deeply furrowed. The lady was slightly roughed, and had the appearance of an old country actress.

"I do not see, sir, what you can say against a marriage such as ours," said the old man to me.

"The laws of Rome forefend!" I cried, laughing.

The marchioness gave me a look filled with inquietude as well as disapprobation, which seemed to say, "Is it possible that at my age I have become but a concubine?"

We sat down upon a bench, in the gloomy clump of trees planted at the corner of the high terrace which commands La Place Louis XV, on the side of the Garde-Meuble. Autumn had already begun to strip the trees of their foliage, and was scattering before our eyes the yellow leaves of his garland; but the sun nevertheless filled the air with grateful warmth.

"Well, is your work finished?" asked the old man, in the unctuous tones peculiar to men of the ancient aristocracy.

And with these words he gave a sardonic smile, as if for commentary.

"Very nearly, sir," I replied. "I have come to the philosophic situation, which you appear to have reached, but I confess that I—"

"You are searching for ideas?" he added—finishing for me a sentence, which I confess I did not know how to end.

"Well," he continued, "you may boldly assume, that on arriving at the winter of his life, a man—a man who thinks, I mean—ends by denying that love has any existence, in the wild form with which our illusions invested it!"

"What! would you deny the existence of love on the day after that of marriage?"

"In the first place, the day after would be the very reason; but my marriage was a commercial speculation," replied he, stooping to speak into my ear. "I have thereby purchased the care, the attention, the services which I need; and I am certain to obtain all the consideration my age demands; for I have willed all my property to my nephew, and as my wife will be rich only during my life, you can imagine how—"

I turned on the old marquis a look so piercing that he wrung my hand and said: "You seem to have a good heart, for nothing is certain in this life—"

"Well, you may be sure that I have arranged a pleasant surprise for her in my will," he replied, gayly.

"Come here, Joseph," cried the marchioness, approaching a servant who carried an overcoat lined with silk. "The marquis is probably feeling the cold."

The old marquis put on his overcoat, buttoned it up, and taking my arm, led me to the sunny side of the terrace.

"In your work," he continued, "you have doubtless spoken of the love of a young man. Well, if you wish to act up to the scope which you give to your work—in the word ec—elec—"

"Eclectic," I said, smiling, seeing he could not remember this philosophic term.

"I know the word well!" he replied. "If then you wish to keep your vow of eclecticism, you should be willing to express certain virile ideas on the subject of love which I will communicate to you, and I will not grudge you the benefit of them, if benefit there be; I wish to bequeath my property to you, but this will be all that you will get of it."

"There is no money fortune which is worth as much as a fortune of ideas if they be valuable ideas! I shall, therefore, listen to you with a grateful mind."

"There is no such thing as love," pursued the old man, fixing his gaze upon me. "It is not even a sentiment, it is an unhappy necessity, which is midway between the needs of the body and those of the soul. But siding for a moment with your youthful thoughts, let us try to reason upon this social malady. I suppose that you can only conceive of love as either a need or a sentiment."

I made a sign of assent.

"Considered as a need," said the old man, "love makes itself felt last of all our needs, and is the first to cease. We are inclined to love in our twentieth year, to speak in round numbers, and we cease to do so at fifty. During these thirty years, how often would the need be felt, if it were not for the provocation of city manners, and the modern custom of living in the presence of not one woman, but of women in general? What is our debt to the perpetuation of the race? It probably consists in producing as many children as we have breasts—so that if one dies the other may live. If these two children were always faithfully produced, what would become of nations? Thirty millions of people would constitute a population too great for France, for the soil is not sufficient to guarantee more than ten millions against misery and hunger. Remember that China is reduced to the expedient of throwing its children into the water, according to the accounts of travelers. Now this production of two children is really the whole of marriage. The superfluous pleasures of marriage are not only profligate, but involve an immense loss to the man, as I will now demonstrate. Compare then with this poverty of result, and shortness of duration, the daily and perpetual urgency of other needs of our existence. Nature reminds us every hour of our real needs; and, on the other hand, refuses absolutely to grant the excess which our imagination sometimes craves in love. It is, therefore, the last of our needs, and the only one which may be forgotten without causing any disturbance in the economy of the body. Love is a social luxury like lace and diamonds. But if we analyze it as a sentiment, we find two distinct elements in it; namely, pleasure and passion. Now analyze pleasure. Human affections rest upon two foundations, attraction and repulsion. Attraction is a universal feeling for those things which flatter our instinct of self-preservation; repulsion is the exercise of the same instinct when it tells us that something is near which threatens it with injury. Everything which profoundly moves our organization gives us a deeper sense of our existence; such a thing is pleasure. It is contracted of desire, of effort, and the joy of possessing something or other. Pleasure is a unique element in life, and our passions are nothing but modifications, more or less keen, of pleasure; moreover, familiarity with one pleasure almost always precludes the enjoyment of all others. Now, love is the least keen and the least durable of our pleasures. In what would you say the pleasure of love consists? Does it lie in the beauty of the beloved? In one evening you may obtain for money the loveliest odalisques; but at the end of a month you will in this way have burnt out all your sentiment for all time. Would you love a women because she is well dressed, elegant, rich, keeps a carriage, has commercial credit? Do not call this love, for it is vanity, avarice, egotism. Do you love her because she is intellectual? You are in that case merely obeying the dictates of literary sentiment."

"But," I said, "love only reveals its pleasures to those who mingle in one their thoughts, their fortunes, their sentiments, their souls, their lives—"

"Oh dear, dear!" cried the old man, in a jeering tone. "Can you show me five men in any nation who have sacrificed anything for a woman? I do not say their life, for that is a slight thing,—the price of a human life under Napoleon was never more than twenty thousand francs; and there are in France to-day two hundred and fifty thousand brave men who would give theirs for two inches of red ribbon; while seven men have sacrificed for a woman ten millions on which they might have slept in solitude for a whole night. Dubreuil and Phmeja are still rarer than is the love of Dupris and Bolingbroke. These sentiments proceed from an unknown cause. But you have brought me thus to consider love as a passion. Yes, indeed, it is the last of them all and the most contemptible. It promises everything, and fulfils nothing. It comes, like love, as a need, the last, and dies away the first. Ah, talk to me of revenge, hatred, avarice, of gaming, of ambition, of fanaticism. These passions have something virile in them; these sentiments are imperishable; they make sacrifices every day, such as love only makes by fits and starts. But," he went on, "suppose you abjure love. At first there will be no disquietudes, no anxieties, no worry, none of those little vexations that waste human life. A man lives happy and tranquil; in his social relations he becomes infinitely more powerful and influential. This divorce from the thing called love is the primary secret of power in all men who control large bodies of men; but this is a mere trifle. Ah! if you knew with what magic influence a man is endowed, what wealth of intellectual force, what longevity in physical strength he enjoys, when detaching himself from every species of human passion he spends all his energy to the profit of his soul! If you could enjoy for two minutes the riches which God dispenses to the enlightened men who consider love as merely a passing need which it is sufficient to satisfy for six months in their twentieth year; to the men who, scorning the luxurious and surfeiting beefsteaks of Normandy, feed on the roots which God has given in abundance, and take their repose on a bed of withered leaves, like the recluses of the Thebaid!—ah! you would not keep on three seconds the wool of fifteen merinos which covers you; you would fling away your childish switch, and go to live in the heaven of heavens! There you would find the love you sought in vain amid the swine of earth; there you would hear a concert of somewhat different melody from that of M. Rossini, voices more faultless than that of Malibran. But I am speaking as a blind man might, and repeating hearsays. If I had not visited Germany about the year 1791, I should know nothing of all this. Yes!—man has a vocation for the infinite. There dwells within him an instinct that calls him to God. God is all, gives all, brings oblivion on all, and thought is the thread which he has given us as a clue to communication with himself!"

He suddenly stopped, and fixed his eyes upon the heavens.

"The poor fellow has lost his wits!" I thought to myself.

"Sir," I said to him, "it would be pushing my devotion to eclectic philosophy too far to insert your ideas in my book; they would destroy it. Everything in it is based on love, platonic and sensual. God forbid that I should end my book by such social blasphemies! I would rather try to return by some pantagruelian subtlety to my herd of celibates and honest women, with many an attempt to discover some social utility in their passions and follies. Oh! if conjugal peace leads us to arguments so disillusionizing and so gloomy as these, I know a great many husbands who would prefer war to peace."

"At any rate, young man," the old marquis cried, "I shall never have to reproach myself with refusing to give true directions to a traveler who had lost his way."

"Adieu, thou old carcase!" I said to myself; "adieu, thou walking marriage! Adieu, thou stick of a burnt-out fire-work! Adieu, thou machine! Although I have given thee from time to time some glimpses of people dear to me, old family portraits,—back with you to the picture dealer's shop, to Madame de T——-, and all the rest of them; take your place round the bier with undertaker's mutes, for all I care!"

MEDITATION XXX.
CONCLUSION.

A recluse, who was credited with the gift of second sight, having commanded the children of Israel to follow him to a mountain top in order to hear the revelation of certain mysteries, saw that he was accompanied by a crowd which took up so much room on the road that, prophet as he was, his *amour-propre* was vastly tickled.

But as the mountain was a considerable distance off, it happened that at the first halt, an artisan remembered that he had to deliver a new pair of slippers to a duke and peer, a publican fell to thinking how he had some specie to negotiate, and off they went.

A little further on two lovers lingered under the olive trees and forgot the discourse of the prophet; for they thought that the promised land was the spot where they stood, and the divine word was heard when they talked to one another.

The fat people, loaded with punches a la Sancho, had been wiping their foreheads with their handkerchiefs, for the last quarter of an hour, and began to grow thirsty, and therefore halted beside a clear spring.

Certain retired soldiers complained of the corns which tortured them, and spoke of Austerlitz, and of their tight boots.

At the second halt, certain men of the world whispered together:

"But this prophet is a fool."

"Have you ever heard him?"

"I? I came from sheer curiosity."

"And I because I saw the fellow had a large following." (The last man who spoke was a fashionable.)

"He is a mere charlatan."

The prophet kept marching on. But when he reached the plateau, from which a wide horizon spread before him, he turned back, and saw no one but a poor Israelite, to whom he might have said as the Prince de Ligne to the wretched little bandy-legged drummer boy, whom he found on the spot where he expected to see a whole garrison awaiting him: "Well, my readers, it seems that you have dwindled down to one."

Thou man of God who has followed me so far—I hope that a short recapitulation will not terrify thee, and I have traveled on under the impression that thou, like me, hast kept saying to thyself, "Where the deuce are we going?"

Well, well, this is the place and the time to ask you, respected reader, what your opinion is with regard to the renewal of the tobacco monopoly, and what you think of the exorbitant taxes on wines, on the right to carry firearms, on gaming, on lotteries, on playing cards, on brandy, on soap, cotton, silks, etc.

"I think that since all these duties make up one-third of the public revenues, we should be seriously embarrassed if—"

So that, my excellent model husband, if no one got drunk, or gambled, or smoked, or hunted, in a word if we had neither vices, passions, nor maladies in France, the State would be within an ace of bankruptcy; for it seems that the capital of our national income consists of popular corruptions, as our commerce is kept alive by national luxury. If you cared to look a little closer into the matter you would see that all taxes are based upon some moral malady. As a matter of fact, if we continue this philosophical scrutiny it will appear that the gendarmes would want horses and leather breeches, if every one kept the peace, and if there were neither foes nor idle people in the world. Therefore impose virtue on mankind! Well, I consider that there are more parallels than people think between my honest woman and the budget, and I will undertake to prove this by a short essay on statistics, if you will permit me to finish my book on the same lines as those on which I have begun it. Will you grant that a lover must put on more clean shirts than are worn by either a husband, or a celibate unattached? This to me seems beyond doubt. The difference between a husband and a lover is seen even in the appearance of their toilette. The one is careless, he is unshaved, and the other never appears excepting in full dress. Sterne has pleasantly remarked that the account book of the laundress was the most authentic record he knew, as to the life of Tristram Shandy; and that it was easy to guess from the number of shirts he wore what passages of his book had cost him most. Well, with regard to lovers the account book of their laundresses is the most faithful historic record as well as the most impartial account of their various amours. And really a prodigious quantity of tippets, cravats, dresses, which are absolutely necessary to coquetry, is consumed in the course of an amour. A wonderful prestige is gained by white stockings, the lustre of a collar, or a shirt-waist, the artistically arranged folds of a man's shirt, or the taste of his necktie or his collar. This will explain the passages in which I said of the honest woman [Meditation II], "She spends her life in having her dresses starched." I have sought information on this point from a lady in order to learn accurately at what sum was to be estimated the tax thus imposed by love, and after fixing it at one hundred francs per annum for a woman, I recollect what she said with great good humor: "It depends on the character of the man, for some are so much more particular than others." Nevertheless, after a very profound discussion, in which I settled upon the sum for the celibates, and she for her sex, it was agreed that, one thing with another, since the two lovers belong to the social sphere which this work concerns, they ought to spend between them, in the matter referred to, one hundred and fifty francs more than in time of peace.

By a like treaty, friendly in character and long discussed, we arranged that there should be a collective difference of four hundred francs between the expenditure for all parts of the dress on a war footing, and for that on a peace footing. This provision was considered very paltry by all the powers, masculine or feminine, whom we consulted. The light thrown upon these delicate matters by the contributions of certain persons suggested to us the idea of gathering together certain savants at a dinner party, and taking their wise counsels for our guidance in these important investigations. The gathering took place. It was with glass in hand and after listening to many brilliant speeches that I received for the following chapters on the budget of love, a sort of legislative sanction. The sum of one hundred francs was allowed for porters and carriages. Fifty crowns seemed very reasonable for the little patties that people eat on a walk, for bouquets of violets and theatre tickets. The sum of two hundred francs was considered necessary for the extra expense of dainties and dinners at restaurants. It was during this discussion that a young cavalryman, who had been made almost tipsy by the champagne, was called to order for comparing lovers to distilling machines. But the chapter that gave occasion for the most violent discussion, and the consideration of which was adjourned for several weeks, when a report was made, was that concerning presents. At the last session, the refined Madame de D———- was the first speaker; and in a graceful address, which testified to the nobility of her sentiments, she set out to demonstrate that most of the time the gifts of love had no intrinsic value. The author replied that all lovers had their portraits taken. A lady objected that a portrait was invested capital, and care should always be taken to recover it for a second investment. But suddenly a gentleman of Provence rose to deliver a philippic against women. He spoke of the greediness which most women in love exhibited for furs, satins, silks, jewels and furniture; but a lady interrupted him by asking if Madame d'O———-y, his intimate friend, had not already paid his debts twice over.

"You are mistaken, madame," said the Provencal, "it was her husband."

"The speaker is called to order," cried the president, "and condemned to dine the whole party, for having used the word *husband*."

The Provencal was completely refuted by a lady who undertook to prove that women show much more self-sacrifice in love than men; that lovers cost very dear, and that the honest woman may consider herself very fortunate if she gets off with spending on them two thousand francs for a single year. The discussion was in danger of degenerating into an exchange of personalities, when a division was called for. The conclusions of the committee were adopted by vote. The conclusions were, in substance, that the amount for presents between lovers during the year should be reckoned at five hundred francs, but that in this computation should be included: (1) the expense of expeditions into the country; (2) the pharmaceutical expenses, occasioned by the colds caught from walking in the damp pathways of parks, and in leaving the theatre, which expenses are veritable presents; (3) the carrying of letters, and law expenses; (4) journeys, and expenses whose items are forgotten, without counting the follies committed by the spenders; inasmuch as, according to the investigations of the committee, it had been proved that most of a man's extravagant expenditure profited the opera girls, rather than the married

MEDITATION XXVII.
OF THE LAST SYMPTOMS.

The author of this book has met in the world so many people possessed by a fanatic passion for a knowledge of the mean time, for watches with a second hand, and for exactness in the details of their existence, that he has considered this Meditation too necessary for the tranquillity of a great number of husbands, to be omitted. It would have been cruel to leave men, who are possessed with the passion for learning the hour of the day, without a compass whereby to estimate the last variations in the matrimonial zodiac, and to calculate the precise moment when the sign of the Minotaur appears on the horizon. The knowledge of conjugal time would require a whole book for its exposition, so fine and delicate are the observations required by the task. The master admits that his extreme youth has not permitted him as yet to note and verify more than a few symptoms; but he feels a just pride, on his arrival at the end of his difficult enterprise, from the consciousness that he is leaving to his successors a new field of research; and that in a matter apparently so trite, not only was there much to be said, but also very many points are found remaining which may yet be brought into the clear light of observation. He therefore presents here without order or connection the rough outlines which he has so far been able to execute, in the hope that later he may have leisure to co-ordinate them and to arrange them in a complete system. If he has been so far kept back in the accomplishment of a task of supreme national importance, he believes, he may say, without incurring the charge of vanity, that he has here indicated the natural division of those symptoms. They are necessarily of two kinds: the unicorns and the bicorns. The unicorn Minotaur is the least mischievous. The two culprits confine themselves to a platonic love, in which their passion, at least, leaves no visible traces among posterity; while the bicorn Minotaur is unhappiness with all its fruits.

We have marked with an asterisk the symptoms which seem to concern the latter kind.

MINOTAURIC OBSERVATIONS.

I.

*When, after remaining a long time aloof from her husband, a woman makes overtures of a very marked character in order to attract his love, she acts in accordance with the axiom of maritime law, which says: *The flag protects the cargo.*

women. The conclusion arrived at from this pecuniary calculation was that, in one way or another, a passion costs nearly fifteen hundred francs a year, which were required to meet the expense borne more unequally by lovers, but which would not have occurred, but for their attachment. There was also a sort of unanimity in the opinion of the council that this was the lowest annual figure which would cover the cost of a passion. Now, my dear sir, since we have proved, by the statistics of our conjugal calculations [See Meditations I, II, and III.] and proved irrefragably, that there exists a floating total of at least fifteen hundred thousand unlawful passions, it follows:

That the criminal conversations of a third among the French population contribute a sum of nearly three thousand millions to that vast circulation of money, the true blood of society, of which the budget is the heart;

That the honest woman not only gives life to the children of the peerage, but also to its financial funds;

That manufacturers owe their prosperity to this *systolic* movement;

That the honest woman is a being essentially *budgetative*, and active as a consumer;

That the least decline in public love would involve incalculable miseries to the treasury, and to men of invested fortunes;

That a husband has at least a third of his fortune invested in the inconstancy of his wife, etc.

I am well aware that you are going to open your mouth and talk to me about manners, politics, good and evil. But, my dear victim of the Minotaur, is not happiness the object which all societies should set before them? Is it not this axiom that makes these wretched kings give themselves so much trouble about their people? Well, the honest woman has not, like them, thrones, gendarmes and tribunals; she has only a bed to offer; but if our four hundred thousand women can, by this ingenious machine, make a million celibates happy, do not they attain in a mysterious manner, and without making any fuss, the end aimed at by a government, namely, the end of giving the largest possible amount of happiness to the mass of mankind?

"Yes, but the annoyances, the children, the troubles—"

Ah, you must permit me to proffer the consolatory thought with which one of our wittiest caricaturists closes his satiric observations: "Man is not perfect!" It is sufficient, therefore, that our institutions have no more disadvantages than advantages in order to be reckoned excellent; for the human race is not placed, socially speaking, between the good and the bad, but between the bad and the worse. Now if the work, which we are at present on the point of concluding, has had for its object the diminution of the worse, as it is found in matrimonial institutions, in laying bare the errors and absurdities due to our manners and our prejudices, we shall certainly have won one of the fairest titles that can be put forth by a man to a place among the benefactors of humanity. Has not the author made it his aim, by advising husbands, to make women more self-restrained and consequently to impart more violence to passions, more money to the treasury, more life to commerce and agriculture? Thanks to this last Meditation he can flatter himself that he has strictly kept the vow of eclecticism, which he made in projecting the work, and he hopes he has marshaled all details of the case, and yet like an attorney-general refrained from expressing his personal opinion. And really what do you want with an axiom in the present matter? Do you wish that this book should be a mere development of the last opinion held by Tronchet, who in his closing days thought that the law of marriage had been drawn up less in the interest of husbands than of children? I also wish it very much. Would you rather desire that this book should serve as proof to the peroration of the Capuchin, who preached before Anne of Austria, and when he saw the queen and her ladies overwhelmed by his triumphant arguments against their frailty, said as he came down from the pulpit of truth, "Now you are all honorable women, and it is we who unfortunately are sons of Samaritan women"? I have no objection to that either. You may draw what conclusion you please; for I think it is very difficult to put forth two contrary opinions, without both of them containing some grains of truth. But the book has not been written either for or against marriage; all I have thought you needed was an exact description of it. If an examination of the machine shall lead us to make one wheel of it more perfect; if by scouring away some rust we have given more elastic movement to its mechanism; then give his wage to the workman. If the author has had the impertinence to utter truths too harsh for you, if he has too often spoken of rare and exceptional facts as universal, if he has omitted the commonplaces which have been employed from time immemorial to offer women the incense of flattery, oh, let him be crucified! But do not impute to him any motive of hostility to the institution itself; he is concerned merely for men and women. He knows that from the moment marriage ceases to defeat the purpose of marriage, it is unassailable; and, after all, if there do arise serious complaints against this institution, it is perhaps because man has no memory excepting for his disasters, that he accuses his wife, as he accuses his life, for marriage is but a life within a life. Yet people whose habit it is to take their opinions from newspapers would perhaps despise a book in which they see the mania of eclecticism pushed too far; for then they absolutely demand something in the shape of a peroration, it is not hard to find one for them. And since the words of Napoleon served to start this book, why should it not end as it began? Before the whole Council of State the First Consul pronounced the following startling phrase, in which he at the same time eulogized and satirized marriage, and summed up the contents of this book:

"If a man never grew old, I would never wish him to have a wife!"

POSTSCRIPT.

"And so you are going to be married?" asked the duchess of the author who had read his manuscript to her.

She was one of those ladies to whom the author has already paid his respects in the introduction of this work.

"Certainly, madame," I replied. "To meet a woman who has courage enough to become mine, would satisfy the wildest of my hopes."

"Is this resignation or infatuation?"

"That is my affair."

"Well, sir, as you are doctor of conjugal arts and sciences, allow me to tell you a little Oriental fable, that I read in a certain sheet, which is published annually in the form of an almanac. At the beginning of the Empire ladies used to play at a game in which no one accepted a present from his or her partner in the game, without saying the word, *Diadeste*. A game lasted, as you may well suppose, during a week, and the point was to catch some one receiving some trifle or other without pronouncing the sacramental word."

"Even a kiss?"

"Oh, I have won the *Diadeste* twenty times in that way," she laughingly replied.

"It was, I believe, from the playing of this game, whose origin is Arabian or Chinese, that my apologue takes its point. But if I tell you," she went on, putting her finger to her nose, with a charming air of coquetry, "let me contribute it as a finale to your work."

"This would indeed enrich me. You have done me so many favors already, that I cannot repay—"

She smiled slyly, and replied as follows:

A philosopher had compiled a full account of all the tricks that women could possibly play, and in order to verify it, he always carried it about with him. One day he found himself in the course of his travels near an encampment of Arabs. A young woman, who had seated herself under the shade of a palm tree, rose on his approach. She kindly asked him to rest himself in her tent, and he could not refuse. Her husband was then absent. Scarcely had the traveler seated himself on a soft rug, when the graceful hostess offered him fresh dates, and a cup of milk; he could not help observing the rare beauty of her hands as she did so. But, in order to distract his mind from the sensations roused in him by the fair young Arabian girl, whose charms were most formidable, the sage took his book, and began to read.

The seductive creature piqued by this slight said to him in a melodious voice:

"That book must be very interesting since it seems to be the sole object worthy of your attention. Would it be taking a liberty to ask what science it treats of?"

The philosopher kept his eyes lowered as he replied:

"The subject of this book is beyond the comprehension of ladies."

This rebuff excited more than ever the curiosity of the young Arabian woman. She put out the prettiest little foot that had ever left its fleeting imprint on the shifting sands of the desert. The philosopher was perturbed, and his eyes were too powerfully tempted to resist wandering from these feet, which betokened so much, up to the bosom, which was still more ravishingly fair; and soon the flame of his admiring glance was mingled with the fire that sparkled in the pupils of the young Asiatic. She asked again the name of the book in tones so sweet that the philosopher yielded to the fascination, and replied:

"I am the author of the book; but the substance of it is not mine: it contains an account of all the ruses and stratagems of women."

"What! Absolutely all?" said the daughter of the desert.

"Yes, all! And it has been only by a constant study of womankind that I have come to regard them without fear."

"Ah!" said the young Arabian girl, lowering the long lashes of her white eyelids.

Then, suddenly darting the keenest of her glances at the pretended sage, she made him in one instant forget the book and all its contents. And now our philosopher was changed to the most passionate of men. Thinking he saw in the bearing of the young woman a faint trace of coquetry, the stranger was emboldened to make an avowal. How could he resist doing so? The sky was blue, the sand blazed in the distance like a scimitar of gold, the wind of the desert breathed love, and the woman of Arabia seemed to reflect all the fire with which she was surrounded; her piercing eyes were suffused with a mist; and by a slight nod of the head she seemed to make the luminous atmosphere undulate, as she consented to listen to the stranger's words of love. The sage was intoxicated with delirious hopes, when the young woman, hearing in the distance the gallop of a horse which seemed to fly, exclaimed:

"We are lost! My husband is sure to catch us. He is jealous as a tiger, and more pitiless than one. In the name of the prophet, if you love your life, conceal yourself in this chest!"

The author, frightened out of his wits, seeing no other way of getting out of a terrible fix, jumped into the box, and crouched down there. The woman closed down the lid, locked it, and took the key. She ran to meet her husband, and after some caresses which put him into a good humor, she said:

"I must relate to you a very singular adventure I have just had."

"I am listening, my gazelle," replied the Arab, who sat down on a rug and crossed his feet after the Oriental manner.

"There arrived here to-day a kind of philosopher," she began, "he professes to have compiled a book which describes all the wiles of which my sex is capable; and then this sham sage made love to me."

"Well, go on!" cried the Arab.

"I listened to his avowal. He was young, ardent — and you came just in time to save my tottering virtue."

The Arab leaped to his feet like a lion, and drew his scimitar with a shout of fury. The philosopher heard all from the depths of the chest and consigned to Hades his book, and all the men and women of Arabia Petraea.

"Fatima!" cried the husband, "if you would save your life, answer me — Where is the traitor?"

Terrified at the tempest which she had roused, Fatima threw herself at her husband's feet, and trembling beneath the point of his sword, she pointed out the chest with a prompt though timid glance of her eye. Then she rose to her feet, as if in shame, and taking the key from her girdle presented it to the jealous Arab; but, just as he was about to open the chest, the sly creature burst into a peal of laughter. Faroun stopped with a puzzled expression, and looked at his wife in amazement.

"So I shall have my fine chain of gold, after all!" she cried, dancing for joy. "You have lost the *Diadeste*. Be more mindful next time."

The husband, thunderstruck, let fall the key, and offered her the longed-for chain on bended knee, and promised to bring to his darling Fatima all the jewels brought by the caravan in a year, if she would refrain from winning the *Diadeste* by such cruel stratagems. Then, as he was an Arab, and did not like forfeiting a chain of gold, although his wife had fairly won it, he mounted his horse again, and galloped off, to complain at his will, in the desert, for he loved Fatima too well to let her see his annoyance. The young woman then drew forth the philosopher from the chest, and gravely said to him, "Do not forget, Master Doctor, to put this feminine trick into your collection."

"Madame," said I to the duchess, "I understand! If I marry, I am bound to be unexpectedly outwitted by some infernal trick or other; but I shall in that case, you may be quite sure, furnish a model household for the admiration of my contemporaries."

PARIS, 1824-29.

PETTY TROUBLES OF MARRIED LIFE

PART FIRST

PREFACE

IN WHICH EVERY ONE WILL FIND HIS OWN IMPRESSIONS OF MARRIAGE.

A friend, in speaking to you of a young woman, says: "Good family, well bred, pretty, and three hundred thousand in her own right." You have expressed a desire to meet this charming creature.

Usually, chance interviews are premeditated. And you speak with this object, who has now become very timid.

YOU.—"A delightful evening!"

SHE.—"Oh! yes, sir."

You are allowed to become the suitor of this young person.

THE MOTHER-IN-LAW (to the intended groom).—"You can't imagine how susceptible the dear girl is of attachment."

Meanwhile there is a delicate pecuniary question to be discussed by the two families.

YOUR FATHER (to the mother-in-law).—"My property is valued at five hundred thousand francs, my dear madame!"

YOUR FUTURE MOTHER-IN-LAW.—"And our house, my dear sir, is on a corner lot."

A contract follows, drawn up by two hideous notaries, a small one, and a big one.

Then the two families judge it necessary to convoy you to the civil magistrate's and to the church, before conducting the bride to her chamber.

Then what? . . . . . Why, then come a crowd of petty unforeseen troubles, like the following:

PETTY TROUBLES OF MARRIED LIFE

THE UNKINDEST CUT OF ALL.

Is it a petty or a profound trouble? I knew not; it is profound for your sons-in-law or daughters-in-law, but exceedingly petty for you.

"Petty! You must be joking; why, a child costs terribly dear!" exclaims a ten-times-too-happy husband, at the baptism of his eleventh, called the little last new-comer,—a phrase with which women beguile their families.

"What trouble is this?" you ask me. Well! this is, like many petty troubles of married life, a blessing for some one.

You have, four months since, married off your daughter, whom we will call by the sweet name of CAROLINE, and whom we will make the type of all wives. Caroline is, like all other young ladies, very charming, and you have found for her a husband who is either a lawyer, a captain, an engineer, a judge, or perhaps a young viscount. But he is more likely to be what sensible families must seek,—the ideal of their desires—the only son of a rich landed proprietor. (See the *Preface*.)

This phoenix we will call ADOLPHE, whatever may be his position in the world, his age, and the color of his hair.

The lawyer, the captain, the engineer, the judge, in short, the son-in-law, Adolphe, and his family, have seen in Miss Caroline:

I.—Miss Caroline;

II.—The only daughter of your wife and you.

Here, as in the Chamber of Deputies, we are compelled to call for a division of the house:

1.—As to your wife.

Your wife is to inherit the property of a maternal uncle, a gouty old fellow whom she humors, nurses, caresses, and muffles up; to say nothing of her father's fortune. Caroline has always adored her uncle,—her uncle who trotted her on his knee, her uncle who—her uncle whom—her uncle, in short,—whose property is estimated at two hundred thousand.

Further, your wife is well preserved, though her age has been the subject of mature reflection on the part of your son-in-law's grandparents and other ancestors. After many skirmishes between the mothers-in-law, they have at last confided to each other the little secrets peculiar to women of ripe years.

"How is it with you, my dear madame?"

"I, thank heaven, have passed the period; and you?"

"I really hope I have, too!" says your wife.

"You can marry Caroline," says Adolphe's mother to your future son-in-law; "Caroline will be the sole heiress of her mother, of her uncle, and her grandfather."

2.—As to yourself.

You are also the heir of your maternal grandfather, a good old man whose possessions will surely fall to you, for he has grown imbecile, and is therefore incapable of making a will.

You are an amiable man, but you have been very dissipated in your youth. Besides, you are fifty-nine years old, and your head is bald, resembling a bare knee in the middle of a gray wig.

III.—A dowry of three hundred thousand.

IV.—Caroline's only sister, a little dunce of twelve, a sickly child, who bids fair to fill an early grave.

V.—Your own fortune, father-in-law (in certain kinds of society they say *papa father-in-law*) yielding an income of twenty thousand, and which will soon be increased by an inheritance.

VI.—Your wife's fortune, which will be increased by two inheritances —from her uncle and her grandfather. In all, thus:

Three inheritances and interest,	750,000
Your fortune,	250,000
Your wife's fortune,	250,000
	————
Total,	1,250,000

which surely cannot take wing!

Such is the autopsy of all those brilliant marriages that conduct their processions of dancers and eaters, in white gloves, flowering at the button-hole, with bouquets of orange flowers, furbelows, veils, coaches and coach-drivers, from the magistrate's to the church, from the church to the banquet, from the banquet to the dance, from the dance to the nuptial chamber, to the music of the orchestra and the accompaniment of the immemorial pleasantries uttered by relics of dandies, for are there not, here and there in society, relics of dandies, as there are relics of English horses? To be sure, and such is the osteology of the most amorous intent.

The majority of the relatives have had a word to say about this marriage.

Those on the side of the bridegroom:

"Adolphe has made a good thing of it."

Those on the side of the bride:

"Caroline has made a splendid match. Adolphe is an only son, and will have an income of sixty thousand, *some day or other!*"

Some time afterwards, the happy judge, the happy engineer, the happy captain, the happy lawyer, the happy only son of a rich landed proprietor, in short Adolphe, comes to dine with you, accompanied by his family.

Your daughter Caroline is exceedingly proud of the somewhat rounded form of her waist. All women display an innocent artfulness, the first time they find themselves facing motherhood. Like a soldier who makes a brilliant toilet for his first battle, they love to play the pale, the suffering; they rise in a certain manner, and walk with the prettiest affectation. While yet flowers, they bear a fruit; they enjoy their maternity by anticipation. All those little ways are exceedingly charming—the first time.

Your wife, now the mother-in-law of Adolphe, subjects herself to the pressure of tight corsets. When her daughter laughs, she weeps; when Caroline wishes her happiness public, she tries to conceal hers. After dinner, the discerning eye of the co-mother-in-law divines the work of darkness.

Your wife also is an expectant mother! The news spreads like lightning, and your oldest college friend says to you laughingly: "Ah! so you are trying to increase the population again!"

You have some hope in a consultation that is to take place to-morrow. You, kind-hearted man that you are, you turn red, you hope it is merely the dropsy; but the doctors confirm the arrival of a *little last one!*

In such circumstances some timorous husbands go to the country or make a journey to Italy. In short, a strange confusion reigns in your household; both you and your wife are in a false position.

"Why, you old rogue, you, you ought to be ashamed of yourself!" says a friend to you on the Boulevard.

"Well! do as much if you can," is your angry retort.

"It's as bad as being robbed on the highway!" says your son-in-law's family. "Robbed on the highway" is a flattering expression for the mother-in-law.

The family hopes that the child which divides the expected fortune in three parts, will be, like all old men's children, scrofulous, feeble, an abortion. Will it be likely to live? The family awaits the delivery of your wife with an anxiety like that which agitated the house of Orleans during the confinement of the Duchess de Berri: a second son would secure the throne to the younger branch without the onerous conditions of July; Henry V would easily seize the crown. From that moment the house of Orleans was obliged to play double or quits: the event gave them the game.

The mother and the daughter are put to bed nine days apart.

Caroline's first child is a pale, cadaverous little girl that will not live.

Her mother's last child is a splendid boy, weighing twelve pounds, with two teeth and luxuriant hair.

For sixteen years you have desired a son. This conjugal annoyance is the only one that makes you beside yourself with joy. For your rejuvenated wife has attained what must be called the *Indian Summer* of women; she nurses, she has a full breast of milk! Her complexion is fresh, her color is pure pink and white. In her forty-second year, she affects the young woman, buys little baby stockings, walks about followed by a nurse, embroiders caps and tries on the cunningest headdresses. Alexandrine has resolved to instruct her daughter by her example; she is delightful and happy. And yet this is a trouble, a petty one for you, a serious one for your son-in-law. This annoyance is of the two sexes, it is common to you and your wife. In short, in this instance, your paternity renders you all the more proud from the fact that it is incontestable, my dear sir!

REVELATIONS.

Generally speaking, a young woman does not exhibit her true character till she has been married two or three years. She hides her faults, without intending it, in the midst of her first joys, of her first parties of pleasure. She goes into society to dance, she visits her relatives to show you off, she journeys on with an escort of love's first wiles; she is gradually transformed from girlhood to womanhood. Then she becomes mother and nurse, and in this situation, full of charming pangs, that leaves neither a word nor a moment for observation, such are its multiplied cares, it is impossible to judge of a woman. You require, then, three or four years of intimate life before you discover an exceedingly melancholy fact, one that gives you cause for constant terror.

Your wife, the young lady in whom the first pleasures of life and love supplied the place of grace and wit, so arch, so animated, so vivacious, whose least movements spoke with delicious eloquence, has cast off, slowly, one by one, her natural artifices. At last you perceive the truth! You try to disbelieve it, you think yourself deceived; but no: Caroline lacks intellect, she is dull, she can neither joke nor reason, sometimes she has little tact. You are frightened. You find yourself forever obliged to lead this darling through the thorny paths, where you must perforce leave your self-esteem in tatters.

You have already been annoyed several times by replies that, in society, were politely received: people have held their tongues instead of smiling; but you were certain that after your departure the women looked at each other and said: "Did you hear Madame Adolphe?"

"Your little woman, she is—"

"A regular cabbage-head."

"How could he, who is certainly a man of sense, choose—?"

"He should educate, teach his wife, or make her hold her tongue."

AXIOMS.

Axiom.—In our system of civilization a man is entirely responsible for his wife.

Axiom.—The husband does not mould the wife.

Caroline has one day obstinately maintained, at the house of Madame de Fischtaminel, a very distinguished lady, that her little last one resembled neither its father nor its mother, but looked like a certain friend of the family. She perhaps enlightens Monsieur de Fischtaminel, and overthrows the labors of three years, by tearing down the scaffolding of Madame de Fischtaminel's assertions, who, after this visit, will treat you will coolness, suspecting, as she does, that you have been making indiscreet remarks to your wife.

On another occasion, Caroline, after having conversed with a writer about his works, counsels the poet, who is already a prolific author, to try to write something likely to live. Sometimes she complains of the slow attendance at the tables of people who have but one servant and have put themselves to great trouble to receive her. Sometimes she speaks ill of widows who marry again, before Madame Deschars who has married a third time, and on this occasion, an ex-notary, Nicolas-Jean-Jerome-Nepomucene-Ange-Marie-Victor-Joseph Deschars, a friend of your father's.

In short, you are no longer yourself when you are in society with your wife. Like a man who is riding a skittish horse and glares straight between the beast's two ears, you are absorbed by the attention with which you listen to your Caroline.

In order to compensate herself for the silence to which young ladies are condemned, Caroline talks; or rather babbles. She wants to make a sensation, and she does make a sensation; nothing stops her. She addresses the most eminent men, the most celebrated women. She introduces herself, and puts you on the rack. Going into society is going to the stake.

She begins to think you are cross-grained, moody. The fact is, you are watching her, that's all! In short, you keep her within a small circle of friends, for she has already embroiled you with people on whom your interests depended.

How many times have you recoiled from the necessity of a remonstrance, in the morning, on awakening, when you had put her in a good humor for listening! A woman rarely listens. How many times have you recoiled from the burthen of your imperious obligations!

The conclusion of your ministerial communication can be no other than: "You have no sense." You foresee the effect of your first lesson. Caroline will say to herself: "Ah I have no sense! Haven't I though?"

No woman ever takes this in good part. Both of you must draw the sword and throw away the scabbard. Six weeks after, Caroline may prove to you that she has quite sense enough to *minotaurize* you without your perceiving it.

Frightened at such a prospect, you make use of all the eloquent phrases to gild this pill. In short, you find the means of flattering Caroline's various self-loves, for:

Axiom.—A married woman has several self-loves.

You say that you are her best friend, the only one well situated to enlighten her; the more careful you are, the more watchful and puzzled she is. At this moment she has plenty of sense.

You ask your dear Caroline, whose waist you clasp, how she, who is so brilliant when alone with you, who retorts so charmingly (you remind her of sallies that she has never made, which you put in her mouth, and, which she smilingly accepts), how she can say this, that, and the other, in society. She is, doubtless, like many ladies, timid in company.

"I know," you say, "many very distinguished men who are just the same."

You cite the case of some who are admirable tea-party oracles, but who cannot utter half a dozen sentences in the tribune. Caroline should keep watch over herself; you vaunt silence as the surest method of being witty. In society, a good listener is highly prized.

You have broken the ice, though you have not even scratched its glossy surface: you have placed your hand upon the croup of the most ferocious and savage, the most wakeful and clear-sighted, the most restless, the swiftest, the most jealous, the most ardent and violent, the simplest and most elegant, the most unreasonable, the most watchful chimera of the moral world—THE VANITY OF A WOMAN!

Caroline clasps you in her arms with a saintly embrace, thanks you for your advice, and loves you the more for it; she wishes to be beholden to you for everything, even for her intellect; she may be a dunce, but, what is better than saying fine things, she knows how to do them! But she desires also to be your pride! It is not a question of taste in dress, of elegance and beauty; she wishes to make you proud of her intelligence. You are the luckiest of men in having successfully managed to escape from this first dangerous pass in conjugal life.

"We are going this evening to Madame Deschars', where they never know what to do to amuse themselves; they play all sorts of forfeit games on account of a troop of young women and girls there; you shall see!" she says.

You are so happy at this turn of affairs, that you hum airs and carelessly chew bits of straw and thread, while still in your shirt and drawers. You are like a hare frisking on a flowering dew-perfumed meadow. You leave off your morning gown till the last extremity, when breakfast is on the table. During the day, if you meet a friend and he happens to speak of women, you defend them; you consider women charming, delicious, there is something divine about them.

How often are our opinions dictated to us by the unknown events of our life!

You take your wife to Madame Deschars'. Madame Deschars is a mother and is exceedingly devout. You never see any newspapers at her house: she keeps watch over her daughters by three different husbands, and keeps them all the more closely from the fact that she herself has, it is said, some little things to reproach herself with during the career of her two former lords. At her house, no one dares risk a jest. Everything there is white and pink and perfumed with sanctity, as at the houses of widows who are approaching the confines of their third youth. It seems as if every day were Sunday there.

You, a young husband, join the juvenile society of young women and girls, misses and young people, in the chamber of Madame Deschars. The serious people, politicians, whist-players, and tea-drinkers, are in the parlor.

In Madame Deschars' room they are playing a game which consists in hitting upon words with several meanings, to fit the answers that each player is to make to the following questions:

How do you like it?

What do you do with it?

Where do you put it?

Your turn comes to guess the word, you go into the parlor, take part in a discussion, and return at the call of a smiling young lady. They have selected a word that may be applied to the most enigmatical replies. Everybody knows that, in order to puzzle the strongest heads, the best way is to choose a very ordinary word, and to invent phrases that will send the parlor Oedipus a thousand leagues from each of his previous thoughts.

This game is a poor substitute for lansquenet or dice, but it is not very expensive.

The word MAL has been made the Sphinx of this particular occasion. Every one has determined to put you off the scent. The word, among other acceptations, has that of *mal* [evil], a substantive that signifies, in aesthetics, the opposite of good; of *mal* [pain, disease, complaint], a substantive that enters into a thousand pathological expressions; then *malle* [a mail-bag], and finally *malle* [a trunk], that box of various forms, covered with all kinds of skin, made of every sort of leather, with handles, that journeys rapidly, for it serves to carry travelling effects in, as a man of Delille's school would say.

For you, a man of some sharpness, the Sphinx displays his wiles; he spreads his wings and folds them up again; he shows you his lion's paws, his woman's neck, his horse's loins, and his intellectual head; he shakes his sacred fillets, he strikes an attitude and runs away, he comes and goes, and sweeps the place with his terrible equine tail; he shows his shining claws, and draws them in; he smiles, frisks, and murmurs. He puts on the looks of a joyous child and those of a matron; he is, above all, there to make fun of you.

You ask the group collectively, "How do you like it?"

"I like it for love's sake," says one.

"I like it regular," says another.

"I like it with a long mane."

"I like it with a spring lock."

"I like it unmasked."

"I like it on horseback."

"I like it as coming from God," says Madame Deschars.

"How do you like it?" you say to your wife.

"I like it legitimate."

This response of your wife is not understood, and sends you a journey into the constellated fields of the infinite, where the mind, dazzled by the multitude of creations, finds it impossible to make a choice.

"Where do you put it?"

"In a carriage."

"In a garret."

"In a steamboat."

"In the closet."

"On a cart."

"In prison."

"In the ears."

"In a shop."

Your wife says to you last of all: "In bed."

You were on the point of guessing it, but you know no word that fits this answer, Madame Deschars not being likely to have allowed anything improper.

"What do you do with it?"

"I make it my sole happiness," says your wife, after the answers of all the rest, who have sent you spinning through a whole world of linguistic suppositions.

This response strikes everybody, and you especially; so you persist in seeking the meaning of it. You think of the bottle of hot water that your wife has put to her feet when it is cold, — of the warming pan, above all! Now of her night-cap, — of her handkerchief, — of her curling paper, — of the hem of her chemise, — of her embroidery, — of her flannel jacket, — of your bandanna, — of the pillow.

In short, as the greatest pleasure of the respondents is to see their Oedipus mystified, as each word guessed by you throws them into fits of laughter, superior men, perceiving no word that will fit all the explanations, will sooner give it up than make three unsuccessful attempts. According to the law of this innocent game you are condemned to return to the parlor after leaving a forfeit; but you are so exceedingly puzzled by your wife's answers, that you ask what the word was.

"Mal," exclaims a young miss.

You comprehend everything but your wife's replies: she has not played the game. Neither Madame Deschars, nor any one of the young women understand. She has cheated. You revolt, there is an insurrection among the girls and young women. They seek and are puzzled. You want an explanation, and every one participates in your desire.

"In what sense did you understand the word, my dear?" you say to Caroline.

"Why, *male!*" [male.]

Madame Deschars bites her lips and manifests the greatest displeasure; the young women blush and drop their eyes; the little girls open theirs, nudge each other and prick up their ears. Your feet are glued to the carpet, and you have so much salt in your throat that you believe in a repetition of the event which delivered Lot from his wife.

You see an infernal life before you; society is out of the question.

To remain at home with this triumphant stupidity is equivalent to condemnation to the state's prison.

Axiom.—Moral tortures exceed physical sufferings by all the difference which exists between the soul and the body.

THE ATTENTIONS OF A WIFE.

Among the keenest pleasures of bachelor life, every man reckons the independence of his getting up. The fancies of the morning compensate for the glooms of evening. A bachelor turns over and over in his bed: he is free to gape loud enough to justify apprehensions of murder, and to scream at a pitch authorizing the suspicion of joys untold. He can forget his oaths of the day before, let the fire burn upon the hearth and the candle sink to its socket,—in short, go to sleep again in spite of pressing work. He can curse the expectant boots which stand holding their black mouths open at him and pricking up their ears. He can pretend not to see the steel hooks which glitter in a sunbeam which has stolen through the curtains, can disregard the sonorous summons of the obstinate clock, can bury himself in a soft place, saying: "Yes, I was in a hurry, yesterday, but am so no longer to-day. Yesterday was a dotard. To-day is a sage: between them stands the night which brings wisdom, the night which gives light. I ought to go, I ought to do it, I promised I would—I am weak, I know. But how can I resist the downy creases of my bed? My feet feel flaccid, I think I must be sick, I am too happy just here. I long to see the ethereal horizon of my dreams again, those women without claws, those winged beings and their obliging ways. In short, I have found the grain of salt to put upon the tail of that bird that was always flying away: the coquette's feet are caught in the line. I have her now—"

Your servant, meantime, reads your newspaper, half-opens your letters, and leaves you to yourself. And you go to sleep again, lulled by the rumbling of the morning wagons. Those terrible, vexatious, quivering teams, laden with meat, those trucks with big tin teats bursting with milk, though they make a clatter most infernal and even crush the paving stones, seem to you to glide over cotton, and vaguely remind you of the orchestra of Napoleon Musard. Though your house trembles in all its timbers and shakes upon its keel, you think yourself a sailor cradled by a zephyr.

You alone have the right to bring these joys to an end by throwing away your night-cap as you twist up your napkin after dinner, and by sitting up in bed. Then you take yourself to task with such reproaches as these: "Ah, mercy on me, I must get up!" "Early to bed and early to rise, makes a man healthy—!" "Get up, lazy bones!"

All this time you remain perfectly tranquil. You look round your chamber, you collect your wits together. Finally, you emerge from the bed, spontaneously! Courageously! of your own accord! You go to the fireplace, you consult the most obliging of timepieces, you utter hopeful sentences thus couched: "Whatshisname is a lazy creature, I guess I shall find him in. I'll run. I'll catch him if he's gone. He's sure to wait for me. There is a quarter of an hour's grace in all appointments, even between debtor and creditor."

You put on your boots with fury, you dress yourself as if you were afraid of being caught half-dressed, you have the delight of being in a hurry, you call your buttons into action, you finally go out like a conqueror, whistling, brandishing your cane, pricking up your ears and breaking into a canter.

After all, you say to yourself, you are responsible to no one, you are your own master!

But you, poor married man, you were stupid enough to say to your wife, "To-morrow, my dear" (sometimes she knows it two days beforehand), "I have got to get up early." Unfortunate Adolphe, you have especially proved the importance of this appointment: "It's to—and to—and above all to—in short to—"

Two hours before dawn, Caroline wakes you up gently and says to you softly: "Adolphy dear, Adolphy love!"

"What's the matter? Fire?"

"No, go to sleep again, I've made a mistake; but the hour hand was on it, any way! It's only four, you can sleep two hours more."

Is not telling a man, "You've only got two hours to sleep," the same thing, on a small scale, as saying to a criminal, "It's five in the morning, the ceremony will be performed at half-past seven"? Such sleep is troubled by an idea dressed in grey and furnished with wings, which comes and flaps, like a bat, upon the windows of your brain.

A woman in a case like this is as exact as a devil coming to claim a soul he has purchased. When the clock strikes five, your wife's voice, too well known, alas! resounds in your ear; she accompanies the stroke, and says with an atrocious calmness, "Adolphe, it's five o'clock, get up, dear."

"Ye-e-e-s, ah-h-h-h!"

"Adolphe, you'll be late for your business, you said so yourself."

"Ah-h-h-h, ye-e-e-e-s." You turn over in despair.

"Come, come, love. I got everything ready last night; now you must, my dear; do you want to miss him? There, up, I say; it's broad daylight."

Caroline throws off the blankets and gets up: she wants to show you that *she* can rise without making a fuss. She opens the blinds, she lets in the sun, the morning air, the noise of the street, and then comes back.

"Why, Adolphe, you *must* get up! Who ever would have supposed you had no energy! But it's just like you men! I am only a poor, weak woman, but when I say a thing, I do it."

You get up grumbling, execrating the sacrament of marriage. There is not the slightest merit in your heroism; it wasn't you, but your wife, that got up. Caroline gets you everything you want with provoking promptitude; she foresees everything, she gives you a muffler in winter, a blue-striped cambric shirt in summer, she treats you like a child; you are still asleep, she dresses you and has all the trouble. She finally thrusts you out of doors. Without her nothing would go straight! She calls you back to give you a paper, a pocketbook, you had forgotten. You don't think of anything, she thinks of everything!

You return five hours afterwards to breakfast, between eleven and noon. The chambermaid is at the door, or on the stairs, or on the landing, talking with somebody's valet: she runs in on hearing or seeing you. Your servant is laying the cloth in a most leisurely style, stopping to look out of the window or to lounge, and coming and going like a person who knows he has plenty of time. You ask for your wife, supposing that she is up and dressed.

"Madame is still in bed," says the maid.

You find your wife languid, lazy, tired and asleep. She had been awake all night to wake you in the morning, so she went to bed again, and is quite hungry now.

You are the cause of all these disarrangements. If breakfast is not ready, she says it's because you went out. If she is not dressed, and if everything is in disorder, it's all your fault. For everything which goes awry she has this answer: "Well, you would get up so early!" "He would get up so early!" is the universal reason. She makes you go to bed early, because you got up early. She can do nothing all day, because you would get up so unusually early.

Eighteen months afterwards, she still maintains, "Without me, you would never get up!" To her friends she says, "My husband get up! If it weren't for me, he never *would* get up!"

To this a man whose hair is beginning to whiten, replies, "A graceful compliment to you, madame!" This slightly indelicate comment puts an end to her boasts.

This petty trouble, repeated several times, teaches you to live alone in the bosom of your family, not to tell all you know, and to have no confidant but yourself: and it often seems to you a question whether the inconveniences of the married state do not exceed its advantages.

SMALL VEXATIONS.

You have made a transition from the frolicsome allegretto of the bachelor to the heavy andante of the father of a family.

Instead of that fine English steed prancing and snorting between the polished shafts of a tilbury as light as your own heart, and moving his glistening croup under the quadruple network of the reins and ribbons that you so skillfully manage with what grace and elegance the Champs Elysees can bear witness—you drive a good solid Norman horse with a steady, family gait.

You have learned what paternal patience is, and you let no opportunity slip of proving it. Your countenance, therefore, is serious.

By your side is a domestic, evidently for two purposes like the carriage. The vehicle is four-wheeled and hung upon English springs: it is corpulent and resembles a Rouen scow: it has glass windows, and an infinity of economical arrangements. It is a barouche in fine weather, and a brougham when it rains. It is apparently light, but, when six persons are in it, it is heavy and tires out your only horse.

On the back seat, spread out like flowers, is your young wife in full bloom, with her mother, a big marshmallow with a great many leaves. These two flowers of the female species twitteringly talk of you, though the noise of the wheels and your attention to the horse, joined to your fatherly caution, prevent you from hearing what they say.

On the front seat, there is a nice tidy nurse holding a little girl in her lap: by her side is a boy in a red plaited shirt, who is continually leaning out of the carriage and climbing upon the cushions, and who has a thousand times drawn down upon himself those declarations of every mother, which he knows to be threats and nothing else: "Be a good boy, Adolphe, or else—" "I declare I'll never bring you again, so there!"

His mamma is secretly tired to death of this noisy little boy: he has provoked her twenty times, and twenty times the face of the little girl asleep has calmed her.

"I am his mother," she says to herself. And so she finally manages to keep her little Adolphe quiet.

You have put your triumphant idea of taking your family to ride into execution. You left your home in the morning, all the opposite neighbors having come to their windows, envying you the privilege which your means give you of going to the country and coming back again without undergoing the miseries of a public conveyance. So you have dragged your unfortunate Norman horse through Paris to Vincennes, from Vincennes to Saint Maur, from Saint Maur to Charenton, from

Charenton opposite some island or other which struck your wife and mother-in-law as being prettier than all the landscapes through which you had driven them.

"Let's go to Maison's!" somebody exclaims.

So you go to Maison's, near Alfort. You come home by the left bank of the Seine, in the midst of a cloud of very black Olympian dust. The horse drags your family wearily along. But alas! your pride has fled, and you look without emotion upon his sunken flanks, and upon two bones which stick out on each side of his belly. His coat is roughened by the sweat which has repeatedly come out and dried upon him, and which, no less than the dust, has made him gummy, sticky and shaggy. The horse looks like a wrathy porcupine: you are afraid he will be foundered, and you caress him with the whip-lash in a melancholy way that he perfectly understands, for he moves his head about like an omnibus horse, tired of his deplorable existence.

You think a good deal of this horse; your consider him an excellent one and he cost you twelve hundred francs. When a man has the honor of being the father of a family, he thinks as much of twelve hundred francs as you think of this horse. You see at once the frightful amount of your extra expenses, in case Coco should have to lie by. For two days you will have to take hackney coaches to go to your business. You wife will pout if she can't go out: but she will go out, and take a carriage. The horse will cause the purchase of numerous extras, which you will find in your coachman's bill,—your only coachman, a model coachman, whom you watch as you do a model anybody.

To these thoughts you give expression in the gentle movement of the whip as it falls upon the animal's ribs, up to his knees in the black dust which lines the road in front of La Verrerie.

At this moment, little Adolphe, who doesn't know what to do in this rolling box, has sadly twisted himself up into a corner, and his grandmother anxiously asks him, "What is the matter?"

"I'm hungry," says the child.

"He's hungry," says the mother to her daughter.

"And why shouldn't he be hungry? It is half-past five, we are not at the barrier, and we started at two!"

"Your husband might have treated us to dinner in the country."

"He'd rather make his horse go a couple of leagues further, and get back to the house."

"The cook might have had the day to herself. But Adolphe is right, after all: it's cheaper to dine at home," adds the mother-in-law.

"Adolphe," exclaims your wife, stimulated by the word "cheaper," "we go so slow that I shall be seasick, and you keep driving right in this nasty dust. What are you thinking of? My gown and hat will be ruined!"

"Would you rather ruin the horse?" you ask, with the air of a man who can't be answered.

"Oh, no matter for your horse; just think of your son who is dying of hunger: he hasn't tasted a thing for seven hours. Whip up your old horse! One would really think you cared more for your nag than for your child!"

You dare not give your horse a single crack with the whip, for he might still have vigor enough left to break into a gallop and run away.

"No, Adolphe tries to vex me, he's going slower," says the young wife to her mother. "My dear, go as slow as you like. But I know you'll say I am extravagant when you see me buying another hat."

Upon this you utter a series of remarks which are lost in the racket made by the wheels.

"What's the use of replying with reasons that haven't got an ounce of common-sense?" cries Caroline.

You talk, turning your face to the carriage and then turning back to the horse, to avoid an accident.

"That's right, run against somebody and tip us over, do, you'll be rid of us. Adolphe, your son is dying of hunger. See how pale he is!"

"But Caroline," puts in the mother-in-law, "he's doing the best he can."

Nothing annoys you so much as to have your mother-in-law take your part. She is a hypocrite and is delighted to see you quarreling with her daughter. Gently and with infinite precaution she throws oil on the fire.

When you arrive at the barrier, your wife is mute. She says not a word, she sits with her arms crossed, and will not look at you. You have neither soul, heart, nor sentiment. No one but you could have invented such a party of pleasure. If you are unfortunate enough to remind Caroline that it was she who insisted on the excursion, that morning, for her children's sake, and in behalf of her milk—she nurses the baby—you will be overwhelmed by an avalanche of frigid and stinging reproaches.

You bear it all so as "not to turn the milk of a nursing mother, for whose sake you must overlook some little things," so your atrocious mother-in-law whispers in your ear.

All the furies of Orestes are rankling in your heart.

In reply to the sacramental words pronounced by the officer of the customs, "Have you anything to declare?" your wife says, "I declare a great deal of ill-humor and dust."

She laughs, the officer laughs, and you feel a desire to tip your family into the Seine.

Unluckily for you, you suddenly remember the joyous and perverse young woman who wore a pink bonnet and who made merry in your tilbury six years before, as you passed this spot on your way to the chop-house on the river's bank. What a reminiscence! Was Madame Schontz anxious about babies, about her bonnet, the lace of which was torn to pieces in the bushes? No, she had no care for anything whatever, not even for her dignity, for she shocked the rustic police of Vincennes by the somewhat daring freedom of her style of dancing.

You return home, you have frantically hurried your Norman horse, and have neither prevented an indisposition of the animal, nor an indisposition of your wife.

That evening, Caroline has very little milk. If the baby cries and if your head is split in consequence, it is all your fault, as you preferred the health of your horse to that of your son who was dying of hunger, and of your daughter whose supper has disappeared in a discussion in which your wife was right, *as she always is*.

"Well, well," she says, "men are not mothers!"

As you leave the chamber, you hear your mother-in-law consoling her daughter by these terrible words: "Come, be calm, Caroline: that's the way with them all: they are a selfish lot: your father was just like that!"

THE ULTIMATUM.

It is eight o'clock; you make your appearance in the bedroom of your wife. There is a brilliant light. The chambermaid and the cook hover lightly about. The furniture is covered with dresses and flowers tried on and laid aside.

The hair-dresser is there, an artist par excellence, a sovereign authority, at once nobody and everything. You hear the other domestics going and coming: orders are given and recalled, errands are well or ill performed. The disorder is at its height. This chamber is a studio from whence to issue a parlor Venus.

Your wife desires to be the fairest at the ball which you are to attend. Is it still for your sake, or only for herself, or is it for somebody else? Serious questions these.

The idea does not even occur to you.

You are squeezed, hampered, harnessed in your ball accoutrement: you count your steps as you walk, you look around, you observe, you contemplate talking business on neutral ground with a stock-broker, a notary or a banker, to whom you would not like to give an advantage over you by calling at their house.

A singular fact which all have probably observed, but the causes of which can hardly be determined, is the peculiar repugnance which men dressed and ready to go to a party have for discussions or to answer questions. At the moment of starting, there are few husbands who are not taciturn and profoundly absorbed in reflections which vary with their characters. Those who reply give curt and peremptory answers.

But women, at this time, are exceedingly aggravating. They consult you, they ask your advice upon the best way of concealing the stem of a rose, of giving a graceful fall to a bunch of briar, or a happy turn to a scarf. As a neat English expression has it, "they fish for compliments," and sometimes for better than compliments.

A boy just out of school would discern the motive concealed behind the willows of these pretexts: but your wife is so well known to you, and you have so often playfully joked upon her moral and physical perfections, that you are harsh enough to give your opinion briefly and conscientiously: you thus force Caroline to put that decisive question, so cruel to women, even those who have been married twenty years:

CAROLINE AND ADOLPHE.

"So I don't suit you then?"

Drawn upon the true ground by this inquiry, you bestow upon her such little compliments as you can spare and which are, as it were, the small change, the sous, the liards of your purse.

"The best gown you ever wore!" "I never saw you so well dressed." "Blue, pink, yellow, cherry [take your pick], becomes you charmingly." "Your head-dress is quite original." "As you go in, every one will admire you." "You will not only be the prettiest, but the best dressed." "They'll all be mad not to have your taste." "Beauty is a natural gift: taste is like intelligence, a thing that we may be proud of."

"Do you think so? Are you in earnest, Adolphe?"

Your wife is coquetting with you. She chooses this moment to force from you your pretended opinion of one and another of her friends, and to insinuate the price of the articles of her dress you so much admire. Nothing is too dear to please you. She sends the cook out of the room.

"Let's go," you say.

She sends the chambermaid out after having dismissed the hair-dresser, and begins to turn round and round before her glass, showing off to you her most glorious beauties.

"Let's go," you say.

"You are in a hurry," she returns.

And she goes on exhibiting herself with all her little airs, setting herself off like a fine peach magnificently exhibited in a fruiterer's window. But since you have dined rather heartily, you kiss her upon the forehead merely, not feeling able to countersign your opinions. Caroline becomes serious.

The carriage waits. All the household looks at Caroline as she goes out: she is the masterpiece to which all have contributed, and everybody admires the common work.

Your wife departs highly satisfied with herself, but a good deal displeased with you. She proceeds loftily to the ball, just as a picture, caressed by the painter and minutely retouched in the studio, is sent to the annual exhibition in the vast bazaar of the Louvre. Your wife, alas! sees fifty women handsomer than herself: they have invented dresses of the most extravagant price, and more or less original: and that which happens at the Louvre to the masterpiece, happens to the object of feminine labor: your wife's dress seems pale by the side of another very much like it, but the livelier color of which crushes it. Caroline is nobody, and is hardly noticed. When there are sixty handsome women in a room, the sentiment of beauty is lost, beauty is no longer appreciated. Your wife becomes a very ordinary affair. The petty stratagem of her smile, made perfect by practice, has no meaning in the midst of countenances of noble expression, of self-possessed women of lofty presence. She is completely put down, and no one asks her to dance. She tries to force an expression of pretended satisfaction, but, as she is not satisfied, she hears people say, "Madame Adolphe is looking very ill to-night." Women hypocritically ask her if she is indisposed and "Why don't you dance?" They have a whole catalogue of malicious remarks veneered with sympathy and electroplated with charity, enough to damn a saint, to make a monkey serious, and to give the devil the shudders.

You, who are innocently playing cards or walking backwards and forwards, and so have not seen one of the thousand pin-pricks with which your wife's self-love has been tattooed, you come and ask her in a whisper, "What is the matter?"

"Order *my* carriage!"

This *my* is the consummation of marriage. For two years she has said "*my husband's* carriage," "*the* carriage," "*our* carriage," and now she says "*my* carriage."

You are in the midst of a game, you say, somebody wants his revenge, or you must get your money back.

Here, Adolphe, we allow that you have sufficient strength of mind to say yes, to disappear, and *not* to order the carriage.

You have a friend, you send him to dance with your wife, for you have commenced a system of concessions which will ruin you. You already dimly perceive the advantage of a friend.

Finally, you order the carriage. You wife gets in with concentrated rage, she hurls herself into a corner, covers her face with her hood, crosses her arms under her pelisse, and says not a word.

O husbands! Learn this fact; you may, at this fatal moment, repair and redeem everything: and never does the impetuosity of lovers who have been caressing each other the whole evening with flaming gaze fail to do it! Yes, you can bring her home in triumph, she has now nobody but you, you have one more chance, that of taking your wife by storm! But no, idiot, stupid and indifferent that you are, you ask her, "What is the matter?"

Axiom.—A husband should always know what is the matter with his wife, for she always knows what is not.

"I'm cold," she says.

"The ball was splendid."

"Pooh! nobody of distinction! People have the mania, nowadays, to invite all Paris into a hole. There were women even on the stairs: their gowns were horribly smashed, and mine is ruined."

"We had a good time."

"Ah, you men, you play and that's the whole of it. Once married, you care about as much for your wives as a lion does for the fine arts."

"How changed you are; you were so gay, so happy, so charming when we arrived."

"Oh, you never understand us women. I begged you to go home, and you left me there, as if a woman ever did anything without a reason. You are not without intelligence, but now and then you are so queer I don't know what you are thinking about."

Once upon this footing, the quarrel becomes more bitter. When you give your wife your hand to lift her from the carriage, you grasp a woman of wood: she gives you a "thank you" which puts you in the same rank as her servant. You understood your wife no better before than you do after the ball: you find it difficult to follow her, for instead of going up stairs, she flies up. The rupture is complete.

The chambermaid is involved in your disgrace: she is received with blunt No's and Yes's, as dry as Brussells rusks, which she swallows with a slanting glance at you. "Monsieur's always doing these things," she mutters.

You alone might have changed Madame's temper. She goes to bed; she has her revenge to take: you did not comprehend her. Now she does not comprehend you. She deposits herself on her side of the bed in the most hostile and offensive posture: she is wrapped up in her chemise, in her sack, in her night-cap, like a bale of clocks packed for the East Indies. She says neither good-night, nor good-day, nor dear, nor Adolphe: you don't exist, you are a bag of wheat.

Your Caroline, so enticing five hours before in this very chamber where she frisked about like an eel, is now a junk of lead. Were you the Tropical Zone in person, astride of the Equator, you could not melt the ice of this little personified Switzerland that pretends to be asleep, and who could freeze you from head to foot, if she liked. Ask her one hundred times what is the matter with her, Switzerland replies by an ultimatum, like the Diet or the Conference of London.

Nothing is the matter with her: she is tired: she is going to sleep.

The more you insist, the more she erects bastions of ignorance, the more she isolates herself by chevaux-de-frise. If you get impatient, Caroline begins to dream! You grumble, you are lost.

Axiom.—Inasmuch as women are always willing and able to explain their strong points, they leave us to guess at their weak ones.

Caroline will perhaps also condescend to assure you that she does not feel well. But she laughs in her night-cap when you have fallen asleep, and hurls imprecations upon your slumbering body.

WOMEN'S LOGIC.

You imagine you have married a creature endowed with reason: you are woefully mistaken, my friend.

Axiom.—Sensitive beings are not sensible beings.

Sentiment is not argument, reason is not pleasure, and pleasure is certainly not a reason.

"Oh! sir!" she says.

Reply "Ah! yes! Ah!" You must bring forth this "ah!" from the very depths of your thoracic cavern, as you rush in a rage from the house, or return, confounded, to your study.

Why? Now? Who has conquered, killed, overthrown you! Your wife's logic, which is not the logic of Aristotle, nor that of Ramus, nor that of Kant, nor that of Condillac, nor that of Robespierre, nor that of Napoleon: but which partakes of the character of all these logics, and which we must call the universal logic of women, the logic of English women as it is that of Italian women, of the women of Normandy and Brittany (ah, these last are unsurpassed!), of the women of Paris, in short, that of the women in the moon, if there are women in that nocturnal land, with which the women of the earth have an evident understanding, angels that they are!

The discussion began after breakfast. Discussions can never take place in a household save at this hour. A man could hardly have a discussion with his wife in bed, even if he wanted to: she has too many advantages over him, and can too easily reduce him to silence. On leaving the nuptial chamber with a pretty woman in it, a man is apt to be hungry, if he is young. Breakfast is usually a cheerful meal, and cheerfulness is not given to argument. In short, you do not open the business till you have had your tea or your coffee.

You have taken it into your head, for instance, to send your son to school. All fathers are hypocrites and are never willing to confess that their own flesh and blood is very troublesome when it walks about on two legs, lays its dare-devil hands on everything, and is everywhere at once like a frisky pollywog. Your son barks, mews, and sings; he breaks, smashes and soils the furniture, and furniture is dear; he makes toys of everything, he scatters your papers, and he cuts paper dolls out of the morning's newspaper before you have read it.

His mother says to him, referring to anything of yours: "Take it!" but in reference to anything of hers she says: "Take care!"

She cunningly lets him have your things that she may be left in peace. Her bad faith as a good mother seeks shelter behind her child, your son is her accomplice. Both are leagued against you like Robert Macaire and Bertrand against the subscribers to their joint stock company. The boy is an axe with which foraging excursions are performed in your domains. He goes either boldly or slyly to maraud in your wardrobe: he reappears caparisoned in the drawers you laid aside that morning, and brings to the light of day many articles condemned to solitary confinement. He brings the elegant Madame Fischtaminel, a friend whose good graces you cultivate, your girdle for checking corpulency, bits of cosmetic for dyeing your moustache, old waistcoats discolored at the arm-holes, stockings slightly soiled at the heels and somewhat yellow at the toes. It is quite impossible to remark that these stains are caused by the leather!

Your wife looks at your friend and laughs; you dare not be angry, so you laugh too, but what a laugh! The unfortunate all know that laugh.

Your son, moreover, gives you a cold sweat, if your razors happen to be out of their place. If you are angry, the little rebel laughs and shows his two rows of pearls: if you scold him, he cries. His mother rushes in! And what a mother she is! A mother who will detest you if you don't give him the razor! With women there is no middle ground; a man is either a monster or a model.

At certain times you perfectly understand Herod and his famous decrees relative to the Massacre of the Innocents, which have only been surpassed by those of the good Charles X!

Your wife has returned to her sofa, you walk up and down, and stop, and you boldly introduce the subject by this interjectional remark:

"Caroline, we must send Charles to boarding school."

"Charles cannot go to boarding school," she returns in a mild tone.

"Charles is six years old, the age at which a boy's education begins."

"In the first place," she replies, "it begins at seven. The royal princes are handed over to their governor by their governess when they are seven. That's the law and the prophets. I don't see why you shouldn't apply to the children of private people the rule laid down for the children of princes. Is your son more forward than theirs? The king of Rome—"

"The king of Rome is not a case in point."

"What! Is not the king of Rome the son of the Emperor? [Here she changes the subject.] Well, I declare, you accuse the Empress, do you? Why, Doctor Dubois himself was present, besides—"

"I said nothing of the kind."

"How you do interrupt, Adolphe."

"I say that the king of Rome [here you begin to raise your voice], the king of Rome, who was hardly four years old when he left France, is no example for us."

"That doesn't prevent the fact of the Duke de Bordeaux's having been placed in the hands of the Duke de Riviere, his tutor, at seven years." [Logic.]

"The case of the young Duke of Bordeaux is different."

"Then you confess that a boy can't be sent to school before he is seven years old?" she says with emphasis. [More logic.]

"No, my dear, I don't confess that at all. There is a great deal of difference between private and public education."

"That's precisely why I don't want to send Charles to school yet. He ought to be much stronger than he is, to go there."

"Charles is very strong for his age."

"Charles? That's the way with men! Why, Charles has a very weak constitution; he takes after you. [Here she changes from *tu* to *vous*.] But if you are determined to get rid of your son, why put him out to board, of course. I have noticed for some time that the dear child annoys you."

"Annoys me? The idea! But we are answerable for our children, are we not? It is time Charles' education was began: he is getting very bad habits here, he obeys no one, he thinks himself perfectly free to do as he likes, he hits everybody and nobody dares to hit him back. He ought to be placed in the midst of his equals, or he will grow up with the most detestable temper."

"Thank you: so I am bringing Charles up badly!"

"I did not say that: but you will always have excellent reasons for keeping him at home."

Here the *vous* becomes reciprocal and the discussion takes a bitter turn on both sides. Your wife is very willing to wound you by saying *vous*, but she feels cross when it becomes mutual.

"The long and the short of it is that you want to get my child away, you find that he is between us, you are jealous of your son, you want to tyrannize over me at your ease, and you sacrifice your boy! Oh, I am smart enough to see through you!"

"You make me out like Abraham with his knife! One would think there were no such things as schools! So the schools are empty; nobody sends their children to school!"

"You are trying to make me appear ridiculous," she retorts. "I know that there are schools well enough, but people don't send boys of six there, and Charles shall not start now."

"Don't get angry, my dear."

"As if I ever get angry! I am a woman and know how to suffer in silence."

"Come, let us reason together."

"You have talked nonsense enough."

"It is time that Charles should learn to read and write; later in life, he will find difficulties sufficient to disgust him."

Here, you talk for ten minutes without interruption, and you close with an appealing "Well?" armed with an intonation which suggests an interrogation point of the most crooked kind.

"Well!" she replies, "it is not yet time for Charles to go to school."

You have gained nothing at all.

"But, my dear, Monsieur Deschars certainly sent his little Julius to school at six years. Go and examine the schools and you will find lots of little boys of six there."

You talk for ten minutes more without the slightest interruption, and then you ejaculate another "Well?"

"Little Julius Deschars came home with chilblains," she says.

"But Charles has chilblains here."

"Never," she replies, proudly.

In a quarter of an hour, the main question is blocked by a side discussion on this point: "Has Charles had chilblains or not?"

You bandy contradictory allegations; you no longer believe each other; you must appeal to a third party.

Axiom.—Every household has its Court of Appeals which takes no notice of the merits, but judges matters of form only.

The nurse is sent for. She comes, and decides in favor of your wife. It is fully decided that Charles has never had chilblains.

Caroline glances triumphantly at you and utters these monstrous words: "There, you see Charles can't possibly go to school!"

You go out breathless with rage. There is no earthly means of convincing your wife that there is not the slightest reason for your son's not going to school in the fact that he has never had chilblains.

That evening, after dinner, you hear this atrocious creature finishing a long conversation with a woman with these words: "He wanted to send Charles to school, but I made him see that he would have to wait."

Some husbands, at a conjuncture like this, burst out before everybody; their wives take their revenge six weeks later, but the husbands gain this by it, that Charles is sent to school the very day he gets into any mischief. Other husbands break the crockery, and keep their rage to themselves. The knowing ones say nothing and bide their time.

A woman's logic is exhibited in this way upon the slightest occasion, about a promenade or the proper place to put a sofa. This logic is extremely simple, inasmuch as it consists in never expressing but one idea, that which contains the expression of their will. Like everything pertaining to female nature, this system may be resolved into two algebraic terms—Yes: no. There are also certain little movements of the head which mean so much that they may take the place of either.

THE JESUITISM OF WOMEN.

The most jesuitical Jesuit of Jesuits is yet a thousand times less jesuitical than the least jesuitical woman, — so you may judge what Jesuits women are! They are so jesuitical that the cunningest Jesuit himself could never guess to what extent of jesuitism a woman may go, for there are a thousand ways of being jesuitical, and a woman is such an adroit Jesuit, that she has the knack of being a Jesuit without having a jesuitical look. You can rarely, though you can sometimes, prove to a Jesuit that he is one: but try once to demonstrate to a woman that she acts or talks like a Jesuit. She would be cut to pieces rather than confess herself one.

She, a Jesuit! The very soul of honor and loyalty! She a Jesuit! What do you mean by "Jesuit?" She does not know what a Jesuit is: what is a Jesuit? She has never seen or heard of a Jesuit! It's you who are a Jesuit! And she proves with jesuitical demonstration that you are a subtle Jesuit.

Here is one of the thousand examples of a woman's jesuitism, and this example constitutes the most terrible of the petty troubles of married life; it is perhaps the most serious.

Induced by a desire the thousandth time expressed by Caroline, who complained that she had to go on foot or that she could not buy a new hat, a new parasol, a new dress, or any other article of dress, often enough:

That she could not dress her baby as a sailor, as a lancer, as an artilleryman of the National Guard, as a Highlander with naked legs and a cap and feather, in a jacket, in a roundabout, in a velvet sack, in boots, in trousers: that she could not buy him toys enough, nor mechanical moving mice and Noah's Arks enough:

That she could not return Madame Deschars or Madame de Fischtaminel their civilities, a ball, a party, a dinner: nor take a private box at the theatre, thus avoiding the necessity of sitting cheek by jowl with men who are either too polite or not enough so, and of calling a cab at the close of the performance; apropos of which she thus discourses:

"You think it cheaper, but you are mistaken: men are all the same! I soil my shoes, I spoil my hat, my shawl gets wet and my silk stockings get muddy. You economize twenty francs by not having a carriage, — no not twenty, sixteen, for your pay four for the cab — and you lose fifty francs' worth of dress, besides being wounded in your pride on seeing a faded bonnet on my head: you don't see why it's faded, but it's those horrid cabs. I say nothing of the annoyance of being tumbled and jostled by a crowd of men, for it seems you don't care for that!"

That she could not buy a piano instead of hiring one, nor keep up with the fashions; (there are some women, she says, who have all the new styles, but just think what they give in return! She would rather throw herself out of the window than imitate them! She loves you too much. Here she sheds tears. She does not understand such women). That she could not ride in the Champs Elysees, stretched out in her own carriage, like Madame de Fischtaminel. (There's a woman who understands life: and who has a well-taught, well-disciplined and very contented husband: his wife would go through fire and water for him!)

Finally, beaten in a thousand conjugal scenes, beaten by the most logical arguments (the late logicians Tripier and Merlin were nothing to her, as the preceding chapter has sufficiently shown you), beaten by the most tender caresses, by tears, by your own words turned against you, for under circumstances like these, a woman lies in wait in her house like a jaguar in the jungle; she does not appear to listen to you, or to heed you; but if a single word, a wish, a gesture, escapes you, she arms herself with it, she whets it to an edge, she brings it to bear upon you a hundred times over; beaten by such graceful tricks as "If you will do so and so, I will do this and that;" for women, in these cases, become greater bargainers than the Jews and Greeks (those, I mean, who sell perfumes and little girls), than the Arabs (those, I mean, who sell little boys and horses), greater higglers than the Swiss and the Genevese, than bankers, and, what is worse than all, than the Genoese!

Finally, beaten in a manner which may be called beaten, you determine to risk a certain portion of your capital in a business undertaking. One evening, at twilight, seated side by side, or some morning on awakening, while Caroline, half asleep, a pink bud in her white linen, her face smiling in her lace, is beside you, you say to her, "You want this, you say, or you want that: you told me this or you told me that:" in short, you hastily enumerate the numberless fancies by which she has over and over again broken your heart, for there is nothing more dreadful than to be unable to satisfy the desires of a beloved wife, and you close with these words:

"Well, my dear, an opportunity offers of quintupling a hundred thousand francs, and I have decided to make the venture."

She is wide awake now, she sits up in bed, and gives you a kiss, ah! this time, a real good one!

"You are a dear boy!" is her first word.

We will not mention her last, for it is an enormous and unpronounceable onomatope.

"Now," she says, "tell me all about it."

You try to explain the nature of the affair. But in the first place, women do not understand business, and in the next they do not wish to seem to understand it. Your dear, delighted Caroline says you were wrong to take her desires, her groans, her sighs for new dresses, in earnest. She is afraid of your venture, she is frightened at the directors, the shares, and above all at the running expenses, and doesn't exactly see where the dividend comes in.

Axiom.—Women are always afraid of things that have to be divided.

In short, Caroline suspects a trap: but she is delighted to know that she can have her carriage, her box, the numerous styles of dress for her baby, and the rest. While dissuading you from engaging in the speculation, she is visibly glad to see you investing your money in it.

FIRST PERIOD.—"Oh, I am the happiest woman on the face of the earth! Adolphe has just gone into the most splendid venture. I am going to have a carriage, oh! ever so much handsomer than Madame de Fischtaminel's; hers is out of fashion. Mine will have curtains with fringes. My horses will be mouse-colored, hers are bay,—they are as common as coppers."

"What is this venture, madame?"

"Oh, it's splendid—the stock is going up; he explained it to me before he went into it, for Adolphe never does anything without consulting me."

"You are very fortunate."

"Marriage would be intolerable without entire confidence, and Adolphe tells me everything."

Thus, Adolphe, you are the best husband in Paris, you are adorable, you are a man of genius, you are all heart, an angel. You are petted to an uncomfortable degree. You bless the marriage tie. Caroline extols men, calling them "kings of creation," women were made for them, man is naturally generous, and matrimony is a delightful institution.

For three, sometimes six, months, Caroline executes the most brilliant concertos and solos upon this delicious theme: "I shall be rich! I shall have a thousand a month for my dress: I am going to keep my carriage!"

If your son is alluded to, it is merely to ask about the school to which he shall be sent.

SECOND PERIOD.—"Well, dear, how is your business getting on?—What has become of it?—How about that speculation which was to give me a carriage, and other things?—It is high time that affair should come to something.—It is a good while cooking.—When *will* it begin to pay? Is the stock going up?—There's nobody like you for hitting upon ventures that never amount to anything."

One day she says to you, "Is there really an affair?"

If you mention it eight or ten months after, she returns:

"Ah! Then there really *is* an affair!"

This woman, whom you thought dull, begins to show signs of extraordinary wit, when her object is to make fun of you. During this period, Caroline maintains a compromising silence when people speak of you, or else she speaks disparagingly of men in general: "Men are not what they seem: to find them out you must try them." "Marriage has its good and its bad points." "Men never can finish anything."

THIRD PERIOD.—*Catastrophe.*—This magnificent affair which was to yield five hundred per cent, in which the most cautious, the best informed persons took part—peers, deputies, bankers—all of them Knights of the Legion of Honor—this venture has been obliged to liquidate! The most sanguine expect to get ten per cent of their capital back. You are discouraged.

Caroline has often said to you, "Adolphe, what is the matter? Adolphe, there is something wrong."

Finally, you acquaint Caroline with the fatal result: she begins by consoling you.

"One hundred thousand francs lost! We shall have to practice the strictest economy," you imprudently add.

The jesuitism of woman bursts out at this word "economy." It sets fire to the magazine.

"Ah! that's what comes of speculating! How is it that *you, ordinarily so prudent,* could go and risk a hundred thousand francs! *You know I was against it from the beginning!* BUT YOU WOULD NOT LISTEN TO ME!"

Upon this, the discussion grows bitter.

You are good for nothing—you have no business capacity; women alone take clear views of things. You have risked your children's bread, though she tried to dissuade you from it.—You cannot say it was for her. Thank God, she has nothing to reproach herself with. A hundred times a month she alludes to your disaster: "If my husband had not thrown away his money in such and such a scheme, I could have had this and that." "The next time you want to go into an affair, perhaps you'll consult me!" Adolphe is accused and convicted of having foolishly lost one hundred thousand francs, without an object in view, like a dolt, and without having consulted his wife. Caroline advises her friends not to marry. She complains of the incapacity of men who squander the fortunes of their wives. Caroline is vindictive, she makes herself generally disagreeable. Pity Adolphe! Lament, ye husbands! O bachelors, rejoice and be exceeding glad!

MEMORIES AND REGRETS.

After several years of wedded life, your love has become so placid, that Caroline sometimes tries, in the evening, to wake you up by various little coquettish phrases. There is about you a certain calmness and tranquillity which always exasperates a lawful wife. Women see in it a sort of insolence: they look upon the indifference of happiness as the fatuity of confidence, for of course they never imagine their inestimable equalities can be regarded with disdain: their virtue is therefore enraged at being so cordially trusted in.

In this situation, which is what every couple must come to, and which both husband and wife must expect, no husband dares confess that the constant repetition of the same dish has become wearisome; but his appetite certainly requires the condiments of dress, the ideas excited by absence, the stimulus of an imaginary rivalry.

In short, at this period, you walk very comfortably with your wife on your arm, without pressing hers against your heart with the solicitous and watchful cohesion of a miser grasping his treasure. You gaze carelessly round upon the curiosities in the street, leading your wife in a loose and distracted way, as if you were towing a Norman scow. Come now, be frank! If, on passing your wife, an admirer were gently to press her, accidentally or purposely, would you have the slightest desire to discover his motives? Besides, you say, no woman would seek to bring about a quarrel for such a trifle. Confess this, too, that the expression "such a trifle" is exceedingly flattering to both of you.

You are in this position, but you have as yet proceeded no farther. Still, you have a horrible thought which you bury in the depths of your heart and conscience: Caroline has not come up to your expectations. Caroline has imperfections, which, during the high tides of the honey-moon, were concealed under the water, but which the ebb of the gall-moon has laid bare. You have several times run against these breakers, your hopes have been often shipwrecked upon them, more than once your desires—those of a young marrying man—(where, alas, is that time!) have seen their richly laden gondolas go to pieces there: the flower of the cargo went to the bottom, the ballast of the marriage remained. In short, to make use of a colloquial expression, as you talk over your marriage with yourself you say, as you look at Caroline, *"She is not what I took her to be!"*

Some evening, at a ball, in society, at a friend's house, no matter where, you meet a sublime young woman, beautiful, intellectual and kind: with a soul, oh! a soul of celestial purity, and of miraculous beauty! Yes, there is that unchangeable oval cut of face, those features which time will never impair, that graceful and thoughtful brow. The unknown is rich, well-educated, of noble birth: she will always be what she should be, she knows when to shine, when to remain in the background: she appears in all her glory and power, the being you have dreamed of, your wife that should have been, she whom you feel you could love forever. She would always have flattered your little vanities, she would understand and admirably serve your interests. She is tender and gay, too, this young lady who reawakens all your better feelings, who rekindles your slumbering desires.

You look at Caroline with gloomy despair, and here are the phantom-like thoughts which tap, with wings of a bat, the beak of a vulture, the body of a death's-head moth, upon the walls of the palace in which, enkindled by desire, glows your brain like a lamp of gold:

FIRST STANZA. Ah, dear me, why did I get married? Fatal idea! I allowed myself to be caught by a small amount of cash. And is it really over? Cannot I have another wife? Ah, the Turks manage things better! It is plain enough that the author of the Koran lived in the desert!

SECOND STANZA. My wife is sick, she sometimes coughs in the morning. If it is the design of Providence to remove her from the world, let it be speedily done for her sake and for mine. The angel has lived long enough.

THIRD STANZA. I am a monster! Caroline is the mother of my children!

You go home, that night, in a carriage with your wife: you think her perfectly horrible: she speaks to you, but you answer in monosyllables. She says, "What is the matter?" and you answer, "Nothing." She coughs, you advise her to see the doctor in the morning. Medicine has its hazards.

FOURTH STANZA. I have been told that a physician, poorly paid by the heirs of his deceased patient, imprudently exclaimed, "What! they cut down my bill, when they owe me forty thousand a year." *I* would not haggle over fees!

"Caroline," you say to her aloud, "you must take care of yourself; cross your shawl, be prudent, my darling angel."

Your wife is delighted with you since you seem to take such an interest in her. While she is preparing to retire, you lie stretched out upon the sofa. You contemplate the divine apparition which opens to you the ivory portals of your castles in the air. Delicious ecstasy! 'Tis the sublime young woman that you see before you! She is as white as the sail of the treasure-laden galleon as it enters the harbor of Cadiz. Your wife, happy in your admiration, now understands your former taciturnity. You still see, with closed eyes, the sublime young woman; she is the burden of your thoughts, and you say aloud:

FIFTH AND LAST STANZA. Divine! Adorable! Can there be another woman like her? Rose of Night! Column of ivory! Celestial maiden! Morning and Evening Star!

Everyone says his prayers; you have said four.

The next morning, your wife is delightful, she coughs no more, she has no need of a doctor; if she dies, it will be of good health; you launched four maledictions upon her, in the name of your sublime young woman, and four times she blessed you for it. Caroline does not know that in the depths of your heart there wriggles a little red fish like a crocodile, concealed beneath conjugal love like the other would be hid in a basin.

A few days before, your wife had spoken of you in rather equivocal terms to Madame de Fischtaminel: your fair friend comes to visit her, and Caroline compromises you by a long and humid gaze; she praises you and says she never was happier.

You rush out in a rage, you are beside yourself, and are glad to meet a friend, that you may work off your bile.

"Don't you ever marry, George; it's better to see your heirs carrying away your furniture while the death-rattle is in your throat, better to go through an agony of two hours without a drop to cool your tongue, better to be assassinated by inquiries about your will by a nurse like the one in Henry Monnier's terrible picture of a 'Bachelor's Last Moments!' Never marry under any pretext!"

Fortunately you see the sublime young woman no more. You are saved from the tortures to which a criminal passion was leading you. You fall back again into the purgatory of your married bliss; but you begin to be attentive to Madame de Fischtaminel, with whom you were dreadfully in love, without being able to get near her, while you were a bachelor.

OBSERVATIONS.

When you have arrived at this point in the latitude or longitude of the matrimonial ocean, there appears a slight chronic, intermittent affection, not unlike the toothache. Here, I see, you stop me to ask, "How are we to find the longitude in this sea? When can a husband be sure he has attained this nautical point? And can the danger be avoided?"

You may arrive at this point, look you, as easily after ten months as ten years of wedlock; it depends upon the speed of the vessel, its style of rigging, upon the trade winds, the force of the currents, and especially upon the composition of the crew. You have this advantage over the mariner, that he has but one method of calculating his position, while husbands have at least a thousand of reckoning theirs.

EXAMPLE: Caroline, your late darling, your late treasure, who is now merely your humdrum wife, leans much too heavily upon your arm while walking on the boulevard, or else says it is much more elegant not to take your arm at all;

Or else she notices men, older or younger as the case may be, dressed with more or less taste, whereas she formerly saw no one whatever, though the sidewalk was black with hats and traveled by more boots than slippers;

Or, when you come home, she says, "It's no one but my husband:" instead of saying "Ah! 'tis Adolphe!" as she used to say with a gesture, a look, an accent which caused her admirers to think, "Well, here's a happy woman at last!" This last exclamation of a woman is suitable for two eras,—first, while she is sincere; second, while she is hypocritical, with her "Ah! 'tis Adolphe!" When she exclaims, "It's only my husband," she no longer deigns to play a part.

Or, if you come home somewhat late—at eleven, or at midnight—you find her—snoring! Odious symptom!

Or else she puts on her stockings in your presence. Among English couples, this never happens but once in a lady's married life; the next day she leaves for the Continent with some captain or other, and no longer thinks of putting on her stockings at all.

Or else—but let us stop here.

This is intended for the use of mariners and husbands who are weatherwise.

THE MATRIMONIAL GADFLY.

Very well! In this degree of longitude, not far from a tropical sign upon the name of which good taste forbids us to make a jest at once coarse and unworthy of this thoughtful work, a horrible little annoyance appears, ingeniously called the Matrimonial Gadfly, the most provoking of all gnats, mosquitoes, blood-suckers, fleas and scorpions, for no net was ever yet invented that could keep it off. The gadfly does not immediately sting you; it begins by buzzing in your ears, and *you do not at first know what it is.*

Thus, apropos of nothing, in the most natural way in the world, Caroline says: "Madame Deschars had a lovely dress on, yesterday."

"She is a woman of taste," returns Adolphe, though he is far from thinking so.

"Her husband gave it to her," resumes Caroline, with a shrug of her shoulders.

"Ah!"

"Yes, a four hundred franc dress! It's the very finest quality of velvet."

"Four hundred francs!" cries Adolphe, striking the attitude of the apostle Thomas.

"But then there are two extra breadths and enough for a high waist!"

"Monsieur Deschars does things on a grand scale," replies Adolphe, taking refuge in a jest.

"All men don't pay such attentions to their wives," says Caroline, curtly.

"What attentions?"

"Why, Adolphe, thinking of extra breadths and of a waist to make the dress good again, when it is no longer fit to be worn low in the neck."

Adolphe says to himself, "Caroline wants a dress."

Poor man!

Some time afterward, Monsieur Deschars furnishes his wife's chamber anew. Then he has his wife's diamonds set in the prevailing fashion. Monsieur Deschars never goes out without his wife, and never allows his wife to go out without offering her his arm.

If you bring Caroline anything, no matter what, it is never equal to what Monsieur Deschars has done. If you allow yourself the slightest gesture or expression a little livelier than usual, if you speak a little bit loud, you hear the hissing and viper-like remark:

"You wouldn't see Monsieur Deschars behaving like this! Why don't you take Monsieur Deschars for a model?"

In short, this idiotic Monsieur Deschars is forever looming up in your household on every conceivable occasion.

The expression—"Do you suppose Monsieur Deschars ever allows himself"—is a sword of Damocles, or what is worse, a Damocles pin: and your self-love is the cushion into which your wife is constantly sticking it, pulling it out, and sticking it in again, under a variety of unforeseen pretexts, at the same time employing the most winning terms of endearment, and with the most agreeable little ways.

Adolphe, stung till he finds himself tattooed, finally does what is done by police authorities, by officers of government, by military tacticians. He casts his eye on Madame de Fischtaminel, who is still young, elegant and a little bit coquettish, and places her (this had been the rascal's intention for some time) like a blister upon Caroline's extremely ticklish skin.

O you, who often exclaim, "I don't know what is the matter with my wife!" you will kiss this page of transcendent philosophy, for you will find in it *the key to every woman's character*! But as to knowing women as well as I know them, it will not be knowing them much; they don't know themselves! In fact, as you well know, God was Himself mistaken in the only one that He attempted to manage and to whose manufacture He had given personal attention.

Caroline is very willing to sting Adolphe at all hours, but this privilege of letting a wasp off now and then upon one's consort (the legal term), is exclusively reserved to the wife. Adolphe is a monster if he starts off a single fly at Caroline. On her part, it is a delicious joke, a new jest to enliven their married life, and one dictated by the purest intentions; while on Adolphe's part, it is a piece of cruelty worthy a Carib, a disregard of his wife's heart, and a deliberate plan to give her pain. But that is nothing.

"So you are really in love with Madame de Fischtaminel?" Caroline asks. "What is there so seductive in the mind or the manners of the spider?"

"Why, Caroline—"

"Oh, don't undertake to deny your eccentric taste," she returns, checking a negation on Adolphe's lips. "I have long seen that you prefer that Maypole [Madame de Fischtaminel is thin] to me. Very well! go on; you will soon see the difference."

Do you understand? You cannot suspect Caroline of the slightest inclination for Monsieur Deschars, a low, fat, red-faced man, formerly a notary, while you are in love with Madame de Fischtaminel! Then Caroline, the Caroline whose simplicity caused you such agony, Caroline who has become familiar with society, Caroline becomes acute and witty: you have two gadflies instead of one.

The next day she asks you, with a charming air of interest, "How are you coming on with Madame de Fischtaminel?"

When you go out, she says: "Go and drink something calming, my dear." For, in their anger with a rival, all women, duchesses even, will use invectives, and even venture into the domain of Billingsgate; they make an offensive weapon of anything and everything.

To try to convince Caroline that she is mistaken and that you are indifferent to Madame de Fischtaminel, would cost you dear. This is a blunder that no sensible man commits; he would lose his power and spike his own guns.

Oh! Adolphe, you have arrived unfortunately at that season so ingeniously called the *Indian Summer of Marriage*.

You must now—pleasing task!—win your wife, your Caroline, over again, seize her by the waist again, and become the best of husbands by trying to guess at things to please her, so as to act according to her whims instead of according to your will. This is the whole question henceforth.

HARD LABOR.

Let us admit this, which, in our opinion, is a truism made as good as new:

Axiom.—Most men have some of the wit required by a difficult position, when they have not the whole of it.

As for those husbands who are not up to their situation, it is impossible to consider their case here: without any struggle whatever they simply enter the numerous class of the *Resigned*.

Adolphe says to himself: "Women are children: offer them a lump of sugar, and you will easily get them to dance all the dances that greedy children dance; but you must always have a sugar plum in hand, hold it up pretty high, and—take care that their fancy for sweetmeats does not leave them. Parisian women—and Caroline is one—are very vain, and as for their voracity—don't speak of it. Now you cannot govern men and make friends of them, unless you work upon them through their vices, and flatter their passions: my wife is mine!"

Some days afterward, during which Adolphe has been unusually attentive to his wife, he discourses to her as follows:

"Caroline, dear, suppose we have a bit of fun: you'll put on your new gown—the one like Madame Deschars!—and we'll go to see a farce at the Varieties."

This kind of proposition always puts a wife in the best possible humor. So away you go! Adolphe has ordered a dainty little dinner for two, at Borrel's *Rocher de Cancale*.

"As we are going to the Varieties, suppose we dine at the tavern," exclaims Adolphe, on the boulevard, with the air of a man suddenly struck by a generous idea.

Caroline, delighted with this appearance of good fortune, enters a little parlor where she finds the cloth laid and that neat little service set, which Borrel places at the disposal of those who are rich enough to pay for the quarters intended for the great ones of the earth, who make themselves small for an hour.

Women eat little at a formal dinner: their concealed harness hampers them, they are laced tightly, and they are in the presence of women whose eyes and whose tongues are equally to be dreaded. They prefer fancy eating to good eating, then: they will suck a lobster's claw, swallow a quail or two, punish a woodcock's wing, beginning with a bit of fresh fish, flavored by one of those sauces which are the glory of French cooking. France is everywhere sovereign in matters of taste: in painting, fashions, and the like. Gravy is the triumph of taste, in cookery. So that grisettes, shopkeepers' wives and duchesses are delighted with a tasty little dinner washed down with the choicest wines, of which, however, they drink but little, the whole concluded by fruit such as can only be had at Paris; and especially delighted when they go to the theatre to digest the little dinner, and listen, in a comfortable box, to the nonsense uttered upon the stage, and to that whispered in their ears to explain it. But then the bill of the restaurant is one hundred francs, the box costs thirty, the carriage, dress, gloves, bouquet, as much more. This gallantry amounts to the sum of one hundred and sixty francs, which is hard upon four thousand francs a month, if you go often to the Comic, the Italian, or the Grand, Opera. Four thousand francs a month is the interest of a capital of two millions. But then the honor of being a husband is fully worth the price!

Caroline tells her friends things which she thinks exceedingly flattering, but which cause a sagacious husband to make a wry face.

"Adolphe has been delightful for some time past. I don't know what I have done to deserve so much attention, but he overpowers me. He gives value to everything by those delicate ways which have such an effect upon us women. After taking me Monday to the *Rocher de Cancale* to dine, he declared that Very was as good a cook as Borrel, and he gave me the little party of pleasure that I told you of all over again, presenting me at dessert with a ticket for the opera. They sang 'William Tell,' which, you know, is my craze."

"You are lucky indeed," returns Madame Deschars with evident jealousy.

"Still, a wife who discharges all her duties, deserves such luck, it seems to me."

When this terrible sentiment falls from the lips of a married woman, it is clear that she *does her duty*, after the manner of school-boys, for the reward she expects. At school, a prize is the object: in marriage, a shawl or a piece of jewelry. No more love, then!

"As for me," —Madame Deschars is piqued—"I am reasonable. Deschars committed such follies once, but I put a stop to it. You see, my dear, we have two children, and I confess that one or two hundred francs are quite a consideration for me, as the mother of a family."

"Dear me, madame," says Madame de Fischtaminel, "it's better that our husbands should have cosy little times with us than with—"

"Deschars!—" suddenly puts in Madame Deschars, as she gets up and says good-bye.

The individual known as Deschars (a man nullified by his wife) does not hear the end of the sentence, by which he might have learned that a man may spend his money with other women.

Caroline, flattered in every one of her vanities, abandons herself to the pleasures of pride and high living, two delicious capital sins. Adolphe is gaining ground again, but alas! (this reflection is worth a whole sermon in Lent) sin, like all pleasure, contains a spur. Vice is like an Autocrat, and let a single harsh fold in a rose-leaf irritate it, it forgets a thousand charming bygone flatteries. With Vice a man's course must always be crescendo!—and forever.

Axiom.—Vice, Courtiers, Misfortune and Love, care only for the PRESENT.

At the end of a period of time difficult to determine, Caroline looks in the glass, at dessert, and notices two or three pimples blooming upon her cheeks, and upon the sides, lately so pure, of her nose. She is out of humor at the theatre, and you do not know why, you, so proudly striking an attitude in your cravat, you, displaying your figure to the best advantage, as a complacent man should.

A few days after, the dressmaker arrives. She tries on a gown, she exerts all her strength, but cannot make the hooks and eyes meet. The waiting maid is called. After a two horse-power pull, a regular thirteenth labor of Hercules, a hiatus of two inches manifests itself. The inexorable dressmaker cannot conceal from Caroline the fact that her form is altered. Caroline, the aerial Caroline, threatens to become like Madame Deschars. In vulgar language, she is getting stout. The maid leaves her in a state of consternation.

"What! am I to have, like that fat Madame Deschars, cascades of flesh a la Rubens! That Adolphe is an awful scoundrel. Oh, I see, he wants to make me an old mother Gigogne, and destroy my powers of fascination!"

Thenceforward Caroline is willing to go to the opera, she accepts two seats in a box, but she considers it very distingue to eat sparingly, and declines the dainty dinners of her husband.

"My dear," she says, "a well-bred woman should not go often to these places; you may go once for a joke; but as for making a habitual thing of it—fie, for shame!"

Borrel and Very, those masters of the art, lose a thousand francs a day by not having a private entrance for carriages. If a coach could glide under an archway, and go out by another door, after leaving its fair occupants on the threshold of an elegant staircase, how many of them would bring the landlord fine, rich, solid old fellows for customers!

Axiom.—Vanity is the death of good living.

Caroline very soon gets tired of the theatre, and the devil alone can tell the cause of her disgust. Pray excuse Adolphe! A husband is not the devil.

Fully one-third of the women of Paris are bored by the theatre. Many of them are tired to death of music, and go to the opera for the singers merely, or rather to notice the difference between them in point of execution. What supports the theatre is this: the women are a spectacle before and after the play. Vanity alone will pay the exorbitant price of forty francs for three hours of questionable pleasure, in a bad atmosphere and at great expense, without counting the colds caught in going out. But to exhibit themselves, to see and be seen, to be the observed of five hundred observers! What a glorious mouthful! as Rabelais would say.

To obtain this precious harvest, garnered by self-love, a woman must be looked at. Now a woman with her husband is very little looked at. Caroline is chagrined to see the audience entirely taken up with women who are *not* with their husbands, with eccentric women, in short. Now, as the very slight return she gets from her efforts, her dresses, and her attitudes, does not compensate, in her eyes, for her fatigue, her display and her weariness, it is very soon the same with the theatre as it was with the good cheer; high living made her fat, the theatre is making her yellow.

Here Adolphe—or any other man in Adolphe's place—resembles a certain Languedocian peasant who suffered agonies from an agacin, or, in French, corn,—but the term in Lanquedoc is so much prettier, don't you think so? This peasant drove his foot at each step two inches into the sharpest stones along the roadside, saying to the agacin, "Devil take you! Make me suffer again, will you?"

"Upon my word," says Adolphe, profoundly disappointed, the day when he receives from his wife a refusal, "I should like very much to know what would please you!"

Caroline looks loftily down upon her husband, and says, after a pause worthy of an actress, "I am neither a Strasburg goose nor a giraffe!"

"'Tis true, I might lay out four thousand francs a month to better effect," returns Adolphe.

"What do you mean?"

"With the quarter of that sum, presented to estimable burglars, youthful jail-birds and honorable criminals, I might become somebody, a Man in the Blue Cloak on a small scale; and then a young woman is proud of her husband," Adolphe replies.

This answer is the grave of love, and Caroline takes it in very bad part. An explanation follows. This must be classed among the thousand pleasantries of the following chapter, the title of which ought to make lovers smile as well as husbands. If there are yellow rays of light, why should there not be whole days of this extremely matrimonial color?

FORCED SMILES.

On your arrival in this latitude, you enjoy numerous little scenes, which, in the grand opera of marriage, represent the intermezzos, and of which the following is a type:

You are one evening alone after dinner, and you have been so often alone already that you feel a desire to say sharp little things to each other, like this, for instance:

"Take care, Caroline," says Adolphe, who has not forgotten his many vain efforts to please her. "I think your nose has the impertinence to redden at home quite well as at the restaurant."

"This is not one of your amiable days!"

General Rule.—No man has ever yet discovered the way to give friendly advice to any woman, not even to his own wife.

"Perhaps it's because you are laced too tight. Women make themselves sick that way."

The moment a man utters these words to a woman, no matter whom, that woman,—who knows that stays will bend,—seizes her corset by the lower end, and bends it out, saying, with Caroline:

"Look, you can get your hand in! I never lace tight."

"Then it must be your stomach."

"What has the stomach got to do with the nose?"

"The stomach is a centre which communicates with all the organs."

"So the nose is an organ, is it?"

"Yes."

"Your organ is doing you a poor service at this moment." She raises her eyes and shrugs her shoulders. "Come, Adolphe, what have I done?"

"Nothing. I'm only joking, and I am unfortunate enough not to please you," returns Adolphe, smiling.

"My misfortune is being your wife! Oh, why am I not somebody else's!"

"That's what *I* say!"

"If I were, and if I had the innocence to say to you, like a coquette who wishes to know how far she has got with a man, 'the redness of my nose really gives me anxiety,' you would look at me in the glass with all the affectations of an ape, and would reply, 'O madame, you do yourself an injustice; in the first place, nobody sees it: besides, it harmonizes with your complexion; then again we are all so after dinner!' and from this you would go on to flatter me. Do I ever tell you that you are growing fat, that you are getting the color of a stone-cutter, and that I prefer thin and pale men?"

They say in London, "Don't touch the axe!" In France we ought to say, "Don't touch a woman's nose."

"And all this about a little extra natural vermilion!" exclaims Adolphe. "Complain about it to Providence, whose office it is to put a little more color in one place than another, not to me, who loves you, who desires you to be perfect, and who merely says to you, take care!"

"You love me too much, then, for you've been trying, for some time past, to find disagreeable things to say to me. You want to run me down under the pretext of making me perfect—people said I *was* perfect, five years ago."

"I think you are better than perfect, you are stunning!"

"With too much vermilion?"

Adolphe, who sees the atmosphere of the north pole upon his wife's face, sits down upon a chair by her side. Caroline, unable decently to go away, gives her gown a sort of flip on one side, as if to produce a separation. This motion is performed by some women with a provoking impertinence: but it has two significations; it is, as whist players would say, either a signal *for trumps* or a *renounce*. At this time, Caroline renounces.

"What is the matter?" says Adolphe.

"Will you have a glass of sugar and water?" asks Caroline, busying herself about your health, and assuming the part of a servant.

"What for?"

"You are not amiable while digesting, you must be in pain. Perhaps you would like a drop of brandy in your sugar and water? The doctor spoke of it as an excellent remedy."

"How anxious you are about my stomach!"

"It's a centre, it communicates with the other organs, it will act upon your heart, and through that perhaps upon your tongue."

Adolphe gets up and walks about without saying a word, but he reflects upon the acuteness which his wife is acquiring: he sees her daily gaining in strength and in acrimony: she is getting to display an art in vexation and a military capacity for disputation which reminds him of Charles XII and the Russians. Caroline, during this time, is busy with an alarming piece of mimicry: she looks as if she were going to faint.

"Are you sick?" asks Adolphe, attacked in his generosity, the place where women always have us.

"It makes me sick at my stomach, after dinner, to see a man going back and forth so, like the pendulum of a clock. But it's just like you: you are always in a fuss about something. You are a queer set: all men are more or less cracked."

Adolphe sits down by the fire opposite to his wife, and remains there pensive: marriage appears to him like an immense dreary plain, with its crop of nettles and mullen stalks.

"What, are you pouting?" asks Caroline, after a quarter of an hour's observation of her husband's countenance.

"No, I am meditating," replied Adolphe.

"Oh, what an infernal temper you've got!" she returns, with a shrug of the shoulders. "Is it for what I said about your stomach, your shape and your digestion? Don't you see that I was only paying you back for your vermilion? You'll make me think that men are as vain as women. [Adolphe remains frigid.] It is really quite kind in you to take our qualities. [Profound silence.] I made a joke and you got angry [she looks at Adolphe], for you are angry. I am not like you: I cannot bear the idea of having given you pain! Nevertheless, it's an idea that a man never would have had, that of attributing your impertinence to something wrong in your digestion. It's not my Dolph, it's his stomach that was bold enough to speak. I did not know you were a ventriloquist, that's all."

Caroline looks at Adolphe and smiles: Adolphe is as stiff as if he were glued.

"No, he won't laugh! And, in your jargon, you call this having character. Oh, how much better we are!"

She goes and sits down in Adolphe's lap, and Adolphe cannot help smiling. This smile, extracted as if by a steam engine, Caroline has been on the watch for, in order to make a weapon of it.

"Come, old fellow, confess that you are wrong," she says. "Why pout? Dear me, I like you just as you are: in my eyes you are as slender as when I married you, and slenderer perhaps."

"Caroline, when people get to deceive themselves in these little matters, where one makes concessions and the other does not get angry, do you know what it means?"

"What does it mean?" asks Caroline, alarmed at Adolphe's dramatic attitude.

"That they love each other less."

"Oh! you monster, I understand you: you were angry so as to make me believe you loved me!"

Alas! let us confess it, Adolphe tells the truth in the only way he can—by a laugh.

"Why give me pain?" she says. "If I am wrong in anything, isn't it better to tell me of it kindly, than brutally to say [here she raises her voice], 'Your nose is getting red!' No, that is not right! To please you, I will use an expression of the fair Fischtaminel, 'It's not the act of a gentleman!'"

Adolphe laughs and pays the expenses of the reconciliation; but instead of discovering therein what will please Caroline and what will attach her to him, he finds out what attaches him to her.

NOSOGRAPHY OF THE VILLA.

Is it advantageous for a man not to know what will please his wife after their marriage? Some women (this still occurs in the country) are innocent enough to tell promptly what they want and what they like. But in Paris, nearly every woman feels a kind of enjoyment in seeing a man wistfully obedient to her heart, her desires, her caprices—three expressions for the same thing!—and anxiously going round and round, half crazy and desperate, like a dog that has lost his master.

They call this *being loved*, poor things! And a good many of them say to themselves, as did Caroline, "How will he manage?"

Adolphe has come to this. In this situation of things, the worthy and excellent Deschars, that model of the citizen husband, invites the couple known as Adolphe and Caroline to help him and his wife inaugurate a delightful country house. It is an opportunity that the Deschars have seized upon, the folly of a man of letters, a charming villa upon which he lavished one hundred thousand francs and which has been sold at auction for eleven thousand. Caroline has a new dress to air, or a hat with a weeping willow plume—things which a tilbury will set off to a charm. Little Charles is left with his grandmother. The servants have a holiday. The youthful pair start beneath the smile of a blue sky, flecked with milk-while clouds merely to heighten the effect. They breathe the pure air, through which trots the heavy Norman horse, animated by the influence of spring. They soon reach Marnes, beyond Ville d'Avray, where the Deschars are spreading themselves in a villa copied from one at Florence, and surrounded by Swiss meadows, though without all the objectionable features of the Alps.

"Dear me! what a delightful thing a country house like this must be!" exclaims Caroline, as she walks in the admirable wood that skirts Marnes and Ville d'Avray. "It makes your eyes as happy as if they had a heart in them."

Caroline, having no one to take but Adolphe, takes Adolphe, who becomes her Adolphe again. And then you should see her run about like a fawn, and act once more the sweet, pretty, innocent, adorable school-girl that she was! Her braids come down! She takes off her bonnet, and holds it by the strings! She is young, pink and white again. Her eyes smile, her mouth is a pomegranate endowed with sensibility, with a sensibility which seems quite fresh.

"So a country house would please you very much, would it, darling?" says Adolphe, clasping Caroline round the waist, and noticing that she leans upon him as if to show the flexibility of her form.

"What, will you be such a love as to buy me one? But remember, no extravagance! Seize an opportunity like the Deschars."

"To please you and to find out what is likely to give you pleasure, such is the constant study of your own Dolph."

They are alone, at liberty to call each other their little names of endearment, and run over the whole list of their secret caresses.

"Does he really want to please his little girly?" says Caroline, resting her head on the shoulder of Adolphe, who kisses her forehead, saying to himself, "Gad! I've got her now!"

Axiom.—When a husband and a wife have got each other, the devil only knows which has got the other.

The young couple are captivating, whereupon the stout Madame Deschars gives utterance to a remark somewhat equivocal for her, usually so stern, prudish and devout.

"Country air has one excellent property: it makes husbands very amiable."

M. Deschars points out an opportunity for Adolphe to seize. A house is to be sold at Ville d'Avray, for a song, of course. Now, the country house is a weakness peculiar to the inhabitant of Paris. This weakness, or disease, has its course and its cure. Adolphe is a husband, but not a doctor. He buys the house and takes possession with Caroline, who has become once more his Caroline, his Carola, his fawn, his treasure, his girly girl.

The following alarming symptoms now succeed each other with frightful rapidity: a cup of milk, baptized, costs five sous; when it is anhydrous, as the chemists say, ten sous. Meat costs more at Sevres than at Paris, if you carefully examine the qualities. Fruit cannot be had at any price. A fine pear costs more in the country than in the (anhydrous!) garden that blooms in Chevet's window.

Before being able to raise fruit for oneself, from a Swiss meadow measuring two square yards, surrounded by a few green trees which look as if they were borrowed from the scenic illusions of a theatre, the most rural authorities, being consulted on the point, declare that you must spend a great deal of money, and—wait five years! Vegetables dash out of the husbandman's garden to reappear at the city market. Madame Deschars, who possesses a gate-keeper that is at the same time a gardener, confesses that the vegetables raised on her land, beneath her glass frames, by dint of compost and top-soil, cost her twice as much as those she used to buy at Paris, of a woman who had rent and taxes to pay, and whose husband was an elector. Despite the efforts and pledges of the gate-keeper-gardener, early peas and things at Paris are a month in advance of those in the country.

From eight in the evening to eleven our couple don't know what to do, on account of the insipidity of the neighbors, their small ideas, and the questions of self-love which arise out of the merest trifles.

Monsieur Deschars remarks, with that profound knowledge of figures which distinguishes the ex-notary, that the cost of going to Paris and back, added to the interest of the cost of his villa, to the taxes, wages of the gate-keeper and his wife, are equal to a rent of three thousand francs a year. He does not see how he, an ex-notary, allowed himself to be so caught! For he has often drawn up leases of chateaux with parks and out-houses, for three thousand a year.

It is agreed by everybody in the parlor of Madame Deschars, that a country house, so far from being a pleasure, is an unmitigated nuisance.

"I don't see how they sell a cabbage for one sou at market, which has to be watered every day from its birth to the time you eat it," says Caroline.

"The way to get along in the country," replies a little retired grocer, "is to stay there, to live there, to become country-folks, and then everything changes."

On going home, Caroline says to her poor Adolphe, "What an idea that was of yours, to buy a country house! The best way to do about the country is to go there on visits to other people."

Adolphe remembers an English proverb, which says, "Don't have a newspaper or a country seat of your own: there are plenty of idiots who will have them for you."

"Bah!" returns Adolph, who was enlightened once for all upon women's logic by the Matrimonial Gadfly, "you are right: but then you know the baby is in splendid health, here."

Though Adolphe has become prudent, this reply awakens Caroline's susceptibilities. A mother is very willing to think exclusively of her child, but she does not want him to be preferred to herself. She is silent; the next day, she is tired to death of the country. Adolphe being absent on business, she waits for him from five o'clock to seven, and goes alone with little Charles to the coach office. She talks for three-quarters of an hour of her anxieties. She was afraid to go from the house to the office. Is it proper for a young woman to be left alone, so? She cannot support such an existence.

The country house now creates a very peculiar phase; one which deserves a chapter to itself.

TROUBLE WITHIN TROUBLE.

Axiom.—There are parentheses in worry.

EXAMPLE—A great deal of evil has been said of the stitch in the side; but it is nothing to the stitch to which we now refer, which the pleasures of the matrimonial second crop are everlastingly reviving, like the hammer of a note in the piano. This constitutes an irritant, which never flourishes except at the period when the young wife's timidity gives place to that fatal equality of rights which is at once devastating France and the conjugal relation. Every season has its peculiar vexation.

Caroline, after a week spent in taking note of her husband's absences, perceives that he passes seven hours a day away from her. At last, Adolphe, who comes home as gay as an actor who has been applauded, observes a slight coating of hoar frost upon Caroline's visage. After making sure that the coldness of her manner has been observed, Caroline puts on a counterfeit air of interest,—the well-known expression of which possesses the gift of making a man inwardly swear,—and says: "You must have had a good deal of business to-day, dear?"

"Oh, lots!"

"Did you take many cabs?"

"I took seven francs' worth."

"Did you find everybody in?"

"Yes, those with whom I had appointments."

"When did you make appointments with them? The ink in your inkstand is dried up; it's like glue; I wanted to write, and spent a whole hour in moistening it, and even then only produced a thick mud fit to mark bundles with for the East Indies."

Here any and every husband looks suspiciously at his better half.

"It is probable that I wrote them at Paris—"

"What business was it, Adolphe?"

"Why, I thought you knew. Shall I run over the list? First, there's Chaumontel's affair—"

"I thought Monsieur Chaumontel was in Switzerland—"

"Yes, but he has representatives, a lawyer—"

"Didn't you do anything else but business?" asks Caroline, interrupting Adolphe.

Here she gives him a direct, piercing look, by which she plunges into her husband's eyes when he least expects it: a sword in a heart.

"What could I have done? Made a little counterfeit money, run into debt, or embroidered a sampler?"

"Oh, dear, I don't know. And I can't even guess. I am too dull, you've told me so a hundred times."

"There you go, and take an expression of endearment in bad part. How like a woman that is!"

"Have you concluded anything?" she asks, pretending to take an interest in business.

"No, nothing,"

"How many persons have you seen?"

"Eleven, without counting those who were walking in the streets."

"How you answer me!"

"Yes, and how you question me! As if you'd been following the trade of an examining judge for the last ten years!"

"Come, tell me all you've done to-day, it will amuse me. You ought to try to please me while you are here! I'm dull enough when you leave me alone all day long."

"You want me to amuse you by telling you about business?"

"Formerly, you told me everything—"

This friendly little reproach disguises the certitude that Caroline wishes to enjoy respecting the serious matters which Adolphe wishes to conceal. Adolphe then undertakes to narrate how he has spent the day. Caroline affects a sort of distraction sufficiently well played to induce the belief that she is not listening.

"But you said just now," she exclaims, at the moment when Adolphe is getting into a snarl, "that you had paid seven francs for cabs, and you now talk of a hack! You took it by the hour, I suppose? Did you do your business in a hack?" she asks, railingly.

"Why should hacks be interdicted?" inquires Adolphe, resuming his narrative.

"Haven't you been to Madame de Fischtaminel's?" she asks in the middle of an exceedingly involved explanation, insolently taking the words out of your mouth.

"Why should I have been there?"

"It would have given me pleasure: I wanted to know whether her parlor is done."

"It is."

"Ah! then you *have* been there?"

"No, her upholsterer told me."

"Do you know her upholsterer?"

"Yes."

"Who is it?"

"Braschon."

"So you met the upholsterer?"

"Yes."

"You said you only went in carriages."

"Yes, my dear, but to get carriages, you have to go and—"

"Pooh! I dare say Braschon was in the carriage, or the parlor was—one or the other is equally probable."

"You won't listen," exclaims Adolphe, who thinks that a long story will lull Caroline's suspicions.

"I've listened too much already. You've been lying for the last hour, worse than a drummer."

"Well, I'll say nothing more."

"I know enough. I know all I wanted to know. You say you've seen lawyers, notaries, bankers: now you haven't seen one of them! Suppose I were to go to-morrow to see Madame de Fischtaminel, do you know what she would say?"

Here, Caroline watches Adolphe closely: but Adolphe affects a delusive calmness, in the middle of which Caroline throws out her line to fish up a clue.

"Why, she would say that she had had the pleasure of seeing you! How wretched we poor creatures are! We never know what you are doing: here we are stuck, chained at home, while you are off at your business! Fine business, truly! If I were in your place, I would invent business a little bit better put together than yours! Ah, you set us a worthy example! They say women are perverse. Who perverted them?"

Here Adolphe tries, by looking fixedly at Caroline, to arrest the torrent of words. Caroline, like a horse who has just been touched up by the lash, starts off anew, and with the animation of one of Rossini's codas:

"Yes, it's a very neat idea, to put your wife out in the country so that you may spend the day as you like at Paris. So this is the cause of your passion for a country house! Snipe that I was, to be caught in the trap! You are right, sir, a villa is very convenient: it serves two objects. But the wife can get along with it as well as the husband. You may take Paris and its hacks! I'll take the woods and their shady groves! Yes, Adolphe, I am really satisfied, so let's say no more about it."

Adolphe listens to sarcasm for an hour by the clock.

"Have you done, dear?" he asks, profiting by an instant in which she tosses her head after a pointed interrogation.

Then Caroline concludes thus: "I've had enough of the villa, and I'll never set foot in it again. But I know what will happen: you'll keep it, probably, and leave me in Paris. Well, at Paris, I can at least amuse myself, while you go with Madame de Fischtaminel to the woods. What is a *Villa Adolphini* where you get nauseated if you go six times round the lawn? where they've planted chair-legs and broom-sticks on the pretext of producing shade? It's like a furnace: the walls are six inches thick! and my gentleman is absent seven hours a day! That's what a country seat means!"

"Listen to me, Caroline."

"I wouldn't so much mind, if you would only confess what you did to-day. You don't know me yet: come, tell me, I won't scold you. I pardon you beforehand for all that you've done."

Adolphe, who knows the consequences of a confession too well to make one to his wife, replies—"Well, I'll tell you."

"That's a good fellow—I shall love you better."

"I was three hours—"

"I was sure of it—at Madame de Fischtaminel's!"

"No, at our notary's, as he had got me a purchaser; but we could not come to terms: he wanted our villa furnished. When I left there, I went to Braschon's, to see how much we owed him—"

"You made up this romance while I was talking to you! Look me in the face! I'll go to see Braschon to-morrow."

Adolphe cannot restrain a nervous shudder.

"You can't help laughing, you monster!"

"I laugh at your obstinacy."

"I'll go to-morrow to Madame de Fischtaminel's."

"Oh, go wherever you like!"

"What brutality!" says Caroline, rising and going away with her handkerchief at her eyes.

The country house, so ardently longed for by Caroline, has now become a dia-bolical invention of Adolphe's, a trap into which the fawn has fallen.

Since Adolphe's discovery that it is impossible to reason with Caroline, he lets her say whatever she pleases.

Two months after, he sells the villa which cost him twenty-two thousand francs for seven thousand! But he gains this by the adventure—he finds out that the country is not the thing that Caroline wants.

The question is becoming serious. Nature, with its woods, its forests, its val-leys, the Switzerland of the environs of Paris, the artificial rivers, have amused

Caroline for barely six months. Adolphe is tempted to abdicate and take Caroline's part himself.

A HOUSEHOLD REVOLUTION.

One morning, Adolphe is seized by the triumphant idea of letting Caroline find out for herself what she wants. He gives up to her the control of the house, saying, "Do as you like." He substitutes the constitutional system for the autocratic system, a responsible ministry for an absolute conjugal monarchy. This proof of confidence —the object of much secret envy—is, to women, a field-marshal's baton. Women are then, so to speak, mistresses at home.

After this, nothing, not even the memory of the honey-moon, can be compared to Adolphe's happiness for several days. A woman, under such circumstances, is all sugar. She is too sweet: she would invent the art of petting and cosseting and of coining tender little names, if this matrimonial sugar-plummery had not existed ever since the Terrestrial Paradise. At the end of the month, Adolphe's condition is like that of children towards the close of New Year's week. So Caroline is beginning to say, not in words, but in acts, in manner, in mimetic expressions: "It's difficult to tell *what* to do to please a man!"

Giving up the helm of the boat to one's wife, is an exceedingly ordinary idea, and would hardly deserve the qualification of "triumphant," which we have given it at the commencement of this chapter, if it were not accompanied by that of taking it back again. Adolphe was seduced by a wish, which invariably seizes persons who are the prey of misfortune, to know how far an evil will go!—to try how much damage fire will do when left to itself, the individual possessing, or thinking he possesses, the power to arrest it. This curiosity pursues us from the cradle to the grave. Then, after his plethora of conjugal felicity, Adolphe, who is treating himself to a farce in his own house, goes through the following phases:

FIRST EPOCH. Things go on altogether too well. Caroline buys little account books to keep a list of her expenses in, she buys a nice little piece of furniture to store her money in, she feeds Adolphe superbly, she is happy in his approbation, she discovers that very many articles are needed in the house. It is her ambition to be an incomparable housekeeper. Adolphe, who arrogates to himself the right of censorship, no longer finds the slightest suggestion to make.

When he dresses himself, everything is ready to his hands. Not even in Armide's garden was more ingenious tenderness displayed than that of Caroline. For her phoenix husband, she renews the wax upon his razor strap, she substitutes new suspenders for old ones. None of his button-holes are ever widowed. His linen is as well cared for as that of the confessor of the devotee, all whose sins are venial. His stockings are free from holes. At table, his tastes, his caprices even, are studied, consulted: he is getting fat! There is ink in his inkstand, and the sponge is always moist. He never has occasion to say, like Louis XIV, "I came near having to wait!" In short, he hears himself continually called *a love of a man*. He is obliged to reproach Caroline for neglecting herself: she does not pay sufficient attention to her own needs. Of this gentle reproach Caroline takes note.

SECOND EPOCH. The scene changes, at table. Everything is exceedingly dear. Vegetables are beyond one's means. Wood sells as if it came from Campeche. Fruit? Oh! as to fruit, princes, bankers and great lords alone can eat it. Dessert is a cause of ruin. Adolphe often hears Caroline say to Madame Deschars: "How do you manage?" Conferences are held in your presence upon the proper way to keep cooks under the thumb.

A cook who entered your service without effects, without clothes, and without talent, has come to get her wages in a blue merino gown, set off by an embroidered neckerchief, her ears embellished with a pair of ear-rings enriched with small pearls, her feet clothed in comfortable shoes which give you a glimpse of neat cotton stockings. She has two trunks full of property, and keeps an account at the savings bank.

Upon this Caroline complains of the bad morals of the lower classes: she complains of the education and the knowledge of figures which distinguish domestics. From time to time she utters little axioms like the following: There are some mistakes you *must* make!—It's only those who do nothing who do everything well.—She has the anxieties that belong to power.—Ah! men are fortunate in not having a house to keep.—Women bear the burden of the innumerable details.

THIRD EPOCH. Caroline, absorbed in the idea that you should eat merely to live, treats Adolphe to the delights of a cenobitic table.

Adolphe's stockings are either full of holes or else rough with the lichen of hasty mendings, for the day is not long enough for all that his wife has to do. He wears suspenders blackened by use. His linen is old and gapes like a door-keeper, or like the door itself. At a time when Adolphe is in haste to conclude a matter of business, it takes him an hour to dress: he has to pick out his garments one by one, opening many an article before finding one fit to wear. But Caroline is charmingly dressed. She has pretty bonnets, velvet boots, mantillas. She has made up her mind, she conducts her administration in virtue of this principle: Charity well understood begins at home. When Adolphe complains of the contrast between his poverty-stricken wardrobe and Caroline's splendor, she says, "Why, you reproached me with buying nothing for myself!"

The husband and the wife here begin to bandy jests more or less acrimonious. One evening Caroline makes herself very agreeable, in order to insinuate an avowal of a rather large deficit, just as the ministry begins to eulogize the tax-payers, and boast of the wealth of the country, when it is preparing to bring forth a bill for an additional appropriation. There is this further similitude that both are done in the chamber, whether in administration or in housekeeping. From this springs the profound truth that the constitutional system is infinitely dearer than the monarchical system. For a nation as for a household, it is the government of the happy balance, of mediocrity, of chicanery.

Adolphe, enlightened by his past annoyances, waits for an opportunity to explode, and Caroline slumbers in a delusive security.

What starts the quarrel? Do we ever know what electric current precipitates the avalanche or decides a revolution? It may result from anything or nothing. But finally, Adolphe, after a period to be determined in each case by the circumstances of the couple, utters this fatal phrase, in the midst of a discussion: "Ah! when I was a bachelor!"

Her husband's bachelor life is to a woman what the phrase, "My dear deceased," is to a widow's second husband. These two stings produce wounds which are never completely healed.

Then Adolphe goes on like General Bonaparte haranguing the Five Hundred: "We are on a volcano!—The house no longer has a head, the time to come to an understanding has arrived.—You talk of happiness, Caroline, but you have compromised, imperiled it by your exactions, you have violated the civil code: you have mixed yourself up in the discussions of business, and you have invaded the conjugal authority. —We must reform our internal affairs."

Caroline does not shout, like the Five Hundred, "Down with the dictator!" For people never shout a man down, when they feel that they can put him down.

"When I was a bachelor I had none but new stockings! I had a clean napkin every day on my plate. The restaurateur only fleeced me of a determinate sum. I have given up to you my beloved liberty! What have you done with it?"

"Am I then so very wrong, Adolphe, to have sought to spare you numerous cares?" says Caroline, taking an attitude before her husband. "Take the key of the money-box back,—but do you know what will happen? I am ashamed, but you will compel me to go on to the stage to get the merest necessaries of life. Is this what you want? Degrade your wife, or bring in conflict two contrary, hostile interests—"

Such, for three quarters of the French people is an exact definition of marriage.

"Be perfectly easy, dear," resumes Caroline, seating herself in her chair like Marius on the ruins of Carthage, "I will never ask you for anything. I am not a beggar! I know what I'll do—you don't know me yet."

"Well, what will you do?" asks Adolphe; "it seems impossible to joke or have an explanation with you women. What will you do?"

"It doesn't concern you at all."

"Excuse me, madame, quite the contrary. Dignity, honor—"

"Oh, have no fear of that, sir. For your sake more than for my own, I will keep it a dead secret."

"Come, Caroline, my own Carola, what do you mean to do?"

Caroline darts a viper-like glance at Adolphe, who recoils and proceeds to walk up and down the room.

"There now, tell me, what will you do?" he repeats after much too prolonged a silence.

"I shall go to work, sir!"

At this sublime declaration, Adolphe executes a movement in retreat, detecting a bitter exasperation, and feeling the sharpness of a north wind which had never before blown in the matrimonial chamber.

THE ART OF BEING A VICTIM.

On and after the Revolution, our vanquished Caroline adopts an infernal system, the effect of which is to make you regret your victory every hour. She becomes the opposition! Should Adolphe have one more such triumph, he would appear before the Court of Assizes, accused of having smothered his wife between two mattresses, like Shakespeare's Othello. Caroline puts on the air of a martyr; her submission is positively killing. On every occasion she assassinates Adolphe with a "Just as you like!" uttered in tones whose sweetness is something fearful. No elegiac poet could compete with Caroline, who utters elegy upon elegy: elegy in action, elegy in speech: her smile is elegiac, her silence is elegiac, her gestures are elegiac. Here are a few examples, wherein every household will find some of its impressions recorded:

AFTER BREAKFAST. "Caroline, we go to-night to the Deschars' grand ball you know."

"Yes, love."

AFTER DINNER. "What, not dressed yet, Caroline?" exclaims Adolphe, who has just made his appearance, magnificently equipped.

He finds Caroline arrayed in a gown fit for an elderly lady of strong conversational powers, a black moire with an old-fashioned fan-waist. Flowers, too badly imitated to deserve the name of artificial, give a gloomy aspect to a head of hair which the chambermaid has carelessly arranged. Caroline's gloves have already seen wear and tear.

"I am ready, my dear."

"What, in that dress?"

"I have no other. A new dress would have cost three hundred francs."

"Why did you not tell me?"

"I, ask you for anything, after what has happened!"

"I'll go alone," says Adolphe, unwilling to be humiliated in his wife.

"I dare say you are very glad to," returns Caroline, in a captious tone, "it's plain enough from the way you are got up."

Eleven persons are in the parlor, all invited to dinner by Adolphe. Caroline is there, looking as if her husband had invited her too. She is waiting for dinner to be served.

"Sir," says the parlor servant in a whisper to his master, "the cook doesn't know what on earth to do!"

"What's the matter?"

"You said nothing to her, sir: and she has only two side-dishes, the beef, a chicken, a salad and vegetables."

"Caroline, didn't you give the necessary orders?"

"How did I know that you had company, and besides I can't take it upon myself to give orders here! You delivered me from all care on that point, and I thank heaven for it every day of my life."

Madame de Fischtaminel has called to pay Madame Caroline a visit. She finds her coughing feebly and nearly bent double over her embroidery.

"Ah, so you are working those slippers for your dear Adolphe?"

Adolphe is standing before the fire-place as complacently as may be.

"No, madame, it's for a tradesman who pays me for them: like the convicts, my labor enables me to treat myself to some little comforts."

Adolphe reddens; he can't very well beat his wife, and Madame de Fischtaminel looks at him as much as to say, "What does this mean?"

"You cough a good deal, my darling," says Madame de Fischtaminel.

"Oh!" returns Caroline, "what is life to me?"

Caroline is seated, conversing with a lady of your acquaintance, whose good opinion you are exceedingly anxious to retain. From the depths of the embrasure where you are talking with some friends, you gather, from the mere motion of her lips, these words: "My husband would have it so!" uttered with the air of a young Roman matron going to the circus to be devoured. You are profoundly wounded in your several vanities, and wish to attend to this conversation while listening to your guests: you thus make replies which bring you back such inquiries as: "Why, what are you thinking of?" For you have lost the thread of the discourse, and you fidget nervously with your feet, thinking to yourself, "What is she telling her about me?"

Adolphe is dining with the Deschars: twelve persons are at table, and Caroline is seated next to a nice young man named Ferdinand, Adolphe's cousin. Between the first and second course, conjugal happiness is the subject of conversation.

"There is nothing easier than for a woman to be happy," says Caroline in reply to a woman who complains of her husband.

"Tell us your secret, madame," says M. de Fischtaminel agreeably.

"A woman has nothing to do but to meddle with nothing to consider herself as the first servant in the house or as a slave that the master takes care of, to have no will of her own, and never to make an observation: thus all goes well."

This, delivered in a bitter tone and with tears in her voice, alarms Adolphe, who looks fixedly at his wife.

"You forget, madame, the happiness of telling about one's happiness," he returns, darting at her a glance worthy of the tyrant in a melodrama.

Quite satisfied with having shown herself assassinated or on the point of being so, Caroline turns her head aside, furtively wipes away a tear, and says:

"Happiness cannot be described!"

This incident, as they say at the Chamber, leads to nothing, but Ferdinand looks upon his cousin as an angel about to be offered up.

Some one alludes to the frightful prevalence of inflammation of the stomach, or to the nameless diseases of which young women die.

"Ah, too happy they!" exclaims Caroline, as if she were foretelling the manner of her death.

Adolphe's mother-in-law comes to see her daughter. Caroline says, "My husband's parlor:" "Your master's chamber." Everything in the house belongs to "My husband."

"Why, what's the matter, children?" asks the mother-in-law; "you seem to be at swords' points."

"Oh, dear me," says Adolphe, "nothing but that Caroline has had the management of the house and didn't manage it right, that's all."

"She got into debt, I suppose?"

"Yes, dearest mamma."

"Look here, Adolphe," says the mother-in-law, after having waited to be left alone with her son, "would you prefer to have my daughter magnificently dressed, to have everything go on smoothly, *without its costing you anything*?"

Imagine, if you can, the expression of Adolphe's physiognomy, as he hears *this declaration of woman's rights*!

Caroline abandons her shabby dress and appears in a splendid one. She is at the Deschars': every one compliments her upon her taste, upon the richness of her materials, upon her lace, her jewels.

"Ah! you have a charming husband!" says Madame Deschars. Adolphe tosses his head proudly, and looks at Caroline.

"My husband, madame! I cost that gentleman nothing, thank heaven! All I have was given me by my mother."

Adolphe turns suddenly about and goes to talk with Madame de Fischtaminel.

After a year of absolute monarchy, Caroline says very mildly one morning:

"How much have you spent this year, dear?"

"I don't know."

"Examine your accounts."

Adolphe discovers that he has spent a third more than during Caroline's worst year.

"And I've cost you nothing for my dress," she adds.

Caroline is playing Schubert's melodies. Adolphe takes great pleasure in hearing these compositions well-executed: he gets up and compliments Caroline. She bursts into tears.

"What's the matter?"

"Nothing, I'm nervous."

"I didn't know you were subject to that."

"O Adolphe, you won't see anything! Look, my rings come off my fingers: you don't love me any more—I'm a burden to you—"

She weeps, she won't listen, she weeps afresh at every word Adolphe utters.

"Suppose you take the management of the house back again?"

"Ah!" she exclaims, rising sharply to her feet, like a spring figure in a box, "now that you've had enough of your experience! Thank you! Do you suppose it's money that I want? Singular method, yours, of pouring balm upon a wounded heart. No, go away."

"Very well, just as you like, Caroline."

This "just as you like" is the first expression of indifference towards a wife: and Caroline sees before her an abyss towards which she had been walking of her own free will.

THE FRENCH CAMPAIGN.

The disasters of 1814 afflict every species of existence. After brilliant days of conquest, after the period during which obstacles change to triumphs, and the slightest check becomes a piece of good fortune, there comes a time when the happiest ideas turn out blunders, when courage leads to destruction, and when your very fortifications are a stumbling-block. Conjugal love, which, according to authors, is a peculiar phase of love, has, more than anything else, its French Campaign, its fatal 1814. The devil especially loves to dangle his tail in the affairs of poor desolate women, and to this Caroline has come.

Caroline is trying to think of some means of bringing her husband back. She spends many solitary hours at home, and during this time her imagination works. She goes and comes, she gets up, and often stands pensively at the window, looking at the street and seeing nothing, her face glued to the panes, and feeling as if in a desert, in the midst of her friends, in the bosom of her luxuriously furnished apartments.

Now, in Paris, unless a person occupy a house of his own, enclosed between a court and a garden, all life is double. At every story, a family sees another family in the opposite house. Everybody plunges his gaze at will into his neighbor's domains. There is a necessity for mutual observation, a common right of search from which none can escape. At a given time, in the morning, you get up early, the servant opposite is dusting the parlor, she has left the windows open and has put the rugs on the railing; you divine a multitude of things, and vice-versa. Thus, in a given time, you are acquainted with the habits of the pretty, the old, the young, the coquettish, the virtuous woman opposite, or the caprices of the coxcomb, the inventions of the old bachelor, the color of the furniture, and the cat of the two pair front. Everything furnishes a hint, and becomes matter for divination. At the fourth story, a grisette, taken by surprise, finds herself—too late, like the chaste Susanne,—the prey of the delighted lorgnette of an aged clerk, who earns eighteen hundred francs a year, and who becomes criminal gratis. On the other hand, a handsome young gentleman, who, for the present, works without wages, and is only nineteen years old, appears before the sight of a pious old lady, in the simple apparel of a man engaged in shaving. The watch thus kept up is never relaxed, while prudence, on the contrary, has its moments of forgetfulness. Curtains are not always let down in time. A woman, just before dark, approaches the window to thread her needle, and the married man opposite may then admire a head that Raphael might have painted, and one that he considers worthy of himself—a National Guard truly imposing when under arms. Oh, sacred private life, where art thou! Paris is a city ever ready to exhibit itself half naked, a city essentially libertine and devoid of modesty. For a person's life to be decorous in it, the said person should have a hundred thousand a year. Virtues are dearer than vices in Paris.

Caroline, whose gaze sometimes steals between the protecting muslins which hide her domestic life from the five stories opposite, at last discovers a young couple plunged in the delights of the honey-moon, and newly established in the first story directly in view of her window. She spends her time in the most exciting observations. The blinds are closed early, and opened late. One day, Caroline, who has arisen at eight o'clock notices, by accident, of course, the maid preparing a bath or a morning dress, a delicious deshabille. Caroline sighs. She lies in ambush like a hunter at the cover; she surprises the young woman, her face actually illuminated with happiness. Finally, by dint of watching the charming couple, she sees the gentleman and lady open the window, and lean gently one against the other, as, supported by the railing, they breathe the evening air. Caroline gives herself a nervous headache, by endeavoring to interpret the phantasmagorias, some of them having an explanation and others not, made by the shadows of these two young people on the curtains, one night when they have forgotten to close the shutters. The young woman is often seated, melancholy and pensive, waiting for her absent husband; she hears the tread of a horse, or the rumble of a cab at the street corner; she starts from the sofa, and from her movements, it is easy for Caroline to see that she exclaims: "'Tis he!"

"How they love each other!" says Caroline to herself.

By dint of nervous headache, Caroline conceives an exceedingly ingenious plan: this plan consists in using the conjugal bliss of the opposite neighbors as a tonic to stimulate Adolphe. The idea is not without depravity, but then Caroline's intention sanctifies the means!

"Adolphe," she says, "we have a neighbor opposite, the loveliest woman, a brunette—"

"Oh, yes," returns Adolphe, "I know her. She is a friend of Madame de Fischtaminel's: Madame Foullepointe, the wife of a broker, a charming man and a good fellow, very fond of his wife: he's crazy about her. His office and rooms are here, in the court, while those on the street are madame's. I know of no happier household. Foullepointe talks about his happiness everywhere, even at the Exchange; he's really quite tiresome."

"Well, then, be good enough to present Monsieur and Madame Foullepointe to me. I should be delighted to learn how she manages to make her husband love her so much: have they been married long?"

"Five years, just like us."

"O Adolphe, dear, I am dying to know her: make us intimately acquainted. Am I as pretty as she?"

"Well, if I were to meet you at an opera ball, and if you weren't my wife, I declare, I shouldn't know which—"

"You are real sweet to-day. Don't forget to invite them to dinner Saturday."

"I'll do it to-night. Foullepointe and I often meet on 'Change."

"Now," says Caroline, "this young woman will doubtless tell me what her method of action is."

Caroline resumes her post of observation. At about three she looks through the flowers which form as it were a bower at the window, and exclaims, "Two perfect doves!"

For the Saturday in question, Caroline invites Monsieur and Madame Deschars, the worthy Monsieur Fischtaminel, in short, the most virtuous couples of her society. She has brought out all her resources: she has ordered the most sumptuous dinner, she has taken the silver out of the chest: she means to do all honor to the model of wives.

"My dear, you will see to-night," she says to Madame Deschars, at the moment when all the women are looking at each other in silence, "the most admirable young couple in the world, our opposite neighbors: a young man of fair complexion, so graceful and with *such* manners! His head is like Lord Byron's, and he's a real Don Juan, only faithful: he's discovered the secret of making love eternal: I shall perhaps obtain a second crop of it from her example. Adolphe, when he sees them, will blush at his conduct, and—"

The servant announces: "Monsieur and Madame Foullepointe."

Madame Foullepointe, a pretty brunette, a genuine Parisian, slight and erect in form, the brilliant light of her eye quenched by her long lashes, charmingly dressed, sits down upon the sofa. Caroline bows to a fat gentleman with thin gray hair, who follows this Paris Andalusian, and who exhibits a face and paunch fit for Silenus, a butter-colored pate, a deceitful, libertine smile upon his big, heavy lips,—in short, a philosopher! Caroline looks upon this individual with astonishment.

"Monsieur Foullepointe, my dear," says Adolphe, presenting the worthy quinquagenarian.

"I am delighted, madame," says Caroline, good-naturedly, "that you have brought your father-in-law [profound sensation], but we shall soon see your husband, I trust—"

"Madame—!"

Everybody listens and looks. Adolphe becomes the object of every one's attention; he is literally dumb with amazement: if he could, he would whisk Caroline off through a trap, as at the theatre.

"This is Monsieur Foullepointe, my husband," says Madame Foullepointe.

Caroline turns scarlet as she sees her ridiculous blunder, and Adolphe scathes her with a look of thirty-six candlepower.

"You said he was young and fair," whispers Madame Deschars. Madame Foullepointe,—knowing lady that she is,—boldly stares at the ceiling.

A month after, Madame Foullepointe and Caroline become intimate. Adolphe,

who is taken up with Madame de Fischtaminel, pays no attention to this danger-
ous friendship, a friendship which will bear its fruits, for—pray learn this—

Axiom.—Women have corrupted more women than men have ever loved.

A SOLO ON THE HEARSE.

After a period, the length of which depends on the strength of Caroline's principles, she appears to be languishing; and when Adolphe, anxious for decorum's sake, as he sees her stretched out upon the sofa like a snake in the sun, asks her, "What is the matter, love? What do you want?"

"I wish I was dead!" she replies.

"Quite a merry and agreeable wish!"

"It isn't death that frightens me, it's suffering."

"I suppose that means that I don't make you happy! That's the way with women!"

Adolphe strides about the room, talking incoherently: but he is brought to a dead halt by seeing Caroline dry her tears, which are really flowing artistically, in an embroidered handkerchief.

"Do you feel sick?"

"I don't feel well. [Silence.] I only hope that I shall live long enough to see my daughter married, for I know the meaning, now, of the expression so little understood by the young—*the choice of a husband*! Go to your amusements, Adolphe: a woman who thinks of the future, a woman who suffers, is not at all diverting: come, go and have a good time."

"Where do you feel bad?"

"I don't feel bad, dear: I never was better. I don't feel anything. No, really, I am better. There, leave me to myself."

This time, being the first, Adolphe goes away almost sad.

A week passes, during which Caroline orders all the servants to conceal from her husband her deplorable situation: she languishes, she rings when she feels she is going off, she uses a great deal of ether. The domestics finally acquaint their master with madame's conjugal heroism, and Adolphe remains at home one evening after dinner, and sees his wife passionately kissing her little Marie.

"Poor child! I regret the future only for your sake! What is life, I should like to know?"

"Come, my dear," says Adolphe, "don't take on so."

"I'm not taking on. Death doesn't frighten me—I saw a funeral this morning, and I thought how happy the body was! How comes it that I think of nothing but death? Is it a disease? I have an idea that I shall die by my own hand."

The more Adolphe tries to divert Caroline, the more closely she wraps herself up in the crape of her hopeless melancholy. This second time, Adolphe stays at home and is wearied to death. At the third attack of forced tears, he goes out without the slightest compunction. He finally gets accustomed to these everlasting murmurs, to these dying postures, these crocodile tears. So he says:

"If you are sick, Caroline, you'd better have a doctor."

"Just as you like! It will end quicker, so. But bring a famous one, if you bring any."

At the end of a month, Adolphe, worn out by hearing the funereal air that Caroline plays him on every possible key, brings home a famous doctor. At Paris, doctors are all men of discernment, and are admirably versed in conjugal nosography.

"Well, madame," says the great physician, "how happens it that so pretty a woman allows herself to be sick?"

"Ah! sir, like the nose of old father Aubry, I aspire to the tomb—"

Caroline, out of consideration for Adolphe, makes a feeble effort to smile.

"Tut, tut! But your eyes are clear: they don't seem to need our infernal drugs."

"Look again, doctor, I am eaten up with fever, a slow, imperceptible fever—"

And she fastens her most roguish glance upon the illustrious doctor, who says to himself, "What eyes!"

"Now, let me see your tongue."

Caroline puts out her taper tongue between two rows of teeth as white as those of a dog.

"It is a little bit furred at the root: but you have breakfasted—" observes the great physician, turning toward Adolphe.

"Oh, a mere nothing," returns Caroline; "two cups of tea—"

Adolphe and the illustrious leech look at each other, for the doctor wonders whether it is the husband or the wife that is trifling with him.

"What do you feel?" gravely inquires the physician.

"I don't sleep."

"Good!"

"I have no appetite."

"Well!"

"I have a pain, here."

The doctor examines the part indicated.

"Very good, we'll look at that by and by."

"Now and then a shudder passes over me—"

"Very good!"

"I have melancholy fits, I am always thinking of death, I feel promptings of suicide—"

"Dear me! Really!"

"I have rushes of heat to the face: look, there's a constant trembling in my eyelid."

"Capital! We call that a trismus."

The doctor goes into an explanation, which lasts a quarter of an hour, of the trismus, employing the most scientific terms. From this it appears that the trismus is the trismus: but he observes with the greatest modesty that if science knows that the trismus is the trismus, it is entirely ignorant of the cause of this nervous affection, which comes and goes, appears and disappears—"and," he adds, "we have decided that it is altogether nervous."

"Is it very dangerous?" asks Caroline, anxiously.

"Not at all. How do you lie at night?"

"Doubled up in a heap."

"Good. On which side?"

"The left."

"Very well. How many mattresses are there on your bed?"

"Three."

"Good. Is there a spring bed?"

"Yes."

"What is the spring bed stuffed with?"

"Horse hair."

"Capital. Let me see you walk. No, no, naturally, and as if we weren't looking at you."

Caroline walks like Fanny Elssler, communicating the most Andalusian little motions to her tournure.

"Do you feel a sensation of heaviness in your knees?"

"Well, no—" she returns to her place. "Ah, no that I think of it, it seems to me that I do."

"Good. Have you been in the house a good deal lately?"

"Oh, yes, sir, a great deal too much—and alone."

"Good. I thought so. What do you wear on your head at night?"

"An embroidered night-cap, and sometimes a handkerchief over it."

"Don't you feel a heat there, a slight perspiration?"

"How can I, when I'm asleep?"

"Don't you find your night-cap moist on your forehead, when you wake up?"

"Sometimes."

"Capital. Give me your hand."

The doctor takes out his watch.

"Did I tell you that I have a vertigo?" asks Caroline.

"Hush!" says the doctor, counting the pulse. "In the evening?"

"No, in the morning."

"Ah, bless me, a vertigo in the morning," says the doctor, looking at Adolphe.

"The Duke of G. has not gone to London," says the great physician, while examining Caroline's skin, "and there's a good deal to be said about it in the Faubourg St. Germain."

"Have you patients there?" asks Caroline.

"Nearly all my patients are there. Dear me, yes; I've got seven to see this morning; some of them are in danger."

"What do you think of me, sir?" says Caroline.

"Madame, you need attention, a great deal of attention, you must take quieting liquors, plenty of syrup of gum, a mild diet, white meat, and a good deal of exercise."

"There go twenty francs," says Adolphe to himself with a smile.

The great physician takes Adolphe by the arm, and draws him out with him, as he takes his leave: Caroline follows them on tiptoe.

"My dear sir," says the great physician, "I have just prescribed very insufficiently for your wife. I did not wish to frighten her: this affair concerns you more nearly than you imagine. Don't neglect her; she has a powerful temperament, and enjoys violent health; all this reacts upon her. Nature has its laws, which, when disregarded, compel obedience. She may get into a morbid state, which would cause you bitterly to repent having neglected her. If you love her, why, love her: but if you don't love her, and nevertheless desire to preserve the mother of your children, the resolution to come to is a matter of hygiene, but it can only proceed from you!"

"How well he understand me!" says Caroline to herself. She opens the door and says: "Doctor, you did not write down the doses!"

The great physician smiles, bows and slips the twenty franc piece into his pocket; he then leaves Adolphe to his wife, who takes him and says:

"What is the fact about my condition? Must I prepare for death?"

"Bah! He says you're too healthy!" cries Adolphe, impatiently.

Caroline retires to her sofa to weep.

"What is it, now?"

"So I am to live a long time—I am in the way—you don't love me any more—I won't consult that doctor again—I don't know why Madame Foullepointe advised me to see him, he told me nothing but trash—I know better than he what I need!"

"What do you need?"

"Can you ask, ungrateful man?" and Caroline leans her head on Adolphe's shoulder.

Adolphe, very much alarmed, says to himself: "The doctor's right, she may get to be morbidly exacting, and then what will become of me? Here I am compelled to choose between Caroline's physical extravagance, or some young cousin or other."

Meanwhile Caroline sits down and sings one of Schubert's melodies with all the agitation of a hypochondriac.

PART SECOND

PREFACE

If, reader, you have grasped the intent of this book,—and infinite honor is done you by the supposition: the profoundest author does not always comprehend, I may say never comprehends, the different meanings of his book, nor its bearing, nor the good nor the harm it may do—if, then, you have bestowed some attention upon these little scenes of married life, you have perhaps noticed their color—

"What color?" some grocer will doubtless ask; "books are bound in yellow, blue, green, pearl-gray, white—"

Alas! books possess another color, they are dyed by the author, and certain writers borrow their dye. Some books let their color come off on to others. More than this. Books are dark or fair, light brown or red. They have a sex, too! I know of male books, and female books, of books which, sad to say, have no sex, which we hope is not the case with this one, supposing that you do this collection of nosographic sketches the honor of calling it a book.

Thus far, the troubles we have described have been exclusively inflicted by the wife upon the husband. You have therefore seen only the masculine side of the book. And if the author really has the sense of hearing for which we give him credit, he has already caught more than one indignant exclamation or remonstrance:

"He tells us of nothing but vexations suffered by our husbands, as if we didn't have our petty troubles, too!"

Oh, women! You have been heard, for if you do not always make yourselves understood, you are always sure to make yourselves heard.

It would therefore be signally unjust to lay upon you alone the reproaches that every being brought under the yoke (*conjugium*) has the right to heap upon that necessary, sacred, useful, eminently conservative institution,—one, however, that is often somewhat of an encumbrance, and tight about the joints, though sometimes it is also too loose there.

I will go further! Such partiality would be a piece of idiocy.

A man,—not a writer, for in a writer there are many men,—an author, rather, should resemble Janus, see behind and before, become a spy, examine an idea in all its phases, delve alternately into the soul of Alceste and into that of Philaenete, know everything though he does not tell it, never be tiresome, and—

We will not conclude this programme, for we should tell the whole, and that would be frightful for those who reflect upon the present condition of literature.

Furthermore, an author who speaks for himself in the middle of his book, resembles the old fellow in "The Speaking Picture," when he puts his face in the hole cut in the painting. The author does not forget that in the Chamber, no one can take the floor *between two votes*. Enough, therefore!

Here follows the female portion of the book: for, to resemble marriage perfectly, it ought to be more or less hermaphroditic.

PETTY TROUBLES OF MARRIED LIFE

HUSBANDS DURING THE SECOND MONTH.

Two young married women, Caroline and Stephanie, who had been early friends at M'lle Machefer's boarding school, one of the most celebrated educational institutions in the Faubourg St. Honore, met at a ball given by Madame de Fischtaminel, and the following conversation took place in a window-seat in the boudoir.

It was so hot that a man had acted upon the idea of going to breathe the fresh night air, some time before the two young women. He had placed himself in the angle of the balcony, and, as there were many flowers before the window, the two friends thought themselves alone. This man was the author's best friend.

One of the two ladies, standing at the corner of the embrasure, kept watch by looking at the boudoir and the parlors. The other had so placed herself as not to be in the draft, which was nevertheless tempered by the muslin and silk curtains.

The boudoir was empty, the ball was just beginning, the gaming-tables were open, offering their green cloths and their packs of cards still compressed in the frail case placed upon them by the customs office. The second quadrille was in progress.

All who go to balls will remember that phase of large parties when the guests are not yet all arrived, but when the rooms are already filled —a moment which gives the mistress of the house a transitory pang of terror. This moment is, other points of comparison apart, like that which decides a victory or the loss of a battle.

You will understand, therefore, how what was meant to be a secret now obtains the honors of publicity.

"Well, Caroline?"

"Well, Stephanie?"

"Well?"

"Well?"

A double sigh.

"Have you forgotten our agreement?"

"No."

"Why haven't you been to see me, then?"

"I am never left alone. Even here we shall hardly have time to talk."

"Ah! if Adolphe were to get into such habits as that!" exclaimed Caroline.

"You saw us, Armand and me, when he paid me what is called, I don't know why, his court."

"Yes, I admired him, I thought you very happy, you had found your ideal, a fine, good-sized man, always well dressed, with yellow gloves, his beard well shaven, patent leather boots, a clean shirt, exquisitely neat, and so attentive—"

"Yes, yes, go on."

"In short, quite an elegant man: his voice was femininely sweet, and then such gentleness! And his promises of happiness and liberty! His sentences were veneered with rosewood. He stocked his conversation with shawls and laces. In his smallest expression you heard the rumbling of a coach and four. Your wedding presents were magnificent. Armand seemed to me like a husband of velvet, of a robe of birds' feathers in which you were to be wrapped."

"Caroline, my husband uses tobacco."

"So does mine; that is, he smokes."

"But mine, dear, uses it as they say Napoleon did: in short, he chews, and I hold tobacco in horror. The monster found it out, and went without out it for seven months."

"All men have their habits. They absolutely must use something."

"You have no idea of the tortures I endure. At night I am awakened with a start by one of my own sneezes. As I go to sleep my motions bring the grains of snuff scattered over the pillow under my nose, I inhale, and explode like a mine. It seems that Armand, the wretch, is used to these *surprises*, and doesn't wake up. I find tobacco everywhere, and I certainly didn't marry the customs office."

"But, my dear child, what does this trifling inconvenience amount to, if your husband is kind and possesses a good disposition?"

"He is as cold as marble, as particular as an old bachelor, as communicative as a sentinel; and he's one of those men who say yes to everything, but who never do anything but what they want to."

"Deny him, once."

"I've tried it."

"What came of it?"

"He threatened to reduce my allowance, and to keep back a sum big enough for him to get along without me."

"Poor Stephanie! He's not a man, he's a monster."

"A calm and methodical monster, who wears a scratch, and who, every night—"

"Well, every night—"

"Wait a minute!—who takes a tumbler every night, and puts seven false teeth in it."

"What a trap your marriage was! At any rate, Armand is rich."

"Who knows?"

"Good heavens! Why, you seem to me on the point of becoming very unhappy—or very happy."

"Well, dear, how is it with you?"

"Oh, as for me, I have nothing as yet but a pin that pricks me: but it is intolerable."

"Poor creature! You don't know your own happiness: come, what is it?"

Here the young woman whispered in the other's ear, so that it was impossible to catch a single word. The conversation recommenced, or rather finished by a sort of inference.

"So, your Adolphe is jealous?"

"Jealous of whom? We never leave each other, and that, in itself, is an annoyance. I can't stand it. I don't dare to gape. I am expected to be forever enacting the woman in love. It's fatiguing."

"Caroline?"

"Well?"

"What are you going to do?"

"Resign myself. What are you?

"Fight the customs office."

This little trouble tends to prove that in the matter of personal deception, the two sexes can well cry quits.

DISAPPOINTED AMBITION.

I. CHODOREILLE THE GREAT.

A young man has forsaken his natal city in the depths of one of the departments, rather clearly marked by M. Charles Dupin. He felt that glory of some sort awaited him: suppose that of a painter, a novelist, a journalist, a poet, a great statesman.

Young Adolphe de Chodoreille—that we may be perfectly understood — wished to be talked about, to become celebrated, to be somebody. This, therefore, is addressed to the mass of aspiring individuals brought to Paris by all sorts of vehicles, whether moral or material, and who rush upon the city one fine morning with the hydrophobic purpose of overturning everybody's reputation, and of building themselves a pedestal with the ruins they are to make,—until disenchantment follows. As our intention is to specify this peculiarity so characteristic of our epoch, let us take from among the various personages the one whom the author has elsewhere called *A Distinguished Provencal*.

Adolphe has discovered that the most admirable trade is that which consists in buying a bottle of ink, a bunch of quills, and a ream of paper, at a stationer's for twelve francs and a half, and in selling the two thousand sheets in the ream over again, for something like fifty thousand francs, after having, of course, written upon each leaf fifty lines replete with style and imagination.

This problem,—twelve francs and a half metamorphosed into fifty thousand francs, at the rate of five sous a line—urges numerous families who might advantageously employ their members in the retirement of the provinces, to thrust them into the vortex of Paris.

The young man who is the object of this exportation, invariably passes in his natal town for a man of as much imagination as the most famous author. He has always studied well, he writes very nice poetry, he is considered a fellow of parts: he is besides often guilty of a charming tale published in the local paper, which obtains the admiration of the department.

His poor parents will never know what their son has come to Paris to learn at great cost, namely: That it is difficult to be a writer and to understand the French language short of a dozen years of heculean labor: That a man must have explored every sphere of social life, to become a genuine novelist, inasmuch as the novel is the private history of nations: That the great story-tellers, Aesop, Lucian, Boccaccio, Rabelais, Cervantes, Swift, La Fontaine, Lesage, Sterne, Voltaire, Walter Scott, the unknown Arabians of the *Thousand and One Nights*, were all men of genius as well as giants of erudition.

Their Adolphe serves his literary apprenticeship in two or three coffee-houses, becomes a member of the Society of Men of Letters, attacks, with or without reason, men of talent who don't read his articles, assumes a milder tone on seeing the powerlessness of his criticisms, offers novelettes to the papers which toss them from one to the other as if they were shuttlecocks: and, after five or six years of exercises more or less fatiguing, of dreadful privations which seriously tax his parents, he attains a certain position.

This position may be described as follows: Thanks to a sort of reciprocal support extended to each other, and which an ingenious writer has called "Mutual Admiration," Adolphe often sees his name cited among the names of celebrities, either in the prospectuses of the book-trade, or in the lists of newspapers about to appear. Publishers print the title of one of his works under the deceitful heading "IN PRESS," which might be called the typographical menagerie of bears.[3] Chodoreille is sometimes mentioned among the promising young men of the literary world.

For eleven years Adolphe Chodoreille remains in the ranks of the promising young men: he finally obtains a free entrance to the theatres, thanks to some dirty work or certain articles of dramatic criticism: he tries to pass for a good fellow; and as he loses his illusions respecting glory and the world of Paris, he gets into debt and his years begin to tell upon him.

A paper which finds itself in a tight place asks him for one of his bears revised by his friends. This has been retouched and revamped every five years, so that it smells of the pomatum of each prevailing and then forgotten fashion. To Adolphe it becomes what the famous cap, which he was constantly staking, was to Corporal Trim, for during five years "Anything for a Woman" (the title decided upon) "will be one of the most entertaining productions of our epoch."

After eleven years, Chodoreille is regarded as having written some respectable things, five or six tales published in the dismal magazines, in ladies' newspapers, or in works intended for children of tender age.

As he is a bachelor, and possesses a coat and a pair of black cassimere trousers, and when he pleases may thus assume the appearance of an elegant diplomat, and as he is not without a certain intelligent air, he is admitted to several more or less literary salons: he bows to the five or six academicians who possess genius, influence or talent, he visits two or three of our great poets, he allows himself, in coffee-rooms, to call the two or three justly celebrated women of our epoch by their Christian names; he is on the best of terms with the blue stockings of the second grade, — who ought to be called *socks*, — and he shakes hands and takes glasses of absinthe with the stars of the smaller newspapers.

Such is the history of every species of ordinary men — men who have been de-

---

[3] A bear (*ours*) is a play which has been refused by a multitude of theatres, but which is finally represented at a time when some manager or other feels the need of one. The word has necessarily passed from the language of the stage into the jargon of journalism, and is applied to novels which wander the streets in search of a publisher.

nied what they call good luck. This good luck is nothing less than unyielding will, incessant labor, contempt for an easily won celebrity, immense learning, and that patience which, according to Buffon, is the whole of genius, but which certainly is the half of it.

You do not yet see any indication of a petty trouble for Caroline. You imagine that this history of five hundred young men engaged at this moment in wearing smooth the paving stones of Paris, was written as a sort of warning to the families of the eighty-six departments of France: but read these two letters which lately passed between two girls differently married, and you will see that it was as necessary as the narrative by which every true melodrama was until lately expected to open. You will divine the skillful manoeuvres of the Parisian peacock spreading his tail in the recesses of his native village, and polishing up, for matrimonial purposes, the rays of his glory, which, like those of the sun, are only warm and brilliant at a distance.

From Madame Claire de la Roulandiere, nee Jugault, to Madame Adolphe de Chodoreille, nee Heurtaut.

"VIVIERS.

"You have not yet written to me, and it's real unkind in you. Don't you remember that the happier was to write first and to console her who remained in the country?

"Since your departure for Paris, I have married Monsieur de la Roulandiere, the president of the tribunal. You know him, and you can judge whether I am happy or not, with my heart *saturated*, as it is, with our ideas. I was not ignorant what my lot would be: I live with the ex-president, my husband's uncle, and with my mother-in-law, who has preserved nothing of the ancient parliamentary society of Aix but its pride and its severity of manners. I am seldom alone, I never go out unless accompanied by my mother-in-law or my husband. We receive the heavy people of the city in the evening. They play whist at two sous a point, and I listen to conversations of this nature:

"'Monsieur Vitremont is dead, and leaves two hundred and eighty thousand francs,' says the associate judge, a young man of forty-seven, who is as entertaining as a northwest wind.

"'Are you quite sure of that?'

"The *that* refers to the two hundred and eighty thousand francs. A little judge then holds forth, he runs over the investments, the others discuss their value, and it is definitely settled that if he has not left two hundred and eighty thousand, he left something near it.

"Then comes a universal concert of eulogy heaped upon the dead man's body, for having kept his bread under lock and key, for having shrewdly invested his little savings accumulated sou by sou, in order, probably, that the whole city and those who expect legacies may applaud and exclaim in admiration, 'He leaves two hundred and eighty thousand francs!' Now everybody has rich relations of whom they say 'Will he leave anything like it?' and thus they discuss the quick as they have discussed the dead.

"They talk of nothing but the prospects of fortune, the prospects of a vacancy in office, the prospects of the harvest.

"When we were children, and used to look at those pretty little white mice, in the cobbler's window in the rue St. Maclou, that turned and turned the circular cage in which they were imprisoned, how far I was from thinking that they would one day be a faithful image of my life!

"Think of it, my being in this condition!—I who fluttered my wings so much more than you, I whose imagination was so vagabond! My sins have been greater than yours, and I am the more severely punished. I have bidden farewell to my dreams: I am *Madame la Presidente* in all my glory, and I resign myself to giving my arm for forty years to my big awkward Roulandiere, to living meanly in every way, and to having forever before me two heavy brows and two wall-eyes pierced in a yellow face, which is destined never to know what it is to smile.

"But you, Caroline dear, you who, between ourselves, were admitted among the big girls while I still gamboled among the little ones, you whose only sin was pride, you,—at the age of twenty-seven, and with a dowry of two hundred thousand francs,—capture and captivate a truly great man, one of the wittiest men in Paris, one of the two talented men that our village has produced.—What luck!

"You now circulate in the most brilliant society of Paris. Thanks to the sublime privileges of genius. You may appear in all the salons of the Faubourg St. Germain, and be cordially received. You have the exquisite enjoyment of the company of the two or three celebrated women of our age, where so many good things are said, where the happy speeches which arrive out here like Congreve rockets, are first fired off. You go to the Baron Schinner's of whom Adolphe so often spoke to us, whom all the great artists and foreigners of celebrity visit. In short, before long, you will be one of the queens of Paris, if you wish. You can receive, too, and have at your house the lions of literature, fashion and finance, whether male or female, for Adolphe spoke in such terms about his illustrious friendships and his intimacy with the favorites of the hour, that I imagine you giving and receiving honors.

"With your ten thousand francs a year, and the legacy from your Aunt Carabas, added to the twenty thousand francs that your husband earns, you must keep a carriage; and since you go to all the theatres without paying, since journalists are the heroes of all the inaugurations so ruinous for those who keep up with the movement of Paris, and since they are constantly invited to dinner, you live as if you had an income of sixty thousand francs a year! Happy Caroline! I don't wonder you forget me!

"I can understand how it is that you have not a moment to yourself. Your bliss is the cause of your silence, so I pardon you. Still, if, fatigued with so many pleasures, you one day, upon the summit of your grandeur, think of your poor Claire, write to me, tell me what a marriage with a great man is, describe those great Parisian ladies, especially those who write. Oh! I should *so* much like to know what they are made of! Finally don't forget anything, unless you forget that you are loved, as ever, by your poor

"CLAIRE JUGAULT."

From Madame Adolphe de Chodoreille to Madame la Presidente de la Roulandiere, at Viviers.

"PARIS.

"Ah! my poor Claire, could you have known how many wretched little griefs your innocent letter would awaken, you never would have written it. Certainly no friend, and not even an enemy, on seeing a woman with a thousand mosquito-bites and a plaster over them, would amuse herself by tearing it off and counting the stings.

"I will begin by telling you that for a woman of twenty-seven, with a face still passable, but with a form a little too much like that of the Emperor Nicholas for the humble part I play, I am happy! Let me tell you why: Adolphe, rejoicing in the deceptions which have fallen upon me like a hail-storm, smoothes over the wounds in my self-love by so much affection, so many attentions, and such charming things, that, in good truth, women—so far as they are simply women—would be glad to find in the man they marry defects so advantageous. But all men of letters (Adolphe, alas! is barely a man of letters), who are beings not a bit less irritable, nervous, fickle and eccentric than women, are far from possessing such solid qualities as those of Adolphe, and I hope they have not all been as unfortunate as he.

"Ah! Claire, we love each other well enough for me to tell you the simple truth. I have saved my husband, dear, from profound but skillfully concealed poverty. Far from receiving twenty thousand francs a year, he has not earned that sum in the entire fifteen years that he has been at Paris. We occupy a third story in the rue Joubert, and pay twelve hundred francs for it; we have some eighty-five hundred francs left, with which I endeavor to keep house honorably.

"I have brought Adolphe luck; for since our marriage, he has obtained the control of a feuilleton which is worth four hundred francs a month to him, though it takes but a small portion of his time. He owes this situation to an investment. We employed the seventy thousand francs left me by my Aunt Carabas in giving security for a newspaper; on this we get nine per cent, and we have stock besides. Since this transaction, which was concluded some ten months ago, our income has doubled, and we now possess a competence, I can complain of my marriage in a pecuniary point of view no more than as regards my affections. My vanity alone has suffered, and my ambition has been swamped. You will understand the various petty troubles which have assailed me, by a single specimen.

"Adolphe, you remember, appeared to us on intimate terms with the famous Baroness Schinner, so renowned for her wit, her influence, her wealth and her connection with celebrated men. I supposed that he was welcomed at her house as a friend: my husband presented me, and I was coldly received. I saw that her rooms were furnished with extravagant luxury; and instead of Madame Schinner's returning my call, I received a card, twenty days afterward, and at an insolently improper hour.

"On arriving at Paris, I went to walk upon the boulevard, proud of my anonymous great man. He nudged me with his elbow, and said, pointing out a fat little ill-dressed man, 'There's so and so!' He mentioned one of the seven or eight illustrious men in France. I got ready my look of admiration, and I saw Adolphe rapturously doffing his hat to the truly great man, who replied by the curt little nod that you vouchsafe a person with whom you have doubtless exchanged hardly four words in ten years. Adolphe had begged a look for my sake. 'Doesn't he know you?' I said to my husband. 'Oh, yes, but he probably took me for somebody else,' replied he.

"And so of poets, so of celebrated musicians, so of statesmen. But, as a compensation, we stop and talk for ten minutes in front of some arcade or other, with Messieurs Armand du Cantal, George Beaunoir, Felix Verdoret, of whom you have never heard. Mesdames Constantine Ramachard, Anais Crottat, and Lucienne Vouillon threaten me with their *blue* friendship. We dine editors totally unknown in our province. Finally I have had the painful happiness of seeing Adolphe decline an invitation to an evening party to which I was not bidden.

"Oh! Claire dear, talent is still the rare flower of spontaneous growth, that no greenhouse culture can produce. I do not deceive myself: Adolphe is an ordinary man, known, estimated as such: he has no other chance, as he himself says, than to take his place among the *utilities* of literature. He was not without wit at Viviers: but to be a man of wit at Paris, you must possess every kind of wit in formidable doses.

"I esteem Adolphe: for, after some few fibs, he frankly confessed his position, and, without humiliating himself too deeply, he promised that I should be happy. He hopes, like numerous other ordinary men, to obtain some place, that of an assistant librarian, for instance, or the pecuniary management of a newspaper. Who knows but we may get him elected deputy for Viviers, in the course of time?

"We live in obscurity; we have five or six friends of either sex whom we like, and such is the brilliant style of life which your letter gilded with all the social splendors.

"From time to time I am caught in a squall, or am the butt of some malicious tongue. Thus, yesterday, at the opera, I heard one of our most ill-natured wits, Leon de Lora, say to one of our most famous critics, 'It takes Chodoreille to discover the Caroline poplar on the banks of the Rhone!' They had heard my husband call me by my Christian name. At Viviers I was considered handsome. I am tall, well made, and fat enough to satisfy Adolphe! In this way I learn that the beauty of women from the country is, at Paris, precisely like the wit of country gentleman.

"In short, I am absolutely nobody, if that is what you wish to know: but if you desire to learn how far my philosophy goes, understand that I am really happy in having found an ordinary man in my pretended great one.

"Farewell, dear Claire! It is still I, you see, who, in spite of my delusions and the petty troubles of my life, am the most favorably situated: for Adolphe is young, and a charming fellow.

"CAROLINE HEURTAUT."

Claire's reply contained, among other passages, the following: "I hope that the indescribable happiness which you enjoy, will continue, thanks to your philosophy." Claire, as any intimate female friend would have done, consoled herself for her president by insinuations respecting Adolphe's prospects and future conduct.

II. ANOTHER GLANCE AT CHODOREILLE.

(Letter discovered one day in a casket, while she was making me wait a long time and trying to get rid of a hanger-on who could not be made to understand hidden meanings. I caught cold—but I got hold of this letter.)

This fatuous note was found on a paper which the notary's clerks had thought of no importance in the inventory of the estate of M. Ferdinand de Bourgarel, who was mourned of late by politics, arts and amours, and in whom is ended the great Provencal house of Borgarelli; for as is generally known the name Bourgarel is a corruption of Borgarelli just as the French Girardin is the Florentine Gherardini.

An intelligent reader will find little difficulty in placing this letter in its proper epoch in the lives of Adolphe and Caroline.

"My dear Friend:

"I thought myself lucky indeed to marry an artist as superior in his talent as in his personal attributes, equally great in soul and mind, worldly-wise, and likely to rise by following the public road without being obliged to wander along crooked, doubtful by-paths. However, you knew Adolphe; you appreciated his worth. I am loved, he is a father, I idolize our children. Adolphe is kindness itself to me; I admire and love him. But, my dear, in this complete happiness lurks a thorn. The roses upon which I recline have more than one fold. In the heart of a woman, folds speedily turn to wounds. These wounds soon bleed, the evil spreads, we suffer, the suffering awakens thoughts, the thoughts swell and change the course of sentiment.

"Ah, my dear, you shall know all about it, though it is a cruel thing to say—but we live as much by vanity as by love. To live by love alone, one must dwell somewhere else than in Paris. What difference would it make to us whether we had only one white percale gown, if the man we love did not see other women dressed differently, more elegantly than we—women who inspire ideas by their ways, by a multitude of little things which really go to make up great passions? Vanity, my dear, is cousin-german to jealousy, to that beautiful and noble jealousy which consists in not allowing one's empire to be invaded, in reigning undisturbed in a soul, and passing one's life happily in a heart.

"Ah, well, my woman's vanity is on the rack. Though some troubles may seem petty indeed, I have learned, unfortunately, that in the home there are no petty troubles. For everything there is magnified by incessant contact with sensations, with desires, with ideas. Such then is the secret of that sadness which you have surprised in me and which I did not care to explain. It is one of those things in which words go too far, and where writing holds at least the thought within bounds by establishing it. The effects of a moral perspective differ so radically between what is said and what is written! All is so solemn, so serious on paper! One cannot commit any more imprudences. Is it not this fact which makes a treasure out of a letter where one gives one's self over to one's thoughts?

"You doubtless thought me wretched, but I am only wounded. You discovered me sitting alone by the fire, and no Adolphe. I had just finished putting the children to bed; they were asleep. Adolphe for the tenth time had been invited out to a house where I do not go, where they want Adolphe without his wife. There are drawing-rooms where he goes without me, just at there are many pleasures in which he alone is the guest. If he were M. de Navarreins and I a d'Espard, society would never think of separating us; it would want us always together. His habits are formed; he does not suspect the humiliation which weighs upon my heart. Indeed, if he had the slightest inkling of this small sorrow which I am ashamed to own, he would drop society, he would become more of a prig than the people who come between us. But he would hamper his progress, he would make enemies, he would raise up obstacles by imposing me upon the salons where I would be subject to a thousand slights. That is why I prefer my sufferings to what would happen were they discovered.

"Adolphe will succeed! He carries my revenge in his beautiful head, does this man of genius. One day the world shall pay for all these slights. But when? Perhaps I shall be forty-five. My beautiful youth will have passed in my chimney-corner, and with this thought: Adolphe smiles, he is enjoying the society of fair women, he is playing the devoted to them, while none of these attentions come my way.

"It may be that these will finally take him from me!

"No one undergoes slight without feeling it, and I feel that I am slighted, though young, beautiful and virtuous. Now, can I keep from thinking this way? Can I control my anger at the thought that Adolphe is dining in the city without me? I take no part in his triumphs; I do not hear the witty or profound remarks made to others! I could no longer be content with bourgeois receptions whence he rescued me, upon finding me *distinguee*, wealthy, young, beautiful and witty. There lies the evil, and it is irremediable.

"In a word, for some cause, it is only since I cannot go to a certain salon that I want to go there. Nothing is more natural of the ways of a human heart. The ancients were wise in having their *gyneceums*. The collisions between the pride of the women, caused by these gatherings, though it dates back only four centuries, has cost our own day much disaffection and numerous bitter debates.

"Be that as it may, my dear, Adolphe is always warmly welcomed when he comes back home. Still, no nature is strong enough to await always with the same ardor. What a morrow that will be, following the evening when his welcome is less warm!

"Now do you see the depth of the fold which I mentioned? A fold in the heart is an abyss, like a crevasse in the Alps—a profundity whose depth and extent we have never been able to calculate. Thus it is between two beings, no matter how near they may be drawn to each other. One never realizes the weight of suffering which oppresses his friend. This seems such a little thing, yet one's life is affected by it in all its length, in all its breadth. I have thus argued with myself; but the more I have argued, the more thoroughly have I realized the extent of this hidden sorrow. And I can only let the current carry me whither it will.

"Two voices struggle for supremacy when—by a rarely fortunate chance —I am alone in my armchair waiting for Adolphe. One, I would wager, comes from Eugene Delacroix's *Faust* which I have on my table. Mephistopheles speaks, that terrible aide who guides the swords so dexterously. He leaves the engraving, and places himself diabolically before me, grinning through the hole which the great artist has placed under his nose, and gazing at me with that eye whence fall rubies, diamonds, carriages, jewels, laces, silks, and a thousand luxuries to feed the burning desire within me.

"'Are you not fit for society?' he asks. 'You are the equal of the fairest duchesses. Your voice is like a siren's, your hands command respect and love. Ah! that arm!—place bracelets upon it, and how pleasingly it would rest upon the velvet of a robe! Your locks are chains which would fetter all men. And you could lay all your triumphs at Adolphe's feet, show him your power and never use it. Then he would fear, where now he lives in insolent certainty. Come! To action! Inhale a few mouthfuls of disdain and you will exhale clouds of incense. Dare to reign! Are you not next to nothing here in your chimney-corner? Sooner or later the pretty spouse, the beloved wife will die, if you continue like this, in a dressing-gown. Come, and you shall perpetuate your sway through the arts of coquetry! Show yourself in salons, and your pretty foot shall trample down the love of your rivals.'

"The other voice comes from my white marble mantel, which rustles like a garment. I think I see a veritable goddess crowned with white roses, and bearing a palm-branch in her hand. Two blue eyes smile down on me. This simple image of virtue says to me:

"'Be content! Remain good always, and make this man happy. That is the whole of your mission. The sweetness of angels triumphs over all pain. Faith in themselves has enabled the martyrs to obtain solace even on the brasiers of their tormentors. Suffer a moment; you shall be happy in the end.'

"Sometimes Adolphe enters at that moment and I am content. But, my dear, I have less patience than love. I almost wish to tear in pieces the woman who can go everywhere, and whose society is sought out by men and women alike. What profound thought lies in the line of Moliere:

"'The world, dear Agnes, is a curious thing!'

"You know nothing of this petty trouble, you fortunate Mathilde! You are well born. You can do a great deal for me. Just think! I can write you things that I dared not speak about. Your visits mean so much; come often to see your poor

"Caroline."

"Well," said I to the notary's clerk, "do you know what was the nature of this letter to the late Bourgarel?"

"No."

"A note of exchange."

Neither clerk nor notary understood my meaning. Do you?

THE PANGS OF INNOCENCE.

"Yes, dear, in the married state, many things will happen to you which you are far from expecting: but then others will happen which you expect still less. For instance—"

The author (may we say the ingenious author?) *qui castigat ridendo mores*, and who has undertaken the *Petty Troubles of Married Life*, hardly needs to remark, that, for prudence' sake, he here allows a lady of high distinction to speak, and that he does not assume the responsibility of her language, though he professes the most sincere admiration for the charming person to whom he owes his acquaintance with this petty trouble.

"For instance—" she says.

He nevertheless thinks proper to avow that this person is neither Madame Foullepointe, nor Madame de Fischtaminel, nor Madame Deschars.

Madame Deschars is too prudish, Madame Foullepointe too absolute in her household, and she knows it; indeed, what doesn't she know? She is good-natured, she sees good society, she wishes to have the best: people overlook the vivacity of her witticisms, as, under louis XIV, they overlooked the remarks of Madame Cornuel. They overlook a good many things in her; there are some women who are the spoiled children of public opinion.

As to Madame de Fischtaminel, who is, in fact, connected with the affair, as you shall see, she, being unable to recriminate, abstains from words and recriminates in acts.

We give permission to all to think that the speaker is Caroline herself, not the silly little Caroline of tender years. But Caroline when she has become a woman of thirty.

"For instance," she remarks to a young woman whom she is edifying, "you will have children, God willing."

"Madame," I say, "don't let us mix the deity up in this, unless it is an allusion—"

"You are impertinent," she replies, "you shouldn't interrupt a woman—"

"When she is busy with children, I know: but, madame, you ought not to trifle with the innocence of young ladies. Mademoiselle is going to be married, and if she were led to count upon the intervention of the Supreme Being in this affair, she would fall into serious errors. We should not deceive the young. Mademoiselle is beyond the age when girls are informed that their little brother was found under a cabbage."

"You evidently want to get me confused," she replies, smiling and showing the loveliest teeth in the world. "I am not strong enough to argue with you, so I beg you to let me go on with Josephine. What was I saying?"

"That if I get married, I shall have children," returns the young lady.

"Very well. I will not represent things to you worse than they are, but it is extremely probable that each child will cost you a tooth. With every baby I have lost a tooth."

"Happily," I remark at this, "this trouble was with you less than petty, it was positively nothing." — They were side teeth. — "But take notice, miss, that this vexation has no absolute, unvarying character as such. The annoyance depends upon the condition of the tooth. If the baby causes the loss of a decayed tooth, you are fortunate to have a baby the more and a bad tooth the less. Don't let us confound blessings with bothers. Ah! if you were to lose one of your magnificent front teeth, that would be another thing! And yet there is many a woman that would give the best tooth in her head for a fine, healthy boy!"

"Well," resumes Caroline, with animation, "at the risk of destroying your illusions, poor child, I'll just show you a petty trouble that counts! Ah, it's atrocious! And I won't leave the subject of dress which this gentleman considers the only subject we women are equal to."

I protest by a gesture.

"I had been married about two years," continues Caroline, "and I loved my husband. I have got over it since and acted differently for his happiness and mine. I can boast of having one of the happiest homes in Paris. In short, my dear, I loved the monster, and, even when out in society, saw no one but him. My husband had already said to me several times, 'My dear, young women never dress well; your mother liked to have you look like a stick, — she had her reasons for it. If you care for my advice, take Madame de Fischtaminel for a model: she is a lady of taste.' I, unsuspecting creature that I was, saw no perfidy in the recommendation.

"One evening as we returned from a party, he said, 'Did you notice how Madame de Fischtaminel was dressed!' 'Yes, very neatly.' And I said to myself, 'He's always talking about Madame de Fischtaminel; I must really dress just like her.' I had noticed the stuff and the make of the dress, and the style of the trimmings. I was as happy as could be, as I went trotting about town, doing everything I could to obtain the same articles. I sent for the very same dressmaker.

"'You work for Madame de Fischtaminel,' I said.

"'Yes, madame.'

"'Well, I will employ you as my dressmaker, but on one condition: you see I have procured the stuff of which her gown is made, and I want you to make me one exactly like it.'

"I confess that I did not at first pay any attention to a rather shrewd smile of the dressmaker, though I saw it and afterwards accounted for it. 'So like it,' I added, 'that you can't tell them apart.'

"Oh," says Caroline, interrupting herself and looking at me, "you men teach us to live like spiders in the depths of their webs, to see everything without seeming to look at it, to investigate the meaning and spirit of words, movements, looks. You say, 'How cunning women are!' But you should say, 'How deceitful men are!'

"I can't tell you how much care, how many days, how many manoeuvres, it cost me to become Madame de Fischtaminel's duplicate! But these are our battles, child," she adds, returning to Josephine. "I could not find a certain little embroidered neckerchief, a very marvel! I finally learned that it was made to order. I unearthed the embroideress, and ordered a kerchief like Madame de Fischtaminel's. The price was a mere trifle, one hundred and fifty francs! It had been ordered by a gentleman who had made a present of it to Madame de Fischtaminel. All my savings were absorbed by it. Now we women of Paris are all of us very much restricted in the article of dress. There is not a man worth a hundred thousand francs a year, that loses ten thousand a winter at whist, who does not consider his wife extravagant, and is not alarmed at her bills for what he calls 'rags'! 'Let my savings go,' I said. And they went. I had the modest pride of a woman in love: I would not speak a word to Adolphe of my dress; I wanted it to be a surprise, goose that I was! Oh, how brutally you men take away our blessed ignorance!"

This remark is meant for me, for me who had taken nothing from the lady, neither tooth, nor anything whatever of the things with a name and without a name that may be taken from a woman.

"I must tell you that my husband took me to Madame de Fischtaminel's, where I dined quite often. I heard her say to him, 'Why, your wife looks very well!' She had a patronizing way with me that I put up with: Adolphe wished that I could have her wit and preponderance in society. In short, this phoenix of women was my model. I studied and copied her, I took immense pains not to be myself—oh!— it was a poem that no one but us women can understand! Finally, the day of my triumph dawned. My heart beat for joy, as if I were a child, as if I were what we all are at twenty-two. My husband was going to call for me for a walk in the Tuileries: he came in, I looked at him radiant with joy, but he took no notice. Well, I can confess it now, it was one of those frightful disasters—but I will say nothing about it —this gentleman here would make fun of me."

I protest by another movement.

"It was," she goes on, for a woman never stops till she has told the whole of a thing, "as if I had seen an edifice built by a fairy crumble into ruins. Adolphe manifested not the slightest surprise. We got into the carriage. Adolphe noticed my sadness, and asked me what the matter was: I replied as we always do when our hearts are wrung by these petty vexations, 'Oh, nothing!' Then he took his eyeglass, and stared at the promenaders on the Champs Elysees, for we were to go the rounds of the Champs Elysees, before taking our walk at the Tuileries. Finally, a fit of impatience seized me. I felt a slight attack of fever, and when I got home, I composed myself to smile. 'You haven't said a word about my dress!' I muttered. 'Ah, yes, your gown is somewhat like Madame de Fischtaminel's.' He turned on his heel and went away.

"The next day I pouted a little, as you may readily imagine. Just as we were finishing breakfast by the fire in my room—I shall never forget it—the embroideress called to get her money for the neckerchief. I paid her. She bowed to my husband as if she knew him. I ran after her on pretext of getting her to receipt the bill, and said: 'You didn't ask *him* so much for Madame de Fischtaminel's kerchief!' 'I assure you, madame, it's the same price, the gentleman did not beat me down a mite.' I returned to my room where I found my husband looking as foolish as—"

She hesitates and then resumes: "As a miller just made a bishop. 'I understand, love, now, that I shall never be anything more than *somewhat like* Madame de Fischtaminel.' 'You refer to her neckerchief, I suppose: well, I *did* give it to her,—it was for her birthday. You see, we were formerly—' 'Ah, you were formerly more intimate than you are now!' Without replying to this, he added, '*But it's altogether moral.*'

"He took his hat and went out, leaving me with this fine declaration of the Rights of Man. He did not return and came home late at night. I remained in my chamber and wept like a Magdalen, in the chimney-corner. You may laugh at me, if you will," she adds, looking at me, "but I shed tears over my youthful illusions, and I wept, too, for spite, at having been taken for a dupe. I remembered the dressmaker's smile! Ah, that smile reminded me of the smiles of a number of women, who laughed at seeing me so innocent and unsuspecting at Madame de Fischtaminel's! I wept sincerely. Until now I had a right to give my husband credit for many things which he did not possess, but in the existence of which young married women pertinaciously believe.

"How many great troubles are included in this petty one! You men are a vulgar set. There is not a woman who does not carry her delicacy so far as to embroider her past life with the most delightful fibs, while you—but I have had my revenge."

"Madame," I say, "you are giving this young lady too much information."

"True," she returns, "I will tell you the sequel some other time."

"Thus, you see, mademoiselle," I say, "you imagine you are buying a neckerchief and you find a *petty trouble* round your neck: if you get it given to you—"

"It's a *great* trouble," retorts the woman of distinction. "Let us stop here."

The moral of this fable is that you must wear your neckerchief without thinking too much about it. The ancient prophets called this world, even in their time, a valley of woe. Now, at that period, the Orientals had, with the permission of the constituted authorities, a swarm of comely slaves, besides their wives! What shall we call the valley of the Seine between Calvary and Charenton, where the law allows but one lawful wife.

THE UNIVERSAL AMADIS.

You will understand at once that I began to gnaw the head of my cane, to consult the ceiling, to gaze at the fire, to examine Caroline's foot, and I thus held out till the marriageable young lady was gone.

"You must excuse me," I said, "if I have remained behind, perhaps in spite of you: but your vengeance would lose by being recounted by and by, and if it constituted a petty trouble for your husband, I have the greatest interest in hearing it, and you shall know why."

"Ah," she returned, "that expression, *'it's altogether moral,'* which he gave as an excuse, shocked me to the last degree. It was a great consolation, truly, to me, to know that I held the place, in his household, of a piece of furniture, a block; that my kingdom lay among the kitchen utensils, the accessories of my toilet, and the physicians' prescriptions; that our conjugal love had been assimilated to dinner pills, to veal soup and white mustard; that Madame de Fischtaminel possessed my husband's soul, his admiration, and that she charmed and satisfied his intellect, while I was a kind of purely physical necessity! What do you think of a woman's being degraded to the situation of a soup or a plate of boiled beef, and without parsley, at that! Oh, I composed a catilinic, that evening—"

"Philippic is better."

"Well, either. I'll say anything you like, for I was perfectly furious, and I don't remember what I screamed in the desert of my bedroom. Do you suppose that this opinion that husbands have of their wives, the parts they give them, is not a singular vexation for us? Our petty troubles are always pregnant with greater ones. My Adolphe needed a lesson. You know the Vicomte de Lustrac, a desperate amateur of women and music, an epicure, one of those ex-beaux of the Empire, who live upon their earlier successes, and who cultivate themselves with excessive care, in order to secure a second crop?"

"Yes," I said, "one of those laced, braced, corseted old fellows of sixty, who work such wonders by the grace of their forms, and who might give a lesson to the youngest dandies among us."

"Monsieur de Lustrac is as selfish as a king, but gallant and pretentious, spite of his jet black wig."

"As to his whiskers, he dyes them."

"He goes to ten parties in an evening: he's a butterfly."

"He gives capital dinners and concerts, and patronizes inexperienced songstresses."

"He takes bustle for pleasure."

"Yes, but he makes off with incredible celerity whenever a misfortune occurs. Are you in mourning, he avoids you. Are you confined, he awaits your churching before he visits you. He possesses a mundane frankness and a social intrepidity which challenge admiration."

"But does it not require courage to appear to be what one really is?" I asked.

"Well," she resumed, after we had exchanged our observations on this point, "this young old man, this universal Amadis, whom we call among ourselves Chevalier *Petit-Bon-Homme-vil-encore*, became the object of my admiration. I made him a few of those advances which never compromise a woman; I spoke of the good taste exhibited in his latest waistcoats and in his canes, and he thought me a lady of extreme amiability. I thought him a chevalier of extreme youth; he called upon me; I put on a number of little airs, and pretended to be unhappy at home, and to have deep sorrows. You know what a woman means when she talks of her sorrows, and complains that she is not understood. The old ape replied much better than a young man would, and I had the greatest difficulty in keeping a straight face while I listened to him.

"'Ah, that's the way with husbands, they pursue the very worst polity, they respect their wives, and, sooner or later, every woman is enraged at finding herself respected, and divines the secret education to which she is entitled. Once married, you ought not to live like a little school-girl, etc.'

"As he spoke, he leaned over me, he squirmed, he was horrible to see. He looked like a wooden Nuremberg doll, he stuck out his chin, he stuck out his chair, he stuck out his hand—in short, after a variety of marches and countermarches, of declarations that were perfectly angelic—"

"No!"

"Yes. *Petit-Bon-Homme-vil-encore* had abandoned the classicism of his youth for the romanticism now in fashion: he spoke of the soul, of angels, of adoration, of submission, he became ethereal, and of the darkest blue. He took me to the opera, and handed me to my carriage. This old young man went when I went, his waistcoats multiplied, he compressed his waist, he excited his horse to a gallop in order to catch and accompany my carriage to the promenade: he compromised me with the grace of a young collegian, and was considered madly in love with me. I was steadfastly cruel, but accepted his arm and his bouquets. We were talked about. I was delighted, and managed before long to be surprised by my husband, with the viscount on the sofa in my boudoir, holding my hands in his, while I listened in a sort of external ecstasy. It is incredible how much a desire for vengeance will induce us to put up with! I appeared vexed at the entrance of my husband, who made a scene on the viscount's departure: 'I assure you, sir,' said I, after having listened to his reproaches, 'that *it's altogether moral*.' My husband saw the point and went no more to Madame de Fischtaminel's. I received Monsieur de Lustrac no more, either."

"But," I interrupted, "this Lustrac that you, like many others, take for a bachelor, is a widower, and childless."

"Really!"

"No man ever buried his wife deeper than he buried his: she will hardly be found at the day of judgment. He married before the Revolution, and your *altogether moral* reminds me of a speech of his that I shall have to repeat for your benefit. Napoleon appointed Lustrac to an important office, in a conquered province. Madame de Lustrac, abandoned for governmental duties, took a private secretary for her private affairs, though it was altogether moral: but she was wrong in selecting him without informing her husband. Lustrac met this secretary in a state of some excitement, in consequence of a lively discussion in his wife's chamber, and at an exceedingly early hour in the morning. The city desired nothing better than to laugh at its governor, and this adventure made such a sensation that Lustrac himself begged the Emperor to recall him. Napoleon desired his representatives to be men of morality, and he held that such disasters as this must inevitably take from a man's consideration. You know that among the Emperor's unhappy passions, was that of reforming his court and his government. Lustrac's request was granted, therefore, but without compensation. When he returned to Paris, he reappeared at his mansion, with his wife; he took her into society—a step which is certainly conformable to the most refined habits of the aristocracy —but then there are always people who want to find out about it. They inquired the reason of this chivalrous championship. 'So you are reconciled, you and Madame de Lustrac,' some one said to him in the lobby of the Emperor's theatre, 'you have pardoned her, have you? So much the better.' 'Oh,' replied he, with a satisfied air, 'I became convinced—' 'Ah, that she was innocent, very good.' 'No, I became convinced that it was altogether physical.'"

Caroline smiled.

"The opinion of your admirer reduced this weighty trouble to what is, in this case as in yours, a very petty one." ·

"A petty trouble!" she exclaimed, "and pray for what do you take the fatigue of coquetting with a de Lustrac, of whom I have made an enemy! Ah, women often pay dearly enough for the bouquets they receive and the attentions they accept. Monsieur de Lustrac said of me to Monsieur de Bourgarel, 'I would not advise you to pay court to that woman; she is too dear.'"

WITHOUT AN OCCUPATION.

"PARIS, 183-

"You ask me, dear mother, whether I am happy with my husband. Certainly Monsieur de Fischtaminel was not the ideal of my dreams. I submitted to your will, as you know. His fortune, that supreme consideration, spoke, indeed, sufficiently loud. With these arguments, —a marriage, without stooping, with the Count de Fischtaminel, his having thirty thousand a year, and a home at Paris—you were strongly armed against your poor daughter. Besides, Monsieur de Fischtaminel is good looking for a man of thirty-six years; he received the cross of the Legion of Honor from Napoleon upon the field of battle, he is an ex-colonel, and had it not been for the Restoration, which put him upon half-pay, he would be a general. These are certainly extenuating circumstances.

"Many women consider that I have made a good match, and I am bound to confess that there is every appearance of happiness,—for the public, that is. But you will acknowledge that if you had known of the return of my Uncle Cyrus and of his intention to leave me his money, you would have given me the privilege of choosing for myself.

"I have nothing to say against Monsieur de Fischtaminel: he does not gamble, he is indifferent to women, he doesn't like wine, and he has no expensive fancies: he possesses, as you said, all the negative qualities which make husbands passable. Then, what is the matter with him? Well, mother, he has nothing to do. We are together the whole blessed day! Would you believe that it is during the night, when we are the most closely united, that I am the most alone? His sleep is my asylum, my liberty begins when he slumbers. This state of siege will yet make me sick: I am never alone. If Monsieur de Fischtaminel were jealous, I should have a resource. There would then be a struggle, a comedy: but how could the aconite of jealousy have taken root in his soul? He has never left me since our marriage. He feels no shame in stretching himself out upon a sofa and remaining there for hours together.

"Two felons pinioned to the same chain do not find time hang heavy: for they have their escape to think of. But we have no subject of conversation; we have long since talked ourselves out. A little while ago he was so far reduced as to talk politics. But even politics are exhausted, Napoleon, unfortunately for me, having died at St. Helena, as is well known.

"Monsieur de Fischtaminel abhors reading. If he sees me with a book, he comes and says a dozen times an hour—'Nina, dear, haven't you finished yet?'

"I endeavored to persuade this innocent persecutor to ride out every day on horseback, and I alleged a consideration usually conclusive with men of forty years,—his health! But he said that after having been twelve years on horseback, he felt the need of repose.

"My husband, dear mother, is a man who absorbs you, he uses up the vital fluid of his neighbor, his ennui is gluttonous: he likes to be amused by those who call upon us, and, after five years of wedlock, no one ever comes: none visit us but those whose intentions are evidently dishonorable for him, and who endeavor, unsuccessfully, to amuse him, in order to earn the right to weary his wife.

"Monsieur de Fischtaminel, mother, opens the door of my chamber, or of the room to which I have flown for refuge, five or six times an hour, and comes up to me in an excited way, and says, 'Well, what are you doing, my belle?' (the expression in fashion during the Empire) without perceiving that he is constantly repeating the same phrase, which is to me like the one pint too much that the executioner formerly poured into the torture by water.

"Then there's another bore! We can't go to walk any more. A promenade without conversation, without interest, is impossible. My husband walks with me for the walk, as if he were alone. I have the fatigue without the pleasure.

"The interval between getting up and breakfast is employed in my toilet, in my household duties; and I manage to get through with this part of the day. But between breakfast and dinner, there is a whole desert to plough, a waste to traverse. My husband's want of occupation does not leave me a moment of repose, he overpowers me by his uselessness; his idle life positively wears me out. His two eyes always open and gazing at mine compel me to keep them lowered. Then his monotonous remarks:

"'What o'clock is it, love? What are you doing now? What are you thinking of? What do you mean to do? Where shall we go this evening? Anything new? What weather! I don't feel well, etc., etc.'

"All these variations upon the same theme—the interrogation point —which compose Fischtaminel's repertory, will drive me mad. Add to these leaden arrows everlastingly shot off at me, one last trait which will complete the description of my happiness, and you will understand my life.

"Monsieur de Fischtaminel, who went away in 1809, with the rank of sub-lieutenant, at the age of eighteen, has had no other education than that due to discipline, to the natural sense of honor of a noble and a soldier: but though he possesses tact, the sentiment of probity, and a proper subordination, his ignorance is gross, he knows absolutely nothing, and he has a horror of learning anything. Oh, dear mother, what an accomplished door-keeper this colonel would have made, had he been born in indigence! I don't think a bit the better of him for his bravery, for he did not fight against the Russians, the Austrians, or the Prussians: he fought against ennui. When he rushed upon the enemy, Captain Fischtaminel's purpose was to get away from himself. He married because he had nothing else to do.

"We have another slight difficulty to content with: my husband harasses the servants to such a degree that we change them every six months.

"I so ardently desire, dear mother, to remain a virtuous woman, that I am going to try the effect of traveling for half the year. During the winter, I shall go every evening to the Italian or the French opera, or to parties: but I don't know whether our fortune will permit such an expenditure. Uncle Cyrus ought to come to Paris—I would take care of him as I would of an inheritance.

"If you discover a cure for my woes, let your daughter know of it —your daughter who loves you as much as she deplores her misfortunes, and who would have been glad to call herself by some other name than that of

"NINA FISCHTAMINEL."

Besides the necessity of describing this petty trouble, which could only be described by the pen of a woman,—and what a woman she was! —it was necessary to make you acquainted with a character whom you saw only in profile in the first half of this book, the queen of the particular set in which Caroline lived,—a woman both envied and adroit, who succeeded in conciliating, at an early date, what she owed to the world with the requirements of the heart. This letter is her absolution.

INDISCRETIONS.

Women are either chaste—or vain—or simply proud. They are therefore all subject to the following petty trouble:

Certain husbands are so delighted to have, in the form of a wife, a woman to themselves,—a possession exclusively due to the legal ceremony,—that they dread the public's making a mistake, and they hasten to brand their consort, as lumber-dealers brand their logs while floating down stream, or as the Berry stock-raisers brand their sheep. They bestow names of endearment, right before people, upon their wives: names taken, after the Roman fashion (columbella), from the animal kingdom, as: my chick, my duck, my dove, my lamb; or, choosing from the vegetable kingdom, they call them: my cabbage, my fig (this only in Provence), my plum (this only in Alsatia). Never: —My flower! Pray note this discretion.

Or else, which is more serious, they call their wives:—Bobonne, —mother,—daughter,—good woman,—old lady: this last when she is very young.

Some venture upon names of doubtful propriety, such as: Mon bichon, ma niniche, Tronquette!

We once heard one of our politicians, a man extremely remarkable for his ugliness, call his wife, *Moumoutte!*

"I would rather he would strike me," said this unfortunate to her neighbor.

"Poor little woman, she is really unhappy," resumed the neighbor, looking at me when Moumoutte had gone: "when she is in company with her husband she is upon pins and needles, and keeps out of his way. One evening, he actually seized her by the neck and said: 'Come fatty, let's go home!'"

It has been alleged that the cause of a very famous husband-poisoning with arsenic, was nothing less than a series of constant indiscretions like these that the wife had to bear in society. This husband used to give the woman he had won at the point of the Code, public little taps on her shoulder, he would startle her by a resounding kiss, he dishonored her by a conspicuous tenderness, seasoned by those impertinent attentions the secret of which belongs to the French savages who dwell in the depths of the provinces, and whose manners are very little known, despite the efforts of the realists in fiction. It was, it is said, this shocking situation,—one perfectly appreciated by a discerning jury,—which won the prisoner a verdict softened by the extenuating circumstances.

The jurymen said to themselves:

"For a wife to murder her husband for these conjugal offences, is certainly going rather far; but then a woman is very excusable, when she is so harassed!"

We deeply regret, in the interest of elegant manners, that these arguments are not more generally known. Heaven grant, therefore, that our book may have an immense success, as women will obtain this advantage from it, that they will be treated as they deserve, that is, as queens.

In this respect, love is much superior to marriage, it is proud of indiscreet sayings and doings. There are some women that seek them, fish for them, and woe to the man who does not now and then commit one!

What passion lies in an accidental *thou*!

Out in the country I heard a husband call his wife: "Ma berline!" She was delighted with it, and saw nothing ridiculous in it: she called her husband, "Mon fiston!" This delicious couple were ignorant of the existence of such things as petty troubles.

It was in observing this happy pair that the author discovered this axiom:

Axiom:—In order to be happy in wedlock, you must either be a man of genius married to an affectionate and intellectual woman, or, by a chance which is not as common as might be supposed, you must both of you be exceedingly stupid.

The too celebrated history of the cure of a wounded self-love by arsenic, proves that, properly speaking, there are no petty troubles for women in married life.

Axiom.—Woman exists by sentiment where man exists by action.

Now, sentiment can at any moment render a petty trouble either a great misfortune, or a wasted life, or an eternal misery. Should Caroline begin, in her ignorance of life and the world, by inflicting upon her husband the vexations of her stupidity (re-read REVELATIONS), Adolphe, like any other man, may find a compensation in social excitement: he goes out, comes back, goes here and there, has business. But for Caroline, the question everywhere is, To love or not to love, to be or not to be loved.

Indiscretions are in harmony with the character of the individuals, with times and places. Two examples will suffice.

Here is the first. A man is by nature dirty and ugly: he is ill-made and repulsive. There are men, and often rich ones, too, who, by a sort of unobserved constitution, soil a new suit of clothes in twenty-four hours. They were born disgusting. It is so disgraceful for a women to be anything more than just simply a wife to this sort of Adolphe, that a certain Caroline had long ago insisted upon the suppression of the modern *thee* and *thou* and all other insignia of the wifely dignity. Society had been for five or six years accustomed to this sort of thing, and supposed Madame and Monsieur completely separated, and all the more so as it had noticed the accession of a Ferdinand II.

One evening, in the presence of a dozen persons, this man said to his wife: "Caroline, hand me the tongs, there's a love." It is nothing, and yet everything. It was a domestic revelation.

Monsieur de Lustrac, the Universal Amadis, hurried to Madame de Fischtaminel's, narrated this little scene with all the spirit at his command, and Madame de Fischtaminel put on an air something like Celimene's and said: "Poor creature, what an extremity she must be in!"

I say nothing of Caroline's confusion,—you have already divined it.

Here is the second. Think of the frightful situation in which a lady of great refinement was lately placed: she was conversing agreeably at her country seat near Paris, when her husband's servant came and whispered in her ear, "Monsieur has come, madame."

"Very well, Benoit."

Everybody had heard the rumblings of the vehicle. It was known that the husband had been at Paris since Monday, and this took place on Saturday, at four in the afternoon.

"He's got something important to say to you, madame."

Though this dialogue was held in a whisper, it was perfectly understood, and all the more so from the fact that the lady of the house turned from the pale hue of the Bengal rose to the brilliant crimson of the wheatfield poppy. She nodded and went on with the conversation, and managed to leave her company on the pretext of learning whether her husband had succeeded in an important undertaking or not: but she seemed plainly vexed at Adolphe's want of consideration for the company who were visiting her.

During their youth, women want to be treated as divinities, they love the ideal; they cannot bear the idea of being what nature intended them to be.

Some husbands, on retiring to the country, after a week in town, are worse than this: they bow to the company, put their arm round their wife's waist, take a little walk with her, appear to be talking confidentially, disappear in a clump of trees, get lost, and reappear half an hour afterward.

This, ladies, is a genuine petty trouble for a young woman, but for a woman beyond forty, this sort of indiscretion is so delightful, that the greatest prudes are flattered by it, for, be it known:

That women of a certain age, women on the shady side, want to be treated as mortals, they love the actual; they cannot bear the idea of no longer being what nature intended them to be.

Axiom.—Modesty is a relative virtue; there is the modesty of the woman of twenty, the woman of thirty, the woman of forty-five.

Thus the author said to a lady who told him to guess at her age: "Madame, yours is the age of indiscretion."

This charming woman of thirty-nine was making a Ferdinand much too conspicuous, while her daughter was trying to conceal her Ferdinand I.

BRUTAL DISCLOSURES.

FIRST STYLE. Caroline adores Adolphe, she thinks him handsome, she thinks him superb, especially in his National Guard uniform. She starts when a sentinel presents arms to him, she considers him moulded like a model, she regards him as a man of wit, everything he does is right, nobody has better taste than he, in short, she is crazy about Adolphe.

It's the old story of Cupid's bandage. This is washed every ten years, and newly embroidered by the altered manners of the period, but it has been the same old bandage since the days of Greece.

Caroline is at a ball with one of her young friends. A man well known for his bluntness, whose acquaintance she is to make later in life, but whom she now sees for the first time, Monsieur Foullepointe, has commenced a conversation with Caroline's friend. According to the custom of society, Caroline listens to this conversation without mingling in it.

"Pray tell me, madame," says Monsieur Foullepointe, "who is that queer man who has been talking about the Court of Assizes before a gentleman whose acquittal lately created such a sensation: he is all the while blundering, like an ox in a bog, against everybody's sore spot. A lady burst into tears at hearing him tell of the death of a child, as she lost her own two months ago."

"Who do you mean?"

"Why, that fat man, dressed like a waiter in a cafe, frizzled like a barber's apprentice, there, he's trying now to make himself agreeable to Madame de Fischtaminel."

"Hush," whispers the lady quite alarmed, "it's the husband of the little woman next to me!"

"Ah, it's your husband?" says Monsieur Foullepointe. "I am delighted, madame, he's a charming man, so vivacious, gay and witty. I am going to make his acquaintance immediately."

And Foullepointe executes his retreat, leaving a bitter suspicion in Caroline's soul, as to the question whether her husband is really as handsome as she thinks him.

SECOND STYLE. Caroline, annoyed by the reputation of Madame Schinner, who is credited with the possession of epistolary talents, and styled the "Sevigne of the note", tired of hearing about Madame de Fischtaminel, who has ventured to write a little 32mo book on the education of the young, in which she has boldly reprinted Fenelon, without the style:—Caroline has been working for six months upon a tale tenfold poorer than those of Berquin, nauseatingly moral, and flamboyant in style.

After numerous intrigues such as women are skillful in managing in the interest of their vanity, and the tenacity and perfection of which would lead you to believe that they have a third sex in their head, this tale, entitled "The Lotus," appears in three installments in a leading daily paper. It is signed Samuel Crux.

When Adolphe takes up the paper at breakfast, Caroline's heart beats up in her very throat: she blushes, turns pale, looks away and stares at the ceiling. When Adolphe's eyes settle upon the feuilleton, she can bear it no longer: she gets up, goes out, comes back, having replenished her stock of audacity, no one knows where.

"Is there a feuilleton this morning?" she asks with an air that she thinks indifferent, but which would disturb a husband still jealous of his wife.

"Yes, one by a beginner, Samuel Crux. The name is a disguise, clearly: the tale is insignificant enough to drive an insect to despair, if he could read: and vulgar, too: the style is muddy, but then it's—"

Caroline breathes again. "It's—" she suggests.

"It's incomprehensible," resumes Adolphe. "Somebody must have paid Chodoreille five or six hundred francs to insert it; or else it's the production of a blue-stocking in high society who has promised to invite Madame Chodoreille to her house; or perhaps it's the work of a woman in whom the editor is personally interested. Such a piece of stupidity cannot be explained any other way. Imagine, Caroline, that it's all about a little flower picked on the edge of a wood in a sentimental walk, which a gentleman of the Werther school has sworn to keep, which he has had framed, and which the lady claims again eleven years after (the poor man has had time to change his lodgings three times). It's quite new, about as old as Sterne or Gessner. What makes me think it's a woman, is that the first literary idea of the whole sex is to take vengeance on some one."

Adolphe might go on pulling "The Lotus" to pieces; Caroline's ears are full of the tinkling of bells. She is like the woman who threw herself over the Pont des Arts, and tried to find her way ten feet below the level of the Seine.

ANOTHER STYLE. Caroline, in her paroxysms of jealousy, has discovered a hiding place used by Adolphe, who, as he can't trust his wife, and as he knows she opens his letters and rummages in his drawers, has endeavored to save his correspondence with Hector from the hooked fingers of the conjugal police.

Hector is an old schoolmate, who has married in the Loire Inferieure.

Adolphe lifts up the cloth of his writing desk, a cloth the border of which has been embroidered by Caroline, the ground being blue, black or red velvet,—the color, as you see, is perfectly immaterial,—and he slips his unfinished letters to Madame de Fischtaminel, to his friend Hector, between the table and the cloth.

The thickness of a sheet of paper is almost nothing, velvet is a downy, discreet material, but, no matter, these precautions are in vain. The male devil is fairly matched by the female devil: Tophet will furnish them of all genders. Caroline has Mephistopheles on her side, the demon who causes tables to spurt forth fire, and who, with his ironic finger points out the hiding place of keys—the secret of secrets.

Caroline has noticed the thickness of a letter sheet between this velvet and this table: she hits upon a letter to Hector instead of hitting upon one to Madame de Fischtaminel, who has gone to Plombieres Springs, and reads the following:

"My dear Hector:

"I pity you, but you have acted wisely in entrusting me with a knowledge of the difficulties in which you have voluntarily involved yourself. You never would see the difference between the country woman and the woman of Paris. In the country, my dear boy, you are always face to face with your wife, and, owing to the ennui which impels you, you rush headforemost into the enjoyment of your bliss. This is a great error: happiness is an abyss, and when you have once reached the bottom, you never get back again, in wedlock.

"I will show you why. Let me take, for your wife's sake, the shortest path—the parable.

"I remember having made a journey from Paris to Ville-Parisis, in that vehicle called a 'bus: distance, twenty miles: 'bus, lumbering: horse, lame. Nothing amuses me more than to draw from people, by the aid of that gimlet called the interrogation, and to obtain, by means of an attentive air, the sum of information, anecdotes and learning that everybody is anxious to part with: and all men have such a sum, the peasant as well as the banker, the corporal as well as the marshal of France.

"I have often noticed how ready these casks, overflowing with wit, are to open their sluices while being transported by diligence or 'bus, or by any vehicle drawn by horses, for nobody talks in a railway car.

"At the rate of our exit from Paris, the journey would take full seven hours: so I got an old corporal to talk, for my diversion. He could neither read nor write: he was entirely illiterate. Yet the journey seemed short. The corporal had been through all the campaigns, he told me of things perfectly unheard of, that historians never trouble themselves about.

"Ah! Hector, how superior is practice to theory! Among other things, and in reply to a question relative to the infantry, whose courage is much more tried by marching than by fighting, he said this, which I give you free from circumlocution:

"'Sir, when Parisians were brought to our 45th, which Napoleon called The Terrible (I am speaking of the early days of the Empire, when the infantry had legs of steel, and when they needed them), I had a way of telling beforehand which of them would remain in the 45th. They marched without hurrying, they did their little six leagues a day, neither more nor less, and they pitched camp in condition to begin again on the morrow. The plucky fellows who did ten leagues and wanted to run to the victory, stopped half way at the hospital.'

"The worthy corporal was talking of marriage while he thought he was talking of war, and you have stopped half way, Hector, at the hospital.

"Remember the sympathetic condolence of Madame de Sevigne counting out three hundred thousand francs to Monsieur de Grignan, to induce him to marry one of the prettiest girls in France! 'Why,' said she to herself, 'he will have to marry her every day, as long as she lives! Decidedly, I don't think three hundred francs too much.' Is it not enough to make the bravest tremble?

"My dear fellow, conjugal happiness is founded, like that of nations, upon ignorance. It is a felicity full of negative conditions.

"If I am happy with my little Caroline, it is due to the strictest observance of that salutary principle so strongly insisted upon in the *Physiology of Marriage*. I have resolved to lead my wife through paths beaten in the snow, until the happy day when infidelity will be difficult.

"In the situation in which you have placed yourself, and which resembles that of Duprez, who, on his first appearance at Paris, went to singing with all the voice his lungs would yield, instead of imitating Nourrit, who gave the audience just enough to enchant them, the following, I think, is your proper course to—"

The letter broke off here: Caroline returned it to its place, at the same time wondering how she would make her dear Adolphe expiate his obedience to the execrable precepts of the *Physiology of Marriage*.

A TRUCE.

This trouble doubtless occurs sufficiently often and in different ways enough in the existence of married women, for this personal incident to become the type of the genus.

The Caroline in question here is very pious, she loves her husband very much, her husband asserts that she loves him too much, even: but this is a piece of marital conceit, if, indeed, it is not a provocation, as he only complains to his wife's young lady friends.

When a person's conscience is involved, the least thing becomes exceedingly serious. Madame de — —- has told her young friend, Madame de Fischtaminel, that she had been compelled to make an extraordinary confession to her spiritual director, and to perform penance, the director having decided that she was in a state of mortal sin. This lady, who goes to mass every morning, is a woman of thirty-six years, thin and slightly pimpled. She has large soft black eyes, her upper lip is strongly shaded: still her voice is sweet, her manners gentle, her gait noble—she is a woman of quality.

Madame de Fischtaminel, whom Madame de — —- has made her friend (nearly all pious women patronize a woman who is considered worldly, on the pretext of converting her),—Madame de Fischtaminel asserts that these qualities, in this Caroline of the Pious Sort, are a victory of religion over a rather violent natural temper.

These details are necessary to describe the trouble in all its horror.

This lady's Adolphe had been compelled to leave his wife for two months, in April, immediately after the forty days' fast that Caroline scrupulously observes. Early in June, therefore, madame expected her husband, she expected him day by day. From one hope to another,

"Conceived every morn and deferred every eve."

She got along as far as Sunday, the day when her presentiments, which had now reached a state of paroxysm, told her that the longed-for husband would arrive at an early hour.

When a pious woman expects her husband, and that husband has been absent from home nearly four months, she takes much more pains with her toilet than a young girl does, though waiting for her first betrothed.

This virtuous Caroline was so completely absorbed in exclusively personal preparations, that she forgot to go to eight o'clock mass. She proposed to hear a low mass, but she was afraid of losing the delight of her dear Adolphe's first glance, in case he arrived at early dawn. Her chambermaid—who respectfully left her mistress alone in the dressing-room where pious and pimpled ladies let no one enter, not even their husbands, especially if they are thin—her chambermaid heard her exclaim several times, "If it's your master, let me know!"

The rumbling of a vehicle having made the furniture rattle, Caroline assumed a mild tone to conceal the violence of her legitimate emotions.

"Oh! 'tis he! Run, Justine: tell him I am waiting for him here." Caroline trembled so that she dropped into an arm-chair.

The vehicle was a butcher's wagon.

It was in anxieties like this that the eight o'clock mass slipped by, like an eel in his slime. Madame's toilet operations were resumed, for she was engaged in dressing. The chambermaid's nose had already been the recipient of a superb muslin chemise, with a simple hem, which Caroline had thrown at her from the dressing-room, though she had given her the same kind for the last three months.

"What are you thinking of, Justine? I told you to choose from the chemises that are not numbered."

The unnumbered chemises were only seven or eight, in the most magnificent trousseau. They are chemises gotten up and embroidered with the greatest care: a woman must be a queen, a young queen, to have a dozen. Each one of Caroline's was trimmed with valenciennes round the bottom, and still more coquettishly garnished about the neck. This feature of our manners will perhaps serve to suggest a suspicion, in the masculine world, of the domestic drama revealed by this exceptional chemise.

Caroline had put on a pair of Scotch thread stockings, little prunella buskins, and her most deceptive corsets. She had her hair dressed in the fashion that most became her, and embellished it with a cap of the most elegant form. It is unnecessary to speak of her morning gown. A pious lady who lives at Paris and who loves her husband, knows as well as a coquette how to choose those pretty little striped patterns, have them cut with an open waist, and fastened by loops to buttons in a way which compels her to refasten them two or three times in an hour, with little airs more or less charming, as the case may be.

The nine o'clock mass, the ten o'clock mass, every mass, went by in these preparations, which, for women in love, are one of their twelve labors of Hercules.

Pious women rarely go to church in a carriage, and they are right. Except in the case of a pouring shower, or intolerably bad weather, a person ought not to appear haughty in the place where it is becoming to be humble. Caroline was afraid to compromise the freshness of her dress and the purity of her thread stockings. Alas! these pretexts concealed a reason.

"If I am at church when Adolphe comes, I shall lose the pleasure of his first glance: and he will think I prefer high mass to him."

She made this sacrifice to her husband in a desire to please him—a fearfully worldly consideration. Prefer the creature to the Creator! A husband to heaven! Go and hear a sermon and you will learn what such an offence will cost you.

"After all," says Caroline, quoting her confessor, "society is founded upon marriage, which the Church has included among its sacraments."

And this is the way in which religious instruction may be put aside in favor of a blind though legitimate love. Madame refused breakfast, and ordered the meal to be kept hot, just as she kept herself ready, at a moment's notice, to welcome the precious absentee.

Now these little things may easily excite a laugh: but in the first place they are continually occurring with couples who love each other, or where one of them loves the other: besides, in a woman so strait-laced, so reserved, so worthy, as this lady, these acknowledgments of affection went beyond the limits imposed upon her feelings by the lofty self-respect which true piety induces. When Madame de Fischtaminel narrated this little scene in a devotee's life, dressing it up with choice by-play, acted out as ladies of the world know how to act out their anecdotes, I took the liberty of saying that it was the Canticle of canticles in action.

"If her husband doesn't come," said Justine to the cook, "what will become of us? She has already thrown her chemise in my face."

At last, Caroline heard the crack of a postilion's whip, the well-known rumbling of a traveling carriage, the racket made by the hoofs of post-horses, and the jingling of their bells! Oh, she could doubt no longer, the bells made her burst forth, as thus:

"The door! Open the door! 'Tis he, my husband! Will you never go to the door!" And the pious woman stamped her foot and broke the bell-rope.

"Why, madame," said Justine, with the vivacity of a servant doing her duty, "it's some people going away."

"Upon my word," replied Caroline, half ashamed, to herself, "I will never let Adolphe go traveling again without me."

A Marseilles poet—it is not known whether it was Mery or Barthelemy —acknowledged that if his best fried did not arrive punctually at the dinner hour, he waited patiently five minutes: at the tenth minute, he felt a desire to throw the napkin in his face: at the twelfth he hoped some great calamity would befall him: at the fifteenth, he would not be able to restrain himself from stabbing him several times with a dirk.

All women, when expecting somebody, are Marseilles poets, if, indeed, we may compare the vulgar throes of hunger to the sublime Canticle of canticles of a pious wife, who is hoping for the joys of a husband's first glance after a three months' absence. Let all those who love and who have met again after an absence ten thousand times accursed, be good enough to recall their first glance: it says so many things that the lovers, if in the presence of a third party, are fain to lower their eyes! This poem, in which every man is as great as Homer, in which he seems a god to the woman who loves him, is, for a pious, thin and pimpled lady, all the more immense, from the fact that she has not, like Madame de Fischtaminel, the resource of having several copies of it. In her case, her husband is all she's got!

So you will not be surprised to learn that Caroline missed every mass and had no breakfast. This hunger and thirst for Adolphe gave her a violent cramp in the stomach. She did not think of religion once during the hours of mass, nor during those of vespers. She was not comfortable when she sat, and she was very uncomfortable when she stood: Justine advised her to go to bed. Caroline, quite overcome, retired at about half past five in the evening, after having taken a light soup: but she ordered a dainty supper at ten.

"I shall doubtless sup with my husband," she said.

This speech was the conclusion of dreadful catalinics, internally fulminated. She had reached the Marseilles poet's several stabs with a dirk. So she spoke in a tone that was really terrible. At three in the morning Caroline was in a profound sleep: Adolphe arrived without her hearing either carriage, or horse, or bell, or opening door!

Adolphe, who would not permit her to be disturbed, went to bed in the spare room. When Caroline heard of his return in the morning, two tears issued from her eyes; she rushed to the spare room without the slightest preparatory toilet; a hideous attendant, posted on the threshold, informed her that her husband, having traveled two hundred leagues and been two nights without sleep, requested that he might not be awakened: he was exceedingly tired.

Caroline—pious woman that she was—opened the door violently without being able to wake the only husband that heaven had given her, and then hastened to church to listen to a thanksgiving mass.

As she was visibly snappish for three whole days, Justine remarked, in reply to an unjust reproach, and with a chambermaid's finesse:

"Why, madame, your husband's got back!"

"He has only got back to Paris," returned the pious Caroline.

USELESS CARE.

Put yourself in the place of a poor woman of doubtful beauty, who owes her husband to the weight of her dowry, who gives herself infinite pains, and spends a great deal of money to appear to advantage and follow the fashions, who does her best to keep house sumptuously and yet economically—a house, too, not easy to manage—who, from morality and dire necessity, perhaps, loves no one but her husband, who has no other study but the happiness of this precious husband, who, to express all in one word, joins the maternal sentiment *to the sentiment of her duties*. This underlined circumlocution is the paraphrase of the word love in the language of prudes.

Have you put yourself in her place? Well, this too-much-loved husband by chance remarked at his friend Monsieur de Fischtaminel's, that he was very fond of mushrooms *a l'Italienne*.

If you have paid some attention to the female nature, in its good, great, and grand manifestations, you know that for a loving wife there is no greater pleasure than that of seeing the beloved one absorbing his favorite viands. This springs from the fundamental idea upon which the affection of women is based: that of being the source of all his pleasures, big and little. Love animates everything in life, and conjugal love has a peculiar right to descend to the most trivial details.

Caroline spends two or three days in inquiries before she learns how the Italians dress mushrooms. She discovers a Corsican abbe who tells her that at Biffi's, in the rue de Richelieu, she will not only learn how the Italians dress mushrooms, but that she will be able to obtain some Milanese mushrooms. Our pious Caroline thanks the Abbe Serpolini, and resolves to send him a breviary in acknowledgment.

Caroline's cook goes to Biffi's, comes back from Biffi's, and exhibits to the countess a quantity of mushrooms as big as the coachman's ears.

"Very good," she says, "did he explain to you how to cook them?"

"Oh, for us cooks, them's a mere nothing," replies the cook.

As a general rule, cooks know everything, in the cooking way, except how a cook may feather his nest.

At evening, during the second course, all Caroline's fibres quiver with pleasure at observing the servant bringing to the table a certain suggestive dish. She has positively waited for this dinner as she had waited for her husband.

But between waiting with certainty and expecting a positive pleasure, there is, to the souls of the elect—and everybody will include a woman who adores her husband among the elect—there is, between these two worlds of expectation, the difference that exists between a fine night and a fine day.

The dish is presented to the beloved Adolphe, he carelessly plunges his spoon in and helps himself, without perceiving Caroline's extreme emotion, to several of those soft, fat, round things, that travelers who visit Milan do not for a long time recognize; they take them for some kind of shell-fish.

"Well, Adolphe?"

"Well, dear."

"Don't you recognize them?"

"Recognize what?"

"Your mushrooms *a l'Italienne*?"

"These mushrooms! I thought they were—well, yes, they *are* mushrooms!"

"Yes, and *a l'Italienne*, too."

"Pooh, they are old preserved mushrooms, *a la milanaise*. I abominate them!"

"What kind is it you like, then?"

"*Fungi trifolati.*"

Let us observe—to the disgrace of an epoch which numbers and labels everything, which puts the whole creation in bottles, which is at this moment classifying one hundred and fifty thousand species of insects, giving them all the termination *us*, so that a *Silbermanus* is the same individual in all countries for the learned men who dissect a butterfly's legs with pincers—that we still want a nomenclature for the chemistry of the kitchen, to enable all the cooks in the world to produce precisely similar dishes. It would be diplomatically agreed that French should be the language of the kitchen, as Latin has been adopted by the scientific for botany and entomology, unless it were desired to imitate them in that, too, and thus really have kitchen Latin.

"My dear," resumes Adolphe, on seeing the clouded and lengthened face of his chaste Caroline, "in France the dish in question is called Mushrooms *a l'Italienne, a la provencale, a la bordelaise*. The mushrooms are minced, fried in oil with a few ingredients whose names I have forgotten. You add a taste of garlic, I believe—"

Talk about calamities, of petty troubles! This, do you see, is, to a woman's heart, what the pain of an extracted tooth is to a child of eight. *Ab uno disce omnes*: which means, "There's one of them: find the rest in your memory." For we have taken this culinary description as a prototype of the vexations which afflict loving but indifferently loved women.

SMOKE WITHOUT FIRE.

A woman full of faith in the man she loves is a romancer's fancy. This feminine personage no more exists than does a rich dowry. A woman's confidence glows perhaps for a few moments, at the dawn of love, and disappears in a trice like a shooting star.

With women who are neither Dutch, nor English, nor Belgian, nor from any marshy country, love is a pretext for suffering, an employment for the superabundant powers of their imaginations and their nerves.

Thus the second idea that takes possession of a happy woman, one who is really loved, is the fear of losing her happiness, for we must do her the justice to say that her first idea is to enjoy it. All who possess treasures are in dread of thieves, but they do not, like women, lend wings and feet to their golden stores.

The little blue flower of perfect felicity is not so common, that the heaven-blessed man who possesses it, should be simpleton enough to abandon it.

Axiom.—A woman is never deserted without a reason.

This axiom is written in the heart of hearts of every woman. Hence the rage of a woman deserted.

Let us not infringe upon the petty troubles of love: we live in a calculating epoch when women are seldom abandoned, do what they may: for, of all wives or women, nowadays, the legitimate is the least expensive. Now, every woman who is loved, has gone through the petty annoyance of suspicion. This suspicion, whether just or unjust, engenders a multitude of domestic troubles, and here is the biggest of all.

Caroline is one day led to notice that her cherished Adolphe leaves her rather too often upon a matter of business, that eternal Chaumontel's affair, which never comes to an end.

Axiom.—Every household has its Chaumontel's affair. (See TROUBLE WITHIN TROUBLE.)

In the first place, a woman no more believes in matters of business than publishers and managers do in the illness of actresses and authors. The moment a beloved creature absents himself, though she has rendered him even too happy, every woman straightway imagines that he has hurried away to some easy conquest. In this respect, women endow men with superhuman faculties. Fear magnifies everything, it dilates the eyes and the heart: it makes a woman mad.

"Where is my husband going? What is my husband doing? Why has he left me? Why did he not take me with him?"

These four questions are the four cardinal points of the compass of suspicion, and govern the stormy sea of soliloquies. From these frightful tempests which ravage a woman's heart springs an ignoble, unworthy resolution, one which every woman, the duchess as well as the shopkeeper's wife, the baroness as well as the stockbroker's lady, the angel as well as the shrew, the indifferent as well as the passionate, at once puts into execution. They imitate the government, every one of them; they resort to espionage. What the State has invented in the public interest, they consider legal, legitimate and permissible, in the interest of their love. This fatal woman's curiosity reduces them to the necessity of having agents, and the agent of any woman who, in this situation, has not lost her self-respect, — a situation in which her jealousy will not permit her to respect anything: neither your little boxes, nor your clothes, nor the drawers of your treasury, of your desk, of your table, of your bureau, nor your pocketbook with private compartments, nor your papers, nor your traveling dressing-case, nor your toilet articles (a woman discovers in this way that her husband dyed his moustache when he was a bachelor), nor your india-rubber girdles — her agent, I say, the only one in whom a woman trusts, is her maid, for her maid understands her, excuses her, and approves her.

In the paroxysm of excited curiosity, passion and jealousy, a woman makes no calculations, takes no observations. She simply wishes to know the whole truth.

And Justine is delighted: she sees her mistress compromising herself with her, and she espouses her passion, her dread, her fears and her suspicions, with terrible friendship. Justine and Caroline hold councils and have secret interviews. All espionage involves such relationships. In this pass, a maid becomes the arbitress of the fate of the married couple. Example: Lord Byron.

"Madame," Justine one day observes, "monsieur really *does* go out to see a woman."

Caroline turns pale.

"But don't be alarmed, madame, it's an old woman."

"Ah, Justine, to some men no women are old: men are inexplicable."

"But, madame, it isn't a lady, it's a woman, quite a common woman."

"Ah, Justine, Lord Byron loved a fish-wife at Venice, Madame de Fischtaminel told me so."

And Caroline bursts into tears.

"I've been pumping Benoit."

"What is Benoit's opinion?"

"Benoit thinks that the woman is a go-between, for monsieur keeps his secret from everybody, even from Benoit."

For a week Caroline lives the life of the damned; all her savings go to pay spies and to purchase reports.

Finally, Justine goes to see the woman, whose name is Madame Mahuchet; she bribes her and learns at last that her master has preserved a witness of his youthful follies, a nice little boy that looks very much like him, and that this woman is his nurse, the second-hand mother who has charge of little Frederick, who pays his quarterly school-bills, and through whose hands pass the twelve hundred or two thousand francs which Adolphe is supposed annually to lose at cards.

"What of the mother?" exclaims Caroline.

To end the matter, Justine, Caroline's good genius, proves to her that M'lle Suzanne Beauminet, formerly a grisette and somewhat later Madame Sainte-Suzanne, died at the hospital, or else that she has made her fortune, or else, again, that her place in society is so low there is no danger of madame's ever meeting her.

Caroline breathes again: the dirk has been drawn from her heart, she is quite happy; but she had no children but daughters, and would like a boy. This little drama of unjust suspicions, this comedy of the conjectures to which Mother Mahuchet gives rise, these phases of a causeless jealousy, are laid down here as the type of a situation, the varieties of which are as innumerable as characters, grades and sorts.

This source of petty troubles is pointed out here, in order that women seated upon the river's bank may contemplate in it the course of their own married life, following its ascent or descent, recalling their own adventures to mind, their untold disasters, the foibles which caused their errors, and the peculiar fatalities to which were due an instant of frenzy, a moment of unnecessary despair, or sufferings which they might have spared themselves, happy in their self-delusions.

This vexation has a corollary in the following, one which is much more serious and often without remedy, especially when its root lies among vices of another kind, and which do not concern us, for, in this work, women are invariably esteemed honest—until the end.

THE DOMESTIC TYRANT.

"My dear Caroline," says Adolphe one day to his wife, "are you satisfied with Justine?"

"Yes, dear, quite so."

"Don't you think she speaks to you rather impertinently?"

"Do you suppose I would notice a maid? But it seems *you* notice her!"

"What do you say?" asks Adolphe in an indignant way that is always delightful to women.

Justine is a genuine maid for an actress, a woman of thirty stamped by the small-pox with innumerable dimples, in which the loves are far from sporting: she is as brown as opium, has a good deal of leg and not much body, gummy eyes, and a tournure to match. She would like to have Benoit marry her, but at this unexpected suggestion, Benoit asked for his discharge. Such is the portrait of the domestic tyrant enthroned by Caroline's jealousy.

Justine takes her coffee in the morning, in bed, and manages to have it as good as, not to say better than, that of her mistress. Justine sometimes goes out without asking leave, dressed like the wife of a second-class banker. She sports a pink hat, one of her mistress' old gowns made over, an elegant shawl, shoes of bronze kid, and jewelry of doubtful character.

Justine is sometimes in a bad humor, and makes her mistress feel that she too is a woman like herself, though she is not married. She has her whims, her fits of melancholy, her caprices. She even dares to have her nerves! She replies curtly, she makes herself insupportable to the other servants, and, to conclude, her wages have been considerably increased.

"My dear, this girl is getting more intolerable every day," says Adolphe one morning to his wife, on noticing Justine listening at the key-hole, "and if you don't send her away, I will!"

Caroline, greatly alarmed, is obliged to give Justine a talking to, while her husband is out.

"Justine, you take advantage of my kindness to you: you have high wages, here, you have perquisites, presents: try to keep your place, for my husband wants to send you away."

The maid humbles herself to the earth, she sheds tears: she is so attached to madame! Ah! she would rush into the fire for her: she would let herself be chopped into mince-meat: she is ready for anything.

"If you had anything to conceal, madame, I would take it on myself and say it was me!"

"Very well, Justine, very good, my girl," says Caroline, terrified: "but that's not the point: just try to keep in your place."

"Ah, ha!" says Justine to herself, "monsieur wants to send me away, does he? Wait and see the deuce of a life I'll lead you, you old curmudgeon!"

A week after, Justine, who is dressing her mistress' hair, looks in the glass to make sure that Caroline can see all the grimaces of her countenance: and Caroline very soon inquires, "Why, what's the matter, Justine?"

"I would tell you, readily, madame, but then, madame, you are so weak with monsieur!"

"Come, go on, what is it?"

"I know now, madame, why master wanted to show me the door: he has confidence in nobody but Benoit, and Benoit is playing the mum with me."

"Well, what does that prove? Has anything been discovered?"

"I'm sure that between the two they are plotting something against you madame," returns the maid with authority.

Caroline, whom Justine watches in the glass, turns pale: all the tortures of the previous petty trouble return, and Justine sees that she has become as indispensable to her mistress as spies are to the government when a conspiracy is discovered. Still, Caroline's friends do not understand why she keeps so disagreeable a servant girl, one who wears a hat, whose manners are impertinent, and who gives herself the airs of a lady.

This stupid domination is talked of at Madame Deschars', at Madame de Fischtaminel's, and the company consider it funny. A few ladies think they can see certain monstrous reasons for it, reasons which compromise Caroline's honor.

Axiom.—In society, people can put cloaks on every kind of truth, even the prettiest.

In short the *aria della calumnia* is executed precisely as if Bartholo were singing it.

It is averred that Caroline cannot discharge her maid.

Society devotes itself desperately to discovering the secret of this enigma. Madame de Fischtaminel makes fun of Adolphe who goes home in a rage, has a scene with Caroline and discharges Justine.

This produces such an effect upon Justine, that she falls sick, and takes to her bed. Caroline observes to her husband, that it would be awkward to turn a girl in Justine's condition into the street, a girl who is so much attached to them, too, and who has been with them sine their marriage.

"Let her go then as soon as she is well!" says Adolphe.

Caroline, reassured in regard to Adolphe, and indecently swindled by Justine, at last comes to desire to get rid of her: she applies a violent remedy to the disease, and makes up her mind to go under the Caudine Forks of another petty trouble, as follows:

THE AVOWAL.

One morning, Adolphe is petted in a very unusual manner. The too happy husband wonders what may be the cause of this development of affection, and he hears Caroline, in her most winning tones, utter the word: "Adolphe?"

"Well?" he replies, in alarm at the internal agitation betrayed by Caroline's voice.

"Promise not to be angry."

"Well."

"Not to be vexed with me."

"Never. Go on."

"To forgive me and never say anything about it."

"But tell me what it is!"

"Besides, you are the one that's in the wrong—"

"Speak, or I'll go away."

"There's no one but you that can get me out of the scrape—and it was you that got me into it."

"Come, come."

"It's about—"

"About—"

"About Justine!"

"Don't speak of her, she's discharged. I won't see her again, her style of conduct exposes your reputation—"

"What can people say—what have they said?"

The scene changes, the result of which is a secondary explanation which makes Caroline blush, as she sees the bearing of the suppositions of her best friends.

"Well, now, Adolphe, it's to you I owe all this. Why didn't you tell me about Frederick?"

"Frederick the Great? The King of Prussia?"

"What creatures men are! Hypocrite, do you want to make me believe that you have forgotten your son so soon, M'lle Suzanne Beauminet's son?"

"Then you know—?"

"The whole thing! And old other Mahuchet, and your absences from home to give him a good dinner on holidays."

"How like moles you pious women can be if you try!" exclaims Adolphe, in his terror.

"It was Justine that found it out."

"Ah! Now I understand the reason of her insolence."

"Oh, your Caroline has been very wretched, dear, and this spying system, which was produced by my love for you, for I do love you, and madly too,—if you deceived me, I would fly to the extremity of creation,—well, as I was going to say, this unfounded jealousy has put me in Justine's power, so, my precious, get me out of it the best way you can!"

"Let this teach you, my angel, never to make use of your servants, if you want them to be of use to you. It is the lowest of tyrannies, this being at the mercy of one's people."

Adolphe takes advantage of this circumstance to alarm Caroline, he thinks of future Chaumontel's affairs, and would be glad to have no more espionage.

Justine is sent for, Adolphe peremptorily dismisses her without waiting to hear her explanation. Caroline imagines her vexations at an end. She gets another maid.

Justine, whose twelve or fifteen thousand francs have attracted the notice of a water carrier, becomes Madame Chavagnac, and goes into the apple business. Ten months after, in Adolphe's absence, Caroline receives a letter written upon school-boy paper, in strides which would require orthopedic treatment for three months, and thus conceived:

"Madam!

"Yu ar shaimphoolly diseeved bi yure huzban fur mame Deux fischtaminelle, hee goze their evry eavning, yu ar az blynde az a Batt. Your gott wott yu dizzurv, and I am Glad ovit, and I have thee honur ov prezenting yu the assurunz ov Mi moaste ds Sting guischt respecks."

Caroline starts like a lion who has been stung by a bumble-bee; she places herself once more, and of her own accord, upon the griddle of suspicion, and begins her struggle with the unknown all over again.

When she has discovered the injustice of her suspicions, there comes another letter with an offer to furnish her with details relative to a Chaumontel's affair which Justine has unearthed.

The petty trouble of avowals, ladies, is often more serious than this, as you perhaps have occasion to remember.

HUMILIATIONS.

To the glory of women, let it be said, they care for their husbands even when their husbands care no more for them, not only because there are more ties, social-ly speaking, between a married woman and a man, than between the man and the wife; but also because woman has more delicacy and honor than man, the chief conjugal question apart, as a matter of course.

Axiom.—In a husband, there is only a man; in a married woman, there is a man, a father, a mother and a woman.

A married woman has sensibility enough for four, or for five even, if you look closely.

Now, it is not improper to observe in this place, that, in a woman's eyes, love is a general absolution: the man who is a good lover may commit crimes, if he will, he is always as pure as snow in the eyes of her who loves him, if he truly loves her. As to a married woman, loved or not, she feels so deeply that the honor and consideration of her husband are the fortune of her children, that she acts like the woman in love,—so active is the sense of community of interest.

This profound sentiment engenders, for certain Carolines, petty troubles which, unfortunately for this book, have their dismal side.

Adolphe is compromised. We will not enumerate all the methods of compro-mising oneself, for we might become personal. Let us take, as an example, the so-cial error which our epoch excuses, permits, understands and commits the most of any—the case of an honest robbery, of skillfully concealed corruption in office, or of some misrepresentation that becomes excusable when it has succeeded, as, for instance, having an understanding with parties in power, for the sale of property at the highest possible price to a city, or a country.

Thus, in a bankruptcy, Adolphe, in order to protect himself (this means to recover his claims), has become mixed up in certain unlawful doings which may bring a man to the necessity of testifying before the Court of Assizes. In fact, it is not known that the daring creditor will not be considered a party.

Take notice that in all cases of bankruptcy, protecting oneself is regarded as the most sacred of duties, even by the most respectable houses: the thing is to keep the bad side of the protection out of sight, as they do in prudish England.

Adolphe does not know what to do, as his counsel has told him not to appear in the matter: so he has recourse to Caroline. He gives her a lesson, he coaches her, he teaches her the Code, he examines her dress, he equips her as a brig sent on a voyage, and despatches her to the office of some judge, or some syndic. The judge is apparently a man of severe morality, but in reality a libertine: he retains his serious expression on seeing a pretty woman enter, and makes sundry very uncomplimentary remarks about Adolphe.

"I pity you, madame, you belong to a man who may involve you in numerous unpleasant affairs: a few more matters like this, and he will be quite disgraced. Have you any children? Excuse my asking; you are so young, it is perfectly natural." And the judge comes as near to Caroline as possible.

"Yes, sir."

"Ah, great heavens! what a prospect is yours! My first thought was for the woman, but now I pity you doubly, I think of the mother. Ah, how you must have suffered in coming here! Poor, poor woman!"

"Ah, sir, you take an interest in me, do you not?"

"Alas, what can I do?" says the judge, darting a glance sidewise at Caroline. "What you ask of me is a dereliction of duty, and I am a magistrate before I am a man."

"Oh, sir, only be a man—"

"Are you aware of the full bearing of that request, fair creature?" At this point the magistrate tremblingly takes Caroline's hand.

Caroline, who remembers that the honor of her husband and children is at stake, says to herself that this is not the time to play the prude. She abandons her hand, making just resistance enough for the old man (happily he is an old man) to consider it a favor.

"Come, come, my beauty," resumes the judge, "I should be loath to cause so lovely a woman to shed tears; we'll see about it. You shall come to-morrow evening and tell me the whole affair. We must look at the papers, we will examine them together—"

"Sir—"

"It's indispensable."

"But, sir—"

"Don't be alarmed, my dear, a judge is likely to know how to grant what is due to justice and—" he puts on a shrewd look here—"to beauty."

"But, sir—"

"Be quite at your ease," he adds, holding her hand closely in his, "and we'll try to reduce this great crime down to a peccadillo." And he goes to the door with Caroline, who is frightened to death at an appointment thus proposed.

The syndic is a lively young man, and he receives Madame Adolphe with a smile. He smiles at everything, and he smiles as he takes her round the waist with an agility which leaves Caroline no time to resist, especially as she says to herself, "Adolphe particularly recommended me not to vex the syndic."

Nevertheless Caroline escapes, in the interest of the syndic himself, and again pronounces the "Sir!" which she had said three times to the judge.

"Don't be angry with me, you are irresistible, you are an angel, and your husband is a monster: for what does he mean by sending a siren to a young man whom he knows to be inflammable!"

"Sir, my husband could not come himself; he is in bed, very sick, and you threatened him so terribly that the urgency of the matter—"

"Hasn't he got a lawyer, an attorney?"

Caroline is terrified by this remark which reveals Adolphe's profound rascality.

"He supposed, sir, that you would have pity upon the mother of a family, upon her children—"

"Ta, ta, ta," returns the syndic. "You have come to influence my independence, my conscience, you want me to give the creditors up to you: well, I'll do more, I give you up my heart, my fortune! Your husband wants to save *his* honor, *my* honor is at your disposal!"

"Sir," cries Caroline, as she tries to raise the syndic who has thrown himself at her feet. "You alarm me!"

She plays the terrified female and thus reaches the door, getting out of a delicate situation as women know how to do it, that is, without compromising anything or anybody.

"I will come again," she says smiling, "when you behave better."

"You leave me thus! Take care! Your husband may yet find himself seated at the bar of the Court of Assizes: he is accessory to a fraudulent bankruptcy, and we know several things about him that are not by any means honorable. It is not his first departure from rectitude; he has done a good many dirty things, he has been mixed up in disgraceful intrigues, and you are singularly careful of the honor of a man who cares as little for his own honor as he does for yours."

Caroline, alarmed by these words, lets go the door, shuts it and comes back.

"What do you mean, sir?" she exclaims, furious at this outrageous broadside.

"Why, this affair—"

"Chaumontel's affair?"

"No, his speculations in houses that he had built by people that were insolvent."

Caroline remembers the enterprise undertaken by Adolphe to double his income: (See *The Jesuitism of Women*) she trembles. Her curiosity is in the syndic's favor.

"Sit down here. There, at this distance, I will behave well, but I can look at you."

And he narrates, at length, the conception due to du Tillet the banker, interrupting himself to say: "Oh, what a pretty, cunning, little foot; no one but you could have such a foot as that—*Du Tillet, therefore, compromised*. What an ear, too! You have been doubtless told that you had a delicious ear—*And du Tillet was right, for judgment had already been given*—I love small ears, but let me have a model of yours, and I will do anything you like—*du Tillet profited by this to throw the whole loss on your idiotic husband*: oh, what a charming silk, you are divinely dressed!"

"Where were we, sir?"

"How can I remember while admiring your Raphaelistic head?"

At the twenty-seventh compliment, Caroline considers the syndic a man of wit: she makes him a polite speech, and goes away without learning much more of the enterprise which, not long before had swallowed up three hundred thousand francs.

There are many huge variations of this petty trouble.

EXAMPLE. Adolphe is brave and susceptible: he is walking on the Champs Elysees, where there is a crowd of people; in this crowd are several ill-mannered young men who indulge in jokes of doubtful propriety: Caroline puts up with them and pretends not to hear them, in order to keep her husband out of a duel.

ANOTHER EXAMPLE. A child belonging to the genus Terrible, exclaims in the presence of everybody:

"Mamma, would you let Justine hit me?"

"Certainly not."

"Why do you ask, my little man?" inquires Madame Foullepointe.

"Because she just gave father a big slap, and he's ever so much stronger than me."

Madame Foullepointe laughs, and Adolphe, who intended to pay court to her, is cruelly joked by her, after having had a first last quarrel with Caroline.

THE LAST QUARREL.

In every household, husbands and wives must one day hear the striking of a fatal hour. It is a knell, the death and end of jealousy, a great, noble and charming passion, the only true symptom of love, if it is not even its double. When a woman is no longer jealous of her husband, all is over, she loves him no more. So, conjugal love expires in the last quarrel that a woman gives herself the trouble to raise.

Axiom.—When a woman ceases to quarrel with her husband, the Minotaur has seated himself in a corner arm-chair, tapping his boots with his cane.

Every woman must remember her last quarrel, that supreme petty trouble which often explodes about nothing, but more often still on some occasion of a brutal fact or of a decisive proof. This cruel farewell to faith, to the childishness of love, to virtue even, is in a degree as capricious as life itself. Like life it varies in every house.

Here, the author ought perhaps to search out all the varieties of quarrels, if he desires to be precise.

Thus, Caroline may have discovered that the judicial robe of the syndic in Chaumontel's affair, hides a robe of infinitely softer stuff, of an agreeable, silky color: that Chaumontel's hair, in short, is fair, and that his eyes are blue.

Or else Caroline, who arose before Adolphe, may have seen his greatcoat thrown wrong side out across a chair; the edge of a little perfumed paper, just peeping out of the side-pocket, may have attracted her by its whiteness, like a ray of the sun entering a dark room through a crack in the window: or else, while taking Adolphe in her arms and feeling his pocket, she may have caused the note to crackle: or else she may have been informed of the state of things by a foreign odor that she has long noticed upon him, and may have read these lines:

"Ungraitfull wun, wot du yu supoz I no About Hipolite. Kum, and yu shal se whether I Love yu."

Or this:

"Yesterday, love, you made me wait for you: what will it be to-morrow?"

Or this:

"The women who love you, my dear sir, are very unhappy in hating you so, when you are not with them: take care, for the hatred which exists during your absence, may possibly encroach upon the hours you spend in their company."

Or this:

"You traitorous Chodoreille, what were you doing yesterday on the boulevard with a woman hanging on your arm? If it was your wife, accept my compliments of condolence upon her absent charms: she has doubtless deposited them at the pawnbroker's, and the ticket to redeem them with is lost."

Four notes emanating from the grisette, the lady, the pretentious woman in middle life, and the actress, among whom Adolphe has chosen his *belle* (according to the Fischtaminellian vocabulary).

Or else Caroline, taken veiled by Ferdinand to Ranelagh Garden, sees with her own eyes Adolphe abandoning himself furiously to the polka, holding one of the ladies of honor to Queen Pomare in his arms; or else, again, Adolphe has for the seventh time, made a mistake in the name, and called his wife Juliette, Charlotte or Lisa: or, a grocer or restaurateur sends to the house, during Adolphe's absence, certain damning bills which fall into Caroline's hands.

PAPERS RELATING TO CHAUMONTEL'S AFFAIR.

(Private Tables Served.)

		Dr
M. Adolphe to Perrault, To 1 Pate de Foie Gras delivered at Madame		
Schontz's, the 6th of January,		fr. 22.50
Six bottle of assorted wines,		70.00
To one special breakfast delivered at Congress Hotel, the 11th of February, at No. 21 — —		
Stipulated price,		100.00
		———
	Total, Francs,	192.50

Caroline examines the dates and remembers them as appointments made for business connected with Chaumontel's affair. Adolphe had designated the sixth of January as the day fixed for a meeting at which the creditors in Chaumontel's affair were to receive the sums due them. On the eleventh of February he had an appointment with the notary, in order to sign a receipt relative to Chaumontel's affair.

Or else—but an attempt to mention all the chances of discovery would be the undertaking of a madman.

Every woman will remember to herself how the bandage with which her eyes were bound fell off: how, after many doubts, and agonies of heart, she made up her mind to have a final quarrel for the simple purpose of finishing the romance, putting the seal to the book, stipulating for her independence, or beginning life over again.

Some women are fortunate enough to have anticipated their husbands, and they then have the quarrel as a sort of justification.

Nervous women give way to a burst of passion and commit acts of violence.

Women of mild temper assume a decided tone which appalls the most intrepid husbands. Those who have no vengeance ready shed a great many tears.

Those who love you forgive you. Ah, they conceive so readily, like the woman called "Ma berline," that their Adolphe must be loved by the women of France, that they are rejoiced to possess, legally, a man about whom everybody goes crazy.

Certain women with lips tight shut like a vise, with a muddy complexion and thin arms, treat themselves to the malicious pleasure of promenading their Adolphe through the quagmire of falsehood and contradiction: they question him (see *Troubles within Troubles*), like a magistrate examining a criminal, reserving the spiteful enjoyment of crushing his denials by positive proof at a decisive moment. Generally, in this supreme scene of conjugal life, the fair sex is the executioner, while, in the contrary case, man is the assassin.

This is the way of it: This last quarrel (you shall know why the author has called it the *last*), is always terminated by a solemn, sacred promise, made by scrupulous, noble, or simply intelligent women (that is to say, by all women), and which we give here in its grandest form.

"Enough, Adolphe! We love each other no more; you have deceived me, and I shall never forget it. I may forgive it, but I can never forget it."

Women represent themselves as implacable only to render their forgiveness charming: they have anticipated God.

"We have now to live in common like two friends," continues Caroline. "Well, let us live like two comrades, two brothers, I do not wish to make your life intolerable, and I never again will speak to you of what has happened—"

Adolphe gives Caroline his hand: she takes it, and shakes it in the English style. Adolphe thanks Caroline, and catches a glimpse of bliss: he has converted his wife into a sister, and hopes to be a bachelor again.

The next day Caroline indulges in a very witty allusion (Adolphe cannot help laughing at it) to Chaumontel's affair. In society she makes general remarks which, to Adolphe, are very particular remarks, about their last quarrel.

At the end of a fortnight a day never passes without Caroline's recalling their last quarrel by saying: "It was the day when I found Chaumontel's bill in your pocket:" or "it happened since our last quarrel:" or, "it was the day when, for the first time, I had a clear idea of life," etc. She assassinates Adolphe, she martyrizes him! In society she gives utterance to terrible things.

"We are happy, my dear [to a lady], when we love each other no longer: it's then that we learn how to make ourselves beloved," and she looks at Ferdinand.

In short, the last quarrel never comes to an end, and from this fact flows the following axiom:

Axiom.—Putting yourself in the wrong with your lawful wife, is solving the problem of Perpetual Motion.

A SIGNAL FAILURE.

Women, and especially married women, stick ideas into their brain-pan precisely as they stick pins into a pincushion, and the devil himself, —do you mind?— could not get them out: they reserve to themselves the exclusive right of sticking them in, pulling them out, and sticking them in again.

Caroline is riding home one evening from Madame Foullepointe's in a violent state of jealousy and ambition.

Madame Foullepointe, the lioness—but this word requires an explanation. It is a fashionable neologism, and gives expression to certain rather meagre ideas relative to our present society: you must use it, if you want to describe a woman who is all the rage. This lioness rides on horseback every day, and Caroline has taken it into her head to learn to ride also.

Observe that in this conjugal phase, Adolphe and Caroline are in the season which we have denominated *A Household Revolution*, and that they have had two or three *Last Quarrels*.

"Adolphe," she says, "do you want to do me a favor?"

"Of course."

"Won't you refuse?"

"If your request is reasonable, I am willing—"

"Ah, already—that's a true husband's word—if—"

"Come, what is it?"

"I want to learn to ride on horseback."

"Now, is it a possible thing, Caroline?"

Caroline looks out of the window, and tries to wipe away a dry tear.

"Listen," resumes Adolphe; "I cannot let you go alone to the riding-school; and I cannot go with you while business gives me the annoyance it does now. What's the matter? I think I have given you unanswerable reasons."

Adolphe foresees the hiring of a stable, the purchase of a pony, the introduction of a groom and of a servant's horse into the establishment—in short, all the nuisance of female lionization.

When a man gives a woman reasons instead of giving her what she wants — well, few men have ventured to descend into that small abyss called the heart, to test the power of the tempest that suddenly bursts forth there.

"Reasons! If you want reasons, here they are!" exclaims Caroline. "I am your wife: you don't seem to care to please me any more. And as to the expenses, you greatly overrate them, my dear."

Women have as many inflections of voice to pronounce these words, *My dear*, as the Italians have to say *Amico*. I have counted twenty-nine which express only various degrees of hatred.

"Well, you'll see," resumes Caroline, "I shall be sick, and you will pay the apothecary and the doctor as much as the price of a horse. I shall be walled up here at home, and that's all you want. I asked the favor of you, though I was sure of a refusal: I only wanted to know how you would go to work to give it."

"But, Caroline—"

"Leave me alone at the riding-school!" she continues without listening. "Is that a reason? Can't I go with Madame de Fischtaminel? Madame de Fischtaminel is learning to ride on horseback, and I don't imagine that Monsieur de Fischtaminel goes with her."

"But, Caroline—"

"I am delighted with your solicitude. You think a great deal of me, really. Monsieur de Fischtaminel has more confidence in his wife, than you have in yours. He does not go with her, not he! Perhaps it's on account of this confidence that you don't want me at the school, where I might see your goings on with the fair Fischtaminel."

Adolphe tries to hide his vexation at this torrent of words, which begins when they are still half way from home, and has no sea to empty into. When Caroline is in her room, she goes on in the same way.

"You see that if reasons could restore my health or prevent me from desiring a kind of exercise pointed out by nature herself, I should not be in want of reasons, and that I know all the reasons that there are, and that I went over with the reasons before I spoke to you."

This, ladies, may with the more truth be called the prologue to the conjugal drama, from the fact that it is vigorously delivered, embellished with a commentary of gestures, ornamented with glances and all the other vignettes with which you usually illustrate such masterpieces.

Caroline, when she has once planted in Adolphe's heart the apprehension of a scene of constantly reiterated demands, feels her hatred for his control largely increase. Madame pouts, and she pouts so fiercely, that Adolphe is forced to notice it, on pain of very disagreeable consequences, for all is over, be sure of that, between two beings married by the mayor, or even at Gretna Green, when one of them no longer notices the sulkings of the other.

Axiom.—A sulk that has struck in is a deadly poison.

It was to prevent this suicide of love that our ingenious France invented boudoirs. Women could not well have Virgil's willows in the economy of our modern dwellings. On the downfall of oratories, these little cubbies become boudoirs.

This conjugal drama has three acts. The act of the prologue is already played. Then comes the act of false coquetry: one of those in which French women have the most success.

Adolphe is walking about the room, divesting himself of his apparel, and the man thus engaged, divests himself of his strength as well as of his clothing. To every man of forty, this axiom will appear profoundly just:

Axiom. — The ideas of a man who has taken his boots and his suspenders off, are no longer those of a man who is still sporting these two tyrants of the mind.

Take notice that this is only an axiom in wedded life. In morals, it is what we call a relative theorem.

Caroline watches, like a jockey on the race course, the moment when she can distance her adversary. She makes her preparations to be irresistibly fascinating to Adolphe.

Women possess a power of mimicking pudicity, a knowledge of secrets which might be those of a frightened dove, a particular register for singing, like Isabella, in the fourth act of *Robert le Diable: "Grace pour toi! Grace pour moi!"* which leave jockeys and horse trainers whole miles behind. As usual, the *Diable* succumbs. It is the eternal history, the grand Christian mystery of the bruised serpent, of the delivered woman becoming the great social force, as the Fourierists say. It is especially in this that the difference between the Oriental slave and the Occidental wife appears.

Upon the conjugal pillow, the second act ends by a number of onomatopes, all of them favorable to peace. Adolphe, precisely like children in the presence of a slice of bread and molasses, promises everything that Caroline wants.

THIRD ACT. As the curtain rises, the stage represents a chamber in a state of extreme disorder. Adolphe, in his dressing gown, tries to go out furtively and without waking Caroline, who is sleeping profoundly, and finally does go out.

Caroline, exceedingly happy, gets up, consults her mirror, and makes inquiries about breakfast. An hour afterward, when she is ready she learns that breakfast is served.

"Tell monsieur."

"Madame, he is in the little parlor."

"What a nice man he is," she says, going up to Adolphe, and talking the babyish, caressing language of the honey-moon.

"What for, pray?"

"Why, to let his little Liline ride the horsey."

OBSERVATION. During the honey-moon, some few married couples, — very young ones, — make use of languages, which, in ancient days, Aristotle classified and defined. (See his Pedagogy.) Thus they are perpetually using such terminations as *lala, nana, coachy-poachy*, just as mothers and nurses use them to babies. This is one of the secret reasons, discussed and recognized in big quartos by the

Germans, which determined the Cabires, the creators of the Greek mythology, to represent Love as a child. There are other reasons very well known to women, the principal of which is, that, in their opinion, love in men is always *small*.

"Where did you get that idea, my sweet? You must have dreamed it!"

"What!"

Caroline stands stark still: she opens wide her eyes which are already considerably widened by amazement. Being inwardly epileptic, she says not a word: she merely gazes at Adolphe. Under the satanic fires of their gaze, Adolphe turns half way round toward the dining-room; but he asks himself whether it would not be well to let Caroline take one lesson, and to tip the wink to the riding-master, to disgust her with equestrianism by the harshness of his style of instruction.

There is nothing so terrible as an actress who reckons upon a success, and who *fait four*.

In the language of the stage, to *faire four* is to play to a wretchedly thin house, or to obtain not the slightest applause. It is taking great pains for nothing, in short a *signal failure*.

This petty trouble—it is very petty—is reproduced in a thousand ways in married life, when the honey-moon is over, and when the wife has no personal fortune.

In spite of the author's repugnance to inserting anecdotes in an exclusively aphoristic work, the tissue of which will bear nothing but the most delicate and subtle observations,—from the nature of the subject at least,—it seems to him necessary to illustrate this page by an incident narrated by one of our first physicians. This repetition of the subject involves a rule of conduct very much in use with the doctors of Paris.

A certain husband was in our Adolphe's situation. His Caroline, having once made a signal failure, was determined to conquer, for Caroline often does conquer! (See *The Physiology of Marriage*, Meditation XXVI, Paragraph *Nerves*.) She had been lying about on the sofas for two months, getting up at noon, taking no part in the amusements of the city. She would not go to the theatre,—oh, the disgusting atmosphere!—the lights, above all, the lights! Then the bustle, coming out, going in, the music,—it might be fatal, it's so terribly exciting!

She would not go on excursions to the country, oh, certainly it was her desire to do so!—but she would like (desiderata) a carriage of her own, horses of her own—her husband would not give her an equipage. And as to going in hacks, in hired conveyances, the bare thought gave her a rising at the stomach!

She would not have any cooking—the smell of the meats produced a sudden nausea. She drank innumerable drugs that her maid never saw her take.

In short, she expended large amounts of time and money in attitudes, privations, effects, pearl-white to give her the pallor of a corpse, machinery, and the like, precisely as when the manager of a theatre spreads rumors about a piece gotten up in a style of Oriental magnificence, without regard to expense!

This couple had got so far as to believe that even a journey to the springs, to Ems, to Hombourg, to Carlsbad, would hardly cure the invalid: but madame would not budge, unless she could go in her own carriage. Always that carriage!

Adolphe held out, and would not yield.

Caroline, who was a woman of great sagacity, admitted that her husband was right.

"Adolphe is right," she said to her friends, "it is I who am unreasonable: he can not, he ought not, have a carriage yet: men know better than we do the situation of their business."

At times Adolphe was perfectly furious! Women have ways about them that demand the justice of Tophet itself. Finally, during the third month, he met one of his school friends, a lieutenant in the corps of physicians, modest as all young doctors are: he had had his epaulettes one day only, and could give the order to fire!

"For a young woman, a young doctor," said our Adolphe to himself.

And he proposed to the future Bianchon to visit his wife and tell him the truth about her condition.

"My dear, it is time that you should have a physician," said Adolphe that evening to his wife, "and here is the best for a pretty woman."

The novice makes a conscientious examination, questions madame, feels her pulse discreetly, inquires into the slightest symptoms, and, at the end, while conversing, allows a smile, an expression, which, if not ironical, are extremely incredulous, to play involuntarily upon his lips, and his lips are quite in sympathy with his eyes. He prescribes some insignificant remedy, and insists upon its importance, promising to call again to observe its effect. In the ante-chamber, thinking himself alone with his school-mate, he indulges in an inexpressible shrug of the shoulders.

"There's nothing the matter with your wife, my boy," he says: "she is trifling with both you and me."

"Well, I thought so."

"But if she continues the joke, she will make herself sick in earnest: I am too sincerely your friend to enter into such a speculation, for I am determined that there shall be an honest man beneath the physician, in me—"

"My wife wants a carriage."

As in the *Solo on the Hearse*, this Caroline listened at the door.

Even at the present day, the young doctor is obliged to clear his path of the calumnies which this charming woman is continually throwing into it: and for the sake of a quiet life, he has been obliged to confess his little error—a young man's error—and to mention his enemy by name, in order to close her lips.

THE CHESTNUTS IN THE FIRE.

No one can tell how many shades and gradations there are in misfortune, for everything depends upon the character of the individual, upon the force of the imagination, upon the strength of the nerves. If it is impossible to catch these so variable shades, we may at least point out the most striking colors, and the principal attendant incidents. The author has therefore reserved this petty trouble for the last, for it is the only one that is at once comic and disastrous.

The author flatters himself that he has mentioned the principal examples. Thus, women who have arrived safely at the haven, the happy age of forty, the period when they are delivered from scandal, calumny, suspicion, when their liberty begins: these women will certainly do him the justice to state that all the critical situations of a family are pointed out or represented in this book.

Caroline has her Chaumontel's affair. She has learned how to induce Adolphe to go out unexpectedly, and has an understanding with Madame de Fischtaminel.

In every household, within a given time, ladies like Madame de Fischtaminel become Caroline's main resource.

Caroline pets Madame de Fischtaminel with all the tenderness that the African army is now bestowing upon Abd-el-Kader: she is as solicitous in her behalf as a physician is anxious to avoid curing a rich hypochondriac. Between the two, Caroline and Madame de Fischtaminel invent occupations for dear Adolphe, when neither of them desire the presence of that demigod among their penates. Madame de Fischtaminel and Caroline, who have become, through the efforts of Madame Foullepointe, the best friends in the world, have even gone so far as to learn and employ that feminine free-masonry, the rites of which cannot be made familiar by any possible initiation.

If Caroline writes the following little note to Madame de Fischtaminel:

"Dearest Angel:

"You will probably see Adolphe to-morrow, but do not keep him too long, for I want to go to ride with him at five: but if you are desirous of taking him to ride yourself, do so and I will take him up. You ought to teach me your secret for entertaining used-up people as you do."

Madame de Fischtaminel says to herself: "Gracious! So I shall have that fellow on my hands to-morrow from twelve o'clock to five."

Axiom.—Men do not always know a woman's positive request when they see it; but another woman never mistakes it: she does the contrary.

Those sweet little beings called women, and especially Parisian women, are the prettiest jewels that social industry has invented. Those who do not adore them, those who do not feel a constant jubilation at seeing them laying their plots while braiding their hair, creating special idioms for themselves and constructing with their slender fingers machines strong enough to destroy the most powerful fortunes, must be wanting in a positive sense.

On one occasion Caroline takes the most minute precautions. She writes the day before to Madame Foullepointe to go to St. Maur with Adolphe, to look at a piece of property for sale there. Adolphe would go to breakfast with her. She aids Adolphe in dressing. She twits him with the care he bestows upon his toilet, and asks absurd questions about Madame Foullepointe.

"She's real nice, and I think she is quite tired of Charles: you'll inscribe her yet upon your catalogue, you old Don Juan: but you won't have any further need of Chaumontel's affair; I'm no longer jealous, you've got a passport. Do you like that better than being adored? Monster, observe how considerate I am."

So soon as her husband has gone, Caroline, who had not omitted, the previous evening, to write to Ferdinand to come to breakfast with her, equips herself in a costume which, in that charming eighteenth century so calumniated by republicans, humanitarians and idiots, women of quality called their fighting-dress.

Caroline has taken care of everything. Love is the first house servant in the world, so the table is set with positively diabolic coquetry. There is the white damask cloth, the little blue service, the silver gilt urn, the chiseled milk pitcher, and flowers all round!

If it is winter, she has got some grapes, and has rummaged the cellar for the very best old wine. The rolls are from the most famous baker's. The succulent dishes, the *pate de foie gras*, the whole of this elegant entertainment, would have made the author of the Glutton's Almanac neigh with impatience: it would make a note-shaver smile, and tell a professor of the old University what the matter in hand is.

Everything is prepared. Caroline has been ready since the night before: she contemplates her work. Justine sighs and arranges the furniture. Caroline picks off the yellow leaves of the plants in the windows. A woman, in these cases, disguises what we may call the prancings of the heart, by those meaningless occupations in which the fingers have all the grip of pincers, when the pink nails burn, and when this unspoken exclamation rasps the throat: "He hasn't come yet!"

What a blow is this announcement by Justine: "Madame, here's a letter!"

A letter in place of Ferdinand! How does she ever open it? What ages of life slip by as she unfolds it! Women know this by experience! As to men, when they are in such maddening passes, they murder their shirt-frills.

"Justine, Monsieur Ferdinand is ill!" exclaims Caroline. "Send for a carriage."

As Justine goes down stairs, Adolphe comes up.

"My poor mistress!" observes Justine. "I guess she won't want the carriage now."

"Oh my! Where have you come from?" cries Caroline, on seeing Adolphe standing in ecstasy before her voluptuous breakfast.

Adolphe, whose wife long since gave up treating *him* to such charming banquets, does not answer. But he guesses what it all means, as he sees the cloth inscribed with the delightful ideas which Madame de Fischtaminel or the syndic of Chaumontel's affair have often inscribed for him upon tables quite as elegant.

"Whom are you expecting?" he asks in his turn.

"Who could it be, except Ferdinand?" replies Caroline.

"And is he keeping you waiting?"

"He is sick, poor fellow."

A quizzical idea enters Adolphe's head, and he replies, winking with one eye only: "I have just seen him."

"Where?"

"In front of the Cafe de Paris, with some friends."

"But why have you come back?" says Caroline, trying to conceal her murderous fury.

"Madame Foullepointe, who was tired of Charles, you said, has been with him at Ville d'Avray since yesterday."

Adolphe sits down, saying: "This has happened very appropriately, for I'm as hungry as two bears."

Caroline sits down, too, and looks at Adolphe stealthily: she weeps internally: but she very soon asks, in a tone of voice that she manages to render indifferent, "Who was Ferdinand with?"

"With some fellows who lead him into bad company. The young man is getting spoiled: he goes to Madame Schontz's. You ought to write to your uncle. It was probably some breakfast or other, the result of a bet made at M'lle Malaga's." He looks slyly at Caroline, who drops her eyes to conceal her tears. "How beautiful you have made yourself this morning," Adolphe resumes. "Ah, you are a fair match for your breakfast. I don't think Ferdinand will make as good a meal as I shall," etc., etc.

Adolphe manages the joke so cleverly that he inspires his wife with the idea of punishing Ferdinand. Adolphe, who claims to be as hungry as two bears, causes Caroline to forget that a carriage waits for her at the door.

The female that tends the gate at the house Ferdinand lives in, arrives at about two o'clock, while Adolphe is asleep on a sofa. That Iris of bachelors comes to say to Caroline that Monsieur Ferdinand is very much in need of some one.

"He's drunk, I suppose," says Caroline in a rage.

"He fought a duel this morning, madame."

Caroline swoons, gets up and rushes to Ferdinand, wishing Adolphe at the bottom of the sea.

When women are the victims of these little inventions, which are quite as adroit as their own, they are sure to exclaim, "What abominable monsters men are!"

ULTIMA RATIO.

We have come to our last observation. Doubtless this work is beginning to tire you quite as much as its subject does, if you are married.

This work, which, according to the author, is to the *Physiology of Marriage* what Fact is to Theory, or History to Philosophy, has its logic, as life, viewed as a whole, has its logic, also.

This logic—fatal, terrible—is as follows. At the close of the first part of the book—a book filled with serious pleasantry—Adolphe has reached, as you must have noticed, a point of complete indifference in matrimonial matters.

He has read novels in which the writers advise troublesome husbands to embark for the other world, or to live in peace with the fathers of their children, to pet and adore them: for if literature is the reflection of manners, we must admit that our manners recognize the defects pointed out by the *Physiology of Marriage* in this fundamental institution. More than one great genius has dealt this social basis terrible blows, without shaking it.

Adolphe has especially read his wife too closely, and disguises his indifference by this profound word: indulgence. He is indulgent with Caroline, he sees in her nothing but the mother of his children, a good companion, a sure friend, a brother.

When the petty troubles of the wife cease, Caroline, who is more clever than her husband, has come to profit by this advantageous indulgence: but she does not give her dear Adolphe up. It is woman's nature never to yield any of her rights. DIEU ET MON DROIT—CONJUGAL! is, as is well known, the motto of England, and is especially so to-day.

Women have such a love of domination that we will relate an anecdote, not ten years old, in point. It is a very young anecdote.

One of the grand dignitaries of the Chamber of Peers had a Caroline, as lax as Carolines usually are. The name is an auspicious one for women. This dignitary, extremely old at the time, was on one side of the fireplace, and Caroline on the other. Caroline was hard upon the lustrum when women no longer tell their age. A friend came in to inform them of the marriage of a general who had lately been intimate in their house.

Caroline at once had a fit of despair, with genuine tears; she screamed and made the grand dignitary's head ache to such a degree, that he tried to console her. In the midst of his condolences, the count forgot himself so far as to say—"What can you expect, my dear, he really could not marry you!"

And this was one of the highest functionaries of the state, but a friend of Louis XVIII, and necessarily a little bit Pompadour.

The whole difference, then, between the situation of Adolphe and that of Caroline, consists in this: though he no longer cares about her, she retains the right to care about him.

Now, let us listen to "What *they* say," the theme of the concluding chapter of this work.

COMMENTARY.

IN WHICH IS EXPLAINED LA FELICITA OF FINALES.

Who has not heard an Italian opera in the course of his life? You must then have noticed the musical abuse of the word *felicita*, so lavishly used by the librettist and the chorus at the moment when everybody is deserting his box or leaving the house.

Frightful image of life. We quit it just when we hear *la felicita*.

Have you reflected upon the profound truth conveyed by this finale, at the instant when the composer delivers his last note and the author his last line, when the orchestra gives the last pull at the fiddle-bow and the last puff at the bassoon, when the principal singers say "Let's go to supper!" and the chorus people exclaim "How lucky, it doesn't rain!" Well, in every condition in life, as in an Italian opera, there comes a time when the joke is over, when the trick is done, when people must make up their minds to one thing or the other, when everybody is singing his own *felicita* for himself. After having gone through with all the duos, the solos, the stretti, the codas, the concerted pieces, the duettos, the nocturnes, the phases which these few scenes, chosen from the ocean of married life, exhibit you, and which are themes whose variations have doubtless been divined by persons with brains as well as by the shallow—for so far as suffering is concerned, we are all equal—the greater part of Parisian households reach, without a given time, the following final chorus:

THE WIFE, *to a young woman in the conjugal Indian Summer*. My dear, I am the happiest woman in the world. Adolphe is the model of husbands, kind, obliging, not a bit of a tease. Isn't he, Ferdinand?

Caroline addresses Adolphe's cousin, a young man with a nice cravat, glistening hair and patent leather boots: his coat is cut in the most elegant fashion: he has a crush hat, kid gloves, something very choice in the way of a waistcoat, the very best style of moustaches, whiskers, and a goatee a la Mazarin; he is also endowed with a profound, mute, attentive admiration of Caroline.

FERDINAND. Adolphe is happy to have a wife like you! What does he want? Nothing.

THE WIFE. In the beginning, we were always vexing each other: but now we get along marvelously. Adolphe no longer does anything but what he likes, he never puts himself out: I never ask him where he is going nor what he has seen. Indulgence, my dear, is the great secret of happiness. You, doubtless, are still in the period of petty troubles, causeless jealousies, cross-purposes, and all sorts of little botherations. What is the good of all this? We women have but a short life, at the best. How much? Ten good years! Why should we fill them with vexation? I was like you. But, one fine morning, I made the acquaintance of Madame de Fischtaminel, a charming woman, who taught me how to make a husband happy. Since then, Adolphe has changed radically; he has become perfectly delightful. He is the first to say to me, with anxiety, with alarm, even, when I am going to the theatre, and he and I are still alone at seven o'clock: "Ferdinand is coming for you, isn't he?" Doesn't he, Ferdinand?

FERDINAND. We are the best cousins in the world.

THE INDIAN SUMMER WIFE, *very much affected*. Shall I ever come to that?

THE HUSBAND, *on the Italian Boulevard*. My dear boy [he has button-holed Monsieur de Fischtaminel], you still believe that marriage is based upon passion. Let me tell you that the best way, in conjugal life, is to have a plenary indulgence, one for the other, on condition that appearances be preserved. I am the happiest husband in the world. Caroline is a devoted friend, she would sacrifice everything for me, even my cousin Ferdinand, if it were necessary: oh, you may laugh, but she is ready to do anything. You entangle yourself in your laughable ideas of dignity, honor, virtue, social order. We can't have our life over again, so we must cram it full of pleasure. Not the smallest bitter word has been exchanged between Caroline and me for two years past. I have, in Caroline, a friend to whom I can tell everything, and who would be amply able to console me in a great emergency. There is not the slightest deceit between us, and we know perfectly well what the state of things is. We have thus changed our duties into pleasures. We are often happier, thus, than in that insipid season called the honey-moon. She says to me, sometimes, "I'm out of humor, go away." The storm then falls upon my cousin. Caroline never puts on her airs of a victim, now, but speaks in the kindest manner of me to the whole world. In short, she is happy in my pleasures. And as she is a scrupulously honest woman, she is conscientious to the last degree in her use of our fortune. My house is well kept. My wife leaves me the right to dispose of my reserve without the slightest control on her part. That's the way of it. We have oiled our wheels and cogs, while you, my dear Fischtaminel, have put gravel in yours.

CHORUS, *in a parlor during a ball*. Madame Caroline is a charming woman.

A WOMAN IN A TURBAN. Yes, she is very proper, very dignified.

A WOMAN WHO HAS SEVEN CHILDREN. Ah! she learned early how to manage her husband.

ONE OF FERDINAND'S FRIENDS. But she loves her husband exceedingly. Besides, Adolphe is a man of great distinction and experience.

ONE OF MADAME DE FISCHTAMINEL'S FRIENDS. He adores his wife. There's no fuss at their house, everybody is at home there.

MONSIEUR FOULLEPOINTE. Yes, it's a very agreeable house.

A WOMAN ABOUT WHOM THERE IS A GOOD DEAL OF SCANDAL. Caroline is kind and obliging, and never talks scandal of anybody.

A YOUNG LADY, *returning to her place after a dance.* Don't you remember how tiresome she was when she visited the Deschars?

MADAME DE FISCHTAMINEL. Oh! She and her husband were two bundles of briars—continually quarreling. [She goes away.]

AN ARTIST. I hear that the individual known as Deschars is getting dissipated: he goes round town—

A WOMAN, *alarmed at the turn the conversation is taking, as her daughter can hear.* Madame de Fischtaminel is charming, this evening.

A WOMAN OF FORTY, *without employment.* Monsieur Adolphe appears to be as happy as his wife.

A YOUNG LADY. Oh! what a sweet man Monsieur Ferdinand is! [Her mother reproves her by a sharp nudge with her foot.] What's the matter, mamma?

HER MOTHER, *looking at her fixedly.* A young woman should not speak so, my dear, of any one but her betrothed, and Monsieur Ferdinand is not a marrying man.

A LADY DRESSED RATHER LOW IN THE NECK, *to another lady dressed equally low, in a whisper.* The fact is, my dear, the moral of all this is that there are no happy couples but couples of four.

A FRIEND, *whom the author was so imprudent as to consult.* Those last words are false.

THE AUTHOR. Do you think so?

THE FRIEND, *who has just been married.* You all of you use your ink in depreciating social life, on the pretext of enlightening us! Why, there are couples a hundred, a thousand times happier than your boasted couples of four.

THE AUTHOR. Well, shall I deceive the marrying class of the population, and scratch the passage out?

THE FRIEND. No, it will be taken merely as the point of a song in a vaudeville.

THE AUTHOR. Yes, a method of passing truths off upon society.

THE FRIEND, *who sticks to his opinion.* Such truths as are destined to be passed off upon it.

THE AUTHOR, *who wants to have the last word.* Who and what is there that does not pass off, or become passe? When your wife is twenty years older, we will resume this conversation.

THE FRIEND. You revenge yourself cruelly for your inability to write the history of happy homes.

THE END

Lector House believes that a society develops through a two-fold approach of continuous learning and adaptation, which is derived from the study of classic literary works spread across the historic timeline of literature records. Therefore, we aim at reviving, repairing and redeveloping all those inaccessible or damaged but historically as well as culturally important literature across subjects so that the future generations may have an opportunity to study and learn from past works to embark upon a journey of creating a better future.

This book is a result of an effort made by Lector House towards making a contribution to the preservation and repair of original ancient works which might hold historical significance to the approach of continuous learning across subjects.

HAPPY READING & LEARNING!

LECTOR HOUSE LLP
E-MAIL: lectorpublishing@gmail.com